LIBRARY LIT. 12- The Best of 1981

edited by

BILL KATZ

and

KATHLEEN WEIBEL

The Scarecrow Press, Inc.
Metuchen, N.J., & London
1982

ISBN 0-8108-1522-2
Library of Congress Catalog Card No. 78-154842

CONTENTS

INTRODUCTION

An even dozen--that's where the 1981 volume brings the Best of Library Literature series. The purpose of this anthology, like the others before it, is to recognize and share what some of us, writers and editors of library literature, consider the year's best writing about libraries and related fields.

When the series began in 1970, editor Bill Katz defined "best" primarily in terms of writing. Over the years another facet of the definition has become visible. Quality of writing remains the first proviso for selection but once that criterion has been met a topical consideration comes into play. A book containing articles solely on historical bibliography, on-line searching, or story telling would not represent the best of the year's literature in a profession as varied and changing as librarianship.

There is a give and take on content and style in the attempt to produce this annual collection of the thirty "best." And so there should be. A competent report of research findings has a form different from a well-stated philosophical argument and must be viewed in that context as well as in relation to the outpouring of a whole year's writing. Certainly there are common requirements: clarity, correct usage, and both consistency and flair in the writer's style. Beyond these there is the requirement of the individual volume and the series--the goal of recognizing the "best," defined both in terms of writing and the many issues and interests in the library field.

The selection criteria and process used for the 1981 collection are essentially those described by series originator Bill Katz in his introduction to the 1980 anthology.

> The usual evaluation was applied to the candidates, i.e. the style of writing and the originality of ideas was the first consideration. After that, the judges examined the topical interest of the material, its potential value to help students and librarians better understand and appreciate their profession, and its significance in the main stream of library literature.

The selection process for 1981 varied from the usual in two ways. The Best of Library Literature year typically runs from November to November. Due to scheduling complications, this year's coverage falls a bit short, ending in mid-October. Articles published after the 1981 volume cutoff date will be considered for the 1982 collection. The second variation is that articles by members of the jury were not considered eligible.

Each year the editor sifts through almost 200 English-language journals in the fields of librarianship, information science, education, communications, and publishing. A watchful eye is kept for the well-written piece addressing areas covered in the anthology. Journals outside the traditional 200 are also scanned for likely candidates. Bill Katz and I split that responsibility this year. He covered the first six months before going on sabbatical; I covered the remainder of the year.

A few individuals submit suggestions, always a welcome addition. Friends and colleagues are also badgered for nominations.

Articles selected by the editor and all suggestions, whether solicited or unsolicited, are reviewed by a jury. It is the jury members who decide the "best of library literature." And believe me, they don't always agree.

Jury members for 1981 were: Deirdre Boyle, Library Media Consultant; Mary K. Chelton, Coeditor, Voice of Youth Advocates; Arthur Curley, Deputy Director, The New York Public Library; William Eshelman, President, Scarecrow Press; Bill Katz, School of Library and Information Science, State University of New York at Albany; Patricia Glass Schuman, President, Neal-Schuman Publishers; Kathleen Weibel, Educational Consultant.

Twice a year the editor packs up copies of candidate articles and mails them off to members of the jury. This year they received 85 articles, a fairly typical number.

The jury gathers in the fall, articles and tally sheets in hand. There is usually agreement on only a few articles. After that it is up for grabs. One juror's favorite is quite likely to be anathema to another. Discussion is spirited and voting frequent. It takes awhile, but 30 selections and 3 alternates are finally decided upon.

This year was no exception. There were convincing and unconvincing arguments, holdouts, recounts, negotiations, and differences of opinion which remained unresolved. Mary K. Chelton did not participate in the discussions but there were frequent cries of "what does Mary K. think" followed by referrals to her tally sheet. The jury did its work well and the requisite number of articles were selected.

Publishers and authors of the 30 articles have all given their permissions to reprint so the collection which follows is truly, in the judgment of the jury, the "best of 1981." You may not agree with the choices but if the anthology causes you to think about your own standards of writing or the practice and profession of librarianship it will have served a purpose.

Please, if in the coming years, you run across an article you think is one of the best, do suggest it to the editor for jury consideration.

When I mentioned to friends that I was editing this year's anthology their responses were typically either of sympathy or outrage at previous volumes. In response to the sympathy I must say that the experience of reading more library literature at one time than I ever had before was not as bad as they, or I, had imagined. This was particularly striking when the library literature was juxtaposed to the masses of inter-organizational relations literature I was reading at the same time. There is life in library literature, a dance in the old dame yet. Ideas, passions, problems, creativity, and concern are present. Sure there are unintelligible articles, vacuous pieces, posturing, and trivia. But I must say that after the worst and best of 1981 I feel better about the potential of librarians to deal with the times ahead.

As to the critical responses this series evokes, let's hear more of it. It is my belief that discussion of the substance and form of our literature can only lead to a greater sense of what the library field should be about. Besides, critical comments on the "best" may lead to better writing.

My thanks to the authors and publishers of the 85 candidate articles for this collection who responded to requests for permission to reprint articles should the jury select them. Jane Arvanites, an Albany independent researcher, gave invaluable assistance in assembling the candidate articles. The jury was magnificent; generous with time, talent and resources. Thank you all.

Kathleen Weibel

Madison, Wisconsin
November 1981

Part I

LIBRARIES AND LIBRARIANS

SUNDAY OBSERVER:

TERMINAL EDUCATION*

Russell Baker

Ever since reading about Clarkson College's plan to replace its library with a computer I have been worrying about what college students will do in the spring. I mean, you can't just haul a computer
out on the campus and plunk it down under a budding elm and lie
there with the thing on your chest while watching the birds at work,
can you?

You can do that with a book, and it is one of the better
things about going to college. With a computer, though you've got
to have a video terminal, which is basically a television set that
rolls little, green, arthritic-looking letters and numbers across a
dark screen.

It's not much fun reading a television screen, since, for one
thing, the print has a terribly tortured look, as if it had spent four
months in a Savak cellar, and since, for another, you always expect
it to be interrupted by a commercial. Which is neither here nor
there, of course, since this kind of reading is not supposed to convey pleasure, but information.

The difficulty is that you can't take your television screen out
under the elm tree and plug it into the computer--the information bank
or the information center or the information conveyor, or whatever they
choose to call it--since (1) television screens are expensive and fragile
and no college president in his right mind is going to let students expose
them to ants, dew and tree sap, and since (2) colleges aren't going
to shortchange the football team to pay for installing electrical outlets in the tree trunks.

What this means for college students of the future--and Clarkson's electronic library is the library of the future, make no mis-
take--what it means is that students are going to be spending their
springs sitting alone in stale air staring at television screens.

*Reprinted by permission from the New York Times Magazine,
November 9, 1980, p. 29. Copyright © 1980 by The New York
Times Company.

Give them a six-pack of beer or a glass of bourbon, you might say, and you have the ideal training program for American adult home life, which, one supposes, they will still be expected to undertake once they leave college stuffed with information. All I can say is: What does this have to do with education?

The answer comes from Dr. Walter Grattidge, director of Clarkson's new Educational Resources Center--Clarkson's term, not mine. "Education," he told a New York Times reporter, "is basically an information-transfer process." At the risk of sounding somewhat snappish, I say, "Fie, Dr. Grattidge! Fie!"

"Information-transfer process" indeed. Education is not like a decal, to be slipped off a piece of stiff paper and pasted on the back of the skull. The point of education is to waken innocent minds to a suspicion of information.

An educated person is one who has learned that information almost always turns out to be at best incomplete and very often false, misleading, fictitious, mendacious--just dead wrong. Ask any seasoned cop or newspaper reporter. Ask anybody who has ever been the defendant in a misdemeanor trial or the subject of a story in a newspaper.

Well, let's grant that Dr. Grattidge's opinion about education being "basically an information-transfer process" is only 80 percent baloney. If you're going to learn the importance of mistrusting information, somebody first has to give you some information, and college is a place where people try to do this, if only so the professors can find out how gullible you are.

Knowing that, they can then begin to try to teach you to ask a few questions before buying the Brooklyn Bridge or the newest theory about the wherefore of the universe. I'm talking about the good professors now, not the ones who spend all their time compiling fresh information to be transferred to the book-buying public. Even the good professors, however, rarely have enough time to teach the whole student body the art of doubting, which leads to the astonishing act of thinking.

This is why so much of whatever educating happens at college happens in places like the grass under the elm where somebody has gone to read a book, just because it seems like a nicer place to read than the library, and has become distracted by the shape of the clouds, or an ant on the elbow, or an impulse to say to the guy or the girl crossing the quadrangle, "Let's chuck the books for a while and get a beer."

If the time is autumn, and the campus has an apple tree, who knows? Maybe somebody half asleep in an informational-transference volume will look up, see an apple fall and revolutionize science. Not much chance of that happening if you're sitting in a room staring at a TV screen plugged into the Educational Resources Center, is there?

In there you are just terribly alone, blotting up information from a machine which, while very, very smart in some ways, has never had an original thought in its life. And no trees grow, and no apples fall.

PRODUCTIVITY, PROFIT, AND LIBRARIES*

Leigh Estabrook

In a formulation that has been enthusiastically embraced by librarians, Daniel Bell has argued that society is moving into a state he
terms "post-industrial." What he sees is a breakdown of the industrial capitalist structure which differentiated between owners of capital and nonowners. In its place he sees ownership or nonownership
of information as forming the critical distinction between individuals
in our society.[1]

    In one respect Bell is correct: information as a resource,
a commodity, or tool has become increasingly important. In both
developed and developing nations in the latter half of the 20th Century, access to information, control of information, management of
information, and production of information have become significant
concerns of government, industry, and the nonprofit sector. It does
not necessarily follow, however, that, as information becomes more
important, those organizations and professionals traditionally involved
in the dissemination of information (for example, libraries and librarians) will assume a more important societal role. Nor does it follow that ownership of capital will be replaced by ownership of knowledge as the basis for societal power. Rather, it can be argued that,
as information becomes more important, the owners of capital will
appropriate the information utilities more directly for their purposes.
This run-on issue will be examined in this article, specifically as
it relates to the pressures and tensions within our current economic
system, and the way in which those dynamics affect the information
industry in general and libraries in particular. A premise of the
argument is that there is an essential difference between libraries
and the information industry. Libraries, as nonprofit organizations,
continue to be bound to certain ideals of service for the public good.
The information industry as defined in this paper is that group of
for-profit organizations which have as their fundamental goal the return of capital to organizational investors.

    The central problem for contemporary capitalism is the long-

---

*Reprinted by permission of the author and publisher from Library
Journal, 106 (July 1981) 1377-80. Published by R. R. Bowker Co.
(a Xerox Company). Copyright © 1981 by Xerox Corporation.

term decline in profits. This is not to say that the oil companies
are not doing very well, but to point to the significant, systemic
change that is affecting the overall profitability of capitalist enterprises.

The problem of profitability must be understood in relationship to two phenomena in the labor market: the relative decline in
productivity and the shift from goods-producing to service-producing
industries. These two changes are interwoven--they affect one another and are in turn related directly back to the question of profits.
Without becoming too technical, an examination of the relationship
between these phenomena--the problem of declining profits and the
associated adjustments being made by capital--is an important first
step to understanding changes in information activities and organization.

The shift to services

There has been a dramatic shift in the labor market from the goods-
producing to the services-producing sector. A number of figures are
available to document the shift. In 1929, for example, approximately
45 percent of the working population was employed in the goods-
producing sector. By 1977 only 32 percent of the working population
was employed in the production of goods. During the same period,
employment in the services-producing sector "increased from 55 to
68 percent of the population."[2] This shift has had an impact on
both profitability and productivity. Technological innovation and other
measures to increase productivity have, until recently, been most
intensively applied to the goods-producing sector. In part, this has
been a function of that sector's providing a direct return on investment, but it has also been a function of the relative difficulty of
adapting certain productivity enhancing measures to the service sector. It is easier to build a robot that will bolt the fenders onto a
new car than to develop one that will be able to determine whether
an individual seeking materials on discrimination is referring to racial, sexual, visual, or some other form of that phenomenon.

However, within the past decade the ability of management
to increase productivity in the production of goods has become limited. The reason for this has been partly that management has
reached the point of diminishing returns in the introduction of pro-
ductivity-boosting measures, and partly that increased production of
goods does not necessarily increase demand for those goods (although
this is disputed by the supply-side economists).

This conjunction of declining profitability, stable industrial
productivity, and a shifting labor force participation has necessitated
various adjustments by business and industry to assure survival.
An important outlet has been the information business, to which the
growth of the information industry is ample testimony. As information has become more central to societal functioning, and as business
and industry seek to maximize profit by directing their attention to

this potentially profitable area, those organizations traditionally involved in the dissemination of information--among them libraries--
are directly affected.   We can see these effects if we look at three
phenomena: 1) the emphasis on productivity in libraries as a function of more limited resources being made available to those organizations; 2) the way in which libraries are used as markets for the
information industry; and 3) the repackaging of library services as
information products.

So long as the service sector of society was relatively small,
and so long as those who worked in the service sector received low
wages, there was little impetus to implement productivity-enhancing
measures in service-producing organizations.   Moreover, as indicated
above, certain measures, such as technological innovation, were seen
to be too expensive to adapt to the service sector.   Libraries were
(and still are) labor intensive, but so long as labor costs were low,
the marginal productivity of an individual worker was not a major
concern.   This is no longer true.   An increasing proportion of workers in the service sector have become unionized; social security
taxes to employers have risen; and library budgets are leaner.   In
response, libraries have become increasingly interested in partici-
patory management, flextime, and other techniques that have been
found to increase the productivity of individual workers.   At the
same time, there is an increasing "rationalization" and specialization of library activities.   No longer can an individual who works
in technical services move easily to a position in public services.

The most significant measure employed to increase productivity has been the rapid adoption of technology.   As labor becomes
more expensive, the incentives to utilize technological measures to
increase productivity become greater.   A $12,000 to $15,000 investment in a circulation control system does not seem that expensive
when it is less than the salary and benefits for one professional for
one year.   Changes in libraries in the past ten years are some indication that the investment in automation has been seen to be worthwhile.

Technological innovation in circulation, cataloging, acquisitions, reference, and other functions changes both the nature of
work and the structure of the work force in libraries.   At the sim-
plest level, the computerization of different library functions has increased the rate of speed at which different operations are performed.
Productivity increases since more work can be completed by fewer
people in less time.   More important has been the effect of technology on the nature and level of library work.   Productivity increases because a skilled, more expensive labor force can be replaced by less skilled workers.   For example, individualized cataloging for different libraries increasingly gives way to acceptance
of MARC records.   Getz found that 19 percent of technical services
staff at libraries using LC MARC cataloging are professionals.[3]
In libraries that do not, 26 percent of the staff are professional.

There are other consequences: rationalization of acquisitions based on circulation records and pacing of the workflow based on differential computer costs or availability of terminals are but two. Each contributes to the more productive use of resources within libraries. At the same time, the information provided to library managers is becoming more accessible and more readily manipulated. It allows them to make decisions regarding costs and benefits of various services and the allocation of human and other resources on a more systematic rather than intuitive basis.

Marketing through libraries

It is a mistake, however, to believe that library management has been adopting new technologies simply for the sake of economy. We must also recognize that libraries are an important market for a variety of products, and the marketing of products by the computer industry has also affected the extent of library investment in technology. This is a somewhat sensitive issue. None of us wishes to believe that either personal or management decisions are affected by a sales pitch. To state the relationship in this fashion is to oversimplify it. Just as libraries have always been a crucial market for the publishing industry, they have also been a very important market for the more widely defined information industry. Libraries provide a limited but nonetheless important outlet for the sales of various types of technological and computer hardware and software. The adoption of these technologies by libraries is important not only for the profits that come to industry from their immediate purchase, but also because library use of such things as online data base searching prepares new markets for the information industry. As individuals become used to obtaining information in an interactive and nonlinear fashion, they are prepared to become customers for such services when they are offered via home computer or cable. One example of the way in which libraries are being used to prepare these markets is the arrangement between OCLC and The Source Telecomputing Company in which terminals are to be placed in public libraries. One goal of The Source Telecomputing Company is to use this project as a means to introduce potential home users to their services.[4] A second example is the encouragement by data base vendors of librarians to use online data bases. At the present time librarians are important intermediaries in the data base search process. At the same time, vendors are exhibiting aggressively at conferences for chemists, psychologists, and other professionals and are working to make their software more "user-cordial."

There exists, then, in the first instance, financial pressures on libraries due to declining profits which lead to intense efforts within libraries to increase productivity. Reinforcing this trend is the expansion of the information industry and a search for new markets for its products. Libraries are used as direct and intermediary outlets.

Repackaging and ownership

The third, and related, development affecting libraries is the repackaging of services as goods. Even in situations in which services are
provided in a direct for-profit context, there are problems in increasing the profitability of those services. Inherent in the nature of
services is the problem of disentangling the person who delivers the
service from the product: the product is a function of the expertise
and skill of the service provider as well as the relationship between
the service provider and the consumer. It is more difficult and
costly to mechanize, standardize, and reproduce services. As a
result, there are pressures on service-producing industries to re-
direct their resources to the production of goods. The recent attempt by OCLC to gain proprietary control over information entered
into the OCLC system is a prime example of such redirection. Although OCLC did not succeed, there is evidence that there will be
increased struggles over the copyright/ownership of these services/
goods.

This repackaging also results from economic pressures on
organizations in the information industry to expand their markets.
There has been enormous growth in the home computer and cable
television markets: both have expanded at a very rapid rate in the
past decade. At the present time, however, each of these businesses is reaching a point of market saturation for the products they
have developed. The home computer industry is still, for the most
part, geared toward educational programs for elementary school children, game playing for all ages, and just plain fiddling around by
people who have always been fascinated by math, logic, and gadgets.
The problem for the industry is that there is a limited segment of
the population willing to invest $1000 or more in sophisticated games.
Producers of home computers are, therefore, actively seeking ways
in which to make their products more desirable for a wider audience
and also to encourage current owners to continue to invest in computer products. A number of services that might otherwise be provided by libraries are being developed by these industries for sales
to the home computer buyers. Compuserv, for example, now sells
a package that one can buy at Radio Shack for $29.95. It allows
the consumer to tie into the Dow Jones service, read the New York
Times, search for encyclopedic information, and obtain a great deal
of other information which has been central to library reference
service. Connect time is currently $6 per hour, and it is estimated
that in five years it will be reduced to nothing.[5]

The cable companies are under similar pressures. In 1980
it was estimated that only about 15 percent of those homes that could
have cable did so.[6] This is partly a function of the delayed development of cable in large urban areas--areas in which there was less
demand for a system whose original function was simply the provision of enhanced television reception. Cable owners have responded
by developing a number of new products, including home banking,
at-home shopping, and (of most importance to this discussion) a

variety of recreational, informational, and educational products that in part duplicate various forms of library services.

At the present time, these new products of the computer and cable businesses are still available to relatively small markets. There is no reason to believe, however, that development and sales of these and similar products will not grow significantly. In the process, the information industry will directly--and probably successfully--compete with library services.

Devaluing expertise

Thus far, a number of ways in which economic pressures of late 20th Century capitalism are affecting libraries and library-related services have been suggested. Of immediate concern, however, is the relationship between these broader changes and consequent changes in the organization of work within libraries and in the patterns of services to library clients.

The way in which libraries are striving to increase productivity, and the effect that is having on the make-up of the work force has been mentioned. What is happening as work becomes more rationalized and systematized is the separation of mental and manual labor within libraries. Fewer individuals are doing professional work--for example, making decisions about how work should be done and interacting with clients. A much higher number of increasingly nonprofessional staff are doing work that requires little independence, little decision making. Even in areas where librarians perceive that they are gaining more independence and professional responsibility, there are indications that this is simply a transitional phenomenon.[7]

As already indicated, these changes within libraries are resulting in increasing managerial control. Perhaps the best example of this is in the area of collection development, where management information systems in the form of computerized acquisition and circulation systems are being utilized. There is no sound reason to defend idiosyncratic collection development as it has too often been carried out, but it should be noted that the employment of these information systems lessens the library worker's autonomy and control and devalues the expertise of those human beings called collection development specialists and acquisitions librarians.

Perhaps the most serious consequence of increased rationalization within libraries is the way in which options for change become limited. If, in fact, there is a certain degradation of work--decreased control of the work force over what work is done and how it is carried out--one solution to the day-to-day boredom is to allow library workers to move among different jobs within their organization or even to exchange jobs with others in other organizations. Some libraries do offer these opportunities. However, since one aspect of increased rationalization of library work is increased specialization

12   Library Lit.-81

and since the financial pressures on libraries necessitate using our
workforce as efficiently as possible, these opportunities are quite
limited.

The triage effect

The pressures on libraries that have been mentioned are also causing changes in patterns of service within all types of libraries.
First, there is an increased emphasis on productive services. Char-
lie Robinson's book-buying policy in the Baltimore County Library
is perhaps the best example of this because one key measure of productivity in libraries has been and continues to be circulation. Concern with productivity affects developments in other areas as well,
insofar as productivity is synonymous with quantity of output. Reference questions that can be answered efficiently are preferred over
ones that are too complex, too vague, or "off-the-wall"! Problems
that take too much staff time are referred to other organizations.
And increasingly it appears that services will be targeted to those
clients known to be the library's most likely customers and to those
who can pay (if not in money, then in community influence and
power). The middle-class patterns of service in public libraries
are well documented.[8] It is a fact familiar to librarians. What
is important for this discussion is that there are a number of indications that libraries are giving up on attempts to serve those individuals who have not or are not likely to be users. One might call
this the triage effect. As pressures increase to make services productive, as resources are diminished, it becomes necessary to treat
or serve those clients who will survive, not those who will probably
fall by the wayside as clients. No effort is made to serve or treat
them.

    Even as this is done, the options become more limited, for
the information industry is rapidly moving to take over the library
services that may be profitable for them. If these businesses continue to develop as they have, and gradually provide greater and
more direct access to data bases and ready reference information,
libraries are going to be pushed into a more limited societal role--
something that will further affect their funding.

    Finally, as the information business becomes big business,
the central problem of access to information becomes even more
critical. At this time there are already many more data bases
which are privately controlled than are available for public access.
Exclusive access to information has been an important asset to corporations for many years. For instance, Merrill Lynch will try to
convince you that it should be your investment broker because of the
quality of its research services, available only to its customers.
Control of information is important for the toy industry and of concern to the defense industry. The issue for this discussion is not
so much these types of proprietary information nor even the cost of
information or client fees. It is, rather, to comment on the more
general effect the changes discussed here will have on the production
and distribution of information.

The economic pressures on both the for-profit information
industry and nonprofit libraries are significantly affecting the nature
of services and the organization of work within libraries. The examples offered in this paper have obviously been selected to substantiate an argument about the nature of these effects. Rigorous and
systematic testing of these hypotheses remains to be done. The
evidence currently available, however, does suggest that the inter-
dependence and latent conflict between the information industry and
libraries are affecting much more than libraries' product offerings.

References

1. Bell, Daniel. The Coming of Post-Industrial Society: a Venture
   in Social Forecasting. Basic, 1973.
2. Ginzberg, Eli & George J. Voijt, "The Service Sector of the
   U. S. Economy, " Scientific American, March 1981, p. 48.
3. Getz, Malcolm. Public Libraries: an Economic View. Johns
   Hopkins Univ. Pr., 1981, p. 137.
4. Press Conference with OCLC, Inc. at National Online Information
   Meeting, New York, March 26, 1980.
5. Ron Schnaper, Marketing Consultant for Radio Shack Computer
   Store, Boston, to Estabrook, March 18, 1981.
6. Future View Panel Discussion, National Information Conference
   and Exposition, Washington, D. C. , May 30, 1980.
7. Nielson, Brian, "Online Bibliographic Searching and the Deprofessionalization of Librarianship, " Online Review, September
   1980, p. 215-24.
8. See, for example, Lawrence J. White's review in "The Public
   Library, Free or Fee: an Economist's Perspective, " in
   Financial Choices for Public Libraries, Chicago: Public
   Library Assn. , 1980.

ONLINE BIBLIOGRAPHIC SEARCHING AND THE
DEPROFESSIONALIZATION OF LIBRARIANSHIP*

Brian Nielsen

Librarianship today is undergoing a great transformation. As an occupational group, we see ourselves on the threshold of tremendous technological changes; we see opportunities before us that were never there before; we see the chance for fulfilling many of our hopes for better access to information, better bibliographic control, and a better social position for ourselves. Feelings of excitement and feelings of hope for our future are now very common among those of us who are involved with new technologies. Technological change is reshaping our occupational landscape, and the optimism that is expressed in our literature and at many of our professional meetings is really quite striking. For many of us this optimism signals the end of the old professional stereotype--the stern spinster wearing a bun, the bookish man too delicate for the business world--and this optimism carries us forward to shape a new, high technology, image of ourselves.

This optimism is, however, only part of the picture. Along with the technological revolution comes a certain amount of anxiety, a feeling that the technology is shaping us more than we are shaping the technology, a feeling of loss of control. These feelings see much less overt expression in the literature of librarianship, but two examples come to mind that show a negative aspect to the technological change we are experiencing. First, there was the remarkable apprehensiveness toward technological innovation expressed by the librarian participants at the 1977 American Library Association President's Program in Detroit[1]. The words used then were malaise, uncertainty, fear, and exasperation when it came to summarizing how librarians felt about the new technologies, library education, social change, and the role of the librarian in the future. A second example illustrative of the negative feelings is the fee-or-free debate. Here we have what seems to be a dwindling minority of vocal librarians decrying the introduction of fees for selected library services that utilize the latest technology. Their position appears more and more quixotic as online bibliographic searching is adopted in more and more libraries.

*Reprinted by permission of the author and publisher from Online Review, 4:3 (September 1980) 215-24.

It is not our purpose to argue one way or another, to be positive or negative about new technologies in librarianship, but to highlight the ambivalence that is evidently being felt if we look at librarianship as a whole. Where are we going? Do we have a good idea about what our future will be or don't we? These questions are important when thinking about the whole collection of information technologies librarians are concerned with, but the questions are perhaps best considered in light of the technology of online bibliographic searching. We will look at the technology of online in detail, but to arrive at a perspective from which to highlight the ambivalence we find, we first turn to some sociological thinking about the future of professions.

A number of sociologists of late have been engaged in a debate about the professions, and a new term, "deprofessionalization," has been coined to evoke the ideas of one side of the debate. The positive side of the debate, the prediction of a future society in which the professions will be important agents for societal decision-making, has received wide attention in the popular press and in librarianship largely through the work of Daniel Bell, the Harvard sociologist who made 'post-industrial society' such a well-known phrase. Bell's work has become known to librarians through his own writing [2-4] and the work of others [5, 6], in part because of the importance he attaches to information as the commodity of value in the future. But there are sociologists who disagree with Bell, who see other trends operating, who view the professions as having a declining social importance.

The view that social change is leading toward deprofessionalization rather than professionalization rests on a number of observations. The most obvious one is that the traditional professions-- medicine, law, and the clergy--are not today so highly regarded as they once were. People are annoyed at their doctors for the exorbitant fees charged, for the political maneuverings undertaken to protect them from lay scrutiny, for the concern with exotic disease at the expense of concern for good health and nutrition. Many see lawyers and their lawsuits as clogging our judicial system, and see claims of ethical good conduct belied by such acts as Watergate and the recent revelations about the back rooms at the Supreme Court. Wilensky [7] noted that for the aspiring professions there was not much room at the top; Freidson [8] views the professions as self-serving; Haug [9] has theorized that a deprofessionalized future will attach less value to the prestige and status of existing professions, leading to more egalitarian relationships between professionals and their clients.

Of the number of sociologists who may be put into the counter-Bell camp, who see deprofessionalization of many occupations as a distinctly likely outcome for the future, Nina Toren of Hebrew University has been one to formalize the thinking about deprofessionalization in a way that is particularly important to our purposes here. Her 1975 paper "Deprofessionalization and its sources: a preliminary analysis" [10] posits two possible sources or root causes of depro-

fessionalization: technological change and public challenges to the
service ideal.   The model she describes takes the two sources as
independent variables, the dependent variable being the loss of professional traits such as the right to hold a monopoly on practice of
particular functions and the expectation by clients of an ethical basis
for professional judgment.   Technological change as a cause of deprofessionalization is of particular interest to us as we examine online bibliographic searching.   Toren reasons that a series of technological advances can make professional knowledge no longer esoteric and special--anybody can push a button--and so society ceases
to recognize the profession's knowledge base as deserving of special
treatment.   The end result is possibly a declining need for an occupation's skill, and thus a declining job market.

What does all this sociological theory mean for librarianship
and online bibliographic searching?   If Toren's model is correct,
and if online searching can be construed as a technological advance
systematizing hitherto esoteric professional knowledge, then librarianship may experience deprofessionalization in the future.   Though
the Toren model does not make explicit which of the occupation's
professional traits will be lost, we are led to foresee a declining
importance for librarianship in the future, perhaps status loss, perhaps a reduced labor market, if we accept the Toren theory and its
relevance to online.

The fascinating thing about this hypothesis is that it is just
the opposite of what so many commentators within librarianship have
been saying about online's professionalizing influence.   Atherton's
field studies [11, 12] turned up time and again the perception among
librarians that their status or prestige in the eyes of patrons rose
with the introduction of online.   Kilgour [13] argues that computer
involvement generally for librarians will mean better salaries.   Numerous case studies in the literature reveal the enthusiasm with
which online is being received both by patrons and by librarians
themselves, and virtually all the commentary on online is glowingly
positive about the technology's future in librarianship.

Who can we believe?   Here we see posed in a more concrete
and reasoned way the ambivalence felt about the new technology and
its meaning for librarianship.   The use of an idea from sociology
helps us illuminate sources of some ambivalence, and with further
analysis we may arrive at a better understanding of where librarianship is going, and what choices it has.

We will now present data on both sides of the issue of professionalization versus deprofessionalization.   The first group of
data confirms Toren's view of deprofessionalization, the second
group supports the more popular technology-as-professionalizing
side.   The data supporting the Toren position are qualitative, high-
lighting technological trends familiar to librarians and information
scientists.   The data on the professionalization side are drawn from
three sources: a national survey conducted in 1976 on opinions reference librarians had about online by Nitecki [14], an impact survey

conducted by the System Development Corporation among intermediary online users and managers in 1974 and 1975[15], and field data
collected by this researcher in December 1978 in one large academic
library heavily involved in online.

In considering the data that support deprofessionalization, we
will not analyze whether or not the Toren theory as a whole holds
up. Let us say for argument's sake that it does; then the relevant
question for consideration is whether online bibliographic searching
can be considered within that theory as a deprofessionalizing technology. We will briefly examine the technology itself, as well as
what we know about developments in information science and theory
of information retrieval, in light of this question.

The sense in which online may be considered a deprofessionalizing technology may be argued in a number of ways. The preparation of made-to-order bibliographies has long been considered a
professional task of a rather high order within librarianship [16,
pp. 188-189; 17, pp. 111-128], but also a time-consuming task, a
luxury for all but the most well-staffed libraries. The task itself
is made much more routine through the computer technology. Online makes explicit and rational the means by which search terms
are manipulated and used to extract bibliographic citations, and
would indicate that "the uncertainty is minimized" [10, p. 330] in
the retrieval process. The choice of database is also routinized in
that it is restricted to those that the systems offer; the potential
user need not be concerned with whether an indexing service exists
but is not available locally, as would be the case in manual bibliographic searching. The process of subject term choice is becoming
more rationalized with the development of more and more thesauri,
many machine-readable, and the choice of database may be routinized by the use of such facilities as BRS's new CROS.

Besides these technical characteristics of the systems themselves that routinize the task of bibliography preparation, there are
economic forces that are tending to diffuse the technology in a variety of settings, not only those in which librarians work. The vendors, competing with each other for maximum system use by all
potential customers, provide training sessions for librarians, as
well as non-librarians employed in research facilities, using the
systems. Database producers, in their workshop efforts, are even
more aggressive in reaching out to non-librarian researchers as a
means of building clientele[18]. The proliferation of databases available in every system has prompted the vendors and producers to
compile and publish more and better manuals, enabling both librarians and nonlibrarians to obtain in many cases more information on
a database than was ever available solely about the printed index[19].
Anticipated changes in online use cost and pricing policies[20], particularly the decreasing reliance on connect time as a major factor
in price determination, may also encourage direct end-user access
to the systems.

Both technological and economic factors make it appear likely

that there will be a declining role for librarian intermediaries in the
future.   It has frequently been admitted in the information science
literature that a technological goal for online development is to create systems which substantially reduce the need for intermediaries
[21].   Further aids to online use are in continuing development, including more published thesauri, computer-assisted instruction in
online use, and common access language development.   The likely
expansion of online-initiated document delivery services such as
DIALORDER and the "Information On Demand" service on THE
SOURCE may allow online users to avoid having to enter libraries
altogether.   All of these factors lead us to the conclusion that online may well be a deprofessionalizing technology in Toren's terms.

        Setting aside this conclusion for the moment, let us turn to
what many librarians are thinking about the professionalizing aspects
of online.   We will look first at some of the Nitecki [14] data, collected via a mail survey of a random sample of American Library
Association Reference and Adult Services Section members.   Five
hundred and forty-two librarians from all types of libraries responded
to the survey, over half of whom were in reference or public services positions, and nearly 75% in public or academic libraries.   Over
40% of the respondents had at least some hands-on experience with
automated IR systems.   Questions on the instrument related to the
respondents' attitudes toward online, their level of experience and
work situations, and their thoughts on online administration and
pricing practices.

        What is most interesting about the data is that there is a
clear pattern of what we might call a commitment process going on
with librarians exposed to online.   As Nitecki [14, p. 42]̄ worded
it, "the greater personal exposure the respondent has to automated
information retrieval, the greater involvement he will express libraries should have with offering such services to users."   This
pattern of commitment may be discerned throughout the data, not
in librarians' advocacy of online alone, but in advocating a number
of positions which have strong implications for administration.   For
instance, (1) the higher exposure to online, the less was the feeling
that the cost of providing the service was a barrier, (2) the higher
exposure to online, the more prepared were librarians to initiate
services without new funding, and (3) reference librarians, who
would presumably be the ones already experienced in online or prime
candidates for becoming intermediaries, were in favor of having a
higher percentage of online costs absorbed by users than were other
types of librarians.   All these findings indicate that becoming involved with online does affect attitudes toward online implementation
and administration.   Librarians who become committed also seek to
involve other librarians in online, and thus the decision to innovate
in this area takes on the quality of a social movement.   This movement to innovate illustrates a value bias inherent in professionalism
to seek the most efficient way to perform a task.   This bias has
been referred to by some as "the technological imperative."

        Two categories of the Nitecki respondents are particularly

interesting to examine. Academic librarians were the most interested in promoting online, and they favor more strongly than others online implementation without new funds. This group is more involved than others in the professionalization drive of the occupation as a whole, as evidenced by the faculty status movement, the emphasis on publication, and the great attention given to continuing education and second master's degrees. Library educators, a very small but interesting group of respondents, also had great interest in online, and felt simultaneously that users should bear a low percentage of online costs and that the service should be initiated without new funds. These respondents' bias toward innovation has apparently dimmed their powers of perception of the fact that the innovation does have accompanying costs. As a profession's educators typically are at the vanguard of professionalization movements [22], we see in this respect that library educators are no exception. For both academic librarians and library educators then, there seems to be a strong association between online and a professionalization movement.

We move on now to a second set of survey data, reported in the SDC impact study [15] that has seen wide circulation in the field. The respondents to this survey, information facility managers and online intermediaries, were also enthusiastic about online, and many of the findings clarify the reasons for this enthusiasm. Interviews supplementing the survey findings revealed a "significant change" in staff morale following online implementation. An "increased sense of professionalism and accomplishment for the staff" was cited most often as a reason for better staff morale, and there was also noted increased productivity, when judged subjectively by respondents.

By comparing various responses of intermediaries and managers, we get some vague indications of tensions between the two groups of respondents. Forty-nine percent of the intermediaries experienced increased workloads with online, yet only 22 percent of the managers believed that introducing online required new staff. Over three quarters of the intermediaries found their productivity levels increased, yet 70 percent felt no need to reduce the size of the reference staff. Despite these tensions, we do see clear satisfaction on the part of both groups, as well as with end-users, with online services.

Both surveys reviewed here present glowing pictures of online and contradict directly the Toren view of a deprofessionalizing technology. What is the reason for the contradiction? To begin to answer this question, we turn to data from a field study conducted by this researcher in late 1978. Based on extended interviews with the reference librarians in a large research library, it is our purpose here to show that online service with intermediaries does have a professionalizing effect, when measured in terms of certain traits commonly viewed as professional. Our findings will be categorized into three areas of impact: impact on time, impact on client relations, and impact on intradepartmental relations.

Time

Noted by all the reference librarians as a significant change accompanying the implementation of online was a substantial increase in the
pace of work. This finding confirms the SDC data. Where jobs in
the past revolved around scheduled hours at the reference desk, online has quickened the pace by involving librarians with lengthy interviews in order to prepare search requests. Involvement with searching necessarily displaces other kinds of work activities. "I do a lot
more delegating of work because it takes so much time to keep up
with online searching," was one comment. To serve those clients
who use online services, more time is required both for interaction
to prepare the searches, as well as time for learning the systems
and relevant vocabularies. "I spend more time trying to learn about
the field," one librarian noted, "so that when someone comes in for
a search and throws out a term I can say that I've seen it somewhere before." Managers have taken note of the new demands for
time, and a senior administrator in this library plans for further
librarian reduction in desk staffing: "Frankly, I'm coming more
and more to the conclusion that if we are going to meet the demand
for the volume of services that we get, that we're going to have to
devote more of our professional staff time to this activity ... and
considerably less professional time to the reference desk. I can
see our going to a situation where the reference desk will be staffed
primarily by nonprofessionals."

Despite the pressures imposed by the added function of online
service, it is interesting to note that to the question "Would you prefer to do more or less online searching?" every librarian queried
preferred to do more. For some the reason was to build their skills
in the use of technology, for others it was the opportunity to promote the new service to clients. Although two librarians noted that
the time spent away from the reference desk and the commonly used
reference books made them not as efficient as they had been at handling these tools in reference work, they still wished to do more online searching.

Client relations

The interactions between librarian and client are changed due to the
nature of online technology. "I spend more time with clients," was
one librarian's comment; "it also changes the attitude that they come
in with. They're much more willing to sit down with me and talk
to me and let me understand what they're doing, whereas before ...
they would show much less tolerance. They sort of respect me
more." A comment by another librarian shows that the demands
for adequate searching give the librarian greater control over the
interaction than might be had in a simpler question-answering interaction: "I dislike it when people assume that you know nothing
when they come to do a search and they want you to be the typist.
But that's generally a misunderstanding that gets ironed out as you
go along."

The length and nature of these encounters have had an impact on how the clients for online service view the librarian. Three of the librarians noted that online patrons came back to them specifically for other types of service, such as interlibrary loan. "They consider me as their contact person," one librarian said, "whether their question related to a literature research or not." Taking on more functions to serve these patrons, such as checking on interlibrary loan requests, adds to the time pressures of the reference librarians' work, but also may redefine their role in the minds of patrons in a way that gives the librarians a greater sense of their importance.

Intradepartmental relations

The introduction of online services has brought about a number of changes in the relationships within the reference department, principal among them being the changing relationship between librarians and the support staff in the department. As the librarians have occupied more of their time with online searching, the support staff have been moved to the reference desk. This has resulted in resentful feelings among the support staff, according to a number of the librarians interviewed. With the attention of administrators focused on online services, and the novelty and prestige value of working with the computer, the support staff likely feel that their contribution and effort to provide services go unrecognized.

The move to online service has also brought about increased specialization in subject fields among the librarians in the department. As is typical in many large reference departments today, subject-related databases are assigned to specific reference librarians, allowing them to be more proficient with vocabularies and protocols. The effects of this division have been to channel search requests to particular librarians and allow greater independence for each librarian in handling requests.

Generalizing from this interview data in all three areas of impact, we see that there are concrete reasons for librarians to feel that their work is more professionalized. Librarians may be working harder, and they are devoting more of their time to patron interactions of a high order. They spend more time with the subject literatures. They spend less time doing routine reference work and supervision. In their interactions with patrons they have found new respect, and have greater control over the interactions than they had over the bulk of traditional reference interactions. In many respects these new interactions can be conceived of as engendering a new fiduciary relationship with patrons [23], much like the doctor-patient or lawyer-client relationship. The technology also changes the librarians' relationships within their department, giving them greater differentiation from support staff and greater independence and autonomy. These data seem to give greater substance to the Nitecki and SDC findings, and like the two earlier studies to refute the deprofessionalization notion of Toren.

22 Library Lit. -81

With all these data brought to bear on a fairly abstract sociological theory, it is now time to apply what Michael Buckland and his
British colleagues call the "so-what test." SO WHAT? So, first of
all, the Toren theory seems inadequate in comprehending the change
that online technology has brought to librarianship up to this point.
So also, librarians who become involved with online experience
changes in relationships that are common in established professions.
So again, librarians, their supervisors, and their end-users all
seem pleased with the new technology.

But does all this allow us to rest easy about the long-range
impact of online? It is this researcher's belief that it does not.
Toren's theory, it will be recalled, is a social change theory that
operates over time, and we are certainly not at the end of development as far as online and libraries go. As is evident with a careful look at the data as we have taken here, a major source of the
enthusiasm librarians hold for online is not enthusiasm for the technology itself but enthusiasm for the roles that librarians enter as
they adopt online. Continuing technological development is in the
direction of end-user access, a service mode that has considerable
implications for future roles of librarians in their relation to online.
Whether the technology does develop to the point where librarians
are not as involved in search formulation and input depends to some
extent on the actions of librarians themselves--whether they will resist such a development or not. Knowing what we do know about
IR systems, relevance judgments, and the little theory we have
about information needs, it seems clear that end-user access has
definite advantages, though with certain costs, for the users; what
we know about the business of online is that end-user access will
likely bring economic advantages to the information industry; what
we are learning about the social aspects of online leads us to think
that end-user access has certain disadvantages for librarians. As
the technology continues to develop, we as librarians will be faced
with critical decisions, decisions that may pit professional judgment
against professional interest. Such decisions may not be easy.

References

1. J. A. Boisse and C. J. Stoffle: "Epilogue, issues and answers:
the participants' views," in E. J. Josey (Ed.), The Information Society: Issues and Answers. Phoenix, AZ: Oryx
Press, 1978.
2. D. Bell: The Coming of Post-industrial Society: A Venture in
Social Forecasting. New York: Basic Books, 1973.
3. D. Bell: The Cultural Contradictions of Capitalism. New York:
Basic Books, 1976.
4. D. Bell: "Teletext and technology," Encounter, June 1977, pp.
9-29.
5. P. Wilson: "Librarianship and ALA in a post-industrial society," American Libraries, 1978, 9, pp. 124-128.
6. K. Musmann: "Will there be a role for librarians and libraries
in the post-industrial society?" Libri, 1978, 28, pp. 228-234.

7. H. Wilensky: "The professionalization of everyone?" Am. J.
    Sociology, 1964, 70, pp. 136-158.
8. E. Freidson: Profession of Medicine: A Study of the Sociology
    of Applied Knowledge. New York: Harper & Row, 1970.
9. M. R. Haug: "The deprofessionalization of everyone?" Socio-
    logical Focus, 1975, 8, pp. 197-213.
10. N. Toren: "Deprofessionalization and its sources: a prelim-
    inary analysis," Sociology of Work and Occupations, 1975,
    2, pp. 327-337.
11. P. Atherton: "Online bibliographic services in academic librar-
    ies: some observations," in P. G. Watson (Ed.), Online
    Bibliographic Services: Where We Are, Where We're Going.
    Chicago: American Library Association, 1977.
12. P. Atherton and R. W. Christian: Librarians and Online Serv-
    ices. White Plains, NY: Knowledge Industries, 1977.
13. F. G. Kilgour: "The impact of technology on libraries," in
    E. J. Josey (Ed.), The Information Society: Issues and
    Answers. Phoenix, AZ: Oryx Press, 1978.
14. D. A. Nitecki: "Opinions toward automated information retrieval
    among reference librarians: a national survey." Unpublished
    master's thesis, University of Tennessee, Knoxville, 1976.
15. J. Wanger, C. A. Cuadra and M. Fishburn: Impact of On-line
    Retrieval Services: A Survey of Users 1974-75. Santa Mon-
    ica, CA: System Development Corporation, 1976.
16. M. Hutchins: Introduction to Reference Work. Chicago: Amer-
    ican Library Association, 1944.
17. W. A. Katz: Introduction to Reference Work, Vol. II: Refer-
    ence Services. New York: McGraw-Hill, 1969.
18. I. Malley: "Educating the special user," Aslib Proceedings,
    1978, 30, pp. 365-372.
19. B. Unruh: "Database user aids and materials: a study." Pa-
    per delivered at the First National Online Information Meet-
    ing, New York, March 27, 1980, to be published in Online
    Review.
20. T. P. Barwise: Online Searching: The Impact on User Charges
    of the Extended Use of Online Information Services. Paris:
    ICSU-AB, 1979.
21. C. T. Meadow: "Online searching and computer programming:
    some behavioral similarities (or why end users will eventu-
    ally take over the terminal)," Online, 1979, 3, pp. 49-52.
22. R. Bucher and A. Strauss: "Professions in process," Am. J.
    Sociology, 1961, 66, pp. 325-334.
23. A. M. Carr-Saunders and P. A. Wilson: The Professions.
    Oxford: Clarendon Press, 1933.

NOT ALL IN THE MIND:

THE VIRILE PROFESSION*

Penelope Cowell

> To most of us public libraries are quiet
> places where nothing ever happens;
> I won't end up stuck in a lousy grot hole
> of a public library;
> Twenty years old and never been rolled. [1]

In our media-orientated, image-conscious contemporary society the
librarian may very well seem particularly unfortunate, reflected in
the imagination of the general public as a fussy old woman of either
sex, myopic and repressed, brandishing or perhaps cowering behind
a date-stamp and surrounded by an array of notices which forbid
virtually every human activity. The media, for whom the librarian
is frustration personified, have reinforced this stereotype, hitherto
transmitted solely by superstition and hearsay; its greatest impact
has no doubt fallen on the two-thirds of the population who never
use the library. One of its effects will be to ensure that they never
do so in the future. As Frank Hatt has pointed out: "The controllers of the new media of communication ... have shown a tendency
to limit choices by using the considerable power of the media to
limit their audience's established attitudes, simply because such limitation is good business."[2] The popular BBC television series,
The last of the summer wine, portrayed a librarian whose vicarious
sex-life through the pages of D. H. Lawrence led to inevitably frustrated attempts to act out his fantasies in occasional under-the-
counter forays with his similarly repressed female assistant. A
Daily mail leader on an appeal against unfair dismissal made by a
London Deputy Borough Librarian reiterates this concept:

> The outsider may not experience much inside a public li-
> brary except an embarrassed wish that his shoes did not
> squeak quite so loudly [where are all these quiet public
> libraries that media-men frequent?] But it's different if
> you work there. The print begins to eat into your soul.

*Reprinted by permission of the author and publisher from Library
Review, 29 (Autumn 1980) 167-175.

Those rows of lurid book jackets start soaking into your blood.... Why should these passion-hungry librarians be compelled to browse in other people's fantasies?

The Mail provides a further refinement in a Harold Robbins/ Spillane pastiche, entitled The librarians: "They did not see the dame behind him, the one who looked as if she had been poured into her cardigan. She held the date-stamp like she knew how to use it."[3] The final effect is comic and not a little vicious in its implications. It confirms some of the most commonly held perceptions exploited so successfully in the once famous Smirnoff advertisement. In the Assistant librarian, Ian Hannah, Product Group Manager for Smirnoff, justified this choice:

> Have another look at it. The advert deliberately encapsulates the old-fashioned, fuddy duddy image of the librarian. The girl who was the mainstay of the public library until she discovered Smirnoff is attractive and obviously emancipated.
> But why feature the public librarian as one of the characters in the series? Because, rightly or wrongly the public at large tend to see the librarian as a person constrained to a boring and humdrum existence, just the sort of person who can benefit from the Smirnoff miracle! [4]

It is by considerations such as these that the media operate: as a correspondent in the Assistant librarian observed: "Even Raquel Welch and Paul Newman would be hardput to create drama and 'human interest' in tracking down a rare pamphlet through interlibrary loans."[5] Literature, although it is comparatively free from these exigencies, has conspicuously failed to produce the three-dimensional librarians who could challenge the cardboard cut-outs of the media. Even Nell Dunn, otherwise noted for her concern with social realism, has conceded to the stereotype in her novel Tear his head off his shoulders. One of the two female characters, a repressed, middle-aged spinster, recovering from the pangs of a torrid love affair in the distant past, which still torments her with erotic fantasies is--surprise--a librarian! This deflects the impact of the novel because it is too facile, but that is not our immediate concern, more pertinent is the demonstration it provides of how pervasive the stereotype is.[6] Similar examples of socially deficient librarians, tinged even here with a faint suggestion of sexual frustration and unattractiveness, are to be found in the more conventional fiction of, for instance, Paul Gallico and Woman's weekly. Janet Goodpenny in Gallico's Trial by terror is "plain looking," presumably "through the lenses of dark, hornrimmed glasses," but she provides restorative love for a brain-washed journalist who refers to her as "that messy little Boston girl with the flat-heeled shoes and the stringy hair."[7]

She has a male counterpart in the pages of Woman's weekly:

John Beckenham watched the quiet drift of people around

the book shelves in the public library and wondered why
he felt no elation on this, his first day as senior librarian.
He had, after all, done extremely well to achieve promotion while still in his early twenties, and he was, after
all, devoted to books of almost any kind....
His accursed shyness was the trouble. It held him back
when everything in him wanted to make a friendly overture,
it tinged his face with pink and it afflicted him with a stam-
mer which was the bane of his life. [8]

Thus, divested of any shreds of glamour, however illusory,
the stereotype has come to be assimilated into the public consciousness. It is worth identifying the factors which have influenced its
origins.

One such is the widespread belief that libraries and librarians are dispensable, a notion which has been put into practice whenever the chips are down. This arose most probably from the context in which the first Public Libraries Act was passed in Britain.
The provision of public libraries was considered desirable but by no
means essential, and the Act made such provision merely permissive. The characteristically Victorian concept of closed access per-
petuated the strict and secret ambience of libraries, enforced by
prohibitive by-laws and aloof librarians, and was no doubt responsible for ignorance on the part of the public about the work carried
on behind the scenes. On the few occasions that authors do stretch
their imaginations to envisage librarians at work they are usually
occupied with either counter-work or cataloguing, tasks guaranteed
to emphasize aspects of the job both trivial and unglamorous.

Both ideas find expression in Hugh Walpole's novel The Cathedral. Miss Milton, the librarian character, spends her time
knitting stockings, and has been on occasion "very near to tears--
also murder" because she "saw the softest, easiest, idlest job in
the world slipping out of her fingers." She thanks God "on her
knees every night" for the Library Committee "by whose graces
she was left in her present position. "[9]

"THE SOFTEST, EASIEST, IDLEST JOB IN THE WORLD"

It's not just a matter of stamping out books.... They
have to be backed and prepared when they arrive from
the publisher and all the cataloguing has to be done. [10]

Thus the drudgery typified by Miss Milton and her fictional colleagues
finds official endorsement in such remarks made--and there is a fine
irony here--by librarians themselves in an attempt to redeem their

image. These statements range from the ingenuous--"The staff here
are mostly young, and even wear trousers to work" [11] to the defensive: "The hair in bun librarian is more likely to be a young
man than an elderly lady--and even the latter has ample reason to
wear her hair in that style as an industrial safety precaution necessitated by library automation. "[12] Most share a somewhat embar-
rassing tendency to backfire, enhancing rather than altering the
stereotype.

Further endeavours which flounder on the rocks of their own
heartiness occur in two works designed to attract new recruits to
the profession, one non-fiction, the other, a career novel. The
first undermines its commendable purpose in a passage of saccharine
brightness:

> A librarian considering applying for a post would probably
> learn more about his likely colleagues before the library
> opens, if only he could see them then, than from any of-
> ficial contacts. The absence of readers removes inhibi-
> tions and friends can talk loudly across the room, some
> even singing at their work. In warm weather assistants
> shelving books may remove coats and work more comfort-
> ably until the friendly attendant gives a general warning
> that he is about to open the doors to the public. If he is
> not friendly he takes a wicked delight in being a few sec-
> onds early to catch the staff off their guard, just one of
> the ways his attitude affects the general well-being and
> happiness of the staff. [13]

The novel, Molly Hilton, library assistant, is an example of
a genre which achieved considerable popularity in the 'fifties. It
tells the story of a young girl who, despite opposition from her parents and friends, and even from her headmistress, is determined to
become a librarian. She presents a stout defence of her chosen profession, but old-fashioned sentiments redolent of the former passage
entirely subvert the novel's good intentions. [14] Paradoxically the
profession has from the first been acutely self-conscious about its
status, role and image, as Panizzi demonstrated in ordering Edward
Edwards to shave off his moustache because it did not befit the status
of a librarian in the British Museum. Less than a hundred years
after the first Public Libraries Act, the stereotype had become
firmly entrenched in public consciousness, for in 1937 McColvin
wrote:

> Curiously enough, the youngsters who most often wish to
> enter library work are frequently of the least suitable type
> --those who are quiet even to the point of shyness, the
> studious, those who prefer their own society to those of
> their fellows, who are "fond of reading" but not of action.
> Perhaps this is partly because with existing low salaries,
> the right people look elsewhere. [15]

Given this situation it is hardly surprising that by 1976
Melvyn Barnes, in rather stronger terms, lamented the fact that:

The typical conception of a public librarian--studious, in-
trovert, colourless, somewhat deficient in the social skills
--has often attracted into the profession recruits who feel
they match this specification. Doctors, parents and well-
intentioned friends attempt to push into Librarianship their
protégées who are admirably suited to our calling, being
shy and retiring, inveterate readers, or recovering from
nervous illnesses. This image deters the extrovert.[16]

Indeed it does, for the inevitable outcome of a stereotype is
that it becomes self-perpetuating. So, despite David Bartlett's claim
that it is "not too late to create a new image for yourselves, or
rather, to convince the public that you are the people you know you
are" [17] the recruits who are attracted by this--to say the least--
unexciting image are liable to continue rather than change the trend,
thereby creating and reinforcing an extremely vicious circle. It is
painful and, it is said, a needless aggravation for librarians to probe
this self-inflicted wound: for the outside world to rub salt into it
is intolerable, as a headmistress' reference received by the College
of Librarianship, Wales unconsciously demonstrates: "The applicant
is a young woman of strong character, great intelligence, wide-
reading and considerable experience: she differs greatly from many
of my pupils who incline to librarianship."[18]

The reaction against being cast in this mould is manifest in
a plethora of editorials, letters and even full length articles in various library journals, which culminated in the early 'seventies and
has faltered somewhat only in the presence of more pressing--that
is, economic--considerations. Although in most respects a natural
progression of McColvin's attempt to refocus the image, they take
issue with his opinion that "it is very rightly said that the librarian
as librarian has no religion, no politics, no class sense and no mor-
als," a stance which Foskett later appropriated. He goes on to say:

No one can prevent a librarian from having his private
opinions, but he should keep them private, since it is in
practice impossible for the librarian, or any other public
servant to dissociate himself from his work in the sight
of the public. Incidentally, it is particularly unsuitable
for a librarian to take any active part in politics.
Physical abnormality is also highly undesirable. Defects of any kind will militate against both personal success and good service. People like to be served by pleasant looking assistants; they are inclined to withdraw themselves and hesitate to make enquiries of any assistant who
is not quite normal.[19]

The Assistant librarian and its sister journals aim to change
such thinking with a new brand of radical chic, providing, for example, "a few sensuous exercises to make the library full with the joy
of life and to make you feel like a real person and not just a role."
Inter alia, one is advised to "get up to show a patron where a book
is located. MOVE your whole body, and not just your index finger.

Dress like Spring, Summer, Winter and Fall, but don't ever dress
like a Librarian."[20]

   Whether such polemic, being of a diffuse and essentially nar-
cissistic nature, will be effective in the long term remains open to
question. If the search for identity is solely of the type which in-
forms Librarians for social change--currently the trendiest British
library journal--and its ilk, the answer is clear.

   There was a time when an ex-policeman, a soldier,
   or someone of equal status, education and training
   was believed to be capable of discharging the duties
   of a Librarian.[21]

Librarianship's ambivalent status is in part the product of an unattractive stereotype as indicated above. The status of a profession
diminishes in relation to the quality of the image which it reflects.
To demonstrate this we must assume that status is simply derived
from image, whereas both are caught in a tangled web of cause and
effect in which various factors are interwoven and their direction
and distinctions accordingly blurred. Certain of these have been influential in the production of both status and stereotype. They include factors such as the low salaries and long working hours necessitated by the permissive nature of the first British Public Libraries
Act, which in turn narrowed the field of potential recruits to the profession.

   Munford cites the example of the appointment in April, 1855,
of a twenty-two-year-old bookseller's assistant to the post of first
librarian of Cambridge Public Library. At least he was in the Trade,
as it were--the runner-up was a retired stage-coachman![22] This
inadequate interpretation of the librarian's role has had more recent
repercussions in the appointment in 1939 of a poet to the post of Librarian of Congress, and again in 1972 of a Civil Servant as Chief
Executive of the British Library. In the first instance President
Roosevelt dismissed librarianship's pretensions to being a profession
as bunkum, a sentiment which must have been echoed in a British
corridor of power some thirty years later: hence the designation of
Chief Executive for the head of the British Library rather than librarian.[23] The British profession did not seem unduly concerned
about the Civil Service snatching this prestigious plum, much to the
surprise of Kenneth Lomas, a Member of Parliament: "Certainly I
can think of very few men in other walks of life who would be prepared to tolerate those responsible juggling with the wording of the
advertisment and then stand around whilst an outsider walked off with
the job from under their very noses." He concludes with what seems
under the circumstances to be unfounded optimism: "I am sure the
librarians' profession will eventually look back in astonishment at the
days when it had to admit it could not provide librarians for the
most demanding tasks at the highest level."[24]

The professional attaches to itself little of the prestige which would enhance its status because moderate salaries and increasing feminisation prevent this.   Making a virtue out of necessity a library manual of 1914 appealed to the altruism of potential employees: "If the service of his fellows is the goal man seeks regardless of the pecuniary rewards accruing then in the librarian's calling will he find a field calling for the exercise of all his powers."[25]   This attitude was to prove damaging in the long term.   Society invests high-salaried professions with a kudos which is in some way derived from the impression that they must partake of glamour, drama and excitement.

The high incidence of women in the profession is both cause and product of modest remuneration.   Such a proportion is by its very existence detrimental to status, as comparison with the nursing profession will demonstrate.   An unwonted emphasis on housekeeping tasks performed in a fussy manner has trivialised library work and produced a bureaucratic structure resistant to changing trends, to pressure and to innovation.   The gradual designation of these tasks as women's work further ensured, in effect, that the library service would be regarded by many as a frill rather than as an integral part of community life.   Melvil Dewey was, it seems, the first on this particular bandwagon too, prophesying that: "A great librarian must have a clear head, a strong hand, and above all, a great heart. Such shall be the greatest among librarians and when I look into the future I am inclined to think that most of the men who achieve this greatness will be women."[26]   This was a means of making a virtue from necessity, as Jesse Shera maintains, not without a touch of acerbity:

> Melvil Dewey is generally charged with bringing women
> into librarianship, but we rather suspect that he was more
> symptomatic than causal.   Melvil was quick to spot a
> trend and capitalize upon it, and he doubtless saw that the
> young ladies of his day were beginning to think of careers
> of their own and that he could profitably exploit this re-
> source by offering them genteel and respectable employ-
> ment. [27]

Indeed not to put too fine a point on it, in Britain and in America too the introduction of women provided cheap labour in a profession where financial limitations imposed low salaries.   Shera continues, outlining the predictable outcome of feminisation: "But despite the movement for the 'liberation' of women, in the popular mind, the hierarchy of the profession is still sex-linked."[28]   Benge corroborates this conclusion in Libraries and cultural change: "From the status point of view this (feminisation) is undesirable not because women make less capable librarians, but because in a world where women are still underprivileged, and likely to abandon a career in favour of marriage, a profession which does not attract men in sufficient numbers inevitably suffers in public esteem."[29]

> The uses of Free Libraries are real and manifold....
> To all sections alike they are accesible, and to say
> that the "great unwashed" alone use them is saying
> what would not be true, especially as on the doors
> and walls of some of the libraries in the manufacturing
> districts a notice enforcing "clean hands and faces" is
> conspicuous and that is rigidly enforced by careful li-
> brarians. [30]

This quotation encapsulates perfectly the ambiguous nature of the
public library movement, on the one hand a product of the emerging
radicalism which precipitated the Factories Acts, State Education and
wider enfranchisement, and on the other, the gift of enlightened and
altruistic Victorian benefactors designed to save the masses from
vice and penury, exemplifying "the nineteenth-century faith in the
public library as a social force that would through the promotion of
reading save mankind from poverty, crime, vice, alcoholism and
almost every other evil to which Flesh is heir."[31] Contemporary
comment reflects both sides of the coin. The existence of demand
is substantiated by the adoption of the unimpressive British Act of
1850 in various areas, despite the difficulties of operation. Its success was no doubt due in part to the failure of the Mechanics' Institutes to provide a service that was both relevant and attractive to
the working classes. A typical contemporary observer made the
point that "a class superior to working men, and a small proportion
of working men receiving comparatively high wages support these
institutions, generally speaking they are not Mechanics' Institutes
and it is a misnomer to designate them as such."[32]

However low the subscriptions, they were prohibitive at a
time when poverty was rife, and if the first public libraries appear
inadequate when compared with those of today, they may well have
seemed superior in every way to the services offered by the Mechanics' Institutes:

> It was and is one thing to offer to a workman free access
> to a Library and Reading Room ... open throughout the
> day, seasoned with bright and gossipy newspapers, illus-
> trated weeklies and grave magazines, and all freer than
> the air he breathes, and it is, or was, quite another thing
> to offer to a workman for 1s. or 1. 6d. a quarter, the
> choice from a third floor apartment ... of a volume at a
> time from a certain section of a somewhat faded collection
> of books. [33]

Hatt sees the impetus for the spread of literacy and the en-
suing reforms as having a base in both the working and the middle-
classes. He argues that the Mechanics' Institutes failed not simply
through providing a relatively costly and unattractive service but because the middle-classes organisers imposed a characteristic ban on
religious and political discussion, thus alienating "suspicious working-
class radicals":

From the point of view of self-defence as well as that of
philanthropy it was desirable that the mob be turned into
something like a collection of respectable Godly people.
This was the hope implicit, and sometimes explicit in most
Victorian reform.   It was certainly one of the dominant
motives for the extension of literacy. [34]

There were those too among the nation's rulers who opposed
reform, however expedient it might be, because they feared that literacy and free libraries would plant the seeds of sedition, but neither
could silence the emerging working-class voice which demanded not
only the right to read, but unlimited access to reading material.
Hatt concludes:

> Public libraries were the response to a need for ... insti-
> tutions publicly owned, providing the public with as wide a
> selection of books, newspapers and periodicals as possible
> and making no effort to influence anybody in the choice of
> what he actually read.   This was essential, for the new
> readers had had enough of being told what was good for
> them. [35]

If the movement was to a large extent middle-class inspired,
the first libraries were very much the province of the working-classes.
On March 5th, 1864, Ewart wrote to the librarian of the Cambridge
Public Library: "So far as my intentions went, Free Libraries were
meant for all classes.   Naturally the most numerous (the working)
class would derive most benefit from them.   But I always thought
one of the good results of such institutions would be the bringing of
all classes together and uniting them by the common bond of literary
pursuits. "[36]

His attempt failed--in the short term at least.   In 1870, the
first year for which occupational tables were prepared, of 710 new
readers joining the Cambridge Public Libraries, less than one hundred
can be identified as other than members of the working-classes.
Munford observed that: "Public libraries were in fact generally regarded as a service for working-class readers until the Act of 1919
had abolished rate limitation and enabled the service to recover from
what a librarian of 1900 could euphemistically diagnose as 'an anae-
mic condition. '"[37]

The origins of the public library, if not entirely radical
therefore, were working-class orientated, a situation which under-
lines how far the pendulum has swung in the opposite direction during
the intervening years, so that the public library has come to be regarded as a bastion of the middle-classes.   Munford implies that,
as the service improved, the middle-classes appropriated it for their
own uses.   But that is only half the story, public libraries themselves a force for conservatism, fossilised by increasing
bureaucracy and tedious contention over professionalism.   Despite
librarianship's low status, it is, by virtue of being a profession,
resolutely middle-class.   The one deters ambitious recruits, and

the other, because of the particular values it embodies, alienates many potential users. Moreover it is characteristic that the campaign for status concerns itself with snobbish rather than more practical ends, as Judith McPheron points out: "What we aspire to is not only the higher good of mankind, but bourgeois respectability and comfort and a sense of insularity and class solidarity which keeps us forever separate from that seamy band, the workers.... The crazy thing about the aspirations of librarians is that they are going for the social status and not the money."[38] The image of librarianship is formed by an amalgam of these disparate influences: an unfortunate stereotype, a low-status profession, and an aura of bourgeois respectability. James Thompson suggests that the remedy lies in the establishment of librarianship as an élite profession, a term somewhat misleading in its implications. The terminology rather than the basic premise is at fault: "The solution must lie in the creation of an élite corps of librarians who are well-educated and committed." He recognizes that the diffidence of non-users and even users towards the library is "deeply rooted in the inequalities of our social system, not in librarianship as such."[39]

To overcome this diffidence is the librarian's primary task. It has expressed itself in tentative attempts at outreach programmes and extension activities. Unless such gestures are accompanied by revision of the image and redefinition of the role, they will be enfeebled; indeed, given the present economic climate they cannot survive. This re-assessment must not take the direction which Judith McPheron derides, as it has so often in the past, a form which Frank Hatt describes as "a kind of narcissism, a painful examination of our 'image' for signs of professional status."[40] That way impotence lies. To remain viable, and to become in all senses more virile, the profession should take heed of the principles of librarianship outlined by Lionel McColvin as long ago as 1942 in terms echoed in more recent years but nowhere bettered:

> The library service exists to serve--to give without question, favour or limitations. It is an instrument for the promotion of all or any of the activities of its readers. Therefore it must be catholic and all-embracing. Whenever, as may often be the case, because of financial or other limitations, it must choose between types of provision, this must always be in accord with the value of the services to the individuals requiring them--not because of our own idea or opinion of what they should be. [41]

References

1. Needle, Jan. Paulo Baby: quoted in Usherwood, Bob. "P.R. and Paulo Baby." Assistant librarian 65, No. 5, May 1972, p. 69.
2. Hatt, Frank. "The Right to Read and the Long Revolution." The Library Association record, 65, No. 1, January, 1963.
3. The daily mail, Saturday, September 13th, 1975, p. 6.

4. Hannah, Ian: quoted in "A Walking Contradiction--The Library Image," Assistant librarian, 65, No. 12, December, 1972, p. 188.
5. "Unsung Libraries." Assistant librarian, 64, No. 12, December, 1971, p. 191.
6. Dunn, Nell. Tear his head off his shoulders. London: Penguin, 1976.
7. Gallico, Paul. Trial by terror: quoted in Hutton, Muriel. "Librarians in Literature," Books, May-June, 1965, p. 101.
8. Tobitt, Yvonne. "Sophie called Sally," Woman's weekly, January 15th, 1977, p. 16.
9. Walpole, Hugh. The Cathedral: quoted in Hutton, Muriel. op. cit. p. 101.
10. Burnley evening star. December 4th, 1973.
11. The Wembley news, September 29th, 1972.
12. Barnes, Melvyn. "The Public Librarian of the Future": in Harrison, K. C., ed. Prospects for British librarianship, London: The Library Association, 1976, p. 247.
13. Maidment, William R. Librarianship. London: David & Charles, 1975, p. 19.
14. Lonsdale, Bertha. Molly Hilton: library assistant. London: Bodley Head, 1954.
15. McColvin, Lionel R. Libraries and the public. London: Allen & Unwin, 1937, p. 75.
16. Barnes, Melvyn. op. cit. p. 260.
17. Bartlett, David. "In Pursuit of a New Image." Assistant librarian, 67, No. 8, August, 1974, p. 128.
18. Quoted in: Ramsden, Michael. "Hanging Together." Assistant librarian, 62, No. 10, November, 1969, p. 164.
19. McColvin, Lionel R. Library staffs. London: Allen & Unwin, 1939, p. 26.
20. Gial, Kathleen. "The Sensuous Librarian": quoted in "A Walking Contradiction--The Library Image," op. cit. p. 189.
21. Munford, W. A. Penny rate, London: The Library Association, 1951.
22. Munford, W. A. op. cit. p. 72.
23. Thompson, James. Library power, London: Clive Bingley, 1974, p. 13.
24. Lomas, Kenneth. "Libraries from an M. P. 's point of view," Library Association record: quoted in Thompson, James. op. cit. p. 14.
25. Roebuck, G. E. Primer of library practice. London: Grafton & Co., 1914, p. 147.
26. Quoted in: Coutts, Henry T. Library jokes and jottings.
27. Shera, Jesse, H. "A Better Class of Mouse": in "The Compleat Librarian" and other essays. London: The Press of Case Western University, 1971, p. 70.
28. Ibid.
29. Benge, Ronald C. Libraries and cultural change. London: Archon Books & Clive Bingley, 1972, p. 215.
30. Greenwood, Thomas. Free public libraries: quoted in Munford W. A. op. cit., p. 61-62.

31. Shera, Jesse H. The foundations of education for librarianship, New York: Becker & Hayes, 1972: quoted in Thompson, James, op. cit. , p. 97.
32. Dawson, G. : quoted in Munford, W. A. op. cit. , p. 138.
33. Milne, J. W. : quoted in Munford, p. 140.
34. Hatt, Frank, op. cit. , p. 14.
35. Ibid. , p. 15.
36. Munford, W. A. op. cit. , p. 63.
37. Ibid. , p. 61.
38. McPheron, Judith. "Peacocks and Posers--Librarianship as a Profession." Assistant librarian. 67, No. 7, July, 1974, p. 116-117.
39. Thompson, James. op. cit. , p. 110.
40. Hatt, Frank. op. cit. , p. 15.
41. McColvin, Lionel R. : quoted in Totterdell, Barry. "Libraries and their Users": in Harrison, K. C. , ed. op. cit. p. 141.

A PROFILE OF ALA PERSONAL MEMBERS*

Leigh S. Estabrook and Kathleen M. Heim

Background of COSWL study and size of sample

In 1979 the Standing Committee on the Status of Women in Librarianship (COSWL) submitted a proposal to the J. Morris Jones and Bailey
K. Howard World Book Encyclopedia ALA Goals Award Committee to
fund a project titled, "A Pilot Profile of the Women Members of the
American Library Association."

The project was supported by a Bailey K. Howard goal award
of $5,000 and services of ALA and the authors' universities. The
committee appointed Kathleen M. Heim, assistant professor at the
Graduate School of Library Science at the University of Illinois/
Urbana-Champaign, and Leigh S. Estabrook, associate professor at
the Syracuse University School of Information Studies, as co-principal
investigators. The investigators developed a seven-page questionnaire, which was sent to 3,000 randomly selected ALA personal
members (excluding foreign, lay, and student) from ALA's total of
28,619 personal members in February 1980. Of the 3,000, 67.1
percent responded.

This article, written for American Libraries, presents initial
descriptive findings of the research (hereafter called the COSWL
Study), based on a subsample of 1,583 full-time, currently employed
ALA members. Responses from retired and part-time members
will be analyzed later.

Female members of the American Library Association earn 25 percent less, have published less, have been less active in professional
associations, and are more occupationally diverse than their male
counterparts. These are some preliminary findings of an award-
funded study of ALA's Standing Committee on the Status of Women
in Librarianship. The COSWL Study provides new kinds of data
about members of ALA. Earlier studies of the characteristics
of librarians have isolated librarians by type (academic, special,

*Reprinted by permission of the American Library Association and
the authors from American Libraries, 12:11 (December 1980) 654-
59. Copyright © 1981 by Leigh Estabrook and Kathleen Heim.

public) or position (directors, reference librarians), or have focused on a few key variables (salary, mobility, personality). [1]

   Concern about the status of women in librarianship over the last decade was apparent in the emergence of the SRRT Feminist Task Force, Women Library Workers, and the Standing Committee on the Status of Women in Librarianship, as well as in articles and conferences. [2]   However, the profession lacked significant data for analyzing factors and trends behind the differences in status according to sex.   The COSWL Study findings reported here will provide information on some of the more salient differences between currently employed, full-time, male and female ALA members, as well as general information on ALA members as compared with the library field at large.

Sex and education

The ALA membership at the time of the COSWL Study was 75. 8-percent female and 24. 1-percent male.   The larger universe of librarians as reported in the 1970 Census is 84-percent female and 16-percent male. [3]   Although ALA does not require any professional credential for membership, 95. 5 percent of its working, U. S. personal members do hold the MLS degree.   Of these, 4. 2 percent of the women and 19. 5 percent of the men hold the Ph. D. , Ed. D. or

ALA's 38.5%
in top-level library positions

All full-time academic, public, school, & special librarians who belong to ALA

(77% women; 23% men)

Directors, 15.3% total

Associate & assistant directors, 5.2% total

Dept. heads, 18% total

American Libraries graphic

Good news and bad news.   As detailed in Table 4, many ALA members are reaching the top echelons; but the percentage of women there falls short of the female percentage of ALA (about 76% in the full sample). In the above subsample of 1, 152 ALA members, each figure represents approximately 100 persons.

DLS. An analysis of library manpower published by the Bureau of
Labor Statistics (BLS) in 1975 noted that "probably no more than 40-
50 percent of all librarians employed in the U.S. have a master's
degree in librarianship." The analysis points to the relatively large
number of school librarians who are not required to have the MLS
as well as the many librarians who completed their professional
training prior to 1951, before standards of accreditation for library
schools endorsed the master's as the first professional degree. [4]
The inability of many small public and special libraries to pay for
a librarian with an MLS is also a factor in the high number of individuals without the MLS who noted their occupation as librarian.

However, since ALA does not require the professional credential for membership, its potential base is that larger pool of 115,000
individuals who reported that they were working as librarians. The
COSWL findings demonstrate that ALA is most successful in attracting those individuals with a master's degree and that men join ALA
in greater numbers than their proportion in the universe of working
librarians.

A slight shift in favor of men's representation in ALA has
occurred since the 1970 ALA salary survey, which found the membership was 76.5-percent female and 23.5-percent male. [5] We do
not yet have the 1980 census data to estimate if we are drawing in
a higher proportion of women, but we know from the placement data
appearing in Library Journal surveys between 1972 and 1980 that the
average percentage of women obtaining degrees from ALA accredited
programs is 79 percent compared to men's 21 percent. [6] Thus,
while ALA membership does not reflect the pool of librarians, it
does reflect the graduates of ALA accredited schools fairly closely.

We may infer from these data that although ALA is open to
all librarians, most of its members hold MLS degrees. ALA's base
is less the universe of librarians than it is those librarians with a
degree from an accredited library school.

Age

The median age of women ALA members was 40; of men, 42. Although the BLS Library Manpower study based on 1970 data found
female librarians to be an older group (48 percent were over 45)
than male librarians (26 percent were over 45), [7] the COSWL Study
shows that ALA members are similar in age, with 42.4 percent of
the women and 41.0 percent of the men over 45.

Race

"Whites" constitute 93.6 percent of the membership; minorities constitute the remaining 6.4 percent (see Table 1). A higher percentage
of female members than of male members are white. Blacks, who
account for 3.3 percent of the total membership, are more often female; Asian-Americans, who account for 1.9 percent of the total,

Table 1: Percentages of librarians by race and sex as indicated in three studies

	1970 Census Data[1]			COSWL Study of ALA			ALA Accredited Master's—OLPR[2]								
							76–77			77–78			78–79		
	M	F	Total	M	F	Total	M	F	T	M	F	T	M	F	T
White	92.3	91.8	91.9	93.6	93.7	93.6	92.1	91.7	91.8	91.3	90.9	91.0	90.1	89.7	89.7
Black	5.7	6.7	6.5	1.6	3.9	3.3	3.4	4.4	4.2	3.0	5.1	4.6	3.5	5.1	4.8
Asian-American	1.3	1.1	1.1	2.9	1.6	1.9	2.0	2.7	2.6	2.3	2.3	2.3	3.8	3.4	3.5
Hispanic	(2.3)	(1.4)	(1.6)[3]	.5	.6	.5	2.5	1.2	1.3	3.4	1.6	1.9	2.6	1.8	1.9

Note: Cells for other ethnic groups are too small for generalization and are omitted so percentages do not add up to 100.

[1] United States, Bureau of the Census. Census of Population: 1970, Occupational Characteristics, Subject Reports, Final Report PC(2)-7A, 1973, p. 12.

[2] American Library Association, Office for Library Personnel Resources. Degrees and Certificates Awarded by U.S. Library Education Program 1976-1979 (Chicago: ALA, 1980); 3-4 (mimeographed).

[3] The 1970 census double-counted persons of Spanish origin since they may be of any race.

are more often male. Hispanics account for only . 5 percent of the
total membership; neither women nor men predominate.

     Turning again to the census data, we see that ALA minority
membership falls below the 8. 1 percent of the total library workforce
reported to be minority librarians in 1970. We do not have any new
data on the total number of minority librarians, but we have data
gathered for the ALA Office for Library Personnel Resources on
degrees and certificates granted. [8] Looking at the racial breakdown
of ALA-accredited master's degree recipients (those most likely to
join ALA), we see that the percentage of minorities receiving degrees has been rising slowly: 8. 2 percent in 76-77; 9 percent in
77-78; and 10. 3 percent in 78-79. It appears that these greater
numbers of minorities graduating with an accredited MLS have not
been drawn to ALA in numbers proportionate to their representation
in the universe of librarians.

                         EMPLOYMENT TRENDS

To labor analysts, librarianship is an occupationally segregated profession because of its predominance of women workers. It is also
occupationally segregated by positions held within libraries; i. e. ,
even though the field itself is a "women's profession," it continues
to have the dual career structure for men and women identified by
Bryan in 1952. [9] The COSWL Study provides a broad view of the
library field by type of employment and a clear picture of positional
segregation.

Type of Library

In the BLS universe of librarians, the school sector accounts for
45. 2 percent of all librarians; public, 23 percent; academic, 17 percent; and special and other, 14. 8 percent. Looking at the same
1970 BLS data for males and females, we find that women predominate in schools (49. 9 percent) and men predominate in academic libraries (36. 7 percent).

     Patterns of employment by type of library are markedly dif-
ferent among current ALA members. Public, academic, and special
and other libraries are represented in greater proportion in ALA
than they are in the population at large, and school libraries account
for only 13. 6 percent of ALA members. Comparing these findings
to those of the 1970 ALA salary survey, we find a shift in ALA
membership by library type over the last decade. The 1970 survey
found 20. 8 percent in schools, 26. 8 percent in public, 29 percent
in special and other (Table 2) (p. 41).

     ALA has become more representative of public, academic,
and special and other librarians while school librarian representation
has declined. [10] If we look at ALA membership by sex and type of
library (Table 3), we find that ALA men predominate in academic

libraries (44. 6 percent), and ALA women predominate in public libraries (30. 7 percent). As expected, women still account for greater
school library membership. More men (3. 4 percent) than women
(2. 2 percent) are employed outside traditional library structures in
such areas as publishing or allied computer industries.

    These trends seem to be holding if we compare them to Li-
brary Journal's most recent placement survey, which found 37. 9
percent of 1979 male graduates in academic libraries, and women
spread more evenly across the four library types. [11]

Table 2: ALA membership by library type

	Academic	Public	School	Special & other
ALA 1979 (COSWL)	31.8	28.8	13.6	25.8
ALA 1970[1]	29.0	26.8	20.8	23.4

[1]Survey did not differentiate by sex.

    The occupational segregation of women that occurs in the
larger labor market, i. e. , the concentration of women in lower-
paying, lower-status jobs, functions clearly in librarianship. The
perceived "higher" status of academic librarianship attracts a greater
proportion of men than any other area of library employment, while
the perceived "lower" status of work with children attracts very few
men. This is already clear from the differentiation of male and female librarians by type of library employment, but it becomes even
clearer when we examine the types of positions librarians hold.

Positions held

To analyze positions held, we looked at a subset of our sample:
those employed in academic, special, school, and public libraries.
The sample was narrowed because the variety of libraries in the
"other" categories required too fine a breakdown of positions to present. Table 4 shows the number and percentages of women and men
in 10 categories of library positions as well as the percentages of
women and men in each position.

    In this analysis we find striking examples of occupational
segregation by position. The "director" level accounts for 28. 9
percent of all reporting ALA male members, but only 11. 2 percent
of females. If we add the "management" categories of "director,"
"assistant/associate director," and "department head," we find that

Table 3: Percentages of librarians by sex in different types of libraries
as indicated in three studies

	Library Manpower Study[1]			COSWL Study of ALA			1979 LJ Placement Study[2]		
	M	W	Total	M	W	Total	M	W	Total
School	20.0	49.9	45.2	3.5	17.0	13.6	8.6	21.5	19.1
Public	20.6	23.5	23.0	22.8	30.7	28.8	25.3	28.0	27.4
Academic	36.7	13.3	17.0	44.6	27.7	31.8	37.6	22.3	25.2
Special & Other	22.7	13.3	14.8	25.7	22.4	23.3	28.5	28.2	28.3
Nonlibrary Other				3.4	2.2	2.5			

Note: Due to the great variety of positions outside of the four major categories of libraries we are displaying here only that subset of the total population employed in the four major categories.

[1] "Librarian-General" includes those individuals who did not differentiate position.

[2] "Librarian-Other" includes a variety of positions allied to the four library types such as bibliographer, information specialist, or consultant.

Table 4: Number and percent of librarians by sex in selected positions
in academic, public, school, and special libraries

	Director	Associate/ Assistant Director	Department Head	Public Services Other	Technical Services Other	School Librarian	Media Specialist	Children's Services	Librarian[1] General	Other[2]
Women (N=886) Number	99	33	157	120	53	17	57	37	256	57
Percent of all women	11.2	3.7	17.8	13.5	6.0	1.9	6.4	4.2	28.9	6.4
Percent in this position who are women	56.3	55.0	75.9	83.3	69.7	94.4	90.5	97.4	87.7	73.1
Men (N=266) Number	77	27	50	24	23	1	6	1	36	21
Percent of all men	28.9	10.2	18.7	9.0	8.6	0.4	2.3	0.4	13.5	7.9
Percent in this position who are men	43.8	45.0	24.1	16.7	30.3	5.6	9.5	2.6	12.3	27.0
Total (N=1152) Percent of total in this position	15.3	5.2	18.0	12.5	6.6	1.6	5.5	3.3	25.3	6.8

Note: Due to the great variety of positions outside of the four major categories of libraries we are displaying here only that subset of the total population employed in the four major categories.

[1]"Librarian-General" includes those individuals who did not differentiate position.

[2]"Librarian-Other" includes a variety of positions allied to the four library types such as bibliographer, information specialist, or consultant.

these account for over half of all ALA men (57. 8 percent) and less than a third (32. 7 percent) of the women. In the two categories that directly relate to children (school librarian and children's services), we find 6. 1 percent women and less than 1 percent (. 8) men. [12] Women also work in public service positions (13. 5 percent) in greater numbers than do men (9 percent).

Of all librarians in ALA, our study indicates that more than one-third (38. 5 percent) are in management positions and about one-fifth (19. 1 percent) in general library work in technical and public services.

We may conclude that librarianship, as represented by ALA, continues to exhibit the occupational, sexual segregation by type of library and position identified by Schiller in 1974. [13]

Within their organization

Another way of looking at "status" is to examine the position of in-dividuals within their organization. We asked a number of questions about position level and individuals supervised in order to discover if there were differences between women and men. We found that the median number of employees in organizations where women worked is 46. 1 versus 48. 5 for men, and that women have been on the job six years and men seven; there are more significant differ-ences between the two in location in the organizational hierarchy and supervisory responsibilities.

In response to the question, "How many levels are there above you in the organization?" 19. 5 percent of the men and 10. 2 percent of the women indicated that they were at the top. Fifty-three per-cent of the men and 66. 8 percent of the women had two or more levels above them. Women have less supervisory responsibility than men. While 38. 5 percent of the men supervised five or more professionals, only 16. 2 percent of the women did so. Men also had more supervisory responsibility for support staff: 45. 1 percent of the men supervised five or more support staff, compared to 25. 8 percent of the women.

We observe that ALA women are less likely to be at the top of their organization and less likely to have supervisory responsi-bility. Later we will measure these factors against the salary var-iable to discover if they contribute to salary differences between women and men.

PROFESSIONAL INVOLVEMENT

We asked questions in two areas to measure professional involve-ment: publication activity and association visibility.

Publications

We looked at a variety of publication formats but include only
three here: books, articles, and book reviews. We found that 5.2
percent of the women versus 17.1 percent of the men had published
books; 24.9 percent of the women versus 52.5 percent of the men
had published articles; and 18.8 percent of the women versus 35.7
percent of the men had published book reviews. We found men publish roughly three times as many books and book reviews and four
times as many articles as women. We have little data with which
to compare these findings, but a recent article by Olsgaard and Olsgaard found that men accounted for about two-thirds (67.4 percent),
and women for about one-third (32.6 percent) of articles in five major library journals. [14]

Professional Visibility

One of the indicators of status within a profession is the degree
of visibility in association activity. We asked our sample to indicate their involvement at two levels: national and state/regional
(Table 5) (below).

Table 5: Percentage of ALA men and women involved in professional activities

	Men	Women
Elected or appointed at national level	31.7	14.6
Chair of committee section, division at national level	28.2	12.1
Member of committee at national level	63.2	42.9
Elected or appointed at state/regional level	55.1	38.7
Chair of committee, section, division at state/regional level	49.9	32.1
Member of committee at state/regional level	71.9	60.5

The percentage of men was higher at every level of professional involvement, including positions in state and regional associations where women have been presumed to be more active.

                              SALARY

Because many previous studies have focused on salaries of librarians
in general, a major concern in the COSWL Study was the salary differential between men and women in ALA. We were not so much interested in confirming what has already been established--that there
are significant differences in earnings of male and female librarians
--as in isolating the factors associated with these differences. Specifically, we examined: 1) whether there has been any convergence
in men's and women's salaries in recent years; 2) whether librarians' salaries have increased at a rate equal to the inflation rate;
and 3) whether there are underlying differences in men's and women's
work patterns that help explain salary inequalities.

Trends in Salaries

The median salary for full-time employed women in the COSWL Study
was $14,700; for men, $19,500. Instead of this dramatic gap, we
had expected to find some convergence between men's and women's
salaries during the past decade, when concern with the status of
women in the profession and the use of affirmative action policies
could have been expected to affect hiring practices and salaries. In
fact, there has been divergence. Comparison of the 1979 COSWL
salary data with that from the 1970 ALA salary survey shows that,
whereas women's salaries in 1970 were 77 percent of men's ($10,400
vs. $13,500), in 1979 they were only 75 percent. [15] In absolute
terms, the median salary for male librarians in 1970 was $3,100
more than that of their female counterparts. In 1979, the difference
was $4,800. These figures parallel recent national data on trends
in the relation of women's earnings to men's.

The impact of inflation on librarians' salaries

The relative loss in earnings that women have experienced over the
past decade is even more shocking when one looks at librarians'
earnings relative to changes in the consumer price index in that
time period. In a study of earnings of various occupational groups,
Blumberg found that between 1967 and 1977 librarians lost 10.3 percent in real earnings when salaries were adjusted for inflation. [16]
When the 1970 ALA membership survey and the COSWL data are
similarly analyzed, the loss between 1970 and 1979 is 25 percent
for the membership as a whole. For female librarians the loss
in earning power was 29 percent.

Differences in salaries within the profession

The central problem for the COSWL Study was to try to understand the reasons for variations in salaries within the profession. How can we explain the major differences between women's and men's salaries? Are the differences a function of women being less mobile or concentrated in different types of organizations, or is gender the major factor in determining a member's salary?

The type of library in which an individual works is one of the strongest determinants of salary; this relationship has been relatively constant over the past 10 years. Academic librarians earn the highest mean salary; school librarians the lowest (Table 6). As noted above, women and men are not proportionally represented in different types of libraries. Almost half the men surveyed work in academic libraries.

Table 6: Mean salary of ALA members by type of library[1]

	Academic	Public	School	Special
ALA 1979 (COSWL)	$16,710	$15,300	$14,700	$15,120
ALA 1970	12,523	11,135	10,623	12,084

[1]In order to make these data comparable, it has been necessary to use mean rather than median salary.

Within library differences

This fundamental difference between women's and men's work patterns was not sufficient, however, to explain the disparities in salaries. Within each type of library (except systems, library education, community colleges, and federal libraries) there were significant differences in compensation of women and men (Table 7).

Our findings that women and men do not have similar rates of publication, nor similar supervisory responsibilities, and that they are not likely to hold similar positions in their organizational hierarchy, suggest that such factors may explain the variance in salary within libraries. In order to examine these relationships more closely, we identified a set of variables thought to explain most fully differences among individual salaries. The variables were age, sex, race, perceived mobility, length of time since receiving the MLS degree, total time spent on leave, number of books published, number of articles published, organization size, number of professionals and number of non-professionals supervised, and

Table 7: Mean salaries of male and female ALA members by type of library employment

	Academic	Public	School
Female	$14,850	$14,236	$14,725
Male	20,520	19,319	18,692

number of levels in the organizational hierarchy above the individual. We looked at simple correlations ("r") between any two of the variables and applied standard multivariate techniques to discover how each group of variables we identified contributed to overall variation in salary in the three major types of libraries. [17]

Our analysis showed wide variation in the relationship between salary and other variables in different types of libraries. Overall, however, personal characteristics--age, sex, race, mobility, and the date of receiving the MLS degree--explained most of the variance in salaries.

Only a few variables besides sex and date of the MLS degree strongly correlated with salary level in the three major types of libraries. In academic libraries the number of professionals supervised (r=. 557) and the number of books published (r=. 320) significantly correlated with earnings. In public libraries both the number of professionals supervised (r=. 324) and the number of non-professionals supervised (r=. 425) bore a relationship to salary; publications did not. Supervisory responsibility in school libraries did not correlate with salary, but the number of books published did (r=. 346).

Because these variables correlate with salary and because we have found that men are likely to publish more and to have greater supervisory responsibility, it was important to determine to what extent salary is related to gender when one controls for the publications and supervision variables. In both academic and public libraries the sex of individuals is a significant predictor of their salary when all the other variables we considered are held constant. Thus we can say that even in circumstances where women and men publish at the same rate, supervise the same number of professionals or non-professionals, receive the MLS at the same time, or are the same age, women are likely to earn lower salaries than men. The only exception is in school libraries. The percentage of male school librarians in our sample was so small that there is not enough variation in male incomes for gender to be a significant predictor of salaries.

Several other comments should be made about our findings. First, in none of the three types of libraries was an individual's level in the organizational hierarchy significantly related to her or his salary. Nonetheless, when we looked at the relationship of the entire set of variables to salary level, we were able to explain almost 50 percent of the variance by our group of personal, professional, and organizational factors. (For school libraries $R^2 = .435$; for academic, $R^2 = .512$; and for public, $R^2 = .506$).

Second, there were differences in salary levels by social group. Most notably, black librarians in school and public libraries are earning significantly higher salaries than white librarians. We would caution, however, against using these findings to support notions of reverse racism. Our evidence suggests that black librarians are underrepresented in ALA (Table 1). If non-members are more likely to hold lower-salaried positions, and if they were counted in our sample, the relationship between race and salary found in our study would probably disappear or be reversed.

ADDITIONAL QUESTIONS

Most important, although our analysis of responses to the COSWL Study has revealed wide variation in the level of participation, compensation, and status of women and men in ALA membership, we still do not know enough to infer causal relationships between many of these variables. If male ALA members receive higher salaries than female ALA members, and if higher salaries are correlated with higher publishing rates, must we infer that men receive higher salaries in part because they publish more? Or is it possible that they publish more because they receive higher salaries and are therefore in a position to secure the support services and encouragement to publish more? To us it is significant to find that even when we control for supervisory responsibilities, publication, age, and other factors associated with higher salaries, women still receive lower salaries than men; but we have not yet identified the circumstances under which these inequities do not prevail.

This article is based on only a portion of the data from the COSWL Study. At a later time we hope to be able to resolve some of these issues by looking, for example, at the effect of total family income on publishing and professional involvement and by looking at the career histories of our respondents. We also hope to examine the effects of family background and family responsibilities on achievement both for currently employed librarians and for the unemployed and retired members in our sample.

The data

The data from the COSWL Study substantiate significant differences in status, accomplishments, and salary between men and women in ALA. We have been able to identify some interrelationships among these factors; however, the question remains of how the association and members of the profession can respond to these findings in a positive and humane manner.

References

1. The COSWL Study final report will include a complete list.
2. See: Kathleen Weibel and Kathleen M. Heim with assistance from Dianne J. Ellsworth, The Role of Women in Librarianship: 1876-1976: The Entry, Advancement and Struggle for Equalization in One Profession. (Phoenix: Oryx Press, 1979); and articles in ALA Yearbooks 1976--present on "Women in Librarianship."
3. United States Bureau of the Census. Census of Population: 1970, Occupational Characteristics, Subject Reports, Final Report PC (2)--7A, 1973, p. 17.
4. United States Bureau of Labor Statistics. Library Manpower: A Study of Demand and Supply. Bulletin 1952, 1975, pp. 16-20.
5. American Library Association. "ALA Salary Survey: Personal Members." American Libraries 2 (April 1971): calculated from Table 9, p. 416.
6. Calculated from annual placement and salary surveys by C. J. Frarey and C. L. Learmont in Library Journal 98 (June 15, 1973); 99 (July 1976); 102 (June 15, 1977); 103 (July 1978); C. L. Learmont and Richard Troiano in Library Journal 104 (July 1979); and C. L. Learmont in Library Journal 105 (Nov. 1, 1980).
7. Bureau of Labor Statistics, Library Manpower, p. 14.
8. American Library Association, Office for Library Personnel Resources. Degrees and Certificates Awarded by U.S. Library Education Programs 1976-1979. (Chicago: ALA, 1980) (mimeographed).
9. Alice I. Bryan, The Public Librarian: A Report of the Public Library Inquiry of the Social Science Research Council, (New York: Columbia University Press, 1952).
10. However, ALA's overall membership included only 6.6 percent who define themselves as special librarians per se. The Special Library Association had 9,442 members when it conducted its 1979 Salary Survey, and the existence of this organization makes it difficult for us to make significant generalizations about the universe of special librarians.
11. Learmont, 1980.
12. We have analyzed position as respondents indicated. While many may work in schools as media specialist or librarian-general, they did not show up under the "school librarian category."
13. Anita R. Schiller, "Women in Librarianship" in Advances in Librarianship, v. 4. Edited by Melvin J. Voigt. (New York: Academic Press, 1974): 103-147.
14. John N. Olsgaard and Jane Kinch Olsgaard. "Authorship in Five Library Periodicals." College and Research Libraries 41 (January 1981): calculated from Table 1, p. 50.

15. "ALA Salary Survey," p. 416.
16. Paul Blumberg. Inequality in an Age of Decline. (New York: Oxford University Press, 1980), p. 79.
17. For simplicity and economy of space, statistical findings from these analyses are not reported in full in this article. Interested readers are invited to write the authors or to consult the final report to the Committee on the Status of Women in Librarianship, ALA (forthcoming). The correlation coefficient ("r") measures the extent to which two variables occur together and ranges from "0" to "1" with "1" representing the situation in which two variables are always associated with one another. Variance (or "R^2") measures the extent to which the change in one (or a group) of variables is associated with a change in another.

PROFESSIONAL IDEALS AND SOCIAL REALITIES:
SOME QUESTIONS ABOUT THE EDUCATION OF LIBRARIANS*

John Calvin Colson

Effective consideration of the problems of education for a profession
must be based in a clear perception of the realities in which the
profession exists. That is, education for a profession is a part of
the profession, and educational problems cannot be examined realis-
tically without attention to the conditions in which the profession exists. There must be medical doctors before there can be a medical
profession before there can be a medical school; similarly, there
must be librarians before there can be a librarianship before there
can be a library school. Thus, effective educational programs for
a profession may not be based only in consideration of an idealized
profession. A concern for reality must be at the core of the development of professional education.

There are two sets of conditions which affect the development
of education for a profession: the intellectual ideals for the profession, and the social conditions in which it exists. The intellectual
ideals are abstractions; and always a matter of debate in the profession, because, for one thing, they are a result of intellectual vision,
and thus not necessarily founded in reality. On the other hand, the
social conditions which affect the development of a profession are
real, but perception of them may be obscured by intellectual vision.
The situation established by this line of argument may seem para-
doxical, but that quality does not reduce the validity of the argument.
Unfortunately, most of the literature about education for librarianship
has been rooted in a concern, usually implicit, to make it intellectually real--that is, in a concern to develop an ideal profession--
rather than in recognition of its social reality. [1] So it is that our
educational programs seriously lag behind the development of librarianship. Some lag (although unmeasured and perhaps unmeasurable)
must be expected, but the amount exhibited in education for librarianship appears to jeopardize the integrity of the profession itself,
if one may accept the explicit (and implicit) beliefs of a number of
critics of library education, from Williamson to Butler to Wasserman to Berry. [2]

*Reprinted by permission of the author and editor of the Association
of American Library Schools' Journal of Education for Librarianship,
21:2 (Fall, 1980) 91-108.

A few examples may illustrate the extent of the lag. It may
be objected that the examples are taken from technology but technological development fundamentally is a social process. The type-
writer was invented in 1885, and its application to card catalogs
became general after 1900 (ironically, after the introduction of printed
cards by the Library of Congress); yet, as late as 1940 the 'library
hand' still was taught in some library schools. Similarly, the use
of the computer began to be introduced extensively into libraries in
the 1960's; a decade-and-a-half later it is possible for a majority
of library school students to graduate without more than an introduction to the computer. Another relevant example is the reorganization
of library and information services being compelled by network and
systems development, which appear to be leading to extensive restructuring of library work, as, for example, the reorganization of
catalog departments usually required when the MARC or OCLC cataloging systems are introduced into a library. The library schools
do not appear to have begun to deal adequately with the opportunities
and problems presented. [3] For a final example, the relationships
of librarians vis-á-vis library technicians appear to be a developing
source of controversy in the field, especially if the technicians continue the rapid professionalization they have exhibited in the past
decade. [4] Other social lags in education for librarianship undoubtedly will become apparent in the next two decades if their effects
are not already.

Half a century ago Pierce Butler published his call for research to establish the science of librarianship, but we appear to be
nowhere near the development of the science he anticipated. [5] Perhaps in our beguilement with the ideal of a library science we have
overlooked concern for some of the social conditions in which library
education must occur. In any case, science, however much scientists may deal with reality, fundamentally is a system of carefully
controlled observation and measurement; and it does not appear that
in librarianship we will be able to develop the control systems necessary for the conduct of rigorous scientific investigation. (Much
scientific investigation, for example, is done through instruments
which can function in a vacuum at extreme temperatures; there is
no analagous condition for the investigation of libraries.) We are
unable to abstract, as scientists are, the objects we investigate from
the normative world in which they exist. Therefore, we cannot create ideal conditions in which libraries may be studied as in a laboratory. Rather, we must develop better ways of accounting for reality.

There are many social conditions which affect the development of education for librarianship, but most of them are beyond
the control of librarians and librarian educators, or are indirect in
their effects. Such are the disruptions brought on by the calamities
of war, depression, and Jarvisian tax rebellions. Also, the disruptions, however hurtful, usually are temporary, followed by recovery
and advance, as in the resurgent development of public libraries in
America after World War II. Other social conditions, such as the
development of industrial society, are of long term but indirect effect
on the field; that is, industrialization results, indirectly, in the need

for more libraries and librarians. Finally, there are the social
conditions inherent to librarianship itself. They are the realities
of librarianship; but be they trees or forest they are not much affected by our perception of them. Rather, it is our perceptions
which determine the ways in which we attempt to deal with them,
and thus in the long run determine the success of our efforts. The
social realities which have direct effect on education for librarianship may be grouped into four classes: the social position of libraries; the work of librarians; the characteristics and nature of library
schools; and the technologies of information.

What is the social position of libraries? The idea that the
library is a social agency is one which has been reiterated beyond
triteness, but there has been inadequate expression of the social positions of libraries. The recitation of shibboleths such as "the heart
of the campus" or "the crowning glory of the schools" is imagism,
not the exposition of ideas. In recent years it has been fashionable
to assert the library's function as a communications agency, or some
such thing, but use of that metaphor has been no more explanatory
than the "crowning glory" statement. Neither tells us much about
the condition, function or status of libraries in society, and it is to
those matters, rather than to the metaphors, our attention should be
directed.

Any library exists in a variety of social conditions. First of
all, it is several things: a facility, a collection of materials, and
an organization of people. It exists without purpose; the purposes
for which a library exists are those of the people who establish,
control, and use libraries; and they are subject to change over time,
and at any time may vary according to circumstances. In other
words, a library is a derivative agency, an instrument created to
the service of particular purposes at particular times. That is the
basic social condition of the library, and makes it nonessential; there
is nothing in mankind's natural condition which creates an absolute
requirement for libraries. They derive from the condition of man
in society, from his culture, and from social attempts to meet human needs. The soundness of the idea may be demonstrated from
the record of mankind's various societies: whenever and wherever
there has been a particular society which required libraries, in some
form, there have been such entities, from Assurbanipal's collection
of clay tablets to the Library of Congress to the Inland Vital Records
Center in the caves of Kansas. As we have developed complex societies from the once universal Neolithic village, they have been followed by a greater number and variety of entities which may be
called libraries.

The social condition of libraries is affected also by other social developments, such as the increasing complexity of the law of
libraries and librarianship. In the America of 1780 there was almost no statute law about libraries, and none about librarians. The
legal status of libraries was determined, when necessary, by reference to the vague corpus known as English Common Law. Now the
condition of library law is remarkably different. There is, for

example, Alex Ladenson's immense compendium of American library law, of which each new edition is more out of date on the day it appears, because library law is changing so rapidly, increasing so greatly. [6] In addition to the statutes there is an increasingly complex body of administrative law, especially in the Federal Government. [7] Finally, librarians have had increasingly to deal with other kinds of law, governing such matters as discrimination, retirement, personal and corporate liability, and a number of other social problems. Yet, the law of libraries and librarianship virtually is ignored in our curricula.

The social condition of libraries also is determined by their social locale; that is, by their places in different segments of society. Even though most libraries possess apparent physical similarities (allowing for differences in such gross measures as the numbers of volumes held, or the scale and grandeur of buildings) their differing social locations make for markedly different operational situations. For examples, the City of Chicago, General Motors, and Harvard University are complex social entities susceptible to reasonably precise definition. Each contains a complex system of libraries. Each is also a remarkably different kind of social entity, and its library system exists in a social condition remarkably different from the others. (To complicate matters even more, some parts of General Motors are in Chicago, although not part of the City of Chicago.) However, it is apparent that library school curricula tend strongly to emphasize the similarities in the three library systems, despite the facts of different social bases, different collections, and different aggregates of users. It is true that our curricula list such courses as academic libraries, public libraries, and special libraries; but that typology itself inadequately describes the diversity within each type; and there is no evidence for a confident assertion that the social diversity in which our profession exists is recognized adequately. Search, for example, the texts on public library administration. You will not find competent discussion of public library law in the various states, nor of many other matters basic to the operation of public libraries. What you will find is discussion of technical matters based on the authors' assumptions about ideal public libraries. Much the same statement may be made about the textbooks on the administration of other library types.

The very idea of the library in society is an abstraction, because our society actually consists of many societies, overlapping and interlocking, competing and cooperating, and in a constant ferment of development. The reality of our profession is many kinds of libraries in different kinds of societies.

What does a librarian do? This is a fundamental question for the education of librarians. What is there about a librarian's work that is unique, and so distinguishes it from other occupations that preparation for the work must be obtained in a unique program? What, for example, distinguishes the work of some librarians from clerks (or department heads, or ultimately, owners) in a bookstore? Aside from the fact that bookstore personnel sell books and librarians

lend them, it is not easy to perceive essential differences in the two
lines of endeavor. There are significant differences in the agencies
in which librarians and booksellers work, but they appear to derive
from the differing social environments in which the related agencies
exist, rather than from different qualities inherent in the work involved. Moreover, as bookstores extend their involvement with
media the similarities appear to be increasing. In either case, the
problems of acquisition of stock, for example do not appear to be
significantly different: the operations involved in the identification,
selection and acquisition of materials for subsequent distribution appear to be remarkably alike for bookstore owner and library director.
Indeed, the buyers for bookstores and libraries use many of the same
selection aids, to the same general end: the development of a useful
stock, or collection. (Many of both also use the same jobbers, such
as Baker & Taylor Company.) So do some of the problems of user
satisfaction appear to be the same for bookstore and library operators. Anyone who has ever used a really well-run bookstore for assistance in locating and obtaining esoteric materials is likely to have
received better bibliographic assistance than would be obtained from
many college and public libraries. Indeed, in many college communities there are local bookstores which serve as necessary supplements to the college libraries precisely because the libraries are
not intended to give the kind of bibliographic services required by
portions of their communities. The same statement may be made
about such distinguished institutions as the University of Chicago:
Woodworth's Bookstore, on East 57th Street, was for decades a necessary adjunct to the university. [8] And, who can think of Oxford
without Blackwell's? On the other hand, many librarians conduct
special operations that bookstore operators commonly do not, e. g. ,
story hours for children, film programs, in-depth reference services
on particular topics, and so on to the limits of imagination and resources. These, however, are not operations conducted in libraries
alone; similar programs are available from museums, newspapers,
public information and service bureaus, and other agencies, sometimes on a basis of reciprocity, sometimes for a fee, sometimes as
a public service.

The question could be elaborated extensively, but the point
seems sufficiently established: the librarian is not uniquely identified by the nature of the work done. Rather, at the root of the
matter, the librarian is identified by the name of the agency in which
the work is done. The work of the librarian is not necessarily identifiable as such. [9]

The problem of identification of work is exacerbated by attempts to distinguish between professional and non-professional work
in libraries. Most of us who teach in librarianship have had experience as librarians and, together with many others, have been unable
to arrive at a satisfactory distinction between the two grades, except
with reference to those libraries which are sufficiently large-scale,
and therefore sufficiently complex, for the division of work. Even
in those cases the divisions frequently have been made arbitrarily,
in assumptions about the status of the work: typing catalog cards

is non-professional; operating a micro-film camera is technical; shelving books is non-professional; operating a computer is technical; bibliography is professional; cataloging is professional; book selection is professional; and so on. Beyond that, it appears that in complex libraries administration and the supervision of other librarians are recognized as the most professional work, in that our hierarchies and salary schedules reflect status more than professional attributes. Yet, there are many small-scale libraries in which one or two librarians must do all the work associated with their positions. They type, they file, they select, they shelve, they catalog, they do reference. In rigorous classification by work we may not call them professional; in justice we may not call them semi- or non-professional. How do we identify them with reference to education? The standard attribute of distinction between professional and other librarians is possession of the M. L. S. degree or equivalent credential from an American Library Association accredited library school, but to make a distinction on that basis is to beg the question of education. What is so unique to librarianship that it can be done effectively only by those who have the proper credential? So far, there is no answer.

What does a librarian need to know? If reference to the identity of librarians does not enable resolution of questions about their education, perhaps it can be done by reference to a set of questions based in tasks and time: what does a librarian need to know; when does the librarian need to know it? Our curricula in librarianship do not appear to have been devised with these questions firmly in mind, except the assumption that the librarian needs to know about books, whatever that may mean. Also, it appears that our curricula are based on an assumption that a librarian is a librarian is a librarian--that is, any librarian's (hence, all librarians') formal education needs may be met by passage through a standardized curriculum for entry into the field; and a corollary assumption: that education necessary subsequently may be gained experientially. To some extent the invalidity of those assumptions is indicated by the current excitement about continuing education, but that appears to be symptomatic rather than systemic, stemming from recognition that the M. L. S. is inadequate for an entire career, rather than from understanding of the inadequacies in the M. L. S. program. The basic assumption is still that a standard curriculum is adequate for entry into any phase of librarianship. It appears to be an ill-founded one; diversity is the reality of our business, at every level. Consider some of the situations into which any one of our graduates may enter as the first job after receiving the M. L. S. degree:

● managing a one-professional public library, with a secretary/clerk assistant;
● managing a one-professional special library, in any field, with a secretary/clerk assistant;
● managing a small library, of any type, with one or three professional or subprofessional assistants, and a few full-time equivalent clerks, secretaries, assistants;
● professional assistant in a subject department in any kind of library;

- branch director in a library system, public or academic,
  with or without a clerk-secretary assistant;
- professional assistant in a bibliographic operations unit--
  acquisitions or cataloging;
- professional assistant in a department organized on the
  basis of form--newspapers, manuscripts, maps, etc.
- professional assistant in a technical systems department--
  computer, photoreproduction, bindery;
- administrative assistant to a senior administrator--that is,
  a position in which one frequently performs tasks the
  senior administrator does not want to do.

The nine examples are only some of the situations in which the beginning librarian may find oneself, and they are organizational situations which do not necessarily describe the work to be done.
There may be a core curriculum which is appropriate for all of them,
but the record of debate on the core concept indicates that we have
not yet found the right one.[10] And, as it is certain that no specific M. L. S. degree curriculum may be regarded as entirely appropriate for any one of these positions, then no specific curriculum may
be appropriate for all of them.   Yet, as we are unable to predict
our graduates' initial job situations, it is precisely that which we expect the M. L. S. program to do: prepare them for any job situation,
in the assumption that a librarian is a librarian is a librarian.

If we are unable to predict the first positions of our graduates,
and devise a curriculum suitable for those positions, we are even
less able to develop educational programs for their subsequent ca-
reers.   Simply, we are unable to predict the diversity of their jobs
after five or ten or fifteen years.   Even so, this year we will graduate some librarians who will be working until the year 2030; and
they have been trained in programs which in many ways are more
appropriate to 1930, or even to 1880.   We cannot resolve this problem by basking in the tribal memories of Melvil Dewey, nor even of
Leon Carnovsky.   Rather, we must begin the development of curricula for a variety of employment situations, now and in the near future; and remain constantly alert to the development of conditions
which will require changes in those curricula.   Education for librarianship is, after all, preparation for work in libraries, not preparation to be a librarian.

What are library schools? The curricula of library education
may be the substance of our educational programs, but they are ap-
purtenances of library schools.   That is, the substance is obtained
in the schools.   What are they? Here it is emphasized that they
are inert entities; unless they have faculties and students they do not
exist.   Although the literature of librarianship is replete with exhor-
tations for the schools to do this or that, and also with some rather
remarkable claims for what they have done, the fact is the schools
do nothing except as it is done by faculties and students.   The schools
do not teach skills, they do not turn out a product, they do not do
research, they do not indoctrinate neophytes in a profession.   These
things are done, if at all, by the men and women who teach and

study in the schools, which themselves are no more than facilities.
Their uses are determined by faculties and students, working in the
overlapping contexts of American librarianship and higher education.
The overlap may be a grinder rather than a source of productive
tension. The schools--at least, those which hold membership, full
or associate, in the Association of American Library Schools--are
graduate institutions and must be operated at least somewhat in accord to the demands of American universities. But the schools exist
for preparation for work in libraries, an occupation which by all accounts suffers in comparison to the other occupations called professions and seated in our universities. At the same time the faculties
and students are held at least somewhat accountable to the profession
--that is, to the authorities who hire and fire librarians. The conflict inherent in this situation should be obvious, but the literature
of education for librarianship displays remarkably little concern for
it. There has been a great deal of attention to what should be taught
in the schools, and at what level; there has been almost no discussion of the roles and functions of faculties in the schools. [11]

What should we expect of the professors of librarianship, individually and collectively? In the conventional wisdom they serve
as the teachers of skills, indoctrinators in the professional ethos,
and students (investigators) of the profession. We have, however,
no firm guidance about the extent to which a single professor is to
engage in each of those roles. In the literature of education for librarianship there is abundant evidence that the professoriat is expected to be all things for all librarians: gifted teachers, creative
scholars, effective administrators, professional activists, and whatever else may be needed for the good of the profession. But these
requirements have been created in the literature's implications about
the schools, not as policy, and there is little in the way of direct
guidance for the individual professor. A wrong guess about priorities may result in serious penalty. For example, a former col-
league taught three courses a semester (one each semester in extension), served on his share of faculty committees, did the other chores
a university expects of its professors, and served actively on ten
professional association committees. During that year he did no research and, in the annual performance review the next year, received
from the administration severe rebuke for his lack of scholarship.
His service to the profession was discounted by an administrator
eager to enhance the school's scholarly reputation. From the folk-
lore of library education we know that is far from an isolated case,
but the people most directly affected, the faculties of library schools,
have not begun to deal with that and related problems.

Nor do we have a clearer view about the collective functions
of faculties. Are they to serve, as one commentator indicated more
than a decade ago, as a sort of Officer Candidate School cadre--the
producers of what she called "the second lieutenants of librarianship?"[12] Or are faculties to serve as instructors in technologism,
concerned only with the production of qualified professionals, as
some other library educators have indicated?[13] Or, as a third
possibility, are faculties to serve as pools of leadership for the

profession, as one may infer from numerous writings about education
for librarianship? We have no firm doctrine on these problems,
perhaps because the questions have not been asked; more likely it
is because the answers have been assumed to be in academic and
library tradition, a much favored source in many writings on both
universities and libraries.

If there is any authoritative statement of the functions and
objectives of the faculties in the library schools it lies in the A. L. A.
Standards for Accreditation. Even there the statement is not explicit,
but must be inferred from analysis of the Standards, which produces
disappointment. Standard III (Faculty) is not one against which the
Committee on Accreditation, nor anyone else, for that matter, may
measure the quality of a faculty. Rather, the Standard is at best a
collection of professional pietisms exhorting ("the school should ...
the faculty as a group should....") faculties to perfectionism; it contains nothing which will help a faculty determine its functions, priorities, and responsibilities. Sadly, there is nothing else in the literature of librarianship to provide that guidance.

If we have been ill-served in the development of doctrine for
faculties, our official knowledge about our students is even less helpful in the development of educational programs appropriate to the
field. One may infer from library school admission requirements
that there exist some fundamental misconceptions about students. It
appears that each year we expect to receive a rather homogeneous
group whose members have been made alike by possession of a common background derived from the experience of something called a
general education. We appear to expect that each new class will
have a common, as well as correct, understanding of the world; and
that in one year we can instill in them not only the knowledge and
skills necessary to the practice of librarianship, but also the ethos
of something called professionalism.[14] The expectations, per se,
are dysfunctional to the development of education for librarianship,
and the misconceptions in which they are rooted compound the problem.

Our students come from variant social backgrounds, even
though the extent and degree of the variances is unmeasured. Although most, if not nearly all, are middle class, that phrase is not
sufficiently descriptive to inform us of their attitudes, expectations,
and values. Nor, to complicate the problem additionally, does the
one year program give us sufficient time to get to know individual
students well enough to accommodate instruction to their variances.
For example, the daughter of a Regular Army officer is apt to have
had a remarkably different upbringing than the son of a university
librarian, and both may be remarkably different from another daughter
of a small city independent insurance broker. Each is middle class,
but they have significantly variant views of the world, and those variances greatly complicate the instillation of a professional ethos.
Of the three examples mentioned above, one was a Marxist, one
was hedonist, and one was pietist, in this writer's opinion. It is
very doubtful that their learning at library school had any effect on
their views about social issues in librarianship.

The idea that our students have had a common general education also is a misconception responsible for serious problems in the
development of education for librarianship. Increasing specialization
has been the hallmark of baccalaureate programs during the past
half-century; and one clear result of the trend has been the obvious,
although unmeasured, decline of knowledge commonly possessed by
beginning graduate students.[15] Indeed, as recent reports from
Harvard University indicate, general education has all but disappeared.[16] One sure result of this is that graduate faculties in
library schools are compelled to spend more time in accommodation
to their students' lack of a common education relevant to the study
of librarianship. What, for example, are the increasing numbers
of foundation courses but necessary attempts to prepare students for
the study of libraries and their workings?

Another ill-considered attribute of our students is that many
have worked in libraries before coming to library school. In this
writer's observation, that experience has been at many levels in a
great variety of libraries. One recent course in adult services, for
example, included: a professional level librarian in a youth correc-
tional center, a former page in an academic library, a de facto assistant director in an Illinois library system, a school media center
director, a reference librarian in a medical library, the director of
a small city public library, and a library assistant.[17] All were
excellent students, in a general sort of way, but they were encum-
bered with biases derived from their work experiences; and it became obvious they had sharply differing expectations of the course.
Adult services is an amorphous concept to begin with, but the problems of instruction and learning were tremendously complicated by
the factors mentioned here.

The foregoing factors may seem to be minor and are perhaps
without effect as far as library education is concerned. Reflection
on the matter should convince us otherwise. It is apparent, if unmeasured in sociological terms, that many of our students arrive
with more or less fixed opinions about libraries and related concerns, such as, for example, intellectual freedom or outreach programs. It is apparent that in too many cases our teaching has done
little to effect change in those opinions. In significant ways our
teaching has been ineffective because it has been perceived as indoc-
trinative. Student opinions on social questions may be irrelevant to
courses in mathematics, or chemistry, perhaps even to the study of
literature. The organization and operations of libraries, and the
services performed in them, however, are social questions per se,
and thus related more or less directly to questions about society.
Librarianship is not a science, nor a mathematic, and it cannot be
taught as such. Thus, much of our teaching is, at one level or
another, a discussion of social questions presented to students whose
minds are made up when they come to us, and who in many cases
are uninterested in making the effort necessary to a test of their
own opinions. At the least, the situation gives a Lear-like quality
to our teaching; at worst it creates in the classroom a condition of
silent, impassive conflict between students and teacher. And, the

conditions in which education for librarianship is operated do not
allow sufficient time for recognition of the conflict in many cases,
let alone its resolution.

What are the functions of professional associations in education? The presumed functions of professional associations are well
known, and need no restatement here. Three of them, however, do
require discussion at this time. They are: the associations' responsibility for leadership; the exertion of professional discipline;
and the control of entry into the profession.

The last responsibility stated here can be disposed of most
easily. The professional associations in librarianship have no real
control over entry into the field. One could rationalize the statement elaborately, but the root of the matter may be stated simply:
anyone who wishes may establish a library, and hire anyone to run
it. Libraries come into existence at the behest of persons or groups
outside librarianship; and through their hiring authority they control
entry into the field. That the professional associations in librarianship have won a measure of influence over entry into portions of the
field is testimony to their ingenuity and persistence, rather than to
their presumed authority; and even that influence is exerted tenuously.
The most recent evidence for the statement is the apparently widespread use of CETA (Comprehensive Employment and Training Act)
personnel as replacements or substitutes for professional librarians
in academic and public libraries. The practice's effect on library
schools is unmeasured but it appears to have disastrous potential.

The matter of professional discipline, as it relates to education for librarianship, is far more complex. Such discipline as the
profession has exercised has until quite recently been achieved
through the accrediting authority of the A. L. A. which only ardent
champtions of A. L. A. would assert has been applied effectively.
The fact, for example, that there are at least 34 unaccredited master's degree programs (some of long standing), compared to 69 accredited ones, is a clear indicator of how little discipline A. L. A.
can exert. Even that is being eroded by the development of certification programs for individual professionals: the Medical Library
Association already has a certification program; the Society of American Archivists is well on the way to the establishment of its own.
And, most, if not all state education authorities have certification
requirements for school librarians. The academic programs in which
the certificates are earned appear to attract more students than the
accredited library schools; and some, at least, of those would not
survive if they were to lose their school library certification programs. The professional associations in librarianship have not exerted an effective educational discipline.

In the theory of professionalism the professional association
is supposed to furnish leadership in the development of educational
programs for it. How have the professional associations in librarianship conformed to the theory? A. L. A. appears to have reacted
to events, rather than to have offered leadership. For example:

The association resisted Melvil Dewey's establishment of a library
school at Columbia College. The subsequent establishment of library
schools in colleges and universities, 1897-1923, appears to have
been a result of individual effort by persons in and out of the profession, e.g., Katherine Sharp at the Armour Institute, and Andrew
Carnegie's grant to Western Reserve University. The Williamson
report of 1923 was a result of the Carnegie Corporation's concern
about the results of the Carnegie gifts for public libraries. The
establishment of the A. L. A. Board of Education for Librarianship
was a response to the Williamson report. The post World War II
establishment of the master's degree programs was resisted by the
A. L. A. Board of Education. In short, the record of A. L. A.'s involvement in education for librarianship, 1887-1955 (when the University of California at Berkeley began to offer the master's degree),
does not indicate a leadership role. For the other professional associations in librarianship, not even that may be said.

Another function in which the professional association is supposed to offer leadership is in research into the opportunities, problems, and operational concerns facing the profession. How have we
in librarianship fared in this matter? Not well. The professional
associations in librarianship have not established research agencies
of significance, whether it has been a result of incapacity or lack
of will. The only major attempts to establish research agencies in
librarianship have been:

The Carnegie Corporation grant to the University of Chicago
in 1926, which amounted to 2.6 million dollars. Fifty years
later 75 percent of the Graduate Library School budget still came
from the grant.[18]
The research funds provided by the Federal Government under
L. S. C. A. Title II. They prompted a significant increase in doc-
toral programs in library schools and also the establishment of
several library research centers. To a large extent the funds
were frittered away and the library research centers have declined as the federal funds were reduced.

Even so, since 1926 there has been a lot of research in librarianship: about 500 doctoral dissertations have been produced, and there
have been thousands of research articles in the journals of librarianship. How has this affected the development of librarianship? We
do not know and perhaps we cannot find out.[19] However, questions
about the utility and effect of research in librarianship are no more
important than questions about the organization of research efforts.
Assuming an ultimate benefit from research, should we expect the
professional associations in librarianship to serve as the focal points
for the development of coherent research programs? Or, as Houser
and Schrader put the question, may we reasonably expect the professional associations to create a "research front" in librarianship?
Given the long-running controversy in A. L. A., whether the association should be involved in research, the answer appears to be no.[20]
And, indeed, since about 1950, the most significant research in library science has been in the branch called information science,

done for the most part in centers outside librarianship, e.g., International Business Machines Corporation, Bell Laboratories, Massachusetts Institute of Technology, etc.; and librarians and librarian educators have been responding to that research. It is, after all, the technologies of information which affect the development of libraries.

What of the technologies of information? In its traditions librarianship is bound to the book and its variants, the periodical, newspapers, and other forms produced on the printing press. The traditions of the book, esthetic and intellectual, are so compelling that other forms of librarianship (archives, media specialty, map librarianship, and so on) conventionally are judged in relation to book librarianship, usually to the detriment of the newer forms, by librarians, at least. In their turns the specialists of the other forms have adopted a defensive wariness toward librarians which amounts almost to hostility. (A librarian need only go to a meeting of archivists to discover the depths of this attitude.) The roots of the librarians' condescension toward other information specialists may lie in the fact that for some two thousand years the book (or some other artifact recognizable as a book, such as the Gilgamesh tablets) was the only form in which a literary work could be reproduced and distributed conveniently. Thus, librarians see themselves as the principal inheritors and guardians of a proudly ancient tradition.

In the past century new reproduction technologies have profoundly affected the status of the book. Film, magnetic tape, and vinyl disc have for many purposes come to supplement or replace the book, in either case eroding its primary position. Librarians, lovers of books, have not come to terms with this development. The extent of their disaffection with the new forms is made apparent by the contemptuous term usually applied to books produced by adaptation from original screenplays or television scripts: non-books. We forget, for a contrary example, the Shakespeare First Folio was an adaptation of dramatic scripts.[21] For a less extreme example, librarians, especially in academic institutions, devote substantial resources to the acquisition and mastery of the bibliography of Shakespeare; few have given much effort or money to the "filmography" of his works. For still another example, in a recent issue of Library Trends a good deal of space was given to defensive assertions that films are appropriate for libraries.[22] Such illustrations could be continued at length, but further exposure of librarians' obstinacy is not the end in view here.

Librarians' attention to the technologies of information is the concern, and it appears that before their attention to that matter can be developed there must be an end to their confusion about media. Others are not less than books; indeed, the book is but another form of media, to use the term in its usual looseness. Books, phonograph records, films, tape cassettes, and other forms are not media, but the artifacts of reproduction technologies. There are only a few media: ink on paper, images on film, magnetic impressions on tape, incisions on wax or vinyl, and radio-telephone signals. We use them in a great variety of ways to reproduce information of many forms and kinds, which then may be distributed or stored, used or not used. The production, distribution, storage, and use of the forms are socially determined processes. Together, the forms and processes constitute the information systems with which we should be concerned.

A library is a component of an information technology and is derived from it. That is, a library is a result of the development of an information technology. (So, for example, are newspapers, television broadcasting stations, motion picture studios, and a number of other social entities, each of which, also, tends to have a library within its particular organization.) Thus, the development of new information technologies has had, and will continue to have, substantial effect upon the development of librarianship, not only in such ways as the development of new kinds of libraries, but in the development of new demands upon existing libraries. So, if the library schools are to remain the principal source of education in librarianship, then their faculties will have to become much more responsive to the effects of the new information technologies. Unfortunately, examination of our curricula reveals that we remain bound to the traditions of the book.

Over the past two or three decades librarian educators have paid increasing attention to a phenomenon called the information explosion, as we have come to appreciation of the really awesome increases in information, knowledge, and the forms in which they are distributed and stored. Properly, much of our attention has been directed toward the problems of achieving bibliographic control over the forms, and some promising attempts toward it have begun. [23] Nevertheless, we continue the use of curricula rooted in the idea that 'a librarian is a librarian'; and to insist concomitantly that our discipline is something unique, with its own intellectual content and zeitgeist. Perhaps. The administration and operation of libraries is a specific form of endeavor, although our developing recognition that there may be something useful for us in the ideas of information science amounts also to a developing doubt about the specificity of our enterprise. [24] Be that as it may, our primary attention remains directed to the artifacts of information rather than on the ways in which people organize themselves for the generation, distribution and use of information, the real source of the information explosion. Despite our half-century old realization that libraries are social agencies, we know relatively little about the social mechanisms by which libraries are created, organized, and operated. Despite our more recently begun understanding that even "escape reading" is educative and informative, we know relatively little about the individual or social imperatives which lead our users into the search for particular information. On the other hand, we know next to nothing about why many people choose not to read, but tend to assume that those who do not read are uncultured. Yet the information explosion has been not only an increase in works in print, but also the introduction of new forms by which people may inform themselves about their jobs, about culture, and about other interests. Our ignorance of these matters is complicated by our reluctance to diminish our reliance on the book.

The information explosion also has meant the development of great amounts of new knowledge about human behavior, recently developed in other disciplines. We have been reluctant to realize its potential relevance for our profession, loath to realize that our subject is librarianship rather than library science. Thus we have tended to foreclose the possibilities of development in our subject, by denial that there is a psychology of librarianship, a sociology of librarianship, an economics of librarianship, perhaps even a physics of librarianship. We do admit history into our academy, but mainly as an ornament. Our curricula, and our research do not give adequate respect to new knowledge of human behavior, despite our protestations of our humanism.

Summation. The proper way to educate for librarianship has been for more than a century a source of controversy among librarians. It, as will controversy on any professional matter, has generated a substantial body of literature, much of which, however, is sterile, historicist, and divergent from the realities of our profession. Such is the case because much of it has been addressed to questions of status, professionalism, and other matters which, intellectually at least, are not central to the work of librarianship. The fundamental questions in education for librarianship are still: what does a librarian need to know and when is it necessary to know it. One prays that long before 2080 we will have a better understanding of those questions than in 1980.

We have the wit to develop that understanding; what we need are the will and the means. The will, of course, can come only from within us. Once it is found the means will follow. They can be developed, just as the library schools of today have been. So, we must use our wits to analyze the foundations of librarianship, and to make public knowledge of our findings. We must study libraries and librarianship, rather than teach library science. We must study the ways in which people create, maintain, and use libraries. We must seek to know the realities of our field.

References and Notes

1. The concern is explicit in: Shera, J. H.: Foundations of Education for Librarianship. New York, Becker & Hayes, 1972. See pp. viii-ix; see also, the "Information Science Series" statement at [v].
2. Specific statements are not cited here, but they may be seen in, or inferred from, a number of works, including: Vann, S. K., ed.: Charles C. Williamson, The Williamson Reports of 1921 and 1923. Metuchen, NJ. Scarecrow Press, 1971; Butler, P.: Introduction to Library Science, Chicago, University of Chicago Press, 1933; Wassermann, P.: The New

Librarianship: A Challenge for Change. New York, R. R.
Bowker, 1972; Berry, J. N.: Open the Faculty Clubs, Library Journal, 101:1679, Sept. 1, 1976.

3. This judgment (and similar ones elsewhere) is based on close
examination of course listings and descriptions in the catalogs, bulletins, announcements, and similar publications
from the library schools accredited by A. L. A., 1978/1979.
Such evidence is not conclusive, but it is powerfully suggestive.

4. See, for example: Council on Library Technical Assistants.
Role of the Professional Librarian in the Training of LTA's.
In: Johnson, D. T., ed.: Proceedings of the Fifth Annual
Meeting, May 6 through 8, 1971. The Council, 1973; and
Evans, C. W.: Library Technical Assistant: a New Profession? In: Adamovick, S. G., ed.: Reader in Library Technology. Englewood, CO, Microcard Editions Books, 1975;
and Jaki, E. B.: Professionalizing the Paraprofessional.
In: Ibid., pp. 85-88. Additionally, the author has talked
with enough technicians to know that many resent bitterly the
put-downs they feel they have received from librarians identified as professional, but unable to do the work of the technicians.

5. Butler, ref. 2.

6. Ladenson, A. D., ed: American Library Laws. 4th ed. Chicago,
American Library Association, 1973.

7. U. S. National Archives and Records Service, Federal Register
Division. Code of Federal Regulations. Washington, 1979.
See, for example, Title 37, Chap. 11, "Copyright Office,
Library of Congress"; and Title 45, Chap. XVII, "National
Commission on Libraries and Information Services."

8. The author, when a student in the University of Chicago Graduate
Library School, was referred to Woodworth's by university
librarians, on two or three occasions.

9. For a good illustration of the variety of work done by librarians
see: Duncan, C. B.: "An Analysis of Tasks Performed by
Reference Personnel in College and University Libraries in
Indiana." Dissertation submitted to Indiana University, Bloom-
ington, 1973.

10. Asheim, L. F., Ed.: The Core of Education for Librarianship.
Chicago, American Library Association, 1954. This work,
the papers presented at the University of Chicago Graduate
Library School Conference in 1953, remains the best introduction to the core concept. Since 1953 concern with the idea
has continued, with a noteworthy attempt at core curriculum
development at Case Western Reserve University, on which
see: Shera, ref. 1, pp. 367-371.

11. See for examples: Carroll, C. E., The Professionalization of
Education for Librarianship. Metuchen, New Jersey, Scarecrow Press, 1971, Chap. V: "Graduate Study and Research
in Library Science"; Davis, D. G., Jr.: Education for Librarianship. Library Trends, 25: 113-134, July 1976; and
Shera, ref. 1, Chap. 13. "The Faculty." The Carroll and
Davis works, both historical, cannot be faulted for the lack;

what has not been cannot be studied. Shera's remarks are,
as always, provocative and stimulating; they are, however,
largely speculative when they touch on the matters considered
here. Of the 70 or so works cited in the chapter, only 15
are from library literature.

12. Bundy, M. L. : The Development of Graduate Education and Research at the University of Maryland School of Library and
Information Services. College Park, 1966, p. 5.

13. Wasserman, P. : The Librarian and the Machine. Detroit,
Gale, 1965, pp. 133-135.

14. For a contrary example, consider the implications of Ervin
Gaines' well known story about a student who got an A in
Gaines' course in intellectual freedom, and later was dis-
covered razoring out the "offensive" passages in Canterbury
Tales.

15. The matter does not seem to have received much attention in librarianship; but, for discussion of a similar problem in another field, see: The Education of Historians in the United
States. New York, McGraw-Hill, 1962. "The Carnegie
Series in American Education," pp. 38-41.

16. New York Times, February 26, 1978, 1:1.

17. The class included two students who appeared to be there on the
principle: "Ever'body gotta be somewhere."

18. Statement to the writer by Dean Howard Winger during the fall
quarter, 1974.

19. Shearer, K. : The Impact of Research on Librarianship: Journal
of Education for Librarianship, 20:114-128, Fall 1979.

20. Houser, L. , and Schrader, A. M. : The Search for a Scientific
Profession: Library Science Education in the U. S. and Canada.
Metuchen, NJ, Scarecrow Press, 1978, p. 125.

21. Burgess, A. : Shakespeare. London, Penguin Books, 1972,
p. 261.

22. Sigler, R. F. : A Rationale for the Film as a Public Library
Resource and Service. Library Trends, 27:9-26 Summer 1978.

23. See, for example: Frost, C. O. : Teaching the Cataloging of
Non-Book Media. Journal of Education for Librarianship,
19:32-39, Summer 1978.

24. Wilson, P. : Public Knowledge, Private Ignorance. Westport,
CT, Greenwood Press, 1977, pp. 13-17.

TAKING THE LIBRARY OUT OF LIBRARY EDUCATION*

Pauline Wilson

Library school is where the formal process of becoming a librarian begins, and where signs of fundamental change in the profession can be expected to occur first. At the Association of American Library Schools annual conference in Washington Jan. 30-Feb. 1, 1981, a restless climate of change pervaded the air.

In the meeting rooms, corridors, and byways of the conference, library educators discussed the ideas and plans they are considering as they grope their way to the future. What caused this restless climate and what might it portend?

Technology is one cause of the climate of change. Most library educators believe all students must acquire knowledge of computer applications for storing and retrieving information, and get "hands-on" experience with these applications. The need to introduce technology requires revision of the curriculum; some old courses must be changed and some new ones developed. This is a time-consuming and costly process. In addition, knowledgeable faculty must be employed and expensive equipment obtained. What this means, in sum, is that the library school cannot tolerate a reduction in support if it is to remain viable. Indeed, it is likely to need an increase of resources if it is to effect meaningful change.

A second cause of change is the worsening financial condition of higher education. Fewer students are enrolling in higher education and the decline is expected to continue throughout the '80s, reaching a steady state of no growth by 1990. [1] Coupled with the decline in students is lessened support for higher education. Budgets can't keep pace with rising costs. Library schools must operate in a highly competitive environment. Within the university they compete with other academic units for resources. Outside the university they compete with other library schools for students. Coupled with this competition is a more constricted job market for librarians.

The discovery that the skills and knowledge of librarians are

*Reprinted by permission of the American Library Association and the author from American Libraries, 12:6 (June 1981) 321-25.

applicable to jobs in industry is a third cause of change. While library educators want to provide more career options for students,
educators also see the opportunities in industry as a way out of their
difficulties. These career options offer the possibility of attracting
more students, thereby keeping enrollment up and placing the schools
in a position to ask for continued or increased resources. Library
schools behave like other organizations faced with a threat: they try
to survive. Because the situation of each library school is somewhat different, depending upon the university in which it is embedded, the schools can be expected to consider and to try different
strategies to survive or to strengthen themselves, as the case may
be.

The two-year program strategy

One of those strategies is to extend the library education program
to two years. In general, the two-year program is intended to provide time for more extensive training in technology, for specialization, and for such course work outside the library school as may be
relevant to a student's career goal. Two-year programs are not
necessarily all alike, however. In one type, a school defines its
mission to be the production of fewer but better-prepared librarians.
This type of two-year program rests on problematic assumptions:
Will there continue to be an adequate market for librarians? (More
about this later.) Will the remuneration for librarians be sufficient
to justify the additional expenditure of money and time?

       Improved remuneration for librarians can be envisioned. Such
improvement, however, probably will depend upon a smaller supply
of librarians. Library service is worth only so much to society.
It has a place in society's hierarchy, but it can never compete with
police and fire protection, for example. Thus libraries may never
receive a proportionately larger share of society's resources, for
these resources are always limited. If librarians are to have better
remuneration, therefore, there must be fewer of them and they must
be better prepared. But there must be a need for them to be better
prepared, otherwise the result will be unnecessary and costly cre-
dentialing. To those who accept this view, the two-year program
designed to produce fewer but better prepared librarians might be
seen as the right path to the future.

       In a second example of a two-year program, the school's
mission or domain has not been clearly defined or fully implemented.
A hypothetical school might decide to switch to a two-year program
with the idea of preparing students to work in industry as well as
in libraries. In such a case, the program can be used to enlarge
the curriculum to cover both fields: One-year programs that already
exist may decide to do the same. In these instances, the programs
could develop into two-track programs and encounter some difficulties.

Curriculum problems and moral values

One such difficulty is curriculum. The jobs available in industry
will deal largely with computer applications for storage and retrieval
of data and information. Students preparing for these positions may
not need some courses now in the core curriculum. Why should
such students take collection development? Bibliography also might
be of little value.

Additionally, most library schools have a socialization course
called Library in Society or some similar name. Its ultimate goal
is to produce an individual who thinks about libraries as a librarian.
In this process, the student is socialized into a discrete profession,
not into the anonymous, undifferentiated world of industry. Shall we
drop this course because of its focus on librarianship? Shall we
take the library out of library education? Shall we teach only skills
courses, adding courses needed by students preparing for industry?
Or shall we try to do both? If the latter, will conflict occur?

Perhaps the answers depend on what one conceives a librarian
to be. Is a librarian a cataloger, a bibliographer, an indexer, an
online searcher, a person who answers questions, a storyteller, a
program planner, an administrator? Is a librarian a congeries of
technical skills or is a librarian something more? We will assume
the latter position: A librarian is a specialist--a library expert,
one who knows how to create, operate, and maintain libraries. A
librarian understands that institution called a library, knows its place
in society, and knows how to make it perform to meet society's expectations.

Given that view of a librarian, we would expect to find that
librarians had organized their work as a profession, and that fact
may give rise to another conflict. Whether librarianship is called
a semi-profession or a profession is not relevant to the issue. Librarianship is organized as a profession and has many characteristics common to occupations so organized. One of those characteristics is the values held in common by its members, values about
the service provided. For our discussion, the salient value is the
moral value that undergirds librarianship, the value of intellectual
freedom, the conviction that users should have open access to library
materials.

The moral value is likely to conflict with the proprietary
values of industry. Such conflict can be illustrated with the copyright issue. Librarians fought long and hard to get section 108 in
the 1976 copyright law. They did not act out of personal self-interest;
no librarian would have lost a job if the issue had been settled dif-
ferently. Librarians fought for section 108 because they knew they
could not provide the library service needed by society without it.

Contrast that belief with the position taken recently by the
American Society for Information Science (ASIS). In hearings before

the Register of Copyrights to determine the effects of section 108,
ASIS stated its position to be one of "neutrality" and went on to say
the "Section 108 principles ... are not observed and 'most users
have no intention of complying with the law' ... According to the
ASIS testimony, the missing ingredient is the payout for the user
that will make compliance with the law 'more attractive than non-
compliance.'"[2] This "neutral" position was taken because of the
"diverse interests and work situations" of ASIS members. More
than a third of its members are from industry.[3] Some of them do
not share the librarian's value of open access. This kind of value
conflict may be resolved in the future, but it could be a potential
problem for library schools which offer or plan to offer two-year
or one-year programs designed to prepare librarians and personnel
for industry.

The "withering away" theory

The two-year program designed to produce fewer but better-prepared
librarians assumes the market for librarians will continue because
libraries will continue to exist.   That assumption has been challenged
by those who argue that technological developments, such as electronic mail, teleconferencing, in-office/in-home videotext systems,
and proliferation of databases will eventually result in the "withering
away" of libraries.[4]   According to this view the librarian will be
"de-institutionalized."   But can the librarian be de-institutionalized?
Perhaps not--if libraries continue to exist.

In considering that question another must be posed: Does
the library provide services computerized information services cannot, and will it continue to do so? A recent market test of OCLC's
Viewtel home information system found the average viewing session
lasted nine minutes.[5] That time span suggests the use of such
systems is not similar to the use of libraries.   Library user studies provide abundant evidence that libraries, with appropriate exceptions, are most used, and most appreciated, for book borrowing.

Books are not likely to disappear in the foreseeable future.
They are still the fastest and easiest-to-use information storage and
retrieval device for a lengthy text and likely to remain so.   Imagine
the situation if one could only read books by sitting before a TV
screen or a microform reader.   Librarians who use a CRT terminal
for extended periods have already discovered headaches and eyestrain
are occupational hazards.[6] Users also experience trouble and express dissatisfaction with such technology.[7]

This technology, however, can be combined with printers to
produce hardcopy. Can that combination solve the problem? Probably not. How long would it take before one were buried beneath a
mountain of printouts? This question assumes endless printouts
would be affordable by the average library user. At present such
an assumption seems incorrect even in the case of those presumably
most able to pay for information. A recent market test of Prestel,

the British videotext information service, identified an economic problem. Although the great majority of Prestel subscribers were business firms, its use was inhibited by the fact that "the meter is always running,"[8] According to the report, users need to be able
to see a clear economic advantage of using the system. Most people
do not use libraries because they see a clear economic advantage.
We might also consider whether the American people who have supported libraries for some 200 years are going to tolerate a system
with a "meter that is always running" between them and information.
All things considered, it seems unlikely libraries will wither away
in the foreseeable future, with the possible exception of small special libraries located in industry.

The libraries least likely to disappear

Perhaps we have confused ourselves in making predictions about the
future of libraries because we have not made sufficient distinctions
between them. The two types of libraries least likely to disappear
are the research library and the public library. Both have a place
and an identity in society setting them apart from other types of
libraries. We might call them generic libraries. Research libraries taken together constitute the library of record. They have a role
in and a responsibility to society in addition to their role in the parent institutions of which they may be a part.

     This is not the case in college, special, and school libraries,
which are support services in the fullest sense of the term. Their
responsibility is narrowly confined to supporting the mission of their
parent institution. They have no meaning or special identity for society apart from their parent institution.

     The public library, on the other hand, is unique. To most
persons, library means the public library. It serves a far higher
proportion of the populace than any other type of library and its
clientele, reflecting the diversity of society itself, is unlike that of
any other library.

     The question these differences raise is again the question of
taking the library out of library education. In making way for new
courses designed for students preparing for positions in industry,
will type-of-library courses be eliminated on the ground that all libraries are the same? In many schools, type-of-library courses
have already been eliminated because they are assumed to be variants of the administration or management courses. Management
courses are not the question, for management principles are the
same for all libraries and can be taught in a general course. But
can management courses, plus the skills courses such as reference,
sufficiently prepare professionals for work in different types of libraries?

The special needs of public librarians

Throughout the history of public libraries, librarians have struggled
to understand and clearly articulate the mission of the public library.
Public librarians need to know what society has expected of the library over time and what its responses have been. Librarians must
understand the environment in which the library operates, its political, economic, demographic, educational, and social environments,
both at the national or macro level and at the local community or
micro level. None of this can be taught in a management course
nor should it be. Students preparing for industry or other types of
libraries have no need for specialized knowledge of the public library.
Are there other bodies of knowledge, apart from skills courses required of all students, that are sufficiently large and specialized to
warrant being taught as a separate course by type of library? Librarians might consider this question, taking care to avoid overstating
the case for their type of library.

    The various types of two- and one-year programs are likely
to be found in predictable areas, for the principal factor determining
their location is financial. Two-year programs are likely to be in
a school with a favorable geographic location, that is, one with little
or no competition from other library schools in its area. Two-year
programs are also more likely to be found in state universities offering low tuition, especially if the school's mission is to prepare
librarians. In a private university, the cost of a two-year program
for librarians would be prohibitive. One-year, two-track programs
preparing students for both libraries and industry are more likely
to be found in a highly competitive situation, where the school com-
petes both within the university and outside. Such a school must
demonstrate a need for its program to justify continued or increased
funding. The best way to demonstrate a continued need is to maintain enrollment or, better, to increase enrollment. Diversification--
preparing students for industry and libraries--offers a possible strategy.

Information affiliates

Other strategies include programs affiliated with or offered in conjunction with an MLS program. Although not library-related, these
programs may have an impact on library education. One such new
program is information resource management, which focuses on the
design and evaluation of information systems regardless of informational content or organizational context. Information resource management is necessarily a two-year program designed to produce a
high level of skill along with the probability of a high-paying position
in industry. If a high-cost program is located in a private university, it must use quality as its drawing card to be competitive. The
cost of quality can be justified only if the outcome is a highly-paid
position.

    Another new program is the undergraduate major in information science, intended to produce a programmer/analyst, a person with data processing skills. Some library educators believe this kind of undergraduate program will receive more emphasis within the new few years. Such programs may not be offered under the auspices of the library schools, however. That will depend on the amount of competition from other academic departments, such as computer science, and on whether the library school has developed a good information science program. Although undergraduate information science is not library science, such a program may have an impact on library education because the nature of the jobs and the career structure for information-related work in industry is not entirely clear. [9] It is possible graduates of these undergraduate programs could fill the jobs in industry for which the two-track, one-year library school programs would prepare students.

Another approach bears watching: a strategy that attempts to increase resources for the library school by combining it with another academic unit with presumably common interests, like a school of communications. Two different outcomes can be imagined. The values and separate identity of the library school might be lost. The library school could be subsumed under the stronger school and, perhaps, in time be phased out. The other outcome would be that librarianship could be strengthened if a synergistic relationship developed between the combined schools.

Shucking the negative stereotype

In addition to the three major causes for the pervasive climate of change noted earlier (technology, competition, and applicability of library skills), a fourth cause might also be considered: the desire of some library educators to disassociate themselves from the word librarian, to be free of the negative stereotype associated with the name. Many librarians share this desire. If one accepts that the stereotype is a handicap, how will it be possible to attract sufficient students to a program resulting in a master of library science degree? If the name of the degree is changed to avoid the stereotype, what happens to library science and the librarian? This change would represent the ultimate in taking the library out of library education.

Everyone in the library profession has at one time or another been bruised by the stereotype. But what are our options? One suggestion has been to subsume everyone whose primary work function is connected with information under the title of information professional. What does that mean? Professional in what profession? Information is not a profession nor an occupation. Neither is it a discipline. By way of contrast even though the dimensions of information science are not entirely clear nor its claim to being a science fully established, it has achieved some recognition as a discipline.

A recent study identified 1. 64 million persons as being

information professionals. [10] Included were occupations such as
librarians and public relations personnel. Though both occupations
are primarily concerned with information, they are quite different.
Can the occupations represented in this study be formed into a recognizable whole that coheres under the rubric of information professional? We would predict this could not be done because when a
field of work or a discipline becomes large and complex, division
of labor--specialization--occurs. Whatever the eventual outcome,
the term information professional has little to offer librarians. It
has no real meaning, no specific referent.

The term information manager has been suggested as another
alternative. This term has somewhat more meaning, but problems
arise here also. Information manager can have more than one referent, which leads to confusion. It could describe a function rather
than an occupation, as in the case of a person who processes information to make it accessible. It could refer to an information officer who interacts with the media on behalf of an organization. It
could mean someone who is the chief administrator of an information agency. The ambiguity of the term manager has already received attention in the literature. [11] Persons using the name information manager are asking what the term means. They are also
seeking job clarification and complaining about lack of status. Lack
of status is an old problem for librarians, but adopting the name of
information manager and switching to industry does not appear to be
a solution.

In any proposal to change the name of librarian a final question must be considered: Can it be done? Can an occupation uni-
laterally change its name and thereby acquire better status? For a
name change to transform an image, it must reflect changed conditions, and be accepted as valid and true by others. Recognition by
others, by society, is crucial, not agreement among one's colleagues
on the name change. Rather than enhancing one's position, names
adopted for cosmetic reasons are apt to brand one as a fraud, for
they fool no one.

Whether library education's flirtation with industry will change
our current situation remains to be seen. Meanwhile, we have plenty
to do and plenty to learn. We find ourselves engaged in a competitive struggle to stake out a place in the new information environment.
In the process of competing, the name of our profession may change,
or the present name may endure with an enhanced, more positive
connotation. In the midst of uncertainty, perhaps we can say at
least this much: When the smoke has cleared and the askes have
settled, there is no presently visible reason to believe librarians
will be listed as missing in action.

References

1. Magarrell, Jack. "The 1980's: Higher Education's 'Not-Me'
    Decade," Chronicle of Higher Education, 19, Jan. 7, 1980,
    6-9.

2. Henderson, Madeline M. "ASIS Testifies at Copyright Hearings," Bulletin of the American Society for Information Science, 7, Dec. 1980, p. 9.
3. King, Donald W., Krauser, Cheri, and Sague, Virginia M., "Profile of ASIS Membership," Bulletin of the American Society for Information Science, 6, Aug. 1980, p. 11. Some 58 percent of the members of the Special Libraries Association work in for-profit organizations, but this type of conflict is not evident. Presumably SLA members have no financial interest in the development and sale of information services and technology.
4. Lancaster, F. Wilfrid, "Whither Libraries? or, Wither Libraries," College and Research Libraries, 39, Sept. 1978, 345-357; "Librarians in 2001: Wilfrid Lancaster's De- and Re-institutionalizing," Hotline, 9, June 30, 1980, p. 2.
5. "Channel 2000 to Add Audio," Advanced Technology Libraries, 9, Dec. 1980, p. 10.
6. Low, Kathleen, "Rx for CRT-Strain," American Libraries, 12, Jan. 1981, p. 18.
7. Dobbs, Jeannine, "Must We Separate Books from Words?" Chronicle of Higher Education, 21, Jan. 26, 1981, p. 23.
8. "Progress of Prestel in England Is Halting," Advanced Technology Libraries, 10, Jan. 1981, p. 9.
9. "Career Advisory Service," Bulletin of the American Society for Information Science, 6, June 1980, p. 29; Spivack, Jane F., "101 Jobs for Information Scientists," Bulletin of the American Society for Information Science, 7, Oct. 1980, p. 31.
10. King, Donald W., Debons, Anthony, Mansfield, Una, and Shirley, Donald L., "A National Profile of Information Professionals," Bulletin of the American Society for Information Science, 6, Aug. 1980, 18-22.
11. Gardner, Roberta J. "Fighting an Image Problem: Information Managers Seek Job Clarity," Information World, 1, April 1979, pp. s/3, s/14; Gardner, Roberta J., "Is Tension Inevitable Between SLA and Associated Information Managers?" Special Libraries, 71, Sept. 1980, 373-378; Penn, Ira A. "Why Information Management?" Information and Records Management, 15, Jan. 1981, pp. 10, 66. For a conception of what information management is, see Smith, Harold, T., "Enter the Information Manager," Management World, 7, July 1978, 22-24. It is conceived of as being at the corporation vice-presidential level.

THE FREE LIBRARY OF PHILADELPHIA:

MAKING THE HARD CHOICES*

Philip Lentz

Philadelphia is a city of neighborhoods and the Free Library of Philadelphia, the city's public library, lives in the cultural neighborhood. Outside its front door in Logan Circle is a sculpture fountain by Alexander Stirling Calder (father of the well-known artist Alexander Calder). Across the street is the Franklin Institute, the science and technology museum. And a mile or so down the Parkway--a wide, tree-line boulevard patterned after Paris' Champs-Elysées--is the Philadelphia Museum of Art.

It's a cozy neighborhood located on the fringes of the downtown business district. But recently it has not been a tranquil one. The problem can be traced to a massive structure several hundred yards to the left of the library, adorned atop with a statute of William Penn. The building is City Hall, upon whose largess the library depends for survival. These days the largess has not been very large.

The fiscal difficulties of big cities have hit public libraries particularly hard, and the Free Library is no exception. Staff have been laid off, hours of service have been curtailed, acquisition budgets have been scaled down, and maintenance has been deferred. All this in a time of inflation.

Still, the Free Library has hung on and kept its head above water. "They are trying to economize where they hurt the essence the least," says Lowell A. Martin, a library consultant currently working on a study of the library. "I think they've been fairly successful so far, but I don't know how long they can do that. They'll get down to the bone pretty soon."

A collection for every occasion

Over the years, the Free Library has gained a reputation as one of

*Reprinted by permission of the author and publisher from Wilson Library Bulletin, 55:1 (September 1980) 35-40. Copyright © 1980 by The H.W. Wilson Company.

America's better public libraries.   It has special collections to de-
light researchers, a vast branch library network that reaches into
virtually every city neighborhood, community services that draw the
public into the branches, and programs that help the disabled, the
unschooled, and the unemployed.

It has nearly 3 million books in stock plus more than 4.3
million photographs, prints, maps, pamphlets, magazines, and other
documents.   Circulation, after taking a dip last year due to cutbacks,
is approaching 5 million again.   The library is used by almost
600,000 cardholders, and it handles nearly 800,000 requests a year,
including 220,000 by telephone.

In addition to the central facility at Logan Circle, there are
three regional libraries that serve as "mini-central" libraries, 49
branch libraries, the Mercantile Library, which serves the business
community, and the Library for the Blind and Physically Handicapped.
But the Free Library's pride and joy are its special collections.

In 1929, Edwin A. Fleisher, a local philanthropist and music
patron, was told by fire marshals that the 4,000 orchestral scores
at his Symphony Club were a fire hazard.   So he gave them to the
Free Library.   Today, in a cluttered room on the library's first
floor, the Fleisher collection stands at 13,000 scores, the largest
collection of its kind in the world.   The works are used by researchers and loaned to music ensembles worldwide, from large city or-
chestras to community symphonies.   (The library also lends unusual
instruments, like an organ grinder, if the score calls for it.)   A
German publisher, whose company was destroyed during World War
II, still calls the Free Library regularly to restore its catalog.
The Fleisher collection has virtually all of the publisher's works.

And then there is the story about Brazilian composer Francisco Mignone, who visited the collection in the 1940s and was asked
if he would like to see his Brazilian Suite.

"I'm afraid you don't mean that," the composer said sadly.
"you see, that is impossible.   It does not exist.   The manuscript
was lost four years ago."

However, curator Arthur Cohn plucked out the score and
handed it to the incredulous composer.   The score had been discovered among some old papers at the Brazilian exhibit at the New York
World's Fair.

For car buffs the library features one of the largest collections of auto reference materials.   It was started in 1948, when
Thomas McKean, a collector of car manuals, was told by his wife
that the pamphlets were cluttering up the house and he had better
get rid of them.   He gave them to the Free Library.   (McKean was
killed a year later in an auto accident.)

The collection, hidden in a small, out-of-the-way room on

the second floor, consists of owners manuals, parts manuals, sales
literature, photographs, magazines, and books on everything from
cars to go-carts to trucks. Like the Fleisher collection, it receives
requests from around the world. Most of the interest comes from
car owners repairing their autos and from antique car collectors
who want their restorations to be accurate.

On the fourth floor, tucked near the rotunda ceiling, is the
Rare Books Department. Valued at $30 million and kept under lock
and key in rooms with special temperature and humidity controls,
most of the collection is displayed in glass-enclosed cases that give
the department the atmosphere of a museum. Prized possessions
range from cuneiform clay tablets relating Nebuchadnezzar's conquest
of Jerusalem in 586 B.C. to first editions of Edgar Allan Poe's "The
Raven." Among the 40,000 books and 30,000 manuscripts are works
by Charles Dickens and Oliver Goldsmith and a respected collection
of children's literature that includes early American children's books
and a collection of Beatrix Potter's works.

A short distance away, in yet another cramped and cluttered
room made messier by construction work on air conditioning ducts,
is the library's renowned theater collection, which includes books,
film stills, reviews, old playbills, rare film magazines, movie pos-
ters, and scrapbooks. The subjects range from plays to vaudeville
to the circus. Only the theater collection of the New York Public
Library's Center for the Performing Arts is larger.

There is much more--from an extensive government publications department to choral music to a directory of local foundations--
but it is time to move on.

The Free Library has several innovative community programs,
though its money woes have kept down their size and made them dependent on private and federal sources. One of the most successful
is the Lifelong Learning Center. Started three years ago, it provides counseling, workshops, and seminars to people who want to
change jobs or re-enter the job market. The center has had some
spectacular success stories, like the middle-aged housewife who became the first woman electrician in a Philadelphia hospital, or the
travel agent who sold his business and went to college to fulfill a
childhood ambition of being a nurse. The program is used primarily by women who are either looking for a job or who long to break
out of the secretary-clerk-typist syndrome.

There are additional programs, such as the Reader Development Program, which provides resources to community organizations
that teach illiterates and poor readers to read, and a "Quadrus and
Friends" program in which comic books were given to ghetto youngsters to encourage them to use the library.

Developing a city institution

For a city preparing to celebrate its 300th birthday, the Free

Library is quite a youngster, as institutions go. It was founded in
1891 with a $250,000 bequest left by George S. Pepper, a member
of a prominent Philadelphia family descended from Benjamin Franklin. Pepper gave the money at the urging of his nephew, William
Pepper, a physician and provost at the University of Pennsylvania,
who became the library's founder.

The bequest set off civic squabbling as existing libraries
fought the city for the money. While the fight raged in court, the
city opened its first three branches. In 1894, it won the court battle
and opened the first main library in three rooms in the west wing
of City Hall with a total of 153,000 books. The Free Library moved
to more spacious quarters a year later and, after more quarreling
and court fights, ground was broken in 1917 for a permanent home.
There were to be still more delays--partially caused by World War
I--but the Free Library's $6.5 million central facility finally opened
its doors on June 2, 1927.

Today the library stands at the gateway to the Parkway, the
Museum of Art and Fairmount Park, and beyond. It is a majestic
neoclassical structure built in the style of public buildings of the
twenties: stately, stolid, and imposing. Patterned after the Ministry of Marine in Paris, its Corinthian columns rise 100 feet, and
stone archways decorate the thick walls of Indiana limestone. Inside,
a terrazzo and quarry tile floor lead to an impressive staircase
made of pink Tennessee marble. A statue of William Pepper, peer-
ing pensively into the main foyer, stands on a staircase landing.

By the late twenties, the library's branch system had begun
to grow, after receiving a $1.5 million gift in 1903 from Andrew
Carnegie. But the central library opened on the eve of the Depression, and decades would pass before it reached its potential. For
the Depression was a time of decline for the Free Library. Budgets
were slashed, expansion stopped, and books were not replaced. Circulation dropped from a record high of 5.7 million in 1931 to 3.1
million in 1937. Its collections too often were filled with castoffs
and hand-me-down books.

It was not until 1951 that the library finally began to rebound.
That year a new city charter was adopted and reformers took over
City Hall, ushering in a renaissance period for Philadelphia and its
cultural institutions. Emerson Greenaway, a Baltimore librarian,
was hired as library director, and using newly available resources
from City Hall he upgraded the library's staff, refurbished deteri-
orating collections, and embarked on an ambitious program of regional and smaller branch libraries. Starting in the late fifties,
hardly a year went by without a new branch opening. Today, nearly
thirty years later, the program is still not finished.

Riding the fiscal roller coaster

The fifties and sixties--the Free Library's "golden years"--were a time of ample resources and seemingly unbounded optimism. Expansion plans, for example, were based on projections that Philadelphia's population would increase by 250,000.

But it was not to be. Toward the end of the sixties, something went wrong. The optimism, the buoyancy, and--most of all--the money disappeared. The city's economy turned sour as jobs left, the population decreased, the tax base shrank, and demand for services increased. By 1971, a hiring freeze was imposed on the library. The austere seventies had begun.

Emerson Greenaway retired in 1969, to be succeeded by Keith Doms, a Wisconsin native who had spent the previous 13 years at Pittsburgh's Carnegie Library, the last five as director. He came to Philadelphia full of enthusiasm and ideas but ran into a brick wall of financial woes: "We had to deal with some problems we didn't anticipate. "

In fact, Doms found himself riding a fiscal roller coaster. One year staff would be cut, the next year the cut would be restored; hours would be reduced one year, restored the next. The number of library employees bounced up and down like a yo-yo. Under Mayor Frank L. Rizzo, police and firemen had priority, which meant the "softer" part of the city budget--like libraries--suffered disproportionately. The problem was exacerbated by federal cutbacks in library funds and a static state aid formula that did not account for inflation.

Doms is sanguine about his problems. Ask him about his accomplishments during his 11-year tenure, and he will thrust forward his square jaw and simply say: "Keeping the library operating. " At sixty, his face is chiseled and marked by the library's past decade of money troubles. He confronts them with a combination of good-natured ebullience and stoicism, though it is not easy.

"Survival in itself is a bit of a challenge now," he says, running his hand through his thick jet-black hair that just hints of grey. "And I think we have accomplished quite a few things. The problem with accomplishments is that while we've demonstrated a lot of positive programming that can and should be done by an urban public library, the city's financial resources have not allowed us to respond to known needs!"

The roller coaster stopped last year when the library budget literally crashed to the ground. Huge wage settlements to city workers forced large cuts citywide. The library's $14.3 million budget was cut by $2 million. These are, says Doms, the "down years. " No part of the library has survived unscathed. Some of the results:

● Staff has been cut from 943 to 680.
● Library hours have been sharply curtailed, including the end of Saturday hours at the branches.

● Bookmobile service was ended, as was book service to prisons, hospitals, and nursing homes.

● Circulation dropped last year from 5.3 million to 4.8 million, and the number of books in stock dropped 140,000, to 2.9 million.

● The library is 11 months behind in sending overdue notices, and there are about 200,000 outstanding overdue books.

● Because of the overdue backlog, collections in some branches have been depleted as much as 50 to 60 percent.

● The budget for buying books and other acquisitions was cut 31 percent last year and has not been allowed to grow since.

● There is a backlog of uncataloged new books, although it has been reduced from the 20,000 books of a year ago.

● No new recordings have been cataloged for the last year.

● Eight branches have leaky roofs that need to be repaired, but there is only money to fix two of them.

● Staffing is so meager at the branches that hardly a week goes by when a branch isn't forced to close because an employee calls in sick or goes on vacation.

● The delay in sending out requested music from the Fleisher collection has increased from a week to a month or two.

In addition, a heavily-used branch burned down last February, and it may be a year or more before it is rebuilt. "We just operate by the skin of our teeth," Doms says. He wrote in the library's 1978-79 annual report: "Available funds fell far short of meeting the minimum amounts needed to provide acceptable levels of library and information service for the people of Philadelphia."

An institution "living beyond its means"

The $2 million budget cut left the library in disarray, requiring a reorganization of remaining staff and resources that badly hurt morale. Only now--more than a year later--is the library beginning to recover. "The chaos element and the instability element have been relieved," says Marie Davis, deputy library director. "But staff and books are at the same level."

Yet at a time when the Free Library finds itself with less and less money, its expansion program begun decades before continues unabated. Fueled by neighborhood support and political pressure, two regional and eight new branch libraries were opened in the last 11 years. This despite the fact that the library does not have the money to fully staff or maintain the branches it already has. Library officials have learned to accept new branches with pained smiles. In the library's 1977-78 annual report, James Alan Montgomery Jr. , then president of the board of trustees, itemized the library's many money problems and noted, "We have been the reluctant beneficiary of a number of new branches."

Lowell Martin, in a background paper, put it more bluntly: "High inflation and an end to steady increases in city appropriations create a situation where the institution is trying to live beyond its means."

Presently the city's financial problems have worsened. This year, while newly elected Mayor William J. Green laid off police and firefighters for the first time in the city's history, the library's 1980-81 budget of $17.8 million kept staff and book budgets at their reduced levels. The library also lost 75 workers from the federally-funded Comprehensive Employment and Training Act (CETA); it will be allowed to replace less than half of them. This will mean more delays in cataloging new books and still further curtailment of hours at the branches.

"We can't operate an overextended system without sufficient funds, and we're without personnel to develop imaginative innovative library services," warns Marie Davis.

"We're standing still," says Randy Rosensteel, administrative assistant to Doms.

Making unpopular choices

Thus the Free Library is faced with a crucial decision: Can it maintain its extensive branch system, impressive collections, and community services at a time of constantly shrinking resources? Of course it cannot, and library officials know it.

With the fiscal crunch becoming a permanent reality, the library hired consultant Lowell Martin to prepare a blueprint for the library for the eighties. The report is due in December, and there are seven or eight options under consideration. They range from emphasizing information and retrieval services with tie-ins to cable television, to concentrating on books for children and young people. But in reality there is only one basic choice to be made: Does the library concentrate on its central library and collections, or does it put its time and money into its branches and community services?

"We may come down to that choice," Martin says. "But I'm desperately searching for a way to save both aspects of the library. It may not be possible."

The argument for the branch library system is that the purpose of the Free Library should be to serve the people in their neighborhoods and provide links to community agencies and activities, rather than to maintain collections that can be duplicated elsewhere. "The branch services should far and away take precedence," argues one local library academician. "It's not a public research facility. The collections are of value to a tiny portion of the public.... They should stop building certain exotic collections. Those research collections entail a continued commitment of resources and at this point in time are a luxury."

Doms does not agree: "I think it's a bad idea, because this library serves a very significant number of constituencies. I can't imagine the city of Philadelphia would virtually want to be without the services of the central library, which is essentially a collection of special collections. They could benefit people directly, and they back up the whole system."

A major element weighing heavily on the side of branch support is politics. City council-members fight very hard to get and then keep branch libraries. "Every councilman wants a branch in every neighborhood," says one library expert. Politics is a powerful force that the library cannot overcome. Over the years Doms has periodically recommended reducing or consolidating branches, and each time the council has found the money to save them. Says Christie Hastings, president of the Friends of the Free Library: "Council argues in terms of, 'You're trying to take something away from the people I represent.'"

Doms understands what he is up against. "Neighborhoods will make every effort to guard against the elimination of any facility, whether it's a post office, a library, an elementary school, an engine house.... They're community symbols. They're symbols of self-respect. So when one talks in terms of closing branch libraries or consolidating staffs, one has to expect that there will be strong, strong neighborhood opposition."

However, the reality is that the Free Library has already made up its mind, at least over the short-term. While all parts of the library have suffered during the last few years, the brunt of the cutbacks have been borne by the branches, where hours have been reduced most severely, where staff has been cut back most drastically, where maintenance has been put off, all to preserve the central library.

"Our priorities have to be--there isn't any choice--the central library and the regional libraries, because that is where our greatest resources are," Doms says. This spring, Doms again recommended closing four branches. But the council shifted enough money around to keep them open. (The result is that hours at the branches have been reduced again.) In addition, the council budgeted funds for two more new branches.

An agenda for the eighties

The Free Library of Philadelphia is now setting itself for the eighties. The central library is undergoing a $7 million facelift, its first full-scale renovation since it was built. The library is also starting a $4 million automation program that, it is hoped, will reduce overdue backlogs, speed acquisitions, and eventually replace the card catalog with computer terminals.

But the key item that will set the agenda is Martin's study,

which is designed to give a philosophical underpinning to whatever
policy the Free Library adopts.   The problem is that the library
serves many publics, and some are undoubtedly going to be left out
of the library's future plans.   And those left out are going to make
sure the rest of the public--and the politicians--know about it.   "At
some point we're going to have to make some terribly unpopular
choices," says Christie Hastings, who is a member of a 38-member
group advising Martin.

The library has been hurt, no doubt, by its fiscal problems.
But its basic strengths remain intact.   As to the future, it may be
that the exact course the Free Library ultimately takes is not really
the important thing.   Rather, it may be that the library has realized,
in a time of financial scarcity, that it can no longer be everything
to everyone, that choices must be made, and that not everyone will
be pleased with the result.   With public libraries in trouble across
the country, Martin says, "If Philadelphia can work out a fresh
program without getting more money, then Philadelphia will be setting a pattern and leading the way into a serious, hard-headed approach for these libraries."

THE ERIC AND LISA DATABASES:

HOW THE SOURCES OF LIBRARY SCIENCE LITERATURE COMPARE*

Tim LaBorie and Michael Halperin

Introduction

Of the many online bibliographic databases currently available, only a few have material of direct relevance to students of library and information science. Two data bases that are of particular importance because of their coverage of this field are ERIC and LISA. This article describes a study conducted at the Drexel University Library assessing the ability of the ERIC and LISA databases to support the research needs of library science students.

In the study, we performed subject searches on the two databases to retrieve citations listed in bibliographies prepared by beginning students in Drexel's School of Library and Information Science. This article gives the precision and recall ratios of the searches conducted and assesses the ability of the databases to retrieve known citations gathered from printed indexes. Other factors such as cost, overlap between the bases, and the relative merits of manual and computer searches are also discussed.

In brief, here are our findings:

● A high percentage of the citations in the student bibliographies were not in the ERIC and LISA databases.

● There is considerable duplication of citations retrieved from the two databases.

● ERIC is the preferred database when an exhaustive search is not required.

Background

The School of Library and Information Science at Drexel University

*Reprinted by permission of the authors and publisher from Database, 4:3 (September 1981) 32-37.

requires an introductory core course for all incoming students. One of the assignments for the course is to conduct a literature review on a selected topic within the field of library and information science (see appendix) and prepare a bibliography with annotations or abstracts. Most topics are chosen from a list of 39 in the syllabus. The bibliography, while being highly selective (typically containing less than 20 citations), should also represent the total scope of the topic. Students are required to conduct a thorough literature search using all pertinent printed bibliographic sources. They are discouraged from using computerized databases until a manual search is completed.

The present study is a test of the ability of the two databases to support the students' research, and, by extension, explores the general adequacy of the bases' coverage of library and information science literature.

The Databases

ERIC--The Educational Resources Information Center database, produced at the National Institute of Education, is composed of two sections represented in printed form by the indexes Resources in Education (RIE) and the Current Index to Journals in Education (CIJE). Although primarily an education database, materials relevant to library and information science are indexed by the Information Resources Clearinghouse. Reports, proceedings, conference papers and other more "fugitive" types of materials have been collected for RIE since 1966. CIJE (published since 1969) indexes, fully or partially, over 700 journals; 55 of these are the responsibility of the Information Resources Clearinghouse.

LISA--This database corresponds to the printed index Library and Information Science Abstracts produced by the Library Association (London). Over 300 journals are reviewed for inclusion and about 210 are indexed completely. The database covers the period from 1969 to the present. Some data elements, however, such as complete abstracts and classification codes, have been included only since 1976. LISA is international in scope and covers all aspects of library and information science.

Although not covered by this study, there are several other useful databases for library and information science:

● INSPEC is produced by the Institution of Electrical Engineers and corresponds to the printed versions of Physics Abstracts, Electrical and Electronic Abstracts and Computer and Control Abstracts. The online version covers the period 1969 to the present. Because of its coverage of electronic and computer journals, it is very useful for information science topics.
● NTIS, the online version of Government Reports Announcements and Index, is produced by the National Technical

Information Service. This database provides acess, since 1964, to technical reports from numerous government agencies. It is a good source for government sponsored research in the library and information science fields.

● SCI, The Science Citation Index, and SSCI, The Social Science Citation Index, are available online since 1974 and 1972 respectively. Between them they index over 4000 journals. Although they have limited subject access, they are very effective for searching key authors and cited references. [1]

Methodology

Fourteen students in the Fundamentals of Library and Information Science course volunteered to take part in our study. They met with us after they had finished their manual literature searches and had handed in their completed bibliographies. We developed search strategies (see appendix) in consultation with the students but without looking at their papers. The students were present when the searches were conducted. In this way we attempted to duplicate our usual online search procedure.

We used the following guidelines when designing search strategies:

● Subject terms from the ERIC thesaurus and descriptors from LISA's subject scheme were preferred to free text terms. [2] Most of these searches, however, contain a mixture of both types.

● If the term was a controlled descriptor in only one base, it was included as a free text term in the search of the second base.

● Time and cost limitations were determined by the amount the typical Drexel student is willing to spend. We have observed that $10.00 is the usual upper limit. This allowed about 6 minutes on each base. Our volunteers were not charged. --A set size that could be printed cost effectively online was aimed for. --Search strategies were altered while online in consultation with the student to broaden or to narrow the search.

We then compared the results of the computer searches with the citations listed in the student bibliographies to determine which citations were retrieved in the online search. A few citations which we expected to retrieve online were not retrieved. For these we did title searches online to see if the citations were in the databases.

Analysis

Relevance is an important although elusive concept in information system evaluation. To make judgements about the adequacy of LISA and ERIC to meet the research needs of library science students requires a standard of relevance.   In this article, a relevant citation is one used in the bibliography of a student taking part in the study. It should be kept in mind that the citations in the bibliographies were selected after an extensive manual search of the literature and represent the students' conception of the "best" group of citations for their topic.   The bibliographies are highly selective, averaging 14 citations each--196 citations in 14 papers.   We found it convenient to organize the relevant citations into three categories.   Quantities are presented in Table 1.

1. Retrieved--relevant citations retrieved by subject searches in the databases.
2. Potentially Retrievable--relevant citations present in the databases but which our subject searches failed to re-trieve.
3. Non-Retrievable--relevant citations not in the databases.

Table 1

RELEVANT CITATIONS

Database	ERIC		LISA		Combined	
Category	#	%	#	%	#	%
Retrieved	36	18	31	16	51	26
Potentially Retrievable	35	18	23	12	49	25
Non-Retrievable	125	64	142	72	96	49

Retrieved Citations--Recall and Precision

Two standard measures of information retrieval effectiveness are recall, the ratio of relevant items retrieved to relevant items in the database, and precision, the ratio of relevant items retrieved to total retrieved.

Recall is usually difficult to measure since the number of relevant items in a database, particularly for a large file, is almost impossible to determine.   For this study, however, we were using known citations as our measure of relevance; therefore, it was possible to verify the existence of these citations in the file through title searches.   Our recall and precision ratios are given in Table 2.

Table 2

RECALL AND PRECISIONS RATIOS

Database	ERIC	LISA	Both Bases
Recall Ratios	51%	57%	54%
Precision Ratios	8%	10%	8%

The ratios serve as an indication that the search strategies were equivalent for the two bases. Beyond this, they tell us more about the definition of relevance and the searcher's skill and objectives than they reveal about the adequacy of the databases. A more direct measurement of the ability of ERIC and LISA to supply library students' needs is discussed next.

Database Coverage

The ability of ERIC and LISA to supply the citations actually used by the students in their bibliographies is a good indication of the databases' adequacy as research tools. For the purpose of this study, "coverage" is simply the number of relevant citations in ERIC or LISA divided by the total number of citations in the students' bibliographies. This measure is not influenced by search formulation or by searcher skill. In fact, it could be calculated with fair accuracy without any online searching by examining lists of journals indexed by the databases. We found that ERIC provided 36% and LISA 28% of the relevant citations: together, the databases contained over half (52%) of the relevant citations. About 31% of the relevant citations retrieved in our subject searches were duplicates. Figure 1 shows the effect of retrieving the duplicate citations as a result of an initial search on either ERIC or LISA.

Figure 1

Percent of unique relevant citations retrieved when ERIC is searched first.

ERIC	LISA
70	30

Percent of unique relevant citations retrieved when LISA is searched first.

LISA	ERIC
60	40

Although ERIC appears to have a slight retrieval advantage, the difference is not statistically significant. In general, the results of this analysis suggest that when both ERIC and LISA are searched about 2/3 of the relevant citations will be retrieved from the first base searched and 1/3 from the second base searched. Because of this duplication, often a search of one base will be sufficient and the choice may be determined by cost. The DIALOG rates for access to the two bases through Telenet are as follows: ERIC $25.00

per hour (.42 per min) and LISA $50.00 per hour (.83 per min).
ERIC is less expensive because no royalties are charged.

Cost is only one consideration in choosing a database. However, for subjects in the "mainstream" of library science it appears
to be more cost effective to search ERIC first and then follow with
a search of LISA only if more comprehensive retrieval is required.

Non-retrievable Citations

An interesting finding of this study is the high number of citations in
the student papers that are not in the databases. Of 196 citations in
14 papers, 125 (64%) are not in ERIC and 142 (72%) are not in LISA.

To gain a better understanding of the types of materials used
by students that were not in the databases we analyzed the non-
retrievable citations by format and age. The result is given in
Table 3.

Table 3

PERCENT OF CITATIONS NOT IN
DATABASES BY TYPE OF MATERIAL

Types of Material	ERIC	LISA
Trade books	21%	19%
Other monographs	26%	33%
Journal	36%	30%
Audiovisual	01%	01%
Too old /too recent	15%	17%

We were surprised at the large number of monographic studies cited by the students. ERIC, as was expected, scored better
in its ability to supply citations to monographs. The number of
journal citations not in the databases is remarkably high, particularly
for LISA. Although Drexel's curriculum emphasizes the use of audio-
visual materials, the few citations to this format may reflect the
lack of published materials as well as the beginning students' print
orientation.

Conclusions

Following are the conclusions of this study:

1. Library science students use a wide variety of materials,
   many of which, especially monographic works, are not
   included in the ERIC and LISA databases or the equivalent
   printed indexes. The two databases contain about half

(52%) of the citations used by the sample of students in our study--ERIC held 36% and LISA 28%. It is remarkable that ERIC, which is primarily an education database, scored as well as LISA, the specialized database for the field.

2. There is considerable overlap between the ERIC and LISA databases. This study found that 31% of the relevant citations retrieved in our subject searches were duplicates. Therefore, the first base searched will retrieve about 2/3 of the relevant citations contained in both bases.

3. The cost of connect time on ERIC is about half the rate of LISA. Since their retrieval is closely comparable, ERIC should be searched in preference to LISA if only one base is to be employed.

References

1. For more detailed information on these databases see Williams, Martha E. , Computer-Readable Data Bases; a Directory and Data Sourcebook, Washington, ASIS, 1979.

2. ERIC documents are indexed according to a controlled list of subject terms. We used the Thesaurus of ERIC Descriptors. New York, Macmillan, 1977. LISA's indexing system uses descriptors, section headings as well as a faceted classification scheme. We used descriptors from the subject indexes in issues of Library and Information Science Abstracts. By "free text terms" we mean terms which occur outside of the database's subject or descriptor fields such as in the title or abstract.

APPENDIX--SEARCH TOPICS AND STRATEGIES

1   Faculty Status and the Academic Librarian

ERIC   (ACADEMIC RANK PROFESSIONAL AND LIBRARIANS/DE)
       OR (FACULTY (W) STATUS (F) LIBRARIAN?)
       result 49
LISA   (ACADEMIC STATUS/DE AND STAFF/DE) OR (FACULTY
       (W) STATUS (F) LIBRARIAN?)
       result 41

2   Legal Library Services to Inmates

ERIC   (PRISONERS OR INMATES) AND (LIBRARY SERVICES) AND
       (LAW? OR LEGAL EDUCATION)
       result 38
LISA   (PRISONER? OR INMATE?) AND (LIBRARY (F) SERVICE?
       OR LEGAL (F) EDUCATION)
       result 29

3   The Young Adult and Intellectual Freedom in the Library

ERIC   (YOUNG ADULTS OR YOUTH/DE OR TEENAGERS/DE OR
       ADOLESCENTS/DE) AND (STUDENT RIGHTS OR CENSOR-
       SHIP OR ACADEMIC FREEDOM OR INTELLECTUAL (W)
       FREEDOM)
       result 30
LISA   (YOUTH/DE OR YOUNG (W) ADULT? OR TEENAGER? OR
       ADOLESCENT?) AND (STUDENT (W) RIGHTS OR CENSOR-
       SHIP OR ACADEMIC (W) FREEDOM OR INTELLECTUAL (W)
       FREEDOM)
       result 7

4   Book Selection and Intellectual Freedom (exclude childrens books
     and school libraries)

ERIC   [(MEDIA SELECTION OR BOOK (W) SELECTION OR LIBRARY
       MATERIAL SELECTION OR READING MATERIAL SELECTION)
       AND (INTELLECTUAL (W) FREEDOM OR CENSOR?)] NOT
       (CHILDREN? OR SCHOOL?)
       result 38
LISA   [(BOOK SELECTION/DE OR MATERIAL? (F) SELECTION OR
       MEDIA (F) SELECTION) AND (INTELLECTUAL (W) FREE-
       DOM OR CENSOR?)] NOT (CHILDREN? OR SCHOOL?)
       result 6

5   Automated Claiming of Serials

ERIC   (SERIALS/DE OR PERIODICALS/DE OR JOURNAL?) AND
       (AUTOMATION AND (CLAIM?)
       result 15
LISA   (SERIAL? OR PERIODICAL? OR JOURNAL?) AND (CLAIM?)
       result 24

6   Library Services to Small Business

ERIC   (SMALL (W) BUSINESS? OR SMALL (W) FIRM?) AND (LI-
       BRARY OR LIBRARIES)
       result 20
LISA   (SMALL (W) BUSINESS? OR SMALL (W) FIRM?) AND (LI-
       BRARY OR LIBRARIES)
       result 10

7   Scientific and Technological Information Centers in Israel

ERIC   (INFORMATION SERVICES OR INFORMATION CENTERS OR
       LIBRARIES) AND (SCIENCE? OR SCIENTIFIC OR TECHNICAL
       OR TECHNOLOGY OR TECHNOLOGICAL) AND (ISRAEL)
       result 12

LISA (INFORMATION SERVICES OR INFORMATION CENTERS OR INFORMATION WORK) AND (SCIENCE? OR SCIENTIFIC OR TECHNICAL OR TECHNOLOGY OR TECHNOLOGICAL) AND (ISRAEL)
result 15

8 National Level Planning for Information Services--the Role of NCLIS

ERIC (NATIONAL (W) COMMISSION (S) INFORMATION (S) LIBRAR-IES OR NCLIS) AND (YR=75:YR=79)
result 29
LISA (NATIONAL (W) COMMISSION (S) INFORMATION OR NCLIS) AND (LA=ENGLISH)
result 41

9 Library Programs and Services to Young Adults

ERIC (YOUNG ADULTS OR YOUTH/DE OR TEENAGERS/DE OR ADOLESCENTS/DE) AND (LIBRARY PROGRAMS OR LIBRARY SERVICES)
result 44
LISA (YOUNG (W) ADULT? OR YOUTH/DE OR TEENAGER? OR ADOLESCENT?) AND (PROGRAM?)
result 21

10 Evaluation and Measurement of Reference Services

ERIC (LIBRARY REFERENCE SERVICES) AND (EVALUATION OR MEASUREMENT)
result 50
LISA (REFERENCE WORK) AND (EVALUATION OR MEASUREMENT)
result 18

11 Evaluation of Children's Services in Public Libraries

ERIC (EVALUATION OR MEASUREMENT) AND (PUBLIC LIBRAR-IES) AND (CHILDREN? (S) SERVICES? OR CHILDREN?(S) PROGRAMS?)
result 24
LISA (PUBLIC LIBRARIES) AND (CHILDREN?) AND (PROGRAM? OR SERVICE?) AND (LA=ENGLISH)
result 38

12 The Library in the Preschool

ERIC (PRESCHOOL PROGRAMS OR PRESCHOOL EDUCATION) AND (LIBRARY) AND (YR=73:YR=79)
result 39

LISA   (PRESCHOOL) AND (LIBRARY)
        result 11

13   The Role of the Media Specialist in the Curriculum Development
     Process

ERIC   (MEDIA SPECIALISTS) AND (CURRICULUM) AND (SCHOOL
       LIBRARIES)
       result 23
LISA   (MEDIA (W) SPECIALIST? OR SCHOOL (W) LIBRARIAN?) AND
       (CURRICULUM)
       result 21

14   Information and Referral Services in Public Libraries

ERIC   (INFORMATION (1W) REFERRAL OR I(1W)R) AND (PUBLIC
       LIBRARIES)
       result 30
LISA   (INFORMATION (1W) REFERRAL OR I(1W)R) AND (PUBLIC
       LIBRARIES)
       result 25

Part II

TECHNICAL SERVICES /READERS' SERVICES

THE PLACE AND ROLE OF BIBLIOGRAPHIC DESCRIPTION

IN GENERAL AND INDIVIDUAL CATALOGUES:

A HISTORICAL ANALYSIS*

Gertrude London

> "The heart of the library problem is in the <u>record</u>
> of recorded information"[1]

1. Introduction: Memory Functions of the Catalogue

Librarians are mediators between inquirers or readers and the books (documents) they need or want for information, knowledge, education, or entertainment and pleasure. In former times when libraries were smaller, a librarian often knew the content of his library by heart and assisted his readers as a sort of "living catalogue."[2] As libraries grew, and more and more books were published all over the world, memory alone was no longer adequate for recollecting the contents of a library. It was, therefore, necessary to externalize the recall procedures of the human memory; this is one of the main functions of the catalogue. It records certain selected and agreed features of a document in a pre-determined pattern and in such a way that (1) the document is identified in a bibliographic description and (2) is made accessible to different approaches by adding a number of explicit access points, such as headings for author, title, subtitle, and subject content. These catalogue records serve also as permanent representations of documents which are not always at hand. The catalogue is thus a register which contains records that are abbreviated and condensed according to a code of rules, the code being a shorthand language for representing documents by a number of significant data elements.

The two objectives of the catalogue record (1) identification by bibliographic description and (2) index pointers or headings have not had equal standing in the discussions of catalog code makers. Those interested mainly in creating a particular form of catalog for a particular library were generally inclined to stress the heading(s)

---

*Reprinted by permission of the author and publisher from <u>Libri</u>, 30:4 (October 1980) 253-84.

and the orginizational aspects of the catalogue, e. g. British Museum and Cutter, while the establishment of the bibliographic description was relegated to second place.   Others, who had in mind union catalogues, national or international, or envisaged basic bibliographic records that could be used for producing a variety of catalogues and/or indexes, thought efficient cataloguing required first the preparation of uniform or standardized bibliographic records, e. g. , the French government in 1791, Jewett in 1850, Crestadoro in 1856, the Prussian Instructions in 1899, the MARC project and other forms of computerized cataloguing, and lastly, the 1978 edition of the Anglo-American Cataloguing Rules.   A great number of index points can be added to or included in these unit records, such as title words, subject headings, classification symbols, authors' names, etc.

2.   Rules for a French general catalogue of confiscated libraries, 1791

One of the first attempts at creating a general catalogue for a group of libraries owes its origin to the social changes brought about by the French Revolution. [3] With the suppression of religious and secular establishments in 1790 and the confiscation of their possessions many rich and important private libraries containing unknown quantities of books and manuscripts had become national property.   The government planned to use these books for founding public libraries, devoted to popular education.   But in order to do so, it had to find out first what books existed in these confiscated libraries.   The French government, therefore, issued in 1791 rules for preparing the catalogue of each confiscated library: "Instruction pour procéder à la confection du catalogue de chacune des bibliothèques sur lesquelles les directoires ont dû ou doivent incessamment apposer des scellés. " The purpose of these catalogues as stated in the first paragraph of the "Instruction" was to obtain "exact information about all the books, printed as well as in manuscript that existed in the libraries of each department and were part of the national property. "[4]

        These rules constitute a carefully drawn up cataloguing code, divided into six clearly defined operations.   (1) First progressively numbered cardboard slips ("fichets") were to be placed into each book in the order of their place on the shelves, with one inventory number only for a work in several volumes.   (2) In the second operation the work was to be catalogued by entering the corresponding inventory number on the first line of a playing card, followed by its exact title, names of the author, place of publication, printer or publisher, date and size, with notes on illustrations, where necessary.   On each card one word was to be underlined, preferably the author's surname, or, if it could not be ascertained, a word in the title which best indicated the subject matter.   (3) After all "titles" had been carefully copied on the cards, they were to be filed alphabetically in the order of the underlined words: either by author's surname or by a significant word of the title proper.   (4) The cards were then to be fastened together into separate packages for each letter of the alphabet.   (5) A copy made on ordinary paper was to

be retained in the district, while the original cards, provided with
location symbols: department number and place of library, were
to be sent to Paris. (6) Lastly, in order to facilitate finding the
catalogued books, labels indicating every hundredth number were to
be fixed on the shelves.

The progress of this vast and well-planned union catalogue of
confiscated libraries was, however, not as rapid as expected. In
1794, Henri Grégoire, constitutional bishop of Blois and deputy to
the National Convention, reported to the Convention that only 1, 200, 000
cards, representing about 3 million books had reached Paris. This
was less than one third of the projected catalogue. Furthermore,
the work was often very badly executed by untrained and ignorant
copyists. In this period of upheaval local officials were much too
busy with their own difficulties and troubles to care about the pres-
ervation and cataloguing of books, so that this enormous project for
a union catalogue of confiscated libraries, initiated and supported by
the central French government came to nothing. ("L'immense tra-
vail entrepris n'aboutit pas.")[5]

3. "Rules for the Compilation of the Catalogue" of the British Museum, 1841

In 1841 the first "codification" of cataloguing rules in English, "the
famous code of ninety-one rules,"[6] was published as the first and
only volume of the Catalogue of Printed Books in the British Museum. [7] These "Rules for the Compilation of the Catalogue," which
have had a strong influence on subsequent cataloguing rules in Europe
and America, were the work of a "committee" which was formed
early in 1839 "for framing the rules for the new General Catalogue"
of the British Museum library. It consisted of Anthony Panizzi,
Thomas Watts, J. Winter Jones, Edward Edwards and John H. Parry;
"each of them was separately to prepare, according to his own views,
rules for the compilation of the projected work. These were afterwards discussed collectively, and when any difference arose, it was
settled by vote. The rules so drawn up were sanctioned by the
Trustees, on the 13th of July, 1839, and printed on the 15th July,
1841."[7a]

An examination of the sequence in which these ninety-one
rules were stated in 1841 does not reveal any clear and logical
structure. Most of the rules are concerned with the organization
of the catalogue and problems of choice and form of the headings
under which "titles" are to be entered and arranged alphabetically
(rule 2). Rules 3 through 8, 10 through 17 deal with the choice,
form, and place of personal author headings in the catalogue. The
rules for headings of anonymous, pseudonymous works, and those
issued by corporate bodies, collections, the Bible, encyclopaedias,
serials, etc. , are given in rules 9, 33 through 53. The preoccupation of this cataloguing code with the heading, the filing tag, can
easily be detected in the recurrent use of phrases, such as "to be
entered under," e.g. , rules 4, 5, 10, 11, 12, 32, 45, 46, 47, 51,

52, 85, 86; or "to be catalogued under," e.g., rules 33, 40, 55,
79, 81, 88; or as "as a (the) heading," e.g., rules 8, 14, 34, 38.

Cross-references of three classes ("No work ever to be entered twice at full length. Whenever requisite, cross-references to
be introduced." Rule 54) are discussed in rules 55 through 68, 83,
87 and 91, while rules concerning the filing order of the entries are
stated in rules 68 through 78.

Rules for the description of the book are relatively few. Specific questions of bibliographic description are treated in only fourteen rules: 18 through 31, just over 15% of the total. The main
concern of the "Ninety-one Rules" was the alphabetical arrangement
of the printed catalogue of one library, in which related entries were
grouped together under headings determined according to the principles enunciated in these rules.

4. Jewett's Plan for the Construction of a General Catalogue from
Separate Bibliographic Units, 1852 and 1853

A different orientation from that of the British Museum's "Rules for
the Compilation of the Catalogue" is soon evident in the next impor-
tant code of cataloguing rules in English: Charles Coffin Jewett's
"On the Construction of Catalogues of Libraries, and of a General
Catalogue, and their Publication by Means of Separate, Stereotyped
Titles, with Rules and Examples." Washington, Smithsonian Institu-
tion, 1852. A second, revised edition was published in 1853: "On
the Construction of Catalogues of Libraries, and their Publication by
Means of Separate, Stereotyped Titles. With Rules and Examples."
Washington, Smithsonian Institution, 1853. Here we find a small,
but significant change in the title; the omission of "and of a General
Catalogue" announces the failure of Jewett's far-reaching project.
(I shall generally quote from the second edition, as it contains the
definitive formulation of Jewett's ideas.)

Jewett's approach differs from that of most Anglo-American
catalog rule makers before and after him. From the beginning he
was less preoccupied with the organizational aspects of the catalogue
and its particular filing arrangement in any one library, nor were
the problems he tried to solve applicable to only one particular form
of catalogue; rather his ultimate aim was to "construct a general
catalogue" step by step from separate, uniform bibliographic units,
a concept very similar to the International Standard Bibliographic
Description (ISBD) of the 1970s.

We can follow the origin of his ideas, their evolution, the
definitive formulation of his plans, and their final defeat in Annual
Reports of the Smithsonian Institution, especially those for the years
1847-1854, Second through Ninth Annual Reports. [8]

In the Preface to the Brown University Library Catalogue of
1843, Jewett had already explained his principles: "The plan of

arrangement has been selected after a wide comparison and with
great deliberation.... It is simple and convenient, and admits of
indefinite extension.... The catalogue consists of two parts: a
descriptive Catalogue of all works, which the Library contains, and
an Index of Subjects. "[9] Shortly before his appointment in 1848 as
"Assistant Secretary of the [Smithsonian] institution, acting as librarian," Jewett had proposed in a letter he sent in 1847 to the Secretary of the Smithsonian Institution, Joseph Henry, [10] to make the
library of the Institution "a centre of bibliographical reference" by
collecting catalogues and "lists of future accessions" from "the principal libraries of the United States." At the same time he recommended that "these supplementary catalogues should all be prepared
on a uniform plan. The titles should be written on cards of the
same size, so that they may be placed together in one alphabetical
arrangement, in order to facilitate research." In the third Annual
Report for 1848, [11] Jewett describes the procedures he employed
during his first year at the Smithsonian in "the systematic arrangement for purposes of comparison of the printed catalogues of the
principal libraries of the United States." The titles are separated,
and each is pasted upon a card, which is then stamped with the ini-
tials of all the libraries owning the same book. In the fourth Annual
Report for 1849, Jewett goes one step further and proposes a "general catalogue of the books contained in all our public libraries" to
be prepared by the Smithsonian Institution. His reasons were as
follows: experience gained during 1849 while transcribing 4,000 of
the 55,000 titles extracted from printed catalogues had shown that
many of them were imperfect or inaccurate. He had, therefore,
conceived a plan "to secure general uniformity among the various
libraries in the preparation of catalogues and to establish a system
of stereotyping them by separate titles, * which will enable each library to print annual editions of its catalogue, incorporating the titles
of the last accessions to the collection; and which will enable us, by
means of the same titles, to print a general catalogue of all the libraries. "[12]

     Jewett's plan for producing a catalogue by "stereotyping of
separate titles" was first made public in August 1850 in a paper which
he read at the Annual Meeting of the American Association for the
Advancement of Science in New Haven. He also gave a detailed account in the Fifth Annual Report of the Smithsonian Institution for
1850 under the heading "General Catalogue,"[13] which according to
a footnote [14] is "substantially" the same as the paper he read to
the AAAS. This year, 1850, was probably the zenith of Jewett's
career. Appendix III [15] of the same Annual Report includes a
"Report of Commissioners to examine the plan for forming a general
stereotype catalogue of Public Libraries in the United States." In a
letter, dated August 16, 1850, the Secretary of the Institution, Joseph
Henry, officially submitted Jewett's proposal to six reviewers. They

---

*In stereotyping a solid printing plate or block is cast from a mold
of a piece of printing which was originally composed in movable type.

commented favorably on it and recommended that "a catalogue of the
Library of Congress" be prepared on Jewett's "plan."

Jewett's proposal consisted of two parts:

1. A plan for stereotyping catalogues of libraries by separate
   movable titles of the books contained in them, and
2. A set of general rules to be recommended for adoption
   by the different public libraries in the United States for
   the preparation of their catalogues. [16]

Among the many advantages derived from such a plan, the Commissioners cited four in particular.   First "the economy of time, labor,
and expense."   When preparing new editions of catalogues, "the new
titles only will be stereotyped and inserted in their proper places
among the former titles, all the titles being on movable plates."
Thus the chief cost of republication, that of composition, revision,
and correction will be avoided, except for the new titles. [17] Secondly, the catalogue record of "the same book, in the same edition,
will of course be cast but once, and will thenceforward serve for
the catalogue of every library possessing that book, which may enter
into that arrangement."   A third advantage will be the versatility of
the procedures.   Using the same plates, the arrangement of catalogues can be varied readily from alphabetical to "a classed catalogue, either of a whole library or any department of it;" or as
Jewett expressed it elsewhere: "Another important benefit of this
system is that it allows us to vary the form of the catalogue, at
will, from the alphabetical to the classed, and to modify the classification as we please.   The titles separately stereotyped may change
their order at command." [18] As a fourth and last point the need
for uniform rules was stressed: "Finally, the plan, of necessity
requires that the titles of the books in the libraries, included in the
arrangement, should be given on uniform principles and according
to fixed rules; an object of no small importance to those who consult them." [19]

     The indispensable prerequisite for the success of Jewett's
plan for a general catalogue is, of course, "a much higher degree
of uniformity" [20] in the bibliographic entities of which it is constructed.   "Minute and stringent rules become absolutely indispensable, when the catalogue of each library is, as upon the proposed
plan, to form part of a general catalogue.   Uniformity is then imperative; ..."[21] In order to assist librarians Jewett drew up a
set of rules with great care.   "They are founded upon those adopted
for the compilation of the catalogue of the British Museum; some of
them are, verbatim, the same.   Others conform more to rules advocated by Mr. Panizzi, than to those finally sanctioned by the
Trustees of the Museum."   But he has also made many modifications
and additions, required by "the peculiar character of the system now
proposed.   Some innovations have been introduced, which, it is hoped,
may be considered improvements."[22] Though many of Jewett's
thirty-nine "Rules for preparing the Catalogue," especially those
dealing with "headings" are derived from the British Museum's

"Ninety-one Rules," the structure and the presentation of Jewett's Rules is clearer, more logical, and the leading ideas are different, because his Rules were intended for a different system: not the catalogue of one particular library, but a national union catalogue. The Rules are neatly divided into four parts:[23]

I.   Titles, i. e. bibliographic description (Rules I-XII)
II. Headings (Rules XIII-XXIX)
III. Cross-references (Rules XXX-XXXI)
IV. Arrangement (Rules XXXII-XXXIX)

They are complemented by examples "for the purpose of illustrating the rules, and of furnishing specimens of different kinds of titles, as well as of showing the general appearance of the proposed catalogues."[24] The alphabetical catalogue is supplemented by an "Index of subjects" with references to the headings, and a "Local Index" with references to the running numbers of the stereotyped plates. (See below.)

From the organization of the Rules it can be seen that the bibliographic description, the transcription of titles, is treated in the first part of the Rules. Many of the rules are fairly extensive and consist of a general rule, which is occasionally followed by exceptions, and often has a number of explanatory remarks in small print. For instance, Rule I states:[25] "I. The Titles are transcribed IN FULL, including the names of Authors, Editors, Translators, Commentators, Continuators, etc. , precisely as they stand upon the title-page." Remark 2 of this rule explains the reasons for inclusion of the author's name: "It is necessary (in this plan) to give the name of the Author, in connection with the title, although it be but a repetition of the heading; for the heading will be stereotyped separate from the title, and, therefore, the title should contain all that is necessary to indicate its proper position, in the alphabetical order, in case of displacement." Other rules deal with "Number of volumes, how to be specified" (VIII), Place and date of publication (IX), Size (X), Number of pages (XI), Additions to Titles (XII).

Headings are treated in the second part of the Rules, after the bibliographic description and comprise rules XIII-XXIX. The first of the rules on "Headings" (XIII) states distinctly that choice and form of the heading should be decided after the description has been completed. "When the title has been transcribed in accordance with the foregoing rules, the heading is to be written above it. This heading determines the place of the title in the alphabetical catalogue and consists in general of the name of the author in its vernacular form. ... "[26] In 1853 cataloguing rules followed "the sequence of the cataloguers' operations," to which Anglo-American cataloguing returned in December 1978 with the publication of the second edition of AACR. [27]

The idea that headings are exclusively organizational devices is developed one step further in rule XXXII which, in the second edition of 1853, introduces the fourth part of Jewett's Rules: "Arrange-

ment." "The order of the Headings will be determined by the plan
of the catalogue, whether alphabetical, classed, or chronological."[28]

The separation of cataloguing into two distinct and separate
procedures (a) bibliographical description ("Titles") and (b) headings
and their place in the catalogue permits also flexibility in printing
and stereotyping. "Titles may be prepared and stereotyped without
regard to their future arrangement." After being set up in type,
the titles are carefully checked and corrected if necessary. They
are then "stereotyped, each upon a separate plate or block." The
headings are processed independently: "The headings (if they be
names) are to stand on plates distinct from the titles." This will
allow to interpose new titles and, in printing, avoid repetition of the
heading for each title. In addition, each title will receive "a running number, according to the order of its being stereotyped." These
numbers will be used for reference to the Local Index of the general
catalogue. Copies of the stereotyped titles will also be kept at the
Smithsonian Institution in their numerical order, so that any particular title can be found by simply referring to its number.[29]

While the Sixth and Seventh Annual Reports for 1851 and 1852
respectively contain rather brief non-progress accounts of Jewett's
"Stereotyped Catalogue" and the delays caused by mechanical difficulties with the stereotyping method he had chosen, the Eighth Annual Report for 1853 notes more positive developments. "Upwards
of 6,000 volumes had been catalogued" during 1853.[30] Jewett had
been elected President at the [first] Librarians' Convention in New
York, September 1853. After listening to Jewett's presentation on
the "Smithsonian Catalogue System," the Convention had adopted
unanimously resolutions calling for the continuation and testing at
the Smithsonian Institution of "the plan for constructing catalogues
of libraries, and a general catalogue of the public libraries of the
United States, by means of separate stereotyped titles, originated
and proposed by Prof. C. C. Jewett, and developed by him while
librarian of the Smithsonian Institution."[31] However, this was to
be Jewett's last report at the Smithsonian Institution. The rift between the Secretary of the Institution, the scientist Joseph Henry,
and the Assistant Secretary and Librarian, C. C. Jewett, had wid-
ened, [32] and in the same Annual Report for 1853, Joseph Henry
alluded to the terms of James Smithson's will "to found at Washington, under the name of the SMITHSONIAN INSTITUTION an establishment for the increase and diffusion of knowledge among men." Henry
observed that while in this country much attention was paid to the
diffusion of knowledge, "comparatively little encouragement was
given to its increase." He did not want to use the Smithsonian funds
for the establishment of a national library, but rather for the support
of original scientific research and the publication of its results.[32a]
In the Ninth Annual Report for 1854 the Secretary reports under "Library. --A difficulty which occurred between the Librarian and myself has led to his separation from the Institution."[33]

This was the end of Jewett's far-reaching plan in which he
had envisaged the construction of a general catalogue of all books

held in American libraries from separate bibliographic entities, out of which would grow "an American bibliography, or a complete account of all books published in America." Using the "separate stereotyped titles," he hoped to issue, at little expense, monthly bulletins, annual lists, and quinquennial catalogues of books copyrighted in America. He also looked beyond national interests "towards the accomplishment of that cherished dream of scholars, a universal catalogue. If the system should be successful, in this country, it may eventually be so in every country of Europe. When all shall have adopted and carried out the plan, each for itself, the aggregate of general catalogues, thus formed--few in number--will embrace the whole body of literature extant, and from them, it will be no impossible task to digest and publish a universal Bibliography."[34] With these enthusiastic words Jewett predicted a universal bibliography, to be extracted from a universal catalogue which, in turn, is formed by the aggregate of national union catalogues, each of them prepared according to uniform rules, a system not unlike that which is now called Universal Bibliographic Control (UBC).

Jewett's plan for a union catalogue of the libraries in the United States seems to have impressed foreigners more than his own fellow librarians in America. In 1877 C. A. Cutter wrote this rather lukewarm and indifferent evaluation:

> Mr. Jewett's plan for a general catalogue of all the libraries in the country is well known. Something might have been done by the aid of the Smithsonian Institution, of which he was then librarian; but as the directors resolutely confined their effort to the propagation of science, and as there was at that time no other national organization sufficiently strong to move in the matter, the plan came to nothing. It has often been mentioned since, in terms of regret and longing; but no one has had the courage or seen the way clear to make any definite proposal.[35]

In his wide-ranging survey of union catalogues and printed cards, [36] the German librarian Fritz Milkau, who was one of the most active members of the subcommittee [37] which drew up the "Instruktionen für die alphabetischen Kataloge der Preuszischen Bibliotheken vom 10. Mai 1899" (the so-called Prussian Instructions), gave a prominent place to Jewett's plan for "Stereotyping Catalogues by Separate Titles...."[38] He praised its vigorous originality ("kraftvolle Eigenart") [39] and its unmistakable genius ("Jewetts Plan, der unverkennbar einen Zug von Genialität an sich trägt ..."). [40] At the same time Milkau expressed his surprise ("Befremden") [41] at the complete failure of this well prepared project, and he was unable to understand why it was never tested in a thorough experiment. [42]

The Prussian Instructions of 1899 were conceived in the tradition of Jewett's Rules, because their purpose, too, was the creation of a union catalogue by means of unit bibliographic records ("Titeldrucke"), which were circulated among participating libraries

and checked against their holdings.   The structure of the Prussian
Instructions of 1899, the second edition of 1908, as well as the new
German Cataloguing Rules of 1974 ("Regeln für die alphabetische
Katalogisierung (RAK)") has always followed "the principles of first
determining the bibliographic description, then the main entry and
secondary entries, which form the main entry and secondary entries
are to take, and finally the order of the concepts...."[43]   This is
the sequence of procedures advocated by Jewett, to which AACR has
also returned in 1978.

5.   Crestadoro's Plan for Separate Inventorial and Finding Catalogues, 1856

Exasperated by the delays in the publication of the printed catalogue
of the British Museum, "a reader therein, " Andrea Crestadoro,
wrote in 1856 an essay entitled "The Art of Making Catalogues of
Libraries; or a Method to Obtain in a Short Time a Most Perfect,
Complete, and Satisfactory Printed Catalogue of the British Museum
Library."[44]   In this essay he attacked the idea that associates
"cataloguing a library ... with the notion of an alphabetical, or indeed any particular arrangement, " the main cause of the interminable
delays in the printing of library catalogues everywhere.   He proposes
instead a clear-cut distinction between the "full and exact description" of each book from its access-points, the headings.   A library
should possess two kinds of lists: one he calls "the CATALOGUE
and the other its INDEX. "   Both have essentially different functions,
"as regards their arrangement and their ultimate purpose. "   A catalogue is a "list of the goods" and its direct object is to make an inventory of the property by recording a full and exact description of
each and every article. "   It "needs no particular arrangement, " except "ticketing for future reference with a progressive number" which
will serve as "its address."[45]   The function of the index is that of
a "finding catalogue, " [46] it is "but a table of contents of the first
[the inventorial catalogue], a hand to show how readily to find any
of the articles as actually entered in the inventory."[47]   While the
inventory-catalogue should be "free from all alphabetical bonds, "
[48] the index "is essentially alphabetical, " [49] and its entries are
much briefer than in the catalogue.   If fuller description of a book
is needed its "inventorial number" becomes "the address" that leads
from the index to its detailed bibliographic description in the catalogue.   Crestadoro insists that "catalogue-inventory" and "catalogue-
index" should always be kept separate because their functions are
different: while the catalogue identifies "a particular book, " the
index identifies "a particular subject or name."[50]   According to
Crestadoro "a good catalogue would be a list of all that exists in
the library, not as a matter of arrangement, but as a matter of
inventory, vouching for the existence of the books in the library by
one full and faithful entry."[51]   It ought to be supplemented "by an
Index for every finding purpose, " which contains as many entries
"as there are words in the inventorial entry that require reference. "
These index entries include subjects as well as names in the form

in which they appear in the "inventorial entry," because "the heading [in the index] refers not to the book but to a word in its title-page."[52]

Crestadoro, who has frequently been cited as the forerunner of permuted title indexing (KWIC, KWOC, etc.) goes, however, one step further than most permutators. He noticed the confusion brought about in titleword indexing by synonyms, near-synonyms, or variant names of authors, and thus recognized the need for the preparation of a second index in addition to the name and word index derived from the titles. This second level index would not only bring together all synonyms and specific terms that are "of a like class," [53] but would also include lists of the names of authors who publish under variant names.[54] The formation of the indexes should be regulated by these general principles: "Every heading is capable of receiving entries of two distinct sorts,--the result of two simple operations, or rather the same operation repeated, that is, an Index to the words of the inventory, and then an Index to the Index itself.... The result of the former is a general alphabetical finding Catalogue; of the latter a complete classification of all the contents of the Library."[55]

Crestadoro concludes his long and sometimes rambling essay with a plea for a "UNIVERSAL CATALOGUE not merely of the books existing in our National Library, but of all the books so far known that have ever been printed in any language in this Country and abroad.... The whole world would thus be converted into a single library, as it were;--all its intellectual contents inventoried:--all these inventories incorporated into one UNIVERSAL INDEX...."[56] The idea of a universal catalogue was then "familiar to many minds." [57] Among those interested in such a project Crestadoro points out that "In America the Librarian of the Smithsonian Institution has been instructed to make a collection of the Catalogues of all the important libraries in the United States, and to compile from them one general Index to all the collections of the Country." In 1856 news did not travel as fast as now. When Crestadoro's pamphlet was published, Jewett had been forced to abandon his project, because in 1854 "a difference of opinion between Professor Henry and Professor Jewett caused the latter's retirement from the Institution."[58]

6.   C. A. Cutter's Rules for a Dictionary Catalogue and its Influence on Cataloguing Codes: 1876-1967

6.1   The American Library Association

After Jewett had given cataloguing rules a logical structure: description first, access points via headings and cross-references afterwards, one cannot help asking, when and why was this natural and sensible sequence abandoned in Anglo-American cataloguing codes?

A new era in American cataloguing began in 1876 with the

publication of the first edition of C. A. Cutter's "Rules for a Printed
Dictionary Catalogue. "[59] (In the three subsequent editions: 1889,
1891, and 1904, the title was shortened to "Rules for a Dictionary
Catalogue, " indicating that the physical form of the printed catalogue
was being replaced by that of the card catalogue). 1876 was a very
important year for American librarianship: the American Library
Association (ALA) was founded in that year, and the Library Journal
began publication. In the Library Journal topics and questions of
interest to American, English, and European librarians were quickly
disseminated; it also served as the publishing medium of the ALA,
in which reports of the various ALA Committees and Conferences
were made public, and it is thus a useful source of information on
deliberations that took place among the Association's leading members. The first managing editor of the Library Journal was Melvil
Dewey: 1876-1880 (vols. 1-5). C. A. Cutter, another co-founder
of the ALA and the Library Journal, was bibliography editor from
1876 to 1880, and its general editor 1881-1893 (vols. 6-18).[60]   In
these positions he had a strong and lasting influence on the development of American and Anglo-American cataloguing rules to 1967.

        The table of "Contents" in all four editions of Cutter's Rules
shows immediately that Cutter's approach to cataloguing differed profoundly from Jewett's. There are two main divisions entitled: "A.
Entry (Where to enter)" and "B. Style (How to enter). " Not only
the sequence of the two parts, but also the choice of words: "Where
to enter" and "How to enter, " reveal that Cutter's main interests
were problems and possible solutions about the choice and form of
the access points for author, title, subject, and literary form entries.   These problems are discussed in often elegantly reasoned
and thoughtful remarks in the five chapters of Part A. "Entry."
They are also overflowing into Part B. "Style, " which deals not only
with the elements of the bibliographic description, such as titles,
editions, imprints, collation, contents, and notes, but also with the
form of the Headings (Part B, section 1), References (Part B, section 6 in the first and second editions, section 7 in the fourth edition) and Arrangement, i. e. filing of the entries (Part B, section 9
in the first and second editions, section 11 in the fourth edition).

        While Jewett was concerned primarily with the preparation
of separate bibliographical records which could be used as building
blocks in the "construction" of many different forms and editions of
catalogues, Cutter's Rules are broader in topics and richer in "reasons on both sides, " [61] but narrower in applications. His foremost interest was directed toward the theory and practice of one
particular form of catalogue, the dictionary catalogue, and the specific information needed by the users to "find a book" or a related
group of books with the help of relatively unambiguous author, title,
and subject headings.   The emphasis throughout is on the access
points in the catalogue, choice and form of the headings, which will
lead the inquirer to the book or books he wants via author, title,
or subject headings.

        In a paper published in one of the first issues of the Library

Journal Melvil Dewey stressed the need for "Co-operative Cataloguing."[62] He also proposed the establishment of a "central cataloguing bureau." The methods he recommended using then were clearly derived from those that Jewett had published over 25 years earlier. "The first step in any plan is to know how the separate titles are to be prepared. Every catalogue is made up of individual titles."[63] The transcription of the title-page summarized Jewett's rules I and II, with two deviations. Dewey would omit "the author's name in the body of the title," [64] while Jewett found it "necessary to give the name of the author in connection with the title," because "the heading will be stereotyped separate from the title."[65] The derivation from Jewett's rules is made explicit, when Dewey continues: "A second change from the common rule as given by Professor Jewett is the omission of stars and dots except when great accuracy is desired."[66]

In the Library Journal's issue for September 1877, [67] the editor (Melvil Dewey?) reviews "the second annual Conference of American Librarians, rounding the first year of the American Library Association." He praises the work of the Co-operation Committee and feels certain that the Association will soon "possess a useful and consistent code of recommendation for uniform cataloguing," which, he hopes, will become "a basis for cataloguing common to the booktrade and libraries." This would be particularly useful for his own venture, the "printed title-slip which it is proposed to ask the publishers to issue." (A forerunner of cataloguing in publication).

In March 1878 the ALA's Committee on Uniform Title Entries, which had been appointed on September 5, 1877, [68] published "Condensed Rules for Cataloguing" [69] in a Report signed by C. A. Cutter, A. R. Spofford, S. S. Green, J. N. Dyer, and L. E. Jones. The sequence of the unnumbered rules is still that of Jewett's Rules, namely first the elements of the bibliographic description: title, edition, imprint, collation, contents, and notes. These are followed by (2) rules of choice and form of heading: "Books are to be entered under...." They conclude with (3) Miscellanea, such as punctuation, numerals, and abbreviations. A note under the title states, however: "(N. B. The marginal references are to the sections of Cutter's Rules.)" In these references to Cutter's Rules the numerical sequence is, of course, reversed, as the highest numbers are those referring to the bibliographic description which, in Cutter's Rules, come after those for "entries under."

In 1883 a revised version, prepared by the Coöperation Committee of the ALA and signed by C. A. Cutter, S. H. Scudder, and C. B. Tillinghast, was published with a significantly changed title: "Condensed Rules for an Author and Title Catalog." It was reprinted in the second edition of Cutter's "Rules for a Dictionary Catalogue" in 1889.[70] In this 1883 version of the ALA rules the sequence of Jewett's cataloguing rules and procedures has definitely been reversed: rules for (1) "Entry" are followed by those for (2) "Headings," while "Titles" come in the third place, followed by (4) "Imprints," (5) "Arrangement. " Thus the ALA adopted in 1883 the sequence of Cutter's Rules.   Choice and form of entry and heading were moved before bibliographic description, a sequence which was faithfully observed until the publication of the revised edition of AACR in 1978.[71]

The powerful position occupied by Cutter and the lasting influence of his Rules on American catalogue rule making are acknowledged in the Preface to the "Catalog Rules: Author and Title Entries" of 1908.   "Mr. Cutter was until his last illness [Cutter died in 1903], one of the most active members of this committee.   His close connection with the work of the revision at a time when the 4th edition of his own rules was in course of preparation had no doubt much to do with bringing about a close agreement between the latter and the new A. L. A.   Rules. "[72]

Forty-one years later the Introduction to the "Rules for Descriptive Cataloging in the Library of Congress" confirms in 1949 that Cutter's influence was still strong.   "The rules which have been followed by the Library of Congress in its descriptive cataloging are easily traced to Charles A. Cutter's Rules for a Dictionary Catalogue first published in 1876 ... ", because in 1898, when the Library of Congress began to print a new catalogue on standard size cards, "the rules adopted [for this work] were those of Cutter with a few emendations from the A. L. A. catalog rules of 1883. "[73]

6. 2   The Library Association of the United Kingdom

Meanwhile, in the Library Association of the United Kingdom parallel developments had taken place, though with a slight delay.   The two editions of the "Cataloguing Rules of the Library Association of the United Kingdom, " of 1881 and 1883 [74] follow the sequence of Jewett's Rules.   The forty-nine cataloguing rules of 1881 are arranged in six sections: 1. Title; 2. Volumes, Size, Place, Date, etc.; 3. Language of Title and Imprint; 4. Contents and Notes; 5. Headings "Books are to be entered--" (this is by far the longest section, it comprises rules 10-35); and 6. Miscellaneous.   In the revised edition of 1883 there are only a few changes: section 3:   Language of Title and Imprint, which was rule 7 in 1881, has become rule 1, and former rules 19 and 20 on headings of sacred books are fused into one rule 19.   In 1883 we have thus forty-eight rules grouped into four sections, with bibliographic description still preceding "Headings. "

However, a changed attitude can be deduced from a paper by L. Stanley Jast, in which he discusses in 1902 "The Library Association Cataloguing Rules. "[75]   Nineteen years after the above-mentioned revision, the emphasis has shifted to "the author-entry [which] is still, and must remain the cataloguer's sheet anchor, whatever additional references are made or descriptive matter is appended to it. "[76]

6.3   Anglo-American Cooperation in "Catalog(uing) Rules: Author and Title Entries, " 1908

This was the time when a thorough revision of the 1883 cataloguing codes was keenly discussed in the library associations of the United States and the United Kingdom. The catalogue rule making activities of the two library associations had been converging toward each other for some time. One of the prime movers in Anglo-American cooperation was Melvil Dewey who, in a letter to L. Stanley Jast, [77] suggested "that the Library Association and the American Library Association should unite in the production of an Anglo-American code with a view to establishing uniformity of practice in cataloguing throughout the English speaking race. "[78] To the (British) Committee on Cataloguing Rules Dewey's proposal did not seem to present any problems, because "there [was] no essential difference of principle to be found in the practice of the two races.... The authority of the late Mr. Cutter [was] as firmly established here as in the United States. "[79]

At its 27th Annual Meeting in Newcastle-upon-Tyne in September 1904 the Library Association approved "Mr. Dewey's suggestion in favour of a common code of cataloguing rules for England and the United States. " It sent a delegate, L. Stanley Jast, to the Annual Meeting of the A. L. A. at St. Louis, Mo. , in October 1904, and the A. L. A. accepted the proposal from the Library Association for "the preparation of a joint code of rules. "[80] Thus a new phase had been initiated which resulted in official Anglo-American cooperation. [81] The code was printed in 1908 in two slightly different versions, entitled "Catalog Rules: Author and Title Entries" in the American edition, and "Cataloguing Rules: Author and Title Entries" in the English edition. In their approach to the sequence of cataloguing procedures both versions follow Cutter's Rules. Entry and Heading precede the elements of the bibliographic description: Titles; Imprint, Collation, Series Note; Contents, Notes are in the third section which contains also Added entries, Analytical entries, and References!

The Catalog Rules Revision Committee was also aware of what was going on in other countries, it "watched with great interest the efforts made in Germany towards a coördination of cataloging practice in Prussian university and government libraries, " in view of the Prussian "Gesamtkatalog"; and it "consulted freely" the Prussian Instructions, published in 1899. In spite of the "two fundamental points of difference between German and Anglo-American rules, viz, entry of anonymous books and corporate entry, " the Committee had borne in mind "the possibility of future international agreement and coöperation. "[82]

In Germany, however, librarians were not yet ready for international cooperation, as F. G. Kaltwasser reports. [83] Though the strong impression made by the great cooperative work of the American and British Library Associations inspired discussions about the possibility of a unified catalogue at the International Bibliographic

114   Library Lit. -81

Congress in 1910, German librarians were resolutely opposed to
this "fantastic idea of uniform international cataloguing rules." ("Den
phantastischen Gedanken einer Einheitsweltkatalogisierung halten wir
für indiskutabel.")[84] International collaboration had to wait another
fifty-three years until the International Conference on Cataloguing
Principles (ICCP) was convened in Paris in 1961.

6.4 American Cataloguing Codes of 1949 and Part II of AACR-1967

After the publication of the "Catalog(uing) Rules: Author and Title
Entries" in 1908 international cooperation decreased.   "The first
World War interrupted international links among libraries for a long
time."[85] During the years 1930-1935 cataloguing groups in the
United States discussed revision of the 1908 Catalogue Rules.   They
were dissatisfied with "its omissions" and demanded "expansion" of
the rules.   With the help of a grant from the Carnegie Corporation
the A.L.A. Catalog Code Revision Committee began work in September 1936.   A preliminary edition of the expanded rules was published
in 1941 with the title "A.L.A. Catalog Rules: Author and Title Entries." It contained two parts: "Part I. Entry and Heading" and
"Part II. Description of Book." As there was general dissatisfaction with these "overelaborate" rules, the A.L.A. undertook to re-
vise "Part I in the light of the criticism available," while "further
work on Part II was deferred." Part I was published in 1949 as
"A.L.A. Cataloging Rules for Author and Title Entries." The preoccupation of catalogers with specific questions and problems of
choice and form of author and title headings culminated in this separate publication.   With regard to Anglo-American cooperation, "the
British Committee, whose cordial cooperation was interrupted in
1939 by the outbreak of war, had been kept informed of progress
and general agreement is assured."[86] However, the 1908 edition
of the "Cataloguing Rules" remained the official cataloguing code in
Great Britain until the publication of AACR in 1967.

        The A.L.A. Cataloging Rules of 1949 dealt only with rules
of entry and heading.   "Rules for Descriptive Cataloging in the Library of Congress" were prepared by the Library's Descriptive Cataloging Division, and also published in 1949.   They were "accepted
by the [American Library] Association as the proposed substitute"
for Part II.[87] They were then incorporated with minor changes
and additions into Part II. Description, of AACR in 1967.   Bernice
Field, who discussed the "rules for description and for non-book
materials" at the workshop on AACR, held at Vancouver, in 1967,
explained that "the descriptive cataloging rules ... are not completely reorganized and rewritten as the rules for entry and heading
have been, but are a revision and expansion of the Rules for Descriptive Cataloging in the Library of Congress in 1949."[88] In the
British text of AACR these rules were "taken as the basis for similar rules." The [British] Descriptive Cataloguing Rules Sub-Com-
mittee "attempted to simplify the Rules where possible, to generalize
them sufficiently for their adoption in various forms of catalogues"
[89] and came up with a version that was in many ways more mod-

ern, clearer and easier to understand, and thus pointed the way to
the more logical rules of the ISBD. "Part II of the [1967] code is
not an international code. "[90]

7. "Toward an International Cataloging Code, " [91] or, The Role of
the Council on Library Resources in International Cataloguing: 1957-
1978

7.1 From the Paris Principles to the ISBD(G)

In 1850 Jewett had thought that his plan for the "construction" of a
general catalogue of American libraries from separate bibliographic
units, prepared according to uniform cataloguing rules would become
the model for similar catalogs of European libraries, all of which
would ultimately be combined into a universal catalogue and bibliography. His ambitious plan failed because of adverse circumstances,
human, financial, and technical. He was Assistant Secretary of the
Smithsonian Institution, working under its powerful Secretary, Joseph
Henry, who had different plans for the disposition of the Smithsonian
funds, and he could not overcome the technical defects of the stereotyping process he had chosen. In short, the time had not yet come
for the execution of this far-reaching bibliographic project.

After World War II a new spirit of international cooperation
manifested itself in the creation of the United Nations and its specialized agencies. Unesco, in particular, has, since its establishment in 1946, initiated and supported many international activities
and meetings concerned with problems of libraries, documentation,
and archives, in science, the social sciences, and the humanities.
International endeavors were also pursued more vigorously by non-
governmental international associations, such as IFLA, FID, ISO,
and ICSU. But these non-governmental bodies generally lacked the
financial backing which is needed to convert ideas into effective and
successful action.

In the field of international library cooperation, particularly
in international cataloguing, sustaining help came in 1958 to IFLA's
Working Group on the Coordination of Cataloguing Principles from
an American nonprofit organization: the Council on Library Resources (CLR) which had been established in September 1956 with
a Ford Foundation grant of $5 million. Its first President, Verner
W. Clapp, was keenly aware of the "actual and potential importance"
that "international uniformity" was acquiring "in our increasingly
'one world.'" In 1957 he observed that, while international interchange of information was progressing in the sciences, "librarians
of each country are still condemned to cataloging afresh those publications of every other country which they acquire as though the
country of origin were not already doing the job and possibly better. "[92] He also recognized the impact that "the fantastic capacities of the giant electronic computers" would have "some day on intellectual operations, such as cataloging and indexing, which are the
real bottlenecks of library work. "[93] At the same time he under-

stood that effective application of computers to library work needed
an "international cataloging code. " Out of these convictions grew
the enduring financial support that the Council gave for research
into the applications of computers to cataloguing and into their pre-
requisite: progress "toward international standardization of cataloging" and toward an "international cataloging code. "[94]

In 1954 IFLA had created a Working Group on the Coordination of Cataloguing Principles with A. H. Chaplin as Executive Secretary. [95] Under a contract with Unesco it was to report "on the
principles to be observed in establishing main entries for anonyma
and works of corporate authorship. " The Working Group found not
only general acceptance of entry of anonymous works under first
word of the title and "a growing tendency to allow entries under
corporate bodies, " but it also recommended that "a worldwide conference should be held to consider cataloguing principles in a more
comprehensive way, " a proposal which was accepted by IFLA in
1957. It was at this time that the Council on Library Resources
acted to assist IFLA and, through IFLA, international cooperation
in cataloguing with generous grants. Chaplin writes: "That this
Conference--the International Conference on Cataloguing Principles
(ICCP)--did in fact take place was due to the emergence of a new
decisive factor: the offer of financial help, on a scale unprecedented
in the history of IFLA, by the Council on Library Resources. " Thus
in 1958 the Council provided IFLA with funds ($19,995) "to plan the
next steps toward the international coordination of cataloging rules. "
[96] The Working Group organized a preparatory meeting in London
in July 1959 and made careful plans for the 1961 International Conference on Cataloguing Principles. In 1959 the Council made a second and larger grant (of $95,420) which contributed greatly to the
success of the Conference, [97] held in 1961 at the Unesco Conference Building in Paris. According to Chaplin, the ICCP was "the
largest and most authoritative meeting of cataloguing specialists ever
held"; it was attended by 105 delegates from 53 countries and 12 international organizations, with 104 observers from 20 countries.
The Statement of Principles (often referred to as the Paris Principles) applied "only to the choice and form of the headings and entry
words--i. e. to the principal elements determining the order of en-
tries--in catalogues of printed books in which entries under authors'
names and, where these are inappropriate or insufficient, under the
titles of works are combined in one alphabetical sequence. "[98] Although the Statement of Principles limited itself to the standardization of headings, the organizational aspects of the alphabetical catalogue, which had been in the foreground for over 100 years, in its
Resolution VI it prepared the way for the future by recommending
a study of "possible repercussions on cataloguing rules" caused by
the use "of electronic machinery and of mechanical procedures in
general. "[99] Perhaps it also convinced participants of the Conference and readers of the Report that international cooperation was
not only possible but necessary and fruitful. It created an international forum for future work on standardization of cataloguing.

The International Meeting of Cataloguing Experts (IMCE) in

Copenhagen, 1969, marks the end of the period in which discussion centered mostly on questions concerning choice and form of catalogue headings. [100] "The purpose of the August 1969 sessions in Copenhagen was to review developments since the 1961 International Conference on Cataloguing Principles and to consider the prospects for further advances through standardization and mechanization. " [101] While the first three sessions were devoted to the provisional text of the Annotated Edition of the Paris Statement of Principles, choice and form of headings, other topics representing recent revolutions in cataloguing attitudes and methods were discussed in seven subsequent sessions. First, the experience of the Library of Congress' Shared Cataloging Program "in making catalogers more aware of existing variations, had also increased their willingness to work towards uniformity. "[102] Then, the final Report on the MARC Pilot Project sponsored by the Council on Library Resources, had recently been published, and it had shown that efficient "use of computers in the recording and exchange of bibliographical information" required "international uniformity in the structure of bibliographical descriptions. "[103] Finally, International Standard Book Numbers (ISBN) provided each book with a unique, permanent, and foolproof number, which was useful to publishers, the booktrade, and librarians, especially for all sorts of computerized transactions. All these developments converged in a new approach to "the record of recorded information, " with the result that consideration of an "international standard for the descriptive content of catalogue entries" became the central theme of the meeting. The participants agreed to work for "the creation of a framework for bibliographical description that would serve the needs of both catalogues and bibliographies. "[104] It was specified that the bibliographic record would contain "all the descriptive data commonly required not only in catalogues and bibliographies, but also in other records used in libraries and elsewhere in the control and handling of books, " such as the ISBN. The main elements of the bibliographic description would be recorded "in a fixed order, " [105] which closely follows established cataloguing practice. The IMCE in 1969 thus was a turning point in modern cataloguing: from the preoccupation with uniform rules for the heading, the entry words that govern the place of the record in the alphabetical catalogue, which climaxed in the Paris Principles, attention shifted to the creation of a standard pattern for the bibliographic description.

Jewett's idea of preparing separate bibliographic units that can be merged into special and general catalogues, out of which would grow "that cherished dream of scholars, a universal catalogue, " is now gradually becoming reality through the medium of electronic computers. But computers are not yet able to connect variant versions by imaginative leaps, they work more efficiently with standardized bibliographic descriptions, in which unambiguous symbols, e.g., position and punctuation, mark and indicate different bibliographic elements. This will, eventually, also permit inquirers to retrieve a document or several documents from many more access points than those traditionally provided in alphabetical catalogues, e.g., author(s), title, subject headings, but also by subtitles,

editions, bibliographies, illustrations, publishers, date of publication.
The potential of computerized catalogues and bibliographies to answer
a multiplicity of queries depends no longer on explicit headings but
rather on carefully described and suitably tagged bibliographical records.

These principles are somewhat similar to those advocated in
1856 by Crestadoro, who proposed an "inventorial unalphabetical catalogue" [106] consisting of "full and exact description of each and
every article, " [107] ticketed "for future reference with a progressive number. " It would be supplemented by (a) an "index for every
finding purpose" [108] where important words found in the inventorial catalogue entry--authors' names, title words--are listed alphabetically and (b) an "index to the index" where these words if they
are synonyms, near-synonyms, names of authors writing under different names are collected into "class lists. "[109] The latter would
now be the function of a thesaurus.

In an important policy statement the IMCE recommended the
creation of "a system for the international exchange of information, "
in which national agencies would prepare standard bibliographical
descriptions of their own publications and distribute them "through
the medium of cards or machine readable records. "[110] "Standardization of the form and content of the bibliographical description"
was, of course, considered indispensable to the success of an international system of shared cataloguing, in the true sense of the word.
Chaplin, in 1974, remarked that this resolution became "one of the
principal components of the broad policy of Universal Bibliographic
Control (UBC) later adopted by IFLA. "[111] He also notes that "now
for the third time the Council on Library Resources played a vital
part" in providing further financial support and thus accelerated the
movement toward an international cataloguing code, or as seen from
the Council's point of view: "The work of the Committee [on Cata-
loguing] during the past decade has resulted in valuable contributions
toward the international standardization of cataloging and bibliographical description. " The Council, therefore, made in 1971 a three-
year grant of $54, 000 "for the establishment and support of a per-
manent Secretariat for [IFLA's] Committee on Cataloguing. "[112]

In the same year the Council awarded to IFLA itself a three-
year grant of $100, 000 in order to "strengthen the organization. "
It had recognized in IFLA "a significant instrument for international
cooperation, discussion and action in library affairs, " which was,
however, unable "to develop its potential" because of financial weakness. Both IFLA and its Committee on Cataloguing, which, in 1974,
was expanded into the IFLA International Office for UBC continued
to receive considerable financial support from the Council.[113] In
its Annual Reports the Council praised "the vital role" of the IFLA
International Office for UBC and its Director Dorothy Anderson in
the development of bibliographic standards and the rapid progress
made in gaining worldwide support for the concept of universal bibliographic control (UBC).[114]

In the nine years following the International Meeting of Cataloguing Experts, 1969, the IFLA Committee on Cataloguing and its successor, the IFLA International Office for UBC, coordinated the several revisions of the International Standard Bibliographical Descriptions (ISBD). The successive stages traversed in the development and adoption of the various types and versions of the ISBD since its inception in 1969 to ca. 1978 are outlined in a recent paper by Dorothy Anderson.[115] A draft of the International Standard Bibliographic Description was published in 1971 and circulated to over seventy national bibliographies. Approval and/or adoption followed quickly. For instance, the British National Bibliography, Deutsche Bibliographie, Australian and South African Bibliographies adopted the ISBD in 1972, Bibliographie de France and Canadiana followed in 1973. The American and [British] Library Associations, the Library of Congress, and the Cataloguing Committee of the USSR approved the standard in principle in 1972.[116] It became the basis for the revision of Chapter 6, Separately Published Monographs, of the Anglo-American Cataloging Rules of 1967, which was published in 1974, shortly after the first standard edition of the ISBD(M) for monographs had been issued. After 1971 Working Groups set up by IFLA began to prepare ISBDs for other types of library materials: for serials ISBD(S), for cartographic material ISBD(CM), and for non-book materials ISBD(NBM). However, the growth of these additional ISBDs aroused criticism and concern because they "were deviating from each other and from the original basis."[117] In August 1975 the Joint Steering Committee for the Revision of the Anglo-American Cataloguing Rules (JSCAACR), therefore, proposed the preparation of a basic ISBD which would provide a "consistent framework for the description of all library materials." At a meeting in Paris, in October 1975 representatives of IFLA and the JSCAACR agreed on a "general framework to be known as ISBD(G)."[118] The annotated text of ISBD(G), prepared by the IFLA Working Group on the ISBD(G), was published in 1977; the rules for description in Part I of the revised edition of the Anglo-American Cataloguing Rules (AACR-1978) are "based on [this] general framework for the description of library materials ... (ISBD(G))."[119]

Considering how strongly traditions govern catalogues and cataloguers--consistency is an integral feature of any useful cataloguing language--the rapid and generally enthusiastic acceptance of the ISBD is truly amazing. There is no doubt that it was timely, if not long overdue, but another reason for its success may be found in its analytic clarity and simplicity, compared to many previous cataloguing codes. In the ISBD, traditional elements of the bibliographic description are separated and grouped into eight distinct areas, each of them is marked by specific and very simple place, space, and punctuation symbols and set out in a sequence which is easy to analyze and to understand by man and computer alike.[120]

7.2 The Second Edition of the Anglo-American Cataloguing Rules, 1978

In 1967 the Anglo-American Cataloging Rules were published in two

versions: North American and British, which differed not only in
some of the rules for entry and heading, [121] but included also in
Part II variant texts for "Description," as mentioned above, p. 115.
1967 was the year in which the International Standard Book Number,
a permanent and unique identifying number for the computerized
handling of books, was applied to new publications, first in Great
Britain, then in the United States, and was soon widely adopted. A
growing number of computerized indexing projects in science and
technology had already been tried out, and many were successful,
e. g. , Chemical Titles and Science Citation Index started in 1961,
Index Medicus in 1964. All were based on computer stored bibliographic records. However, in the 1967 edition of AACR interest in
automation appears still to be confined to filing, to "the problems
of machine arrangement of entries in automated systems."[122]
Standardization is mentioned only in relation to the general need
"for a standard mode of identifying bibliographical entities" in all
library, bibliographical and book-trade activities, a need which is
to be satisfied by the rules "prescribing what shall be the main entry."[123] The structure of the AACR reveals not only the emphasis on the finding catalogue, but also inability or unwillingness to
apply uniform methods to all types of library materials. It was
thus prevented from producing a unified and simplified coding system. "The rules are divided into three main parts, the first two
dealing with books and book-like materials. Part I is concerned
with entry and heading; Part II with description," while the six chapters of Part III (chapters 10 through 15) are concerned with the cataloguing of "specific types of non-book materials," each of them having additional rules for entry and description.[124]

The Council on Library Resources whose financial support had
helped to focus trends toward an international cataloguing code into
the creation of an international standard bibliographic description in
1971, had also funded many studies and experiments in library automation.[125] In its Tenth Annual Report for 1966 the "Council's program with respect to library automation" was surveyed. It had been
"guided by the conviction that any meaningful automation in libraries
is dependent upon the machine-handling of bibliographic records.
These records (typically the product of cataloging or other kinds of
bibliographic description) identify and describe books, periodicals
and other library materials. Unless such records can be handled
automatically it is of only minor importance for a library to be able
to automate its business or other records." Genuine progress in
solving present-day library problems depends on a standard for transcribing bibliographic information into machine-readable format.[126]

In view of the Council's active support and sustained involvement with (a) the development of an international cataloguing code
and (b) the automation of bibliographic records, it was natural to
expect that the Council would also support the official revision process of the 1967 edition of the Anglo-American Cataloging Rules,
which had begun unofficially soon after publication.

In March 1974 representatives of the American Library Association, British Library, National Library of Canada, and the Library of Congress met in Chicago, formulated and announced four objectives of this planned revision:

1. Reconcile the North American and British texts of AACR (1967);
2. Incorporate all amendments approved since 1967;
3. Consider for inclusion proposed amendments currently under discussion originating from either the three participating countries or other countries using the AACR;
4. "provide for international interests in AACR ... "[127]

When the American Library Association, on behalf of the Joint Steering Committee for Revision of AACR (JSCAACR), applied in November 1974 for funding to the Council on Library Resources, the fourth objective was "intensified, to one of making a contribution to the development of an international cataloguing code."[128] (Italics mine). As a result of this condition, the objectives announced in 1974 were modified and broadened, and in 1975 the following "four position statements" were announced as the guidelines for the revision policy:

1. Maintenance of general conformity with the Paris Principles of 1961, as manifested in the first edition
2. Particular attention to developments in the machine processing of bibliographic records
3. Continuance of conformity with the ISBD(M) as a basis for the bibliographic description of monographs, and commitment to the principle of standardization in the bibliographic description of all types of materials
4. Determination of the treatment of nonbook materials primarily from a consideration of the published cataloging rules ... [129]

None of these four guidelines initiates radically new policies, they are continuations of existing trends. They were, however, "intensified" and made more explicit, and thus resulted in a more logical, unified, and comprehensive structure of the 1978 edition of AACR. At a time when computerized bibliographic networks had been in operation for several years "particular attention to developments in the machine processing of bibliographic records" was unavoidable. The ISBD(M) had already been incorporated into the revised version of Chapter 6, Description of Separately Published Monographs, which had been published in 1974. The systematic application of ISBD principles to other library materials, which was one of the goals of this revision, soon revealed divergencies between the various international standard bibliographic descriptions which were being developed by different IFLA Working Groups for serials, non-book and cartographic materials, music and old books. Consequently, the Anglo-American catalogue code makers, "mindful of [their] undertaking to the Council on Library Resources" to contribute "to the development of an international cataloguing code," proposed, as mentioned above

p. 119, the establishment of "a generalized structure for bibliographic description, " to which all specialized ISBDs would conform.   In this way "uniformity might be achieved within AACR, within ISBDs, and between ISBDs and AACR. "[130]   The General International Standard Bibliographic Description (ISBD(G)) which resulted from the cooperation of the JSCAACR and the IFLA Committee on Cataloguing was not only an important step towards an international cataloguing code, it also provided the principles for uniform bibliographical treatment of all types of library materials.

Edwin Buchinski, chairman of the Canadian Committee on Cataloguing, reporting in 1976 on "Developments in the Revision of AACR, " describes what one might call a turning point in the structuring of the AACR.   "JSCAACR has agreed that the revised AACR should have a general chapter based on ISBD(G) which is devoted to descriptive cataloguing common to all types of materials.   To emphasize the international nature of the revised code, JSCAACR agreed that since the principles of the ISBD have gained worldwide acceptance that rules for description should precede rules for choice of entry and form of names."[131]   The acceptance of the ISBD framework thus led to a complete reversal in the structure of the AACR. For the first time since 1883 rules for description precede rules for choice of entry and form of name in American cataloguing rules. After over ninety years Anglo-American cataloguing rules have returned to the normal "sequence of cataloguers' operations" by giving bibliographic description its logical place in Part I, which "deals with the provision of information describing the item being catalogued, " while "the determination and establishment of headings, or access points in the catalogue, under which the descriptive information is to be presented" comes afterwards in Part II.[132]

The arrangement of the general table of "Contents" displays the basic division of the rules into two parts and the logical sequence of chapters within each part.   The clarity and simplicity of its layout contrast significantly with the confusing array of headings, subheadings, intermediate headings, chapters, superior, intermediate, and inferior sections in the 1967 edition of AACR.

*   *   *

In 1850/1853 C. C. Jewett, while planning the construction of a "general catalogue, " saw and recommended that cataloguing be divided into three parts.   First the establishment of separate stereotyped titles, according to uniform rules, i. e. standard bibliographic descriptions.   After the transcription of the titles had been completed, headings were to be added in a second operation, and finally, in a third operation the "arrangement" of the bibliographic entities was to be determined by "the plan of the catalogue, whether alphabetical, classed, or chronological. "   The uniform, separate bibliographic descriptions are seen as the principal and versatile elements (building blocks) from which a general catalogue can be constructed, which may in turn become part of a universal catalogue. They can also be used for a variety of different forms and types of special catalogues.

Since the publication of Cutter's "Rules for a Printed Dictionary Catalogue" in 1876 this basic division between bibliographic description and index or access points had become blurred in Anglo-American cataloguing rules and attitudes. "The ISBD clearly recognized the independence of bibliographic description as distinct from the access points by which catalogue users find those descriptions." [133] As a result of experience with computerized and shared cataloguing and the ISBD "the multiple-use bibliographic record" has now returned to its logical place in Part I of the 1978 edition of AACR. Its application has been enlarged to cover many other types of library materials, according to the same uniform pattern of ISBD(G). The access points for the alphabetical author and title catalogue: headings, uniform titles, and references (excluding subject headings and classification symbols) by which bibliographic records may be recalled, and which may vary in different languages and cultures, are to be chosen only after the standardized bibliographic description has been established.

AACR (1978) continues not only "the tradition of Panizzi, Cutter, and Lubetzky," [134] but perhaps its most important contribution to international cataloguing consists in the restatement of the basic principle, proclaimed by Jewett in 1850/1853, that the establishment of separate, uniform bibliographic records, which can be freely interchanged and variously arranged, is the first requirement for the construction of general, special, national, and universal catalogues and bibliographies.

References

1. Verner W. Clapp, in Council on Library Resources, Second Annual Report for the Period Ending June 30, 1958 (Washington, D.C.: 1958), p.8.
2. Dorothy May Norris, A History of Cataloguing and Cataloguing Methods, 1100-1850 ... (London: Grafton, 1939), p.204.
3. This brief survey is based on Verner W. Clapp, "Retrospect and Prospect," Library Trends 16: 165-166, (July 1967); George Watson Cole, "An Early French 'General Catalog.'" Library Journal 25: 329-331 (July 1900); Fritz Milkau, Centralkataloge und Titeldrucke ... Beiheft zum Centralblatt für Bibliothekswesen, 20. (Leipzig; O. Harrassowitz, 1898), pp.52-53; V. et Ch. Mortet, "Des Catalogues Collectifs ou Communs à Plusieurs Bibliothèques," Revue Internationale des Bibliothèques, 1895-1896 (Paris: H. Wetter, 1897), pp.171-175; and Ulysse L. L. Robert, Recueil des Lois, Décrets, Ordonnances, Arrêtés, Circulatires, etc., Concernant les Bibliothèques Publiques ... (Paris: H. Champion, 1883), pp.11-19.
4. Robert, p.11.

5. Mortet, p. 174.
6. Henry B. Wheatley, How to Catalogue a Library (2d ed. London: Elliot Stock, 1889), p. 25.
7. "Rules for the Compilation of the Catalogue," Catalogue of Printed Books in the British Museum (London: Printed by Order of the Trustees, 1841), vol. 1, pp. v-ix.
7a. Louis Fagan, The Life of Sir Anthony Panizzi ... (2d ed. London: Remington, 1880), describes the committee's work on pp. 168-169. Similar accounts are given by Edward Edwards, Lives of the Founders of the British Museum ... (London: Trübner; New York: J. W. Bruton, 1870), pp. 567-569, and by Henry B. Wheatley, How to Catalogue a Library, pp. 26-28.
8. Smithsonian Institution, ... Annual Report of the Board of Regents of the Smithsonian Institution ... (Washington, D. C. : 1847-1854). Second through Ninth Annual Reports, hereafter cited SI/AR-2--SI/AR-9.
9. Michael H. Harris, The Age of Jewett: Charles Coffin Jewett and American Librarianship, 1841-1868 (Littleton: Libraries Unlimited, 1975), p. 60.
10. SI/AR-2 (1847), p. 60.
11. SI/AR-3 (1848), p. 191.
12. SI/AR-4 (1849), p. 45.
13. SI/AR-5 (1850), pp. 32-41.
14. Ibid. , Footnote p. 81.
15. Ibid. , pp. 80-83.
16. Ibid. , p. 81.
17. Ibid. , p. 34.
18. Ibid. , p. 39; also in Charles Coffin Jewett, On the Construction of Catalogues of Libraries, and their Publication by Means of Separate, Stereotyped Titles ... (2d ed. ; Washington, D. C. : Smithsonian Institution, 1853), p. 8.
19. SI/AR-5 (1850), p. 82.
20. Jewett, On the Construction ... 2d. ed. , p. 8.
21. Ibid. , p. 18.
22. Ibid.
23. Ibid. , pp. 29-64.
24. Ibid. , p. 67.
25. Ibid. , pp. 29-31.
26. Ibid. , p. 45.
27. Anglo-American Cataloguing Rules (2d ed. ; Chicago: A. L. A. , 1978), p. 1.
28. Jewett, On the Construction ... 2d ed. , p. 59.
29. Ibid. , pp. 23-24.
30. SI/AR-8 (1853), pp. 27 and 33.
31. Ibid. , p. 34; See also Librarians' Convention, New York City, 1853, Proceedings (s. l. : Reprinted for William Murray, 1915), pp. 17-32.
32. Joseph A. Borrome, Charles Coffin Jewett (Chicago: A. L. A. , 1951) gives, in Chapter 7: "Compromise falls to the ground," (pp. 74-106) a deeper insight into the complex reasons that led to the controversy between J. Henry and C. C. Jewett which, in 1854, forced Jewett to resign, and thus resulted in the abandonment of his plan for a national union catalogue.

32a. SI/AR-8 (1853), p. 10.
33. SI/AR-9 (1854), p. 21.
34. Jewett, On the Construction ... 2d ed., p. 9.
35. Charles A. Cutter, "Dr. Hagen's Letter on Cataloguing," Library Journal 1: 220 (1870).
36. Fritz Milkau, Centralkataloge und Titeldrucke: Geschichtliche Erörterungen und praktische Vorschläge im Hinblick auf die Herstellung eines Gesamtkatalogs der preussischen wissenschaftlichen Bibliotheken, Beiheft zum Centralblatt für Bibliothekswesen, 20. (Leipzig: O. Harrassowitz, 1898), pp. 27-33.
37. Horst Kunze, Grundzüge der Bibliothekslehre (3. Aufl.; Leipzig: Bibliographisches Institut, 1969), p. 317.
38. Milkau, Centralkataloge, pp. 27-33.
39. Ibid., p. 28.
40. Ibid., p. 30.
41. Ibid., pp. 28 and 30.
42. Ibid., p. 30.
43. F. G. Kaltwasser, "The New German Cataloging Rules: Regeln für die alphabetische Katalogisierung (RAK): 1. Background and description: summary and extracts," International Cataloguing 3: 2 (October/December 1974).
44. [Andrea Crestadoro], The Art of Making Catalogues of Libraries, or, A Method to Obtain in a Short Time a Most Perfect, Complete, and Satisfactory Printed Catalogue of the British Museum Library, by A Reader therein, (London: The Literary, Scientific & Artistic Reference Office, 1856), 60 p. During the 19th century titles were often longer and more meaningful than today. They summarized the contents of the work or stated the aims of the author. Cf. the titles of the two editions of Jewett's report "On the Construction of Catalogues...," p. 102 above.
45. Ibid., pp. 9-10.
46. Ibid., p. 20.
47. Ibid., p. 10.
48. Ibid., p. 14.
49. Ibid., p. 10.
50. Ibid., p. 14.
51. Ibid., p. 17.
52. Ibid., p. 20.
53. Ibid., p. 23.
54. Ibid., p. 24.
55. Ibid., p. 25.
56. Ibid., p. 59.
57. Ibid. See also Torstein Jahr and Adam Julius Strohm, Bibliography of Cooperative Cataloguing and the Printing of Catalogue Cards, with Incidental References to International Bibliography and the Universal Catalogue: (1850-1902) (Washington, D. C.: Govt. Print. Off., 1903). This excellent annotated bibliography contains many references to the concept of the "Universal Catalogue" in the period covered. They are indexed on p. 115.
58. Cyrus Adler, The Smithsonian Library, in The Smithsonian

Institution, 1846-1896: the History of its First Half Century, (Washington, D. C. :   1897), p. 283.

59.   Charles A. Cutter, Rules for a Printed Dictionary Catalogue, in U. S. Bureau of Education, Public Libraries in the United States of America ... Special Report, Part II (Washington, D. C. :   Govt. Print. Off. , 1876).

60.   R. R. Bowker, "The Library Journal and Library Organization: a Twenty Years' Retrospect," Library Journal 21:5-9 (January 1896).

61.   Charles A. Cutter, Rules for a Dictionary Catalog (4th ed. , rewritten; Washington, D. C. :   Govt. Print. Off. , 1904), p. 6.

62.   Melvil Dewey, "Co-operative Cataloguing," American Library Journal 1: 170-175 (January 1877).

63.   Ibid. , p. 171.

64.   Ibid.

65.   Jewett, On the Construction ... 2d ed. , 1853, p. 30.

66.   Dewey, "Co-operative Cataloguing," p. 172.

67.   Library Journal 2:14 (September 1877).

68.   Library Journal 2:28 (September 1877).

69.   American Library Association.   Committee on Uniform Title Entries, "Condensed Rules for Cataloguing," Library Journal 3:12-14 (March 1878).

70.   American Library Association.   Coöperation Committee, "Condensed Rules for an Author and Title Catalog," Library Journal 8:251-254 (1883).   Reprinted in Charles A. Cutter, Rules for a Dictionary Catalogue (2d ed. , with corrections and additions; Washington, D. C. :   Govt. Print. Off. , 1889), pp. 99-103.

71.   Kathryn Luther Henderson, in her paper "... Descriptive Cataloging in the United States, 1876-1975," Library Trends 25: 229 (July, 1976) reports that statistical surveys made in 1893 and 1894 had shown that "Cutter's rules were 'most generally followed' " in American libraries.   "Also widely used was 'Condensed Rules for an Author and Title Catalog,' issued in 1883 by the ALA Cooperative Committee. "   The latter was prepared in accordance with Cutter's Rules, to which users were referred if they needed further information.

72.   Catalog Rules: Author and Title Entries (American ed. ; Boston: A. L. A. Publishing Board, 1908), p. ix.

73.   Library of Congress.   Descriptive Cataloging Division, Rules for Descriptive Cataloging in the Library of Congress (Washington, D. C. :   Govt. Print. Off. , 1949), p. 1.

74.   "Cataloguing Rules of the Library Association of the United Kingdom," Library Journal 6:315-316 (1881); "Cataloguing Rules of the Library Association of the United Kingdom.   (As revised at Liverpool, 1883)," Library Chronicle 2:25-28 (1885).

75.   L. Stanley Jast, "The Library Association Cataloguing Rules," Library Association Record 4:579-582 (1902).

76.   Ibid. , p. 580.

77.   At the A. L. A. 's Annual Conference, at St. Louis, Mo. , in October 1904, the delegate of the Library Association, L. Stanley Jast, mentions in his report on the "Revision of the

Cataloguing Rules of the Library Association of the United Kingdom," that he "received a letter from Mr. Dewey," in which the latter was "urging the importance of establishing a common code between the two countries." Library Journal 29, no. 12:231 (December 1904).

78. Library Association. 27th Annual Meeting, Newcastle-upon-Tyne, September 1904, "Report of the Committee on Cataloguing Rules," Library Association Record 6:485 (1904); See also Cataloguing Rules: Author and Title Entries. (English ed.; London: Library Association, 1908), p. iii.

79. Library Association. 27th Annual Meeting ... Library Association Record 6:485 (1904).

80. American Library Association. Annual Conference, St. Louis, Mo., October 1904, Proceedings ... Library Journal 29, no. 12:234 (December 1904); and L. Stanley Jast. "Delegate's Report to the Council of the Library Association," Library Association Record 7:362 (1905).

81. Catalog Rules: Author and Title Entries. (American ed.; Chicago; A. L. A., 1908), p. vii.

82. Ibid., p. x.

83. Franz Georg Kaltwasser, "Entstehung, Strukturen und Anwendung der neuen 'Regeln für die alphabetische Katalogisierung (RAK),'" Zeitschrift für Bibliothekswesen und Bibliographie 21:2 (1974).

84. A. Hilsenbeck, "Zur Frage einheitlicher Katalogisierungsregeln," Zentralblatt für Bibliothekswesen 29:311 (1912), cited in Kaltwasser, Entstehung ... Zeitschrift für Bibliothekswesen und Bibliographie 21:2 (1974).

85. Margarita I. Rudomino, "The Prehistory of IFLA ..." in IFLA's First Fifty Years, (München: Verlag Dokumentation, 1977) p. 75.

86. This brief survey is based on the Preface to the A. L. A. Cataloging Rules for Author and Title Entries (Chicago: A. L. A., 1949), pp. v-x.

87. Library of Congress. Descriptive Cataloging Division, Rules for Descriptive Cataloging in the Library of Congress. (Adopted by the American Library Association) (Washington, D. C. : 1949), p. 5.

88. F. Bernice Field, "The Rules for Description and for Non-Book Materials," in New Rules for an Old Game ... (Vancouver: University of British Columbia, 1967), pp. 81-95. The discussion of descriptive cataloguing occupies 15 pages or less than 10%, out of a total of 159 pages of text, excluding bibliography and index, while choice and form of the heading dominate over 90% of the text.

89. Anglo-American Cataloguing Rules, 1967, British text, p. vi.

90. Field, The Rules ..., p. 89.

91. Council on Library Resources. First Annual Report for the period ending June 30, 1957 (Washington, D. C., 1957), p. 26.
   In the following references the Council's Annual Reports are abbreviated CLR/AR- , e.g. CLR/AR-1:26.

92. Ibid., p. 27.

93. Ibid. , p. 18.
94. Ibid. , p. 28 and CLR/AR-16:37. One of the Council's first
    grants was made to A. L. A. so that its representative could
    participate in a meeting of the German Library Association
    in June 1957 in the interest of "international standardization
    of cataloging." At this meeting German librarians voted to
    abandon their traditional "grammatical" order of filing in
    favor of the "mechanical" method used in French and English
    speaking countries, a first step toward agreement between the
    two most influential codes.
95. A. H. Chaplin, "IFLA Committee on Cataloguing 1954-1974.
    2. A Retrospective View." International Cataloguing 3, no.
    1:7-8 (January/March 1974).
96. CLR/AR-2:10.
97. Chaplin, IFLA ..., p. 8. See also International Conference on
    Cataloguing Principles, Paris, October 1961, Report (London:
    IFLA, 1963), Resolution IX, p. 98.
98. International Conference on Cataloguing Principles, Report, p.
    91.
99. Ibid. , p. 98.
100. International Meeting of Cataloguing Experts (IMCE), Copenha-
    gen, 1969, "Report," Libri 20, no. 1:105-132 (1970).
101. CLR/AR-13:23.
102. IMCE 1969, "Report," Libri 20:113.
103. Ibid. , p. 114.
104. Ibid. , p. 111.
105. Ibid. , p. 112.
106. Crestadoro, p. 17.
107. Ibid. , p. 10.
108. Ibid. , p. 16.
109. Ibid. , pp. 23-32.
110. IMCE 1969, "Report," Libri 20:115-116.
111. Chaplin, IFLA ..., p. 8.
112. CLR/AR-15:37, 45.
113. The IFLA International Office for UBC has received three
    grants totalling $364,000 for the period 1 July 1974-30 June
    1981, in addition to the grant of $54,000 which was made
    to its predecessor, the IFLA Cataloguing Secretariat in 1971.
114. CLR/AR-19: 38; See also CLR/AR-20: 71-74, and CLR/AR-21:
    51-53.
115. Dorothy Anderson, "IFLA's programme of ISBD's," Unesco
    Bulletin for Libraries 32, no. 3:144-150 (1978); See also
    IFLA International Office for UBC, An Annotated Bibliography
    of the International Standard Bibliographic Description (Lon-
    don: IFLA International Office for UBC, 1977).
116. C. Summer Spalding, "ISBD: its Origin, Rationale, and Impli-
    cations," Library Journal 98:122 (January 15, 1973).
117. Anderson, IFLA's programme ..., p. 147.
118. Ibid. and AACR (1978), p. viii.
119. AACR (1978), p. 7.
120. For details see ISBD(G): General International Standards Bibli-
    ographic Description (London: IFLA International Office for
    UBC, 1977).

121. AACR (1967), North American Text, p.371 and British Text, pp.v-vi and pp.297-303.
122. Ibid., North American Text, p.vi.
123. Ibid., p.2.
124. Ibid., p.6.
125. For instance, Automation and the Library of Congress, the so-called "King Report," was published in 1963 (CLR/AR-5: 29 and CLR/AR-8: 41); Lawrence F. Buckland, The Recording of Library of Congress Bibliographical Data in Machine Form, in 1964 (CLR/AR-9: 9). The MARC Pilot Project was funded in 1966 (CLR/AR-10: 126).
126. CLR/AR-10: 40-41. This CLR report was written in 1966, one year before the publication of the first edition of AACR.
127. Carol R. Kelm, "The Historical Development of the Second Edition of the Anglo-American Cataloguing Rules," Library Resources & Technical Services 22:23 (Winter 1978).
128. AACR (1978), p.vii.
129. Ibid.
130. Ibid., p.viii.
131. Edwin Buchinski, "Developments in the Revision of AACR," Canadian Library Journal 33:465 (October 1976).
132. AACR (1978), p.1.
133. Michael Gorman, "The Anglo-American Cataloguing Rules, Second Edition," Library Resources & Technical Services 22:211 (Summer 1978).
134. Ibid., p.225.

Acknowledgment: I am grateful to Virginia Cunningham for critical reading of the manuscript and her helpful and encouraging remarks.

BOOK JOBBERS--THERE YESTERDAY,

HERE TODAY, GONE TOMORROW?*

Dana L. Alessi

The book jobber has always been perceived as the middleman, the
go-between for the publisher and the library. New relationships,
new technology may change those intrinsic relationships. Book jobbers were there yesterday, they are here today, but will they be
gone tomorrow?

In the past, libraries frequently sought to order books through
a book jobber instead of directly from the publisher. It is obviously
much cheaper to mail a batch of 30 orders for 30 different publishers to one place instead of 30 places. Likewise, the cost of receiving orders from a few wholesalers instead of many publishers
decreased, with fewer invoices, fewer payments, and centralized
communication if problems arose. Thus, wholesalers existed to
simplify the routine tasks of many library acquisitions departments
by order consolidation.

Libraries began to apply the techniques of computerization in
the 1960s to their ordering processes--the generation of purchase
orders, claims and cancellations, fund accounting, vendor statistics,
and the like. The most common acquisitions system during the 1960s
was the off-line, batch processing type, usually reliant on punch card
input. Because the techniques of automation are well-suited for the
business arena, jobbers too began to automate--purchase order generation, billing, reports, inventory. Jobbers also began to offer more
services to the libraries they served--partly because of increased competition, partly because of technological advances, and partly because
of the rapid growth of libraries, both in numbers and in financial support. Book jobbers began to supply more than just books to libraries
in the first attempts at integration of services. Libraries could now
receive processing and cataloging along with the books ordered from
jobbers. The creation of machine-readable records enabled the development of cataloging data bases which could retain standardized
records in machine-readable form. In addition, some vendors developed their own systems and made them available to libraries seeking
a turnkey system in lieu of developing such a system themselves.

*Reprinted by permission of the author and publisher from Library
Acquisitions: Practice and Theory, 5 (1981) 21-25. Copyright ©
1981 by Pergamon Press, Ltd.

Also in the 1960s, a new concept of acquisitions arose--the approval plan. Approval plans were the logical culmination of these phenomena of the 1960s:

1. Automation of jobber functions;
2. Increased reliance on book wholesalers by libraries due to:
3. Increased book budgets but not always:
4. Corresponding increases in staff.

Thus, it became possible for a jobber to identify a library's collecting interests, both subject and level (i. e., profile), store the library's profile in the computer, correspondingly profile new books as they were published, and voilá! ship books into the library at or near publication date. The advantages of this computer-based approval plan were many for the library:

1. Speed of delivery;
2. Savings of clerical costs, as a good portion of order preparation routines could be eliminated;
3. Selection with book in hand and the capacity to reject a title if it did not meet the needs of the library;
4. Freeing of time for bibliographers.

With the advent of machine-readable data, however, a new entity developed--the bibliographic utility or network. As the 1960s were for libraries a period of growth, financial plenty, and initial development and application of computer technology; so the 1970s were a period of retrenchment, declining budgets, and enhancements to technology. Thus, the attractiveness of the networks, offering the possibility of resource-sharing, cooperative acquisitions, and the elimination of the need to "do-it-yourself." The logical application of the on-line machine-readable data bases of networks was cataloging, thus largely eliminating, at least as far as many large public and academic libraries were concerned, the need for at least one frequently jobber-supplied service. At this point, the offering of acquisitions and collection development services is becoming more of a reality, which the next section of this article covers. This brings us to the present state of acquisitions, vendors, collection development, and technology.

Libraries today have a variety of choices should they desire to automate their acquisitions functions. But while they may find their choices wide, they may not always find that any one system can meet all of their needs. Essentially, book vendors are back in there pitching with their own systems to sell to libraries, much as they had cataloging and processing to sell before the advent of bibliographic utilities (lest we forget, book jobbers still do sell cataloging). Currently, there are the following systems available through book vendors:

1. Baker & Taylor offers the BATAB system, a batch-processing system that will generate purchase orders, offer fund

accounting, maintain order history, and produce a variety of statistical reports. Baker & Taylor has also recently introduced Libris, an on-line system which enables libraries to search Baker & Taylor's data base (constructed of MARC and B&T records), generate orders, and maintain a record file. In addition, a fund accounting package is offered.

2. Bodart offers OLAS, its On-Line Acquisitions System, which will search the Brodart data base, generate orders, maintain on-order file status, provide fund accounting, etc.

3. Blackwell North America offers Easy Access, an ordering system only, which is not on-line. This system will transmit orders by diskette for searching in the B/NA data base and will provide, through teletype emulators and other modules, additional functions for libraries such as word processing and access to reference data bases.

4. B. H. Blackwell has made its 650,000 title data base (Bookline) accessible to British libraries, and it is possible for a library to link up to this data base for pre-order searching and order generation. At the present time this system does not do fund accounting.

In essence, jobbers' systems offer certain advantages to a library--access to the jobber's data base, on-line or diskette ordering to the jobber, some fund accounting features, and limited access to inventory. But in considering a jobber oriented system, a library must look at certain other factors:

1. Will the jobber's system interface with any other automated system the library uses? Can it interface with the circulation system--or the cataloging system?
2. Will the jobber's system allow for flexibility in vendor selection? (After all, for all the fancy technology, a book jobber is going to want to sell his books first, or he wouldn't stay in business.)
3. Will the jobber system allow for cataloging and processing?
4. Will the jobber system maintain machine-readable records for COM generation?
5. How much will it cost? Is it cost-effective in releasing personnel for other duties?
6. What kind of management statistics will the system provide?
7. Will the system provide access to inventory?
8. If the jobber maintains an inventory in more than one location, will it access one or all locations?
9. What provisions will there be for enhancement?
10. How efficient is the jobber's fulfillment of the type of materials the library usually acquires?
11. Once orders are transmitted, are the orders filled promptly and correctly?

What of the competitors to jobber acquisitions systems? Now

that circulation and cataloging systems have matured, it's time for
libraries and vendors to turn to raise their new child--automated
acquisitions. In addition to book vendors, there are certainly enough
offers for parenthood. There are, in no particular order:

1. Vendor (nonbook) supplied turnkey systems such as CLSI and
   Dataphase;
2. Bibliographic utilities, such as OCLC, UTLAS, WLN and
   RLG (RLIN);
3. Specialty houses such as Sigma Delta;
4. Service houses such as Bowker with its BIP data base;
5. Of course, there is always the "do-it-yourself" approach.

The point is that no one system currently offers everything a library
could want or desire. Some of these systems are expensive--beyond
the means of a small academic library. Some of these systems
won't fit a library's current acquisitions procedures. Some of these
systems may fail. In point of fact, the current state of technology
and jobbers' systems available to libraries is in flux. That's not
good news to libraries trying to cope with shrinking book budgets
and the need to manage their collections efficiently as never before.
Such have been the developments of the 1970s--a time of multitudinal
enhancements due to automation, but still an imperfect world for
acquisitions and collection development.

What of the 1980s? What will the future hold for jobbers as
they interface with publishers, networks, and libraries? It seems
that jobbers have essentially three options as they face the future.
Jobbers, especially small ones, can stubbornly resist all attempts
at automation. They can maintain their manual files, ordering systems and inventory, and manual (or only semi-automated) billing
procedures. They will offer minimal services to libraries, other
than receiving and filling orders--in much the same way as the
1950s. While these jobbers may claim that they can offer "personalized" services, and because of this "personalization," better service, librarians will be attempting to develop collections with shrinking resources, smaller print runs from publishers, with the need
for systems which integrate into their own automated systems. In
other words, the jobber who refuses the future may find that the
future refuses him.

Secondly, other jobbers may choose to continue development
of jobber systems and actively market them to libraries in direct
competition with bibliographic utilities, circulation system vendors
and the like. Jobbers choosing this route must have a highly developed automated in-house system as well as adequate technical
support staff to service library installations. At some point, libraries must ask themselves if vendor systems will allow them the flexibility and control of decision-making they desire. If the answer is
yes, this type of system may be the solution to a library's acquisitions needs. There are risks involved for the jobber choosing to
develop his own system--the need for capitalization and the risk
that it won't be there when it's required; the risk that the system

will prove unresponsive to the needs of libraries; the risk that better systems will be developed and that libraries will take themselves elsewhere; and the risk that too much investment will be put into a service which is peripheral to the central business of the book jobber.

Finally, there is the middle road. It is clear from the above that the jobber of the 1980s must have automated internal procedures. It is obvious that the procedures of the jobber--order fulfillment, inventory control, stock pick, billing--readily lend themselves to automation. It is clear that automation should be within the financial realm of every book jobber. It is clear that publishers and libraries, with whom jobbers do business, are becoming increasingly automated, and that this automation is available at a cheaper price than before. It is also clear that a large part of the acquisition procedure may be automated by bibliographic utilities, turnkey systems, and individual libraries. Some jobbers, it is to be hoped, will respond to the various needs of libraries, receiving orders on-line or by tape for invoicing, inventory status, reporting, etc. This presumes cooperation on the part of those middlemen such as networks and other purveyors of acquisitions systems with jobbers--and leads to questions of governance, compatibility, and standardization. It also presumes the recognition that jobbers can provide necessary and vital services other than mere order fulfillment, and that jobbers have a role to play as an adjunct to publishers. Perhaps down the road will come the great day in the future when there is one common data base with indication of distribution, status of publication, current prices, etc., to which both libraries and jobbers have access.

How will these developments affect collection development and acquisition activities in libraries? Whatever system a library chooses should provide better management statistics and more accountability for monies spent, enabling libraries to husband scarce resources. Automation, both internally and externally, will provide easier access and delivery of materials; it will allow libraries to have more control over past purchases and those in-process. And ultimately, it should provide for cooperative collection development, whether through linkups through a common jobber or other acquisition system.

In the light of the future, what of one of the now traditional methods of collection development--the approval plan? With current capabilities and future enhancements, approval plans will remain strong in the face of any automated system. Through machine-readable data, it should be possible for the approval vendor to feed data to the library's chosen acquisitions system. It should be possible for the jobber to identify titles which have been selected for the library to minimize or totally eliminate duplication with firm orders. Approval plans will remain a cost effective way for libraries to acquire materials, particularly since print runs are becoming smaller and the risk becomes greater that titles will go rapidly out-of-print.

All of this paints a sanguine picture for libraries and jobbers. But what of the library which has only minimal financial resources? How can such a library take advantage of automation without paying painfully? In the best of all possible worlds, some sort of automation will be affordable for even the poorest library. But until that best of all possible worlds turns, it will be necessary for the library to rely upon the jobber and his own management statistics. The jobber, in other words, should be able to supply at least some of the management statistics that any automated system would provide; the jobber might even be able to offer limited fund control. If you are in a library with limited resources, ask your jobber what he can do for you--and take your business to those who can meet your needs.

Finally, some critical questions. How do libraries want jobbers to respond to new technology? Make no mistake about it, most book jobbers are in a position only to respond and not to lead. Do libraries have unrealistic expectations of book jobbers? Book jobbing, contrary to popular belief, is not a high-profit business. To demonstrate, look at the demise within the past 10 years of McClurg's, Dimondstein, Josten's, Grayson's, Makely's, Carol Cox and Richard Abel. Yet libraries are seeking ever higher discounts, and these cut into the money, often large sums of it, needed to automate existing internal procedures, enhance existing automation, and develop libraries' ideal systems. Do libraries want their book jobbers to be booksellers first and foremost, utilizing technology to provide the most efficient fulfillment, or do they want them to provide the access to the system as well? If booksellers are to be systems purveyors as well, are libraries prepared to sacrifice some discounts to enable book jobbers to have the research and development money necessary to create the systems?

And if book jobbers delegate the development of access systems to the bibliographic utilities, circulation vendors, etc. , will they lose one of their primary raisons d'être? Is it pessimistic for book jobbers to fear that electronic transmission of orders from library to acquisition system to publisher will result in a new middleman who can provide the statistics while the publisher can supply the invoice (electronically), the book, and hefty discount?

SECONDARY SERVICES IN THE SOCIAL SCIENCES:

THE NEED FOR IMPROVEMENT AND THE ROLE OF LIBRARIANS*

Maurice B. Line

Secondary services, primarily indexing and abstracting services, in
the social sciences are numerous, seriously imperfect, both individually and collectively, and grossly underused. The present system
(or non-system) is highly unsatisfactory for users and libraries, and
in commercial terms is profitable to only a few producers. It is
not difficult to conceive of a system that would be far more effective
and far less costly. There are several practical obstacles in the
way of improvement, but improvement is nevertheless vital. It cannot depend solely on market forces, but must be planned.

These blunt statements require justification, though anyone
who has worked extensively with indexing and abstracting services
in the social sciences, especially anyone who has tried to serve
users as an intermediary, will need little convincing. The evidence
presented here is taken largely from an extensive research programme into information problems and systems in the social sciences,
carried out between 1967 and 1975, mainly at the University of Bath.
All of the programme was funded by the Office for Scientific and
Technical Information and its successor, the British Library Research and Development Department.

The first project in the programme, the Investigation into
Information Requirements of the Social Sciences (INFROSS),[1] studied, mainly by questionnaire, a large sample of British social scientists, most of them in academic institutions but including also government researchers, social workers, and school teachers. The results gave an "aerial view" of information habits and needs of users
of social science information. The conclusions have been presented
elsewhere, both in detail and in summary; for present purposes the
most relevant finding is that secondary services were relatively very
little used. The average number of indexing and abstracting services used was 1. 7; 22% of respondents used none at all, and 65%

*Reprinted by permission of the author and publisher from Behavioral
and Social Sciences Librarian, 1:4 (Summer 1980) 263-73, © 1981
by the Haworth Press, Inc. All rights reserved.

used only one. Even well established services, such as <u>Sociological</u> <u>Abstracts</u> and the <u>Journal of Economic Abstracts</u>, were used respec- tively by only 16% of sociologists and 15% of economists.

The object of finding out about the information needs and the uses of social scientists was not to satisfy curiosity but to see how their particular requirements might be met. There were good the- oretical reasons for believing that the solutions that had been devel- oped and found more or less satisfactory in science would not be appropriate in the social sciences, and INFROSS reinforced this be- lief. One finding of INFROSS, that informal sources of information were extensively favored, was anticipated to some extent by the sec- ond research project, which tested the concept of information offi- cers. [2] An experimental information service was offered between 1969 and 1971 to social science researchers at the University of Bath and to some at the University of Bristol. This project showed the value and acceptability of such a service, provided detailed data on the information habits of several social scientists, and also gave the two information officers a great deal of first-hand experience of secondary services. The concept of information officers was subse- quently further pursued by two other "action research" projects, both in local authority social service departments; these were based at the Universities of Sheffield and Bath respectively. [3-5]

Alongside the informal system, and behind it in the sense that personal information services may be largely based on formal secondary services, is the formal system. The main successor to INFROSS, and the third project in the research programme, aimed mainly at seeing how secondary services could be improved. [6] It seemed clear that whether it was much used or not, an extensive formal system existed, that it cost both producers and purchasers (mainly libraries) a great deal of money, and that it might be sub- stantially improved with much less effort than would be needed to improve the informal system. Indeed, there are limits to how far the informal system can be developed or improved without introduc- ing some formality, which might thereby deprive it of some of its special and attractive features.

This third project, called Design of Information Systems in the Social Sciences (DISISS), was in fact a set of several related studies. Although most of the work was completed by 1975, the final report was not issued until 1980. The project was based at the University of Bath, but it also involved researchers at the Poly- technic of North London and the Open University, and made use of students from other library schools. The results of the research, though hardly conclusive, indicate very clearly the unsatisfactory nature of the present system and provide good pointers as to how it might be improved.

One part of the DISISS programme studied the size, growth, and structure of social science literature. [7] This showed rapid growth since World War II, more rapid than either in science and technology or in the humanities, though growth rates vary greatly

between subjects and between countries. One unexpected finding was
a great and apparently increasing concentration of production in a
relatively few developed countries; in 1970, 10 countries accounted
for 52% of serials published and for 70% of monographs. The most
striking finding however was the large number and increasing proportion of secondary serials. Nearly 1,000 serials containing lists
of references or abstracts of social science literature were counted
as being alive in 1970, and of these 200 consisted exclusively of
references or abstracts. The ratio of secondary services to primary
journals had changed from 1:42 in 1920 to 1:15 in 1970. Allowing
for the fact that many indexing and abstracting sections in journals
are small and not very significant (in which case their value is questionable), there does seem to be a proliferation of secondary services.

     Another part of DISISS studied coverage and overlap in two
social science subjects, criminology and public administration. [8]
Of the 670 journals covered, 531 were covered by only one of the
six criminology services and only two by all six. The 21 secondary
services relevant to public administration covered 5,053 journals;
many of these were of marginal relevance, but of the 21 most frequently covered titles, only 10 were covered by as many as 11 of
the 21 services. Many of the services appeared to serve little useful purpose, but nearly all of them covered at least one or two unique
titles. To achieve good coverage in either subject it would be necessary to use several services--certainly more than the average
one or two that INFROSS showed social scientists to use. Total
lack of coordination between the services was evident, and although
some of them were aimed at specialist audiences, it was far from
clear what the audience for many of the services was. It should be
noted that neither of the studies aimed to identify journals in the
field that were covered by none of the services, but a supplementary
test with a small sample of articles central to each subject showed
the same picture of poor and scattered coverage.

     Criminology and public administration were chosen as subjects
that drew on other disciplines and that were therefore likely to present special problems for indexing and abstracting services. It cannot be assumed that the situation in all social science fields is equally
unsatisfactory, but since most if not all social science subjects have
a strong interdisciplinary element, it is unlikely that the situation
in criminology and public administration is exceptional.

     A third part of DISISS looked at the design of individual sec-
ondary services. [9] All secondary services have certain character-
istics--coverage, frequency of issue, content of entry (abstracts, citations with keywords, citations only, etc.), the presence or absence
of an index. To maximize all these characteristics would make a
service impossibly costly; it would be difficult to imagine a weekly
service with comprehensive coverage and full abstracts of every item.
Ideally, therefore, an optimum combination of characteristics should
be sought, and an experiment with Geo Abstracts was designed with
this in mind. With the full cooperation of the producer, 48 different

combinations of the above characteristics were produced and sent to a sample of 192 planners in practice, research, and teaching. The results were evaluated by tear-off sheets attached to each issue and by a questionnaire at the end of the experimental period.

The tear-off sheets, which reported the extent to which each issue was used, yielded rather different results from the final questionnaire, which asked what users actually preferred: they by no means always preferred what they found most productive or used most (people do not always like what is good for them). There was a fairly strong bias towards the frequency of issue received by recipients; but allowing for this, the favored frequency seemed to be about monthly, and the optimum number of entries per issue between 100 and 200. The presence or absence of an index to individual issues was almost immaterial, but this does not of course mean that annual or less frequent indexes are not useful. Abstracts were preferred over keyword-enriched titles, but on the other hand only a quarter of the users found titles alone inadequate. It was interesting that although many of the recipients had never used a secondary service before, most of them found it useful.

Whether these results are applicable to other subjects cannot be known without further experimentation, which would be expensive. However, common experience and reflection would suggest that both very frequent and very infrequent issues are not ideal, nor are issues containing either very few or a great many references ideal -- with the proviso that a much larger service broken down into sections, of which users can select only those of relevance to them, may be quite acceptable. This proviso is an important one, because if, as the coverage and overlap study suggested, fewer and larger services would be preferable to the existing multiplicity of uncoordinated services, such larger services should be designed for optimum ease of use, which may require very careful planning.

The further and largest part of DISISS was a large citation analysis. [10] Unlike nearly all previous studies, this used references drawn not only from a few high-ranking serials but from serials selected at random and from monographs. In all, 59,000 references were analyzed. Eleven thousand of these were taken from nearly 300 British and American monographs. One hundred and forty serials were used as sources, including 47 high-ranking serials and 47 selected at random, yielding in all nearly 48,000 references. It may be noted that the analysis of references drawn from monographs produced strikingly different results from analysis of references from serials, and there were also significant differences between the results of analyses of references drawn from high-ranking serials and from serials drawn at random. [11] This suggests that citation analyses based, as most are, only on high-ranking serials must be regarded with strong suspicion, at least in the social sciences.

The results of the citation analyses provide much information on the date distribution of references in different subjects, on concentration and scatter of citations among serials, on relationships

between different subjects, countries, and languages, and on different
forms of material cited (serials, reports, monographs, etc). Some
of this information is highly relevant to the design of secondary services. For example, it is clearly easier to design a service in a
subject where there is a very high concentration of use on a relatively small number of serials, as in economics and psychology, than
in subjects with a wide scatter, such as sociology and political science. However, although in economics and psychology 75% coverage
can be achieved fairly easily, the high concentration means that they
have very long "tails" of little-cited serials, so that it is at least
as hard to achieve 90% coverage in them as in subjects with a low
concentration.

It is also much easier to achieve good coverage in subjects
such as psychology, where the great majority of references are to
serials, than in political science, where monographs are much more
heavily cited--not to mention official publications, newspapers, and
other forms of material. However, in all social science subjects,
forms other than serials are heavily cited; and any service that re-
stricts itself (as most do) to serials only is dealing with only a portion of the relevant literature.

Psychology and economics had a very high self-sufficiency;
that is, most of the items cited by psychology and economics were
in those subjects. At the other extreme, criminology, geography,
social policy, sociology, political science, and education made relatively few references to themselves. A secondary service that covered only the core literature of sociology would be of very limited
value to the sociologist; what is really needed is abstracts for sociologists rather than abstracts of sociological literature. The problems that this poses for the designer of secondary services are obvious.

The literature of each language had a strong tendency to cite
literature in that language; this was overwhelmingly true in the case
of English and to a lesser extent of other languages. Whether this
is partially or largely a result of the linguistic bias of secondary
services, or whether the secondary services merely reflect common
use, is not easy to say. A similar though less pronounced country
bias existed: publications of a particular country tended to cite
other publications of that country.

The date distributions are hardly relevant to current secondary services, but have implications for retrospective bibliographies
and for the maintenance of machine-readable files. The rank lists
of journals cited in each subject, although they are now somewhat
out of date, could be used to select titles for coverage by secondary
services; indeed, it would be very interesting to compare the coverage of journals in specific subjects with the rank lists produced
by DISISS.

Several conclusions could be drawn from these results. It
could, for example, be argued that the very poor coverage of non-

serial literature by most secondary services cannot matter very much, because writers would not be able to cite monographs, official publications, etc. so extensively if they did not have adequate bibliographic access to them in other ways. It could equally be argued that users may have to spend far more time and effort tracking down relevant monographs, reports, etc. , and less effectively, than if secondary services covered them properly. It does seem that on the whole secondary services do not reflect the uses of social scientists, and that where they do (as in the parochial biases towards language and country) they may be narrowing users' horizons when they could be widening them.

The poor match of services to use may go some way towards explaining why the secondary services themselves are much under-used, but an equally good explanation would be their proliferation and the difficulty of knowing which ones to use. DISISS made little attempt to establish the true costs of secondary services. An effort was made to identify the costs of three secondary services, but this proved an extremely difficult exercise, because the producers themselves had never attempted (or needed) to find out the costs. A commercial organization could probably provide a reasonable costing, but many secondary services in the social sciences are at best semi-commercial, and many of their costs are hidden or unknown. For example, scanning of primary serials, abstracting of articles, etc. may be done by voluntary helpers; much of the copy may be typed within the producers' institutions and no financial account may need to be rendered for it. It seems doubtful whether most secondary services are very effective; it is almost impossible to establish whether they are cost-effective when costs cannot be ascertained.

If the situation is unsatisfactory, as it appears to be, why should this be so? After all, the situation in the sciences is by comparison quite good, with many fewer and much more comprehensive services. One reason is that, as suggested above, a good many secondary services in the social sciences are semi-commercial, and some are in effect cottage industries. Indeed, some of them have their origin in personal files and indexes that were distributed first to a few colleagues and then more widely, until they eventually came to be published. Since there is no need for such services to recover more than the overt direct cost, the sale price is often quite low, and a few hundred purchasers can make it appear that the service is fulfilling a real need.

Unfortunately, this appearance may be misleading, because the buyers are not the users, and the market therefore provides no real test of the viability of any given service. The purchasers are nearly all libraries, which rarely have much idea whether or how much particular services are used, and which do not know which ones are "best buys." As for the users, their access is largely confined to what their libraries buy; and unless they have used other and better services elsewhere, they are not in a position to suggest changes.

If it can easily be understood how large numbers of uncoordinated services have sprung up, it still needs to be explained why
they continue to exist when bigger and better services could easily
make them unnecessary. However, the large and relatively wealthy
market for secondary services in science and technology does not
exist in the social sciences, which have no equivalent of, say, the
large pharmaceutical companies. Very large and expensive services
could therefore find it very difficult to gain a market; at any rate,
publishers and institutions do not appear willing to take the risk,
with the striking exception of the APA's Psychological Abstracts.

Yet another reason is the lack of general consensus in the
social sciences. A variety of ideological approaches is possible,
and this may affect profoundly both the classification and terminology
of a subject, with obvious implications for the construction of a secondary service.

Because many producers of secondary services in the social
sciences are not commercial organizations and have little or no
profit motive, they have little incentive to improve their own services, to cooperate with other services, or even to economize very
much. If they do wish to cooperate, there is virtually no machinery
for doing so.

If librarians do not know which services to buy, users are
remarkably inarticulate. In science one would have expected users
to demand (as many of them did) far better services long ago; in
the social sciences they seem remarkably complacent. One reason
for this may be that the penalties for missing relevant material are
far less than in science, where duplication of research is expensive
and the publication of duplicated research both very difficult and
highly undesirable. By the very nature of the subject matter of the
social sciences, replication of research is virtually impossible; and
if it does happen the chances of obtaining the same results are extremely low.

Does it really matter that the system is such a mess? After
all, social scientists continue to get by somehow. Surely it does
matter--for producers, libraries, and users. For the producers, it
can hardly be satisfying to issue underused and perhaps largely unnecessary products, when much better services could be produced
for considerably less money. Among all those involved in indexing
and abstracting, there must be a massive amount of duplicated effort. Users must either spend a great deal of effort tracking down
relevant material or miss much of it through inadequate secondary
services. Most of all, perhaps, the present unsatisfactory situation
matters to librarians. No library can acquire more than a very
limited range of secondary services, and in everyone's interest the
choice should be made as carefully as possible. Not only have librarians little to guide them in their selection, but they may easily
select inferior services, with a result that better services may collapse for lack of a market. One of the two best secondary services
in criminology that DISISS identified went out of existence a year

later: would this have happened if librarians had known it was superior to some of the other services? Unless some way is found either to improve services dramatically or to determine which are best buys, the situation may get worse rather than better: there may be fewer services produced as libraries become able to spend less in real terms, but those that survive may not be the fittest. This is a matter not only of importance but of some urgency.

What can be done to improve matters? In the longer term, it is possible to conceive of a vastly improved system. The development of high-density storage of information and direct access to such stores opens up new possibilities, including the gradual development of a comprehensive data bank, into which references and abstracts could be put (possibly indexed and abstracted for different audiences and from different approaches) and from which they could be retrieved. Some standardization of format would be necessary, but once the data bank reached a certain size it should attract input from other sources on its own terms. The problems of terminology and subject indexing would remain formidable, but their importance would be reduced by the alternative means of access offered by citation indexes. Duplication and unnecessary overlap could be virtually eliminated, and access to references in one discipline that were relevant to others --one of the largest problems facing information systems in the social sciences--would be far easier. Access could be on-line, or by means of published "packages" of references or abstracts suited to particular user groups. These would be adjusted continually to changing demand, which could be monitored through on-line access.

A system of this kind could meet most if not all of the requirements of secondary services in the social sciences--flexibility, the ability to adapt readily to changing needs, freedom of movement across subject boundaries, the ability to provide comprehensiveness or selectivity, speed (through on-line access), browsing (on-line or in published packages), and a variety of access points. The realization of such a system would require a great deal of cooperation, but this should develop as its virtues became apparent. One of the biggest stumbling blocks, the cost of input in an appropriate form, will diminish in importance as more and more secondary services go through a machine-readable stage; this will happen initially as a more satisfactory and economic means of achieving ordinary printed publication, and once it has happened the input of files into the data bank becomes much easier. The cost would probably be much less than that of the total cost of the present system, but the capital and development costs would still be high, and--a rather bigger obstacle --it would be very hard to conceal many of the costs that are hidden in the present systems, and that would have to be passed on to the purchaser and user. Whatever the difficulties, the future does seem to lie in this direction, and it is very difficult to see how improvements to secondary services on the scale ideally required can be achieved along conventional lines.

Meanwhile, conventional secondary services exist, and large improvements in them can undoubtedly be made. One significant gap in the present system is review articles, which are far less common than in science and technology. Another possibility is a publication consisting of contents pages of social science monographs, possibly with keyword indexes to chapter headings. Report literature, official publications, and other forms could be far better covered by secondary services. However, none of these measures would overcome the lack of coordination that is responsible for many of the present deficiencies.

One theoretically possible way of achieving better coordination is to bring secondary service producers together. However, there are large numbers of them, and it would be difficult to gather more than a few together at a time. One attempt to do so could claim only a very limited success as a seminar, and resulted in no positive action. [12] Moreover, even if secondary service horses can be brought to the water of cooperation, there is little incentive to make them drink, for the reasons suggested earlier in this paper. Why should an "inferior" service aid a "better" service by contributing to it some extra references and putting itself out of business? There may be no profit in continuing the service, but there may be quite a lot of prestige. Coordination even within a country would be difficult enough; between countries speaking different languages, and, even more important, with different ideologies, the prospects seem very unpromising.

A better prospect may be offered by the deliberate improvement of selected services to a level where they put inferior services out of business. For the good to drive out the bad, the good must not only become really good but must be seen to be good (and the bad must be seen to be bad). Some means of evaluation would therefore be necessary. Persuading good services to become better would not be easy, especially if they are among the semi-commercial, surreptitiously subsidized services that constitute such a large proportion of secondary services in the social sciences. The financial and organizational basis for their improvement may not be present; it would take them two or three years at least to recover the cost of development, and the money may not be available for this. The best hope would therefore lie in a take-over of some of the better services by a commercial organization, or preferably by a large institution on the scale of the American Psychological Association. However, the forces of inertia are very strong, and it would be foolish to be too hopeful.

Can librarians do anything to help? After all, they are the main purchasers of secondary services; they are the main losers from their inefficiencies, and have most to gain from their improvement. One obvious measure that librarians can take is to evaluate the services they acquire. Evaluation can be done either by objective tests of overlap and coverage or by direct use of evaluation within libraries. Objective evaluations can be carried out as research projects, which are much more likely to be funded if librarians realize their importance and make suitable research proposals. In-house evaluation is much more difficult, especially if ultimate users have to be studied; the difficulties of studying them accurately and unobtrusively hardly need to be stressed. However, several libraries have information officers who use secondary services on behalf of users, and it should not be impossible for them to assess their relative qualities--their productiveness in terms of relevant references, their usability, their currency, etc. A cooperative programme of evaluation studies of both kinds seems to be an urgent necessity.

The second step that librarians can take is a more immediate and practical one. Some services are fairly obviously inferior, and are bought only because subscriptions to them were started a long time ago or because particular users happened to suggest them. Librarians could cooperate in cancelling such subscriptions, thereby putting the services out of business. At the other end, they could identify services that are commonly agreed to be among the better ones, and press in concert for their improvement. Action in isolation is unlikely to be profitable, but librarians may well underestimate the impact they could have if they made a concerted effort. Since librarians are the main market for secondary services, they can and should put appropriate pressure on the producers.

Finally, it was noted earlier that social scientists are remarkably inarticulate, even apathetic, about the inefficiencies of the present system. Is it too much to hope that they could be gradually educated to realize there could be something better and to make greater demands? It is not easy to show them in the abstract what might be; ideally, they would be exposed to better services and compare them with inferior ones. However, where information officers exist they can do much to counter the inefficiencies of the present system, and in doing so point out that they could give an even better service with much less effort if they had better material to work on.

Excessive optimism that the system will be improved would be foolish, but excessive pessimism would be a counsel of despair. Whether change occurs depends only partly on whether the requisite technology and machinery are available: the decisive factor is whether enough people actually want change to happen. It is hard to believe that, once the inadequacies of the present system of secondary services in the social sciences were widely enough publicized, a large body of opinion in favor of change could not be mustered.

References

1. Line, M. B. "The Information Uses and Needs of Social Scientists: an Overview of INFROSS. " Aslib Proceedings 23 (September 1971):412-434.
2. Evans, S. M. , and Line, M. B. "A Personalized Service to Social Science Researchers: the Experimental Information Service in the Social Sciences at the University of Bath. " Journal of Librarianship 5 (July 1973):214-232.
3. Blake, B. , Markham, T. , and Skinner, A. "Inside Information:

Social Welfare Practitioners and their Information Needs."
Aslib Proceedings 31 (June 1979):275-283.
4. Wilson, T. D., and Streatfield, D. R. "Information Needs in
Local Authority Social Services Departments: an Interim Report on Project INISS." Journal of Documentation 33 (December 1977):277-293.
5. Wilson, T. D., Streatfield, D. R., and Mullings, C. "Information Needs in Local Authority Social Services Departments:
a Second Report on Project INISS." Journal of Documentation 33 (December 1977):277-293.
6. Design of Information Systems in the Social Sciences. Research
Report A1:Towards the Improvement of Social Sciences Information Systems. Bath University Library, 1980. This summarizes the detailed findings, which are contained in Research
Reports A2-A5 and B1-B7.
7. Line, M. B., and Roberts, S. "The Size, Growth and Composition of Social Science Literature." International Social Science Journal 28 (1976):122-159.
8. Design of Information in the Social Sciences. Research Report
A5: The Planning of Indexing and Abstracting Services in
the Social Sciences: Coverage, Overlap and Content. Bath
University Library, April 1976. (BL R&D Report 5290).
9. Arms, W. Y. "Usefulness and Style of Secondary Publication:
an Experimental Information Service," in EURIM II: A European Conference on the Application of Research in Information
Services and Libraries, 23-25 March 1976. London: Aslib,
1977, 159-164. This summarizes the main findings, reported
extensively in DISISS Research Report B3 and in shorter form
in DISISS Research Report A4.
10. Line, M. B. "The Structure of Social Science Literature as
Shown by a Large Scale Citation Analysis." (Submitted for
publication.) This summarizes the main findings, reported
in DISISS Research Reports A3 and B7.
11. Line, M. B. "The Influence of the Type of Sources Used on
the Results of Citation Analyses." Journal of Documentation
35 (December 1979):265-284.
12. International Workshop of Secondary Service Producers, York,
1975. Edited by Peter M. Ketley. London: British Library,
1976 (BL R&D Report 5289).

WHY BOTHER WITH READER EDUCATION?*

Neil A. Radford

The question posed in the title of this paper, if asked in polite company, invariably produces two reactions. Initially a hush falls, eyebrows are raised, and mouths gape at such a display of impudence and ignorance. Swiftly, though, comes a torrent of platitudes, generalisations, and unsupported ex cathedra pronouncements from those who feel that a sacred trust is threatened.

Reader education enjoys, among librarians, the happy status of being a "Good Thing." But perhaps we accept it as such too uncritically. Perhaps in our eagerness to educate our readers we have given insufficient thought to such questions as whether they need educating; if so, why; whether they want to be educated; if so, how best to do it; and whether it is all really worth the time and effort it takes. No doubt there are other questions we have neglected to examine carefully and thoughtfully as we scrambled aboard the reader-education bandwaggon, but these will do as a representative sample. Almost every academic library is a passenger on the reader-education bandwaggon. Certainly the University of Sydney Library is, and I expect it to remain there. Nevertheless, in order to do the best work one must know not only how to do it, but why it is being done, and to do that we need to consider some of these neglected questions. In doing so in this paper I will assume a devil's advocate role, concentrating on the problems rather than the solutions. Certainly the problems are easier to identify.

Being a well-educated library user I have surveyed the literature on reader education. This literature has two outstanding characteristics: it is formidable in quantity, and it is mostly appalling in quality. With respect to the latter, the literature on reader education is boring, repetitive, self-serving, and frequently of trivial consequence. It comprises a great many articles of the "how we do it good at our library" type, a smaller number of attempts at evaluation of the effectiveness of reader education (mostly of doubtful quality or not proving much), and quite a deal of allegedly philosophical articles which boil down to a collection of high-sounding generalisations. The literature of reader education is also distinguished by an apparent ignorance of the literature of such fields as

*Reprinted by permission of the author and publisher from New Zealand Libraries, 43:4 (December 1980) 53-56.

education itself and psychology. If the quality of the literature of a
profession is a measure of the sophistication and maturity of that
profession, then librarianship does not make an impressive showing.

The reasons popularly adduced for mounting reader-education
activities in academic libraries can be summarised as follows:
First, the explosion of knowledge places greater stress on the ability to learn throughout life. (I rather like the way the American
humourist James Thurber expressed this. He said: "So much has
been written about everything that it is difficult to find out anything
about it.") Second, knowing how to use a library is essential for
successful life-long education. Third, modern education practice
places greater stress on self-directed learning and less reliance on
formal lectures. Therefore students need to be taught information-
finding skills. Fourth, librarians must become agents for the retrieval of information rather than guardians of the books.

There is possibly a fifth, and seldom admitted, reason for
the zeal with which librarians pursue reader-education work. It
is their eagerness to be accepted by academics as teachers, and
therefore as equals, since respect and recognition in an academic
community are seen to attach much more readily to academics than
to non-academic support staff such as librarians. The myth of the
librarian as a teacher has been propagated and nourished by the profession for years and was analysed and soundly rejected by Pauline
Wilson in a recent issue of Library Quarterly. [1]

Whatever the reasons, be they altruistic or self-serving, why
do we do it? Casting aside the high-sounding reasons given in the
literature, we do it because most people find libraries difficult to
use. This is due to the complexity and inefficiency of the systems
employed by librarians. Perfectionist cataloguers and constantly
changing cataloguing codes have succeeded in making the catalogue
incomprehensible to most people, who require only a simple finding-
list and subject headings which use a terminology they understand.
Architects and librarians have often collaborated to ensure that the
interior arrangements of the library are such as to preclude any but
the most determined explorer from discovering the whereabouts of
service points or the shelf-arrangement of the collections. Consequently, enormous amounts of time and effort are devoted to guiding
users through complexities of the library's own devising. This effort would in many cases be better spent on designing catalogues and
libraries for ease of use--in dismantling the barriers rather than in
training people to clamber over them.

Certain obvious steps, such as adequate signposting within
the building, can be taken to remove some of these barriers to ex-
ploitation of the collections. The goal should be, as one librarian
put it, that "if all the library staff were propped up dead at their
posts ... it should still be possible for a student on his first visit
to the library to find his way to the books he needs."[2] So far as
the catalogue is concerned, it must be admitted, regretfully, that
the problems are too deeply rooted to make them susceptible of easy

solution. Like the poor, the incomprehensible catalogue will probably always be with us. Other barriers, not of the librarian's
making, are also difficult to dismantle. Some indexing services
are notoriously complex, and the mysterious arrangement of government publications inspires dread even in librarians, to take just
two examples.

What should be our response to these difficulties? Should
we try to teach the user how to master them for himself, or should
we ensure that librarians are competent to do it for him? The
reader educators would vote for the first of these; I submit that a
case can be made for the second. William Katz believes that reader
education is not necessarily the answer to the user's needs. He
favours giving the user a choice. "The user should have the option
either (1) to learn how to use the library or any of its parts, or
(2) not to learn how and still to expect a full, complete, and total
answer to his or her question(s) from the reference librarian."[3]
In this context Maurice Line uses the analogy of driving a car versus taking a taxi. [4] Although it can be useful to know how to drive
it is sometimes more convenient to be driven. Like driving, library-
information use is a skill which requires regular practice for best
results. The occasional library user will probably neither wish to
learn it nor be able to do it very effectively because of insufficient
practice.

In fact, the great majority of the population has no interest
in learning how to use a library effectively. Almost everyone goes
through life without much knowledge of what libraries can offer or
how to tap their resources, and they are perfectly happy and successful in life despite this. Even if we restrict ourselves to the elite--
the tertiary student who should be motivated to efficient library use
--we still find a crushing apathy. In one recent study, [5] although
about 60 per cent of the students surveyed said that the library
should offer reader-education courses, about 40 per cent said that
they would not bother to attend such courses. Perhaps more alarm-
ing was the result of another survey which found that of 600 university students questioned, only 94 (or 15 per cent) agreed that reader
education had been of benefit to them. The other 85 per cent said
that reader education had either not helped them or that they had
no opinion either way. [6]

It is also disquieting for the academic librarian to face the
fact that research on the relationship between library use and academic achievement has largely failed to identify any causal connection.

The problem of motivation is well known. Unless the student
really needs information-finding skills to pass his courses the acquisition of these skills will be perceived as an unnecessary frill.
Very few courses at the undergraduate level require any library
skills more sophisticated than the location and use of the reserve-
book collection, the circulation desk, and the photocopying machines,
no matter how much we might wish the truth was otherwise. I won-

der how many undergraduates have failed their examinations because
they did not receive any reader education beyond the traditional
guided tour of the library in orientation week?

The guided tour itself is not a particularly effective teaching
instrument. Almost every study which has ever been done on this
finds out two things--one, the guided tour and lectures to new students are largely in vain; and two, despite this, almost every library
provides orientation tours and lectures. The self-guided tour, as
distinct from the organised crocodile which shuffles through the building with a librarian way out in front, is a more promising development, but requires infinitely more time and effort for its preparation. As a way of orienting new students to the layout of the library
and the location of its service points the self-guided tour on paper
or audio-cassette can be both popular and effective if properly done.
But care must be taken to restrict the tour to physical orientation.
The impulse to cram into it instruction on how to use the catalogue,
the periodical indexes and so on is strong--almost overwhelming--
but pointless. Such instruction is better done at the point of use
by means of audio-tape, tape-slide, or printed instructions which the
user can follow at his own pace. One learns how to use these tools
by actually working with them under guidance, not by listening to a
lecture about them or watching someone use them on a film.

Beyond physical orientation and point-of-use instruction in
specific library tools or services comes what is generally termed
"bibliographic instruction"--the introduction to the user of the information resources available in particular subject disciplines and the
techniques of making use of those resources. It is here that the
library can do most good, but it is also here that our most spectacular failures occur. So convinced are we of the righteousness
of the mission of educating the user that we too often fail to think
clearly about the goals of our reader-education activities. Unless
we know the objectives of the exercise, the content, method, and
evaluation of what is done are in danger. It is apparent from the
literature that relatively few reader-education programmes start
from this basic first principle. Instead, the typical approach appears to be to cram as much detail as possible into the time available in the hope that some of it, at least, might sink in and be useful. This is akin to attacking a blaze with a lawn sprinkler rather
than a fire hose. If one is going to hit the target, one has to concentrate one's ammunition and aim the weapon properly. With such
a "hit or miss" approach it is little wonder that a majority of students and academics are apathetic about reader education. The cooperation of the teaching staff is particularly vital for effective bibliographic instruction. Not only must they be persuaded to make
class time available, but their assistance is needed to ensure that
the instruction given is directly relevant to the course, and that
successful library use is a required part of success in the course.
These are difficult things to arrange, and we have mostly failed.

An oft-repeated theme in the literature on reader education
is that relatively few students are actually reached, and of those

who are, a sizeable proportion--often a majority--are hardly fired
with enthusiasm by the experience.   This is all the more worrying
when one considers the tremendous investment of time and energy
which goes into the typical reader-education programme.   Is it a
wise use of scarce resources to invest so heavily in something which
has such a relatively small return?

To answer this question, of course, one must be able to assess the return derived.   History shows that attempts to evaluate the
effectiveness of reader education frequently sink into the same quick-
sands which have swallowed up attempts to evaluate the educative
process generally.   Although there are many examples of attempts to
evaluate the success of reader education it seems that we have not
yet devised a reliable test.   For example, a comprehensive survey
of tests of library-use competence concluded that few, if any, of
them adequately tested ability to use various information resources,
and to intellectualise a library-use problem. [7]   Examples of muddled testing leading to muddled results are rampant.   The wonder
is that so many of them get into print!

A classic example appeared recently in RQ, the journal of
the Reference and Adult Services Division of ALA.   The author [8]
tested students at her university over a three-year period, dividing
them into groups which had received either no reader-education, or
a tour only, or a tour plus classroom instruction.   She found, I suspect to her dismay and mystification, that in nearly one third of the
cases the students who had had no reader education at all out-per-
formed those who had received assistance, and that the "tour only"
groups knew more than the "tour plus classroom" groups one third
of the time.   Unwilling to admit what may well be the truth--that
the reader-education methods were deficient--the author concluded
with a call for better evaluative measures.   One cannot argue with
that.

It is chastening to note that a number of researchers have
found that students learn at least as much, and often more, from
various methods of machine instruction as they do from live lectures by librarians.   Indeed, the majority of students appear to prefer the machines to the librarians!   All the evaluative measures
known to me are designed to test the immediate effects of reader
education--whether the student can find such and such a book in the
catalogue, or six journal articles on this topic, and so on.   While
these are important, it seems to me that we should be equally, if
not more, interested in the long-term lasting effects of reader education.   A tour, a lecture and perhaps an hour or two of bibliographic
instruction seem an insufficient preparation for a lifetime of successful use of such a complicated instrument as a library.   I am reminded of the perhaps familiar remark that use of a library is like
making love; everybody has some idea of how it is done, but expertise comes only with practice.   The sad fact is, though, that unlike
making love most people are not greatly interested in practising and
improving their library skills.

Additionally, it is pertinent to ask whether, with the advance
of automation, most people will <u>need</u> to use libraries for the rest
of their lives. It does seem highly likely that, within my lifetime
for example, access to information will become a home-oriented or
office-oriented activity via computer terminals, rather than a library-
oriented activity. People will need to know how to operate the terminal rather than how to use the card catalogue or the reader's
guide. It is probably outside the scope of this paper to make predictions about the library of the future, but I point out merely that
it, and the methods of accessing the information it contains, are
sure to be rather different from that to which we have become ac-
customed.

Of course, unless the library meets the challenge of providing information to the enquirer rather than a lecture on how he can
find it himself, the library will be passed over in favour of other
institutions which <u>will</u> give the answer. Community information and
advice services are already enjoying popular support. Information
has a future, but does the library?

To sum up: It seems to me that we engage in reader-
education activities for three main reasons:

1. Although we can't prove it, we think it must be good for
people to know how to use libraries.
2. We are guilty of making our libraries unnecessarily difficult for people to use. And
3. We crave acceptance in the role of teacher because of
its more comforting self-image.

In our uncritical acceptance of reader education as a "Good
Thing," we have paid insufficient attention to the demonstrable fact
that the vast majority of the population does not wish to know how
to use a library and, even if compelled to learn, will not practise
the skills in order to maintain their competence. Even in the more
elite population of tertiary students, motivation to learn library-use
techniques is generally lacking--especially at the undergraduate level
--because it is a proven fact that examination success is achievable
without it. Only the elite of this elite--the postgraduate student and
the researcher--can see a clear benefit from bibliographic instruction.

The reader education we engage in is, generally speaking,
nothing to be proud of. The guided tour during orientation week is
universally condemned but almost universally provided. Basic instruction on such topics as use of the catalogue is generally crammed
with the most intricate details, which defeats rather than supports
the purpose. Bibliographic instruction, though undoubtedly helpful
to many recipients, founders on the rocks of lack of staff, lack of
time, and lack of co-operation and interest from the academic staff.
Attempts to evaluate the success of reader education--the only way
in which the need for improvement can be properly gauged--suffer
from a lack of definition of success itself, and a confusion as to the

goals of the typical reader education programme. In short, we are spending a tremendous amount of time and money and effort in an enterprise the reason for which we cannot rationally define, using methods which are questionable at least and possibly counter-productive, involving individuals the majority of whom neither need nor want to be involved, and at the end of all this we have no reliable method of judging our success. In times of scarce resources, can this be justified?

Surely the answer has to be that teaching the use of libraries is justifiable and desirable, but only if it is done well. Goals must be set, and they must be realistic; methods must be selected and used carefully and thoughtfully; the target audience needs better definition, and we must know its information needs before we design any programme of education. Finally the work must be monitored constantly, and refined in the light of this experience. To do reader education properly will be expensive of both time and money. But poor reader education is extravagant and wasteful, and unjustifiable.

As well as my work at the University of Sydney I have the job of being Chairman of the Board of Education of the LAA. Among other things the Board administers an external examination system for aspiring librarians. Several years ago one examiner wanted to set a question in his paper which asked simply "Why libraries?" A majority of the Board vetoed this, but I and some others argued that it had considerable merit. Aspiring entrants to the profession should be asking themselves that very question, and should certainly be able to answer it. Thinking carefully and critically about "Why libraries?" seemed to me to be a very necessary preparation for the profession of librarianship. Similarly, I believe it is healthy for reader-education librarians to stop now and then and ask "Why reader education?." Periodic introspection and evaluation of this kind can only be beneficial in ensuring that we identify what is worth doing, and then do it well.

References

1. Pauline Wilson, "Librarians as teachers: the study of an organisational fiction," Library Quarterly, v. 49, no. 2 (April 1979), p. 146-162.
2. C. E. N. Childs, quoted in User Education in Libraries, by N. Fjallbrant and M. Stevenson (London: Bingley, 1978), p. 11.
3. William A. Katz, Introduction to Reference Work (3rd ed. New York: McGraw-Hill, 1978) v. 2, p. 261.
4. Maurice B. Line, "The case for information officers," in Educating the Library User, ed. by John Lubans (New York: Bowker 1974), p. 385.
5. John Lubans, "Library use instruction needs from the library users'/nonusers' point of view: a survey report," in Lubans, op. cit. , p. 408.
6. John Lubans, "Evaluating library-use education programmes," in Lubans, op. cit. , p. 236.

7. Masse Bloomfield, "Testing for library use competence," in
    Lubans, op. cit. , p. 221-231.
8. Ellen R. Patterson, "How effective is library instruction?,"
    RQ, v. 18, no. 4 (Summer 1979), p. 376-377.

THE MYTH OF BIBLIOTHERAPY*

Lucy Warner

Massage, meditation, sex, screaming ... today practically anything
can be thought of as therapy. There are even published accounts
of shopping, camping, sailing, skydiving, and pets as psychological
treatments. [1] The question is whether bibliotherapy is simply a
similar fad that elevates a pleasurable pastime or release of feelings
to the ranks of therapy? This suggestion may, at first, seem in-
sulting to professionals involved with the printed word. Books can
sway, enlighten, move emotions, change attitudes and opinions. It
is on such undeniable premises that bibliotherapists base their claims.
However, it is a long step from those conventional wisdoms to the
"prescription" of books to solve or prevent problems, especially when
the so-called therapy is practiced, outside of a clinical setting, on
normal people, and particularly when those people are a captive audience of school children being "treated" by teachers and librarians.

A survey of the professional literature on bibliotherapy is
impressive only in the volume of articles. There is confusion over
what the term means and little evidence to prove that it really works.
Discussions of using bibliotherapy in the schools are loaded with di-
dacticism and value judgements; much of what passes for treatment
seems to be old-fashioned moralizing in modern garb. Superficial,
negative labeling, and coercion are implicit in many of the practices
described. In fact, educators, armed with the false sense of confidence their self-styled role as therapists gives them, may be doing
more harm than good.

Bibliotherapy has been around a long time. A list of works
on the subject compiled in 1962 records over 300 titles going back
to 1900. [2] Another 1968 bibliography cites 138 published since the
'40s. [3] In the last decade, proselytizing articles have appeared regularly in education and psychology journals.

However, bibliotherapy has strayed a long way from its origins. Its use began in hospitals, and seems at first to have been a

*Reprinted by permission of the author and publisher from School
Library Journal, 27:2 (October 1980) 107-11. Published by R. R.
Bowker Co. (a Xerox Company). Copyright © 1980 by Xerox Cor-
poration.

fancy term for what librarians in medical and psychiatric clinics did.
In the '30s, Dr. William G. Menninger gave bibliotherapy a new intellectual respectability: The five-year program at the Menninger
Clinic involved many of the assumptions about the therapeutic value
of reading that are still popular today, although his program was
clearly designed in the medical model. "Reading is a treatment
method and as such must be directed by a physician," was Menninger's dictum. In his program, doctors approved library purchases,
went over patients' reading assignments, and held book discussions.
The librarian's role was subsidiary. [4]

   In the '50s and '60s, bibliotherapy was expanded beyond the
confines of the hospital and beyond the medical model. The term
preventive bibliotherapy was coined to include any reading program
that might prevent future problems not only among hospital patients
but anywhere that books and readers could be brought together. Educators began to embrace bibliotherapy as a means of helping young
people to adjust to and adopt acceptable social values.

   Today, bibliotherapy has taken on the mantle of contemporary
social concerns. Best-selling, self-help psychology books on everything from sexuality to assertiveness lend the concept immediacy.
The current trend toward social realism in children's fiction in the
schools has encouraged teachers and librarians to view books as
aids in dealing with such diverse social issues as broken homes,
racial discrimination, alcohol and drug addiction, and teenage sexuality. But, despite such ambitious goals, there is much confusion
over what bibliotherapy is, how it works, or whether it works at
all. The definition adopted almost universally in the literature is
one expressed by Caroline Shrodes in 1949: "a process of dynamic
interaction between the personality of the reader and literature which
may be utilized for personality assessment and growth."[5] She pin-
points the stages involved in this process as identification, catharsis
and insight, paralleling the progression of insight therapy as a whole.
The theory relies on such firm precepts of psychodynamics as abre-
action, sublimation, repression, and projection.

   The dynamics of reading, however, cannot be as easily reduced to such principles as it might at first appear. An overview
of research concerned with the impact of reading concludes, "We
have never had a complete demonstration that a story of courage
and friendship will communicate ideas of courage and friendship in
every reader, much less result in courageous or friendly behavior."
[6] Studies indicate that the more highly charged an issue appears
to the reader, the less likely he or she is to interpret written material accurately. Factors leading to distortion include strong personal associations, conflict between the reader's beliefs and those
of the author, and the use of value-laden words. David Russell believes that readers respond to literature in "unique and selective
ways.... Some of these relate to the reading skill and personality
of the reader, some to the characteristics of the material read, and
some to the environmental setting in which the reading is done."[8]

Although the concept of catharsis dates from Aristotle, re-cent research has called into question whether exposure to vicarious experiences really purges intense emotions or merely stirs them up. A study of aggression in movies and on television concludes that the media, in fact, increase aggression in viewers. [9] And a recent ex-periment into treatment of school anxiety through reading found that children were more anxious after bibliotherapy than before. [10]

On a practical level, there is a good deal of confusion about what constitutes bibliotherapy and even about which is the therapist--the book or the person directing the reading. To proponents of pre-ventive bibliotherapy, the reading of any book that may potentially change anyone's perspective or stir feelings seems to fall into this vast, amorphous category. Forums for bibliotherapy range from counseling sessions to classroom discussions and story hours with preschoolers. Therapy is often indistinguishable from conventional teaching and library work. One might ask, "What isn't bibliother-apy?"

Joy K. Roy, in her article "Bibliotherapy: An Important Service to Self," recommends that burned-out teachers "prescribe" for themselves travel books, humor, novels, and other writings to "restore l'esprit."[11] This version of bibliotherapy seems indis-tinguishable from recreational reading. A minister recommends the Bible for parishioners' spiritual guidance, a form of therapy that used to be called devotional reading. [12] A researcher refers to the use of a weight reduction manual in a weight reduction group as bibliotherapy. [13] In this case, the therapy may be simple informa-tional reading. A psychotherapist recommends supplying patients with "literary gems," short quotations on cards for the patients to carry around with them. [14] This Reader's Digest form of biblio-therapy does not even require books.

To further muddy the waters, there is little documented evi-dence that bibliotherapy actually works. One observer states, "Faith in it [bibliotherapy] as a means of solving certain emotional problems is great, yet the concrete evidence for its effectiveness is small." [15] Many writers decry the lack of hard data on the validity of bibliotherapy. Until recently, many claims were based on testimon-ials about "books that changed my life" and case studies relating successful pairings of readers and books. The works of Zaccaria and Moses, Russell and Shrodes, Darling, and Sclabassi review the research done in this area. [16]

A search of Dissertation Abstracts International, however, reveals that recently there have been a number of controlled experi-ments into the efficacy of bibliotherapy, a body of research not prev-iously mentioned in the professional literature. Since 1969, 28 doc-toral theses on bibliotherapy have been reported; all but one of them were controlled experiments. While space does not allow a thesis by thesis review of them, a summary of the overall findings is in-structive.

The experiments are not of uniform quality. Many do not pinpoint what books were used, as though the technique could stand above the material in question. Research design for such experiments is fairly standard. A group of subjects selected by one of various methods is assessed before the experiment begins to determine baseline measures for the traits being examined. Subjects are then divided so that some receive a course of therapy and others (the control) do not. At the end, the assessment is repeated to see if there has been any change. The subjects of these studies range from preschoolers to adults. Diverse issues such as marital conflict, assertiveness training, weight reduction, childhood fears, and attitudes toward the handicapped are explored.

In 10 of these studies, bibliotherapy was not found to be successful. [17] Among researchers reporting some success, almost all qualified their conclusions. In four studies, short-term gains were not maintained at followup. [18] In two, theoretical improvement did not translate into a change in behavior. [19] Four produced results only with subjects who had acknowledged a problem and expressed a desire to change. [20] Four found other techniques to be more successful than bibliotherapy. [21] Two endorsed it in conjunction with other techniques. [22] In all, only two studies claimed unqualified success for bibliotherapy. One of these, a study of the use of storytelling to reduce the fears of preschoolers, did not attempt follow-up or a translation of test scores into behavior. [23] The other, which reported a "significant main effect for reading," was in fact testing to see if reading ability made any difference to the effectiveness of bibliotherapy. It didn't. Details of the "main effect" were not provided. [24]

It appears, then, that if bibliotherapy is to succeed at all, the results may be short-term and may not translate into changes in behavior. Bibliotherapy may work best in conjunction with other techniques among people who have acknowledged that they have a problem and want to change. The prospects for bibliotherapy seem limited, though they appear brighter when used as an adjunct to counseling than as a more general technique.

Bibliotherapy may never meet the heavy burden of proof researchers have placed on it. More than 40 years after the death of Freud, insight therapy as a whole has still not been proved effective. [25] A senate committee concluded that there are "virtually no controlled clinical studies ... which confirm the efficacy, safety and appropriateness of psychotherapy as it is conducted today." [26] Many psychotherapists allege that complex behavior cannot be neatly reduced to controlled experimentation. The talents of the therapist, the timing of therapeutic techniques, and other subtle factors must all be taken into account.

In view of the complexities of the issue, the best writers on bibliotherapy are measured in their endorsements and cautious in their recommendations. As one has said, "Bibliotherapy ... should not be oversimplified. And it should be implemented by educators

who are humane, intelligent, and informed about human behavior and
books."[27]

However, as the literature on the subject proliferates, sim-
plistic treatments multiply. Many writers discuss bibliotherapy as
though it were a simple process of labeling a problem and plugging
in a book with the appropriate theme. One article includes a reproduction of a bibliotherapy plan sheet for teachers with blank lines
for filling in problems, objectives, and recommended materials.[28]
Another suggests that teachers use personality tests to diagnose
problems in their classes.[29] Such sweeping statements as "The
library ... is a major bulwark against mental illness," [30] and
"Education is not clearly separable from therapy" [31] do not encourage caution.

Reacting to these wholesale endorsements, one writer has
gone to the other extreme in suggesting rigorous qualifications to
practice bibliotherapy. She suggests that one begin with qualities
such as emotional stability, physical well-being, sound personal
practices, a belief in democratic precepts, and then take courses
in psychiatry, psychology, anatomy and physiology, aging, rehabil-
itation, minority studies, literature, librarianship, and other subjects.[32]

Such a utopian screening and training program may seem
laughably impractical, but it underscores a critical point. Librarians and educators are not, either by training or often by temperament, prepared to be therapists. Despite their concern for their
charges' sometimes heavy problems, they ought to tread lightly. If
they choose to see themselves as agents for social and personal
change, they should examine their methods and expectations carefully. A class or story hour is not a therapy group. Far from
promoting mutual understanding, an adult may encourage children
to tease (and make scapegoats) peers whose problems have been
given public recognition. If a seemingly benign label is in fact a
stigma in disguise, then the damage is compounded.

Booklists, classing titles by problem areas, encourage this
labelling process. A good deal of attention needs to be paid to the
implicit content of these categories and the use to which they are
put. For example, one article on bibliotherapy suggests that teachers
keep card files on books, classified by problem, to be used for small
group discussions among children with that problem. Some suggested
categories: personal appearance, physical handicaps, siblings, acceptance by peer groups, unhappy home situations, economic insecurity, foreign or different backgrounds, and need for diversion.[33]
Many of these labels may apparently be applied with no knowledge of
the child and sensitivity to his or her feelings. What harm does
grouping together all the children the teacher feels have problems
with their personal appearances and then handing them books on
ugly or sloppy people do to their self-images? The labeling process
will dwarf any possible benefits of reading and discussion. To single
out "economic insecurity" and "foreign or different backgrounds" may

be class and race discrimination masking as therapy. Presumably,
only the neat, affluent, popular, middle-class Americans with happy
homes and all their faculties will be rewarded by membership in the
"need for diversion" group.

Similarly, an advocate of preventive bibliotherapy recommends
that teachers be "good teaching 'doctors'" by recognizing and treat-
ing characteristics that might not be causing problems yet, but have
that potential. Her categories include: fatness, plainness, harelip,
scar, poverty, and broken home. [34] One may well wonder what
kind of therapy it is to point out a scar, a plain face, or a poor
family to someone who doesn't consider it a problem.

Most writers agree that, for bibliotherapy to work, readers
must be free to choose their own books. However, an element of
coercion quickly creeps into discussions of how to promote appropriate selections. For example, "It is usually best for the child
himself incidentally to 'discover' the book."[35] Or "If books are
displayed or discussed so that the content is known, often a child
will choose to read a story about a child in a similar situation. If
this is not the case, then obviously your guidance is needed."[26]
Such guidance is in danger of becoming offensively heavy-handed.

One writer comments, "If the child is overweight, it is obvious that one shouldn't compound the problem by recognizing it and
making a comment such as 'Why don't you read this book? It is
about a fat person just like you.' The less said about the problem
the better.... The book need not be only about fat children but
could have illustrations which show a fat child as a member of a
group."[37]

Unfortunately, one man's kid glove is another man's sledge-
hammer. To sensitive children, the teacher's message will be clear
whether the medium is a picture of a fat kid or a book about one.
If the problem hasn't been brought up by the child, maybe it's the
teacher's hang-up. Or maybe the children have valid reasons to
want to read for escape from their problems.

The messages we expect books to communicate need close
examination. Much of what passes for bibliotherapy is thinly disguised preaching aimed at teaching children to behave the way adults
want them to. Children will quickly become wary of such judgemen-
tal biases. One example is: "If we can give children and young
people proper principles of conduct, we can alter their behavior and
make it more desirable. One of the best ways of altering their conduct is by implanting desirable ideas gained in books."[28] Bibliotherapy has been defined as "a technique for the development of
wholesome principles of conduct and the prevention of delinquency."[39]

Much of what passes for therapy seems in fact to be aimed
at instilling particular values. While it may be more difficult to
see the slant in writings that mirror contemporary views, it is easy
to see the loaded messages in discussions of bibliotherapy a genera-

tion ago. In an article written in 1940, bibliotherapy is seen as a
means of teaching teen-agers charm, grace, and (reading between
the lines) sexual restraint. "Such problems have been more adequately treated in books designed for girls than for boys, partly in
recognition of the fact that the girl must, probably, make more decisions in regard to behavior than boys."[40] Bibliotherapy programs
of the '50s frequently attempted to instill an appreciation of democ-
racy. An understanding of the dangers of drug and alcohol addiction,
a respect for ethnic diversity, a tolerance of the handicapped--these
are some of the goals of modern bibliotherapy programs. Laudable
as such goals may be, they are simply part of the traditional process of teaching social values in schools and should not be confused
with psychotherapy.

Often bibliotherapy is used not to introduce sensitive issues
but to avoid having to deal with them head on. The analogy to books
on the birds and bees is clear. Many of the subjects in modern
children's and young adult books--drugs, sex, child abuse, suicide
--are issues educators and parents don't feel comfortable talking
about directly, and decide that it is better that children be exposed
to these subjects through books than not at all. But books should
not be expected to carry too heavy a burden. Vicarious experiences
may give readers a profound insight into situations they have not
known first-hand. However, books should not be expected to resolve
every issue they bring up. A reader's interpretation may not fit the
intended moral. Intense feelings may be stirred up by reading rather than calmed. More questions may be raised than answered.

A recent piece of research illustrates the point. A Ph.D.
candidate from the University of Southern California spent eight
weeks in second- and third-grade classrooms reading and discussing
books dealing with school anxieties. At the end of the course of
bibliotherapy, the children were vocal in their complaints about
school and showing higher anxiety levels in tests than before the
experiment began. Parents and teachers protested to the principal.
[41] Perhaps the anticipated catharsis from reading did not take
place and anxieties were made worse by bibliotherapy. Perhaps, as
the researcher concluded, enough time was not spent in discussion.
It is also possible that the process of students verbalizing their complaints about school would have been anxiety reducing only if teachers and parents had been prepared to listen. In fact, the researcher
may have been giving her students false expectations by encouraging
them to fight a frustrating, losing battle. Before embarking on a
course of bibliotherapy, the would-be therapist must be prepared to
deal with such complex situations inside and outside the classroom.

Fear of the effects of reading sometimes makes writers on
bibliotherapy sound like enemies of the printed word. If there is
good reading for instilling good behavior, the logic goes, then there
must be bad reading too. For example, "The right kind of reading
may inculcate worthy ambitions and result in a healthy activity; the
wrong kind may lead to fantastic or unwholesome conceptions of reality."[42] Or "Caution must be exercised with some children ... to

guard against their withdrawing into a world of fantasy. "[43] A librarian in a VA hospital cautions against contact with harmful materials which tend to excite the patient's condition, [44] and a psy-
chiatrist speaks of "the hazards of the wrong kind of reading. "[45]
One writer goes so far as to recommend only factual material such
as "how to" books for disturbed children with whom follow-up discussion is not possible. [46]

Surely all of this goes against the thrust of a librarian's true
calling--to encourage reading and the proliferation of good books.
To see literature purely as a means to an end and not as something
intrinsically worthwhile erodes intellectual freedom. It is not the
place of librarians, psychiatrists, or anyone to protect people from
books.

It sometimes seems that advocates of bibliotherapy have abandoned their faith in the imagination altogether. Books about stutterers are prescribed for stutterers. [47] Publishers are exhorted to
provide more materials about the learning disabled for children with
such problems. [48] One author comments, "A physically handicapped
child from the slums would not relate to a story of a similarly handicapped child from a prosperous middle-class suburb. "[49] Can a
polio victim gain insight from the problems of a thalidomide child?
Can a fat kid sympathize with malnutrition?

Who can say what elements in a book are going to touch a
reader's deepest feelings? To be relevant to its reader, a book
need not be new as any reader of the classics will testify. The
ham-fisted use of books to mirror our own didactic purposes distorts
their artistic integrity.

By expecting too much of books, bibliotherapists may paradoxically be diminishing their importance. Books can provide pleasure and emotional release, bring about insights, and foster new un-
derstandings, but they are not a bad influence if they stir up violent
feelings. They do not fail if they cannot change a person's score on
a psychological test or change his or her behavior. In fact, it is a
credit to the human spirit that it resists such flagrant propagandiz-
ing.

Occasionally teachers and librarians can be a great emotional
support to the children they care about and who care about them.
Such a relationship is a gift to adult and child alike. But the emotional and social development of children is far too complex for many
educators to cope with, and certainly too complex to be left to books.
Bibliotherapy is a fashion of dubious value. Society will be better
served if it is forgotten and educators concentrated instead on good
books and good teaching.

References

1.   Thomas Szasz, The Myth of Psychotherapy (Garden City, N.Y.:
     Anchor Books, 1979), pp. 200-16.

2. Bibliotherapy in Hospitals: an Annotated Bibliography, 1900-1961 (Washington, D. C. : Veterans Administration, 1962). Cited in Fred McKinney, "Explorations in Bibliotherapy: Personal Involvement in Short Stories and Cases," Psychotherapy: Theory, Research and Practice 12, no. 1 (Spring 1975):110.
3. Corinne W. Riggs, comp., Bibliotherapy: an Annotated Bibliography (Newark, Del. : International Reading Assn., 1968).
4. William C. Menninger, "Bibliotherapy," Bulletin of the Menninger Clinic 1 (November 1937): 267-68. Cited in Margaret C. Hannigan, "The Librarian in Bibliotherapy: Pharmacist or Bibliotherapist?" Library Trends II (October 1962):187.
5. Caroline Shrodes, "Bibliotherapy: a Theoretical and Clinical-Experimental Study" (Ph. D. diss., University of California at Berkeley, 1949). Cited in David H. Russell and Caroline Shrodes, "Contributions of Research in Bibliotherapy to the Language Arts Program I," School Review (September 1950), p. 336.
6. David H. Russell, "Some Research on the Impact of Reading, English Journal 47 (October 1958):409.
7. Ibid., p. 404, 405.
8. David H. Russell, The Dynamics of Reading, ed. Robert B. Ruddell (Waltham, Mass. : Ginn-Blaisdell, 1970), p. 176.
9. McKinney, "Explorations in Bibliotherapy," p. 111.
10. Anne F. Marrelli, "Bibliotherapy and School Anxiety in Young Children," Dissertation Abstracts International 40, no. 4A: 1965.
11. Joy K. Roy, "Bibliotherapy: An Important Service to Self," English Journal (March 1979), pp. 57-62.
12. Orlo Strunk, "Bibliotherapy Revisited," Journal of Religion and Health 11 (July 1972):224.
13. Lester L. Tobias, "The Relative Effectiveness of Behavioristic Bibliotherapy versus Contingency Contracting and Suggestions of Self-Control in Weight Reduction," Dissertation Abstracts International 33, no. 10B:5028.
14. John R. Lickorish, "The Therapeutic Use of Literature," Psychotherapy: Therapy Research and Practice 12, no. 1 (Spring 1975):108.
15. Richard L. Darling, "Mental Hygiene and Books: Bibliotherapy as Used with Children and Adolescents," in Better Libraries Make Better Schools. Selected by Charles L. Trinkner (Hamden, Conn. : Shoe String Press, 1962), p. 299.
16. Joseph S. Zaccaria and Harold A. Moses, Principles and Practices of Bibliotherapy: a Resource Book for Teachers and Counselors (Champaign, Ill. : Stipes Publishing Co., 1968). David H. Russell and Caroline Shrodes, "Contributions of Research in Bibliotherapy to the Language Arts Program," School Review (September & October 1950), pp. 335-42, 411-20. Darling, "Mental Hygiene and Books." Sharon H. Sclabassi, "Literature as a Therapeutic Tool: a Review of the Literature on Bibliotherapy," American Journal of Psychotherapy 27 (1973):70-77.
17. Garold C. Barton, "The Effects of Bibliotherapy vs. Videotape

Feedback and Bibliotherapy on Problem Solving Behaviors and on Marital Conflict," Dissertation Abstracts International 38, no. 8A:5074.

Donna A. Beardsley, "The Effects of Using Fiction in Bibliotherapy to Alter Attitudes of Regular Third Grade Students toward Their Handicapped Peers," DAI 40, no. 9A:1980.

Claude E. Caffee, "Bibliotherapy: Its Effect on Self-Concept and Self-Actualization," DAI 36, no. 8A:5034-35.

Martha J. B. Cook, "Effect of Bibliotherapy on College Students as Revealed in Their Emotional Acceptance of Death and Dying," DAI 40, no. 2A:565.

Marelli, "Bibliotherapy and School Anxiety."

Peter M. Monti, "Effect of Social Skills Training Groups and Social Skills Bibliotherapy with Psychiatric Patients," Journal of Consulting Clinical Psychology 47 (February 1979):189-91.

Ella M. Shearon, "The Effects of Psychodrama Treatment on Professed and Inferred Self-Concepts of Selected Fourth Graders in Elementary School," DAI 36, no. 8A:5161-62.

Jacquelyn W. Stephens, "An Investigation into the Effectiveness of Bibliotherapy on the Reader's Self-Reliance," DAI 35, no. 4A:1971.

Gloria J. Templeton, "The Impact of the Culture of a Cottage in a Residential Treatment Center on the Implementation of a Bibliotherapy Program for Delinquent Girls," DAI 40, no. 8A:4505.

James D. White, "The Assessment of a Program in Bibliotherapy for Black Helpers," DAI 34, no. 2A:628.

18. Michael Baum, "The Short Term, Long Term and Differential Effects of Group vs. Bibliotherapy Relationship Enhancement Program for Couples," DAI 38, no. 12B:6132-33.

David G. Jarmon, "Differential Effectiveness of Rational-Emotive Therapy, Bibliotherapy and Attention Placebo in the Treatment of Speech Anxiety," DAI 33, no. 9B:4510.

Robert A. Muehleissen, "Reducing the Risk of Health Change Associated with Critical Life Stress," DAI 37, no. 6B:3088-89.

Anita L. Phinney, "Effects of Assertion Training and Bibliotherapy with Married Women," DAI 38, no. 6B:2879.

19. David L. Bass, "A Comparison of Eastern Bibliotherapy and Western Bibliotherapy on Counsellor Effectiveness," DAI 37, no. 11A:6947.

Cassandra J. McGovern. "The Relative Efficacy of Bibliotherapy and Assertion Training on Assertiveness Levels of a General Population and a Library Personnel Population," DAI 37, no. 11A:6954-55.

20. Charme S. Davidson, "Learned Internalization as a Treatment Strategy for Obesity in Women: a Comparative Analysis," DAI 39, no. 4B:1948-49.

Joyce Kanaan, "The Application of Adjuvant Bibliotherapeutic Techniques in Resolving Peer Acceptance Problems," DAI 36, no. 9A:5826.

James J. Quale, "The Effects of Bibliotherapy and Audio-Tape Treatments in Reduction of Test Anxiety among Clients Possessing Varying Degrees of Dogmatism," DAI 40, no. 32A: 1288.

Tobias, "Behavioristic Bibliotherapy vs. Contingency Contracting."

21. Richard D. Allen, "An Analysis of Two Forms of Assertiveness Training," DAI 39, no. 4A:2058.
John R. Dixon, "The Effects of Four Methods of Group Reading Therapy on the Level of Reading, Manifest Anxiety, Self-Concept, and School Personal-Social Adjustment among Fifth and Sixth Grade Children in a Central City Setting," DAI 35, no. 6A:3511-12.
Muehleissen, "Reducing Health Risk."
Eric B. Nesbitt, "Comparison of Two Measures of Assertiveness and the Modification of Non-Assertive Behaviors," DAI 38, no. 12A:7236.

22. William J. Lutz, Marriage Enrichment with and without Bibliotherapy," DAI 40, no. 2A:678.
Kent F. Mahoney, "The Effects of Adlerian Groups on the Authoritarian Child Rearing Practices of Parents," DAI 35, no. 7A:4161.

23. Esther R. Ongoa, "The Effect of Bibliotherapy through Listening in Reducing Fears of Young Children," DAI 40, no. 3A:1258.

24. Thomas R. Zentner, "Effects of Bibliotherapy and Level of Reading Ability on Self-Concept," DAI 35, no. 5B:2455-56.

25. Lewis R. Wolberg, The Technique of Psychotherapy, 3d ed. (New York: Grune & Stratton, 1977), pp. 50-67.

26. Psychiatric News, 21 March 1980, p. 4.

27. Patricia J. Ciancolo, "Interaction Between the Personality of the Reader and Literature," School Libraries (Spring 1968), p. 17.

28. Virgil M. Howes, "Guidance through Books," in Better Libraries Make Better Schools, p. 291.

29. Delwyn G. Schubert, "The Role of Bibliotherapy in Reading Instruction," Exceptional Children (April 1975), p. 498.

30. Ruth M. Tews, "Introduction," Library Trends 11 (October· 1962):98.

31. Evalene P. Jackson, "Bibliotherapy and Reading Guidance: a Tentative Approach to Theory," Library Trends 11 (October 1962):118.

32. Margaret M. Kinney, "The Bibliotherapy Program: Requirements for Training," Library Trends 11 (October 1962):127-35.

33. Henry O. Olsen, "Bibliotherapy to Help Children Solve Problems," Elementary School Journal (April 1975), pp. 423-29.

34. Matilda Bailey, "Therapeutic Reading," in Evelyn R. Robinson, ed., Readings about Children's Literature (New York: McKay, 1967), pp. 31-40.

35. Ibid., p. 33.

36. Terry Shepherd and Lynn B. Iles, "What is Bibliotherapy?" Language Arts 53 (May 1976):571.

37. Ibid., pp. 570-71.

38. T. V. Moore, "Bibliotherapy," Catholic Elementary School Library (Washington, D.C.: Catholic University of America Press, 1945). Quoted in Darling, "Mental Hygiene and Books," p. 295.

39. Clara J. Kircher, comp., Behavior Patterns in Children's Books:

a Bibliography (Washington, D. C. : Catholic University of
America Press, 1966), p. iii.
40. Willard A. Heaps, "Bibliotherapy and the School Librarian,"
Library Journal 1 (October 1940), p. 791.
41. Marelli, "Bibliotherapy and School Anxiety."
42. Beverly S. Edwards, "The Therapeutic Value of Reading," Elementary English 49 (March 1972):213.
43. Cheryl Corman, "Bibliotherapy--Insight for the Learning Handicapped," Language Arts 52 (October 1975):936.
44. Hannigan, "The Librarian in Bibliotherapy."
45. Ruth M. Tews, "Questionnaire on Bibliotherapy," Library Trends
11 (October 1962):221.
46. Sharon R. Morgan, "Bibliotherapy: a Broader Concept," Journal
of Clinical Child Psychology 5 (Fall 1976):42.
47. Schubert, "Bibliotherapy in Reading Instruction," p. 497.
48. Barbara E. Lenkowsky and Ronald S. Lenkowsky, "Bibliotherapy
for the LD Adolescent," Academic Therapy 14 no. 2 (November 1978):184.
49. Shepherd and Iles, "What is Bibliotherapy?" p. 571.

Part III

COMMUNICATION AND EDUCATION

CHILDREN'S SERVICE AND POWER:

KNOWLEDGE TO SHAPE THE FUTURE*

Pauline Wilson

Introduction

In a talk before the White House Conference on Library and Information Services held last November in Washington, D. C. , Canada's
deputy prime minister of communications, Bernard Ostry, had what
he termed friendly but "blunt" words for Americans. Among those
blunt words were these: "Canadians are not ... mere passive consumers of knowledge and culture packaged outside the borders by
purveyors who have no interest in their concerns and little or no
knowledge of their political, economic, and cultural identity."[1]
The purveyors referred to, of course, were Americans. [The term
Americans is used to refer to residents of the United States. It is
recognized that residents of all three Americas are Americans, but
residents of the United States have no other term for themselves;
they have never been called United Statesians.] Ostry's comments
were not without some historical precedent, for in the 1890s when
the children's reform movement got underway in Canada, one of its
goals was "to prevent poisonous literature ... from being imported
from the United States."[2] And apparently that is not the only poi-
son capable of being imported from the U. S. The late Donald Creighton, distinguished Canadian historian, was in the process of preparing an account of the corruption of Canadian speech patterns by "per-
nicious influences" from the United States when he died in December
1979. [3]

Professor Creighton was not alone in his dismay about our
language. An American historian, Christopher Lasch, recently
noted that the language of the "violent world of the ghetto ... now
pervades American society as a whole."[4] In any case, Americans
are not unmindful of their faults. Indeed, we never cease worrying
and talking about them. This paper will be no exception. However,
an effort to address complaints has been made in its preparation.

*Reprinted by permission of the author and publisher from Top of
the News, 37:2 (Winter 1981) 115-25. The article originally appeared
in the Canadian Library Journal, 37 (October 1980) 321-26. Copyright © 1980 by the Canadian Library Association and Pauline Wilson.

The result of that effort to learn about Canadian political, economic, and cultural identity was the realization that while Canada and the United States differ in many ways, they are, in other ways, similar. We have social problems in common that bear on our common problem with library service to children.

The Common Problem of Children's Service

Before considering those problems we first need to sketch the general outlines of our common predicament in children's service. The situation in both Canada and the United States is that children's service is thought, if not to be in actual decline, to be in ill health. There is evidence that too often children's service is understaffed and improperly staffed;[5] there is evidence that children's service may be underfunded. [6] Children's service has been termed a "high output-low input service," because its contribution to a library's productivity is thought to be proportionately higher than its support from the library's budget. [7] Another element in the problem is a decline in circulation from the children's room. This varies from library to library, but the circulation statistics for the United States as a whole show a decline from 52 percent of total public library loans in 1964 to 32 percent in 1976. [8] Yet another element of the problem can be seen in the fact that the wisdom of providing a separate children's room is being questioned, [9] and recently the Baltimore (Maryland) County Library began to experiment with what it terms a "generalist approach" to providing library service in branches. [10] This is library service without age-level specialists; a generalist staff serves all users alike regardless of age. Another unsettled question indicating some trouble is that of coordinators. The need for them is being questioned. [11]

In addition to such problems, there is the long-standing perception of children's librarians that historically, and today, children's service and the expertise of children's librarians are not appreciated by administrators and other librarians. [12] Children's librarians believe they are too often treated with friendly condescension. [13] The situation has been summed up by one writer who noted that children's service, which had been "one of the glories" of the public library, a "jewel in the crown of the local public library," may have become "tarnished," may have deteriorated over the years into a "tawdry and shopworn" piece of "costume jewelry. "[14]

That is the situation of children's service and our common predicament. How can it be remedied? For any profession there are two sources of power--organization and knowledge. [15] Knowledge is the subject of this paper. Undergirding the paper's point of view, but not discussed, are two postulates: it is postulated that children's librarians have too limited a view of the intellectual content of their field, thinking it to consist largely of knowing the content of a great many children's books. It is further postulated that this too-narrow view may lead to a lack of self-confidence, which in turn may hamper children's librarians in their relationship to

library administrators and other librarians.   The purpose of this
paper is to suggest that the intellectual scope of knowledge in children's service is larger than the content of children's books.   It
extends to knowledge of society and all of its concerns.   While granting that some criticism of children's service as the crown jewel of
the public library is justified, it will be suggested here that the
present situation is not primarily a case of tarnish on the jewel but
rather a case of tarnish on the setting in which the jewel is embedded.   Perhaps the jewel can help remove some of that tarnish from
its setting.

The Common Problems

The tarnish on our social setting, the economic, political, and cultural structures that make up our society, can be seen in an examination of some of our common problems.   To avoid misunderstanding, it is necessary first to state a caveat and to state the assumption on which the argument rests.   The caveat is that no statement
should be interpreted as implying the possibility of a return to some
golden age.   A true assessment of our limitations was well expressed
in the title of Thomas Wolfe's novel You Can't Go Home Again.   The
assumption underlying the argument is that we have some power over
the future, that the world is not totally deterministic.   There are
limitations, of course.   The library is only one agency that plays
a part in shaping our common life.   Others are the family, the
school, the economy, the government, and the media, to name a
few.   Each must do its part, but given that limitation, it is assumed
that we have at least some power to influence the course of events.
The power of knowledge with which this paper is concerned is knowledge needed to shape the future.

    Where are we now, Canada and the United States, on the road
to the future?   The first thing we might note is that Canada and the
United States have both reached a state wherein they are now referred
to as postindustrial. [16]   The significance of a postindustrial economy
is that such an economy rests on theoretical knowledge.   This high-
level abstract knowledge is needed to produce the continuing scientific and technological innovation that is the basis of our economies.
[17]   To produce that sort of knowledge requires persons with imagination, creativity, and intelligence, highly educated and trained
persons.   How are such persons developed?   Does one develop such
persons when they reach the age of eighteen or twenty-one, or must
their development begin in childhood?   Consider the question of language, which, as noted, has deteriorated.   Language is the thinking
tool, par excellence.   When a language becomes muddled, so do the
people using it.   Biologist Lewis Thomas has expressed it this way:
"Language is the mind actually working. "[18]   How does one acquire
language skill so that one can formulate ideas and express them?
Is such skill acquired when one is an adult or must the pattern be
set in childhood?   According to a Canadian educator, "By the time
students reach high school, any of their 'bad' reading and writing
habits are so ingrained as to be virtually irreversible in the normal

high school situation. Even remedial classes at that level in the
past have been of only marginal success. "[19] Acquisition of reading skills and a lifelong habit of reading have long been goals of
children's service, but do we really understand the relationship of
those important goals to the well-being of the larger society?

There is another aspect of children's acquiring the habit of
reading and the presumably related habit of library usage that we
need to understand better. At what age is the library-usage habit
formed? Adele Fasick and Claire England's study of the Regina,
Saskatchewan, Public Library produced some suggestive findings
that lead one to speculate that the library-use habit may be established at a very early age. [20] When the profile of the child library
users of the study is compared with the profile of adult users of the
public library, striking similarities are seen. Like adult library
users, child users not only read more books, they read more gen-
erally--more news stories and more sports stories in newspapers.
[21] Child users also had higher vocational aspirations than child nonusers, and this is analogous to the higher educational and vocational
attainments of adult users. [22] Child users, like adult users, belong
to more clubs. [23] That finding suggests that child users may grow up
to become community leaders as many adult users are. Child nonusers
seem to share characteristics of adult nonusers as well. The reasons
for not using the library given by child nonusers fall into the very same
category of socially acceptable excuses given by adult nonusers--no
time, no need, not interested. [24] In sum, the possibility that the
library-use habit is established early during childhood is a topic
worthy of further study, for it is highly relevant to all library service.

We have said that persons needed to create the theoretical
knowledge necessary in postindustrial society must be imaginative.
The development of imagination in children through literature has
long been a goal of children's service. An internationally known
Canadian scholar, Northrop Frye, has commented on its importance:
"... imagination is what man constructs with; and therefore human
society is essentially an imaginative construct, and it is by imagination that man participates in society. Consequently a training of the
imagination, particularly through literature, is the central means of
understanding of one's own social role. "[25] Children's librarians
understand the role of literature in developing imagination, but that
understanding could be buttressed with further understanding of the
place of imagination in such practical and popular concerns as the
economy. This would help children's librarians interpret their service to others, perhaps to library administrators who, upon reading
the Fasick and England study and finding that children borrowed
three times as much fiction as nonfiction, might conclude that children's service was frivolous--mere entertainment. [26] Such erroneous conclusions or assumptions need to be corrected effectively and
authoritatively.

Moving on to other areas of our life that are relevant to children's service, we can note the presence of disturbing social problems. We both have problems with youth. Canadian youth have been

termed "rude, arrogant, supercilious--a pleasure seeking 'now' generation"--both "ignorant" and "lazy."[27] Those are terms used by
a Canadian but they have been applied equally to American youth by
Americans.

In both our countries also there is a concern for the values
we hold in common, the value system that motivates and molds our
behavior. In the United States it appears that we are no longer certain that we have a common value system. In Canada concern for
moral values is manifest in the human-values education programs in
the schools.[28] A Canadian educator has noted, however, that
"moral education will make sense to youth only when the wider society demonstrates a higher degree of morality itself."[29] And an
American children's librarian, commenting on moral values, observed
that "children value what adults value, accept what adults accept,
discard what adults discard."[30]

Another problem we share is drug abuse and alcoholism.
This problem is evidenced in Canada by alcohol and drug education
programs in the schools and by a recent report that estimated there
are one million current users of marijuana below the age of eighteen
in Canada.[31] It is estimated that a decade-long attempt to regulate
the use of this substance has cost Canadians $400 million.[32]

Urban decay with its accompanying crime and violence is
another problem we have in common. The United States is further
along in this process. Our urban crisis, in fact, presents an example of a process that Canadian urban planners are attempting to
prevent in Canada.[33] Nevertheless, trouble is visible, especially
in the larger cities such as Toronto, Montreal, and Vancouver.
"Paki-busting," acts of violence against immigrants from Pakistan
and other East Asian countries, occurs. In some cities, blacks
have been attacked and their homes vandalized. Signs reading Keep
Canada White have appeared.[34] In Winnipeg the influx of native
people to the city apparently is contributing to the growth of an urban ghetto. It has been reported that Main Street in Winnipeg is a
familiar scene--"It could be the main street in the dying downtown
of any northern American industrial city."[35] In any event, it seems
clear that in both our countries we are having difficulty getting along
with one another, not only in the case of urban racial groups but in
other areas of our common life in which groups interact. Canada
has declared itself to be a multicultural country, while in the United
States we say we have pluralism.[36] In the United States, however,
we have single-issue groups of every kind, each determined that its
demands be met without thought or care for the commonweal. Consequently, our pluralism is beginning more nearly to resemble the
Hobbesian condition--a war of all against all.[37]

There is yet another problem we share, and that is education.
Both countries have experienced a decline in educational standards
in our public schools. Children and youth are learning less; in the
United States our national Scholastic Aptitude Test (SAT) scores have
fallen steadily for two decades.[38] In both our countries the decline

in educational achievement has led to a demand to go back to the basics. [39] A final, and related, problem we have in common is illiteracy--that prison in which too many of our people are trapped. Recently the National Assessment of Educational Progress reported that adult reading skills in the United States had declined over a six-year period, 1970-77. [40] And, perhaps most significant, the greatest decline has been in skills of interpretation and inference, that is, the skills that indicate whether you can learn or are learning anything from what you read. Can you use your reading to think and to understand or is it simply a mechanical processing of words? Canadian and American librarians have begun to address the problem of illiteracy. [41] In these efforts we must never forget the crucial importance of language for the human being. Enough examples have now been cited to demonstrate that the setting in which the jewel-- children's service--is embedded is showing a bad case of tarnish. What caused it? What can be done about it?

The causes of the tarnish surely are multiple and complex. [42] We will consider only one possible contributing factor. It is a factor on which children's librarians conceivably might have some influence, for it is highly relevant to children's service. It is the change in communication, specifically, the advent of the electronic medium of television. It was a Canadian--a true prophet if ever there was one --who first alerted us to the power of that mediated visual medium. Marshall McLuhan did that when he observed more than a decade ago that the medium is the message. At that time most of us did not understand the meaning of his observation. In fact, many librarians hailed it as the dawning of a bright new day. It would free us from our stereotype of keepers of musty, dusty books, free us from that classic image so long endured--print-oriented, bespectacled, gum- shoed old maid. Today, however, we are just beginning to under- stand the possible ramifications of this new medium, just beginning to get some research evidence that causes an alarm to ring. Re- search being done at Harvard University is producing some interest- ing findings. [43] Two groups of children were exposed to a televi- sion version and a book version of a children's story. Subsequently, their recall and reactions were compared. They were different. The book children were able to recall information given in the story as well as figures of speech and precise wording that were used. The television children, on the other hand, were less able to recall verbal information given in the film, and even when they could recall it they tended to paraphrase it. They did not recall precise word- ing and figures of speech. [44] At the least, that finding suggests that language enrichment was more apt to occur with the book chil- dren. Another finding was that the reasoning process by which the two groups of children made inferences from the stories were dif- ferent. The book children tested what they had seen by relating it to their personal experience and to their knowledge of the world; in other words, they tested it against reality. The television children relied almost wholly on the visual image for inference. They judged on the basis of how a person looked on the screen, facial expression, for example. They did not test their inferences against the reality of their own experience or their knowledge of the world. [45] If one

could rely upon the expression on a face, the game of poker would
not long endure nor would actors have employment.   Recalling to
mind the finding of the National Assessment of Educational Progress,
that the ability of adults to interpret and made inferences from their
reading has declined, causes one to wonder if there is not a connection between the findings of these two studies; to wonder if both are
not related to the electronic medium.   One thing is clear: we need
better understanding of the differences between the media, their limitations, and their possible long-term effects.

Many persons have expressed concern about the possibly
harmful effects of television.   Most of the concern has been about
violence and sex.   One person who has expressed concern is Lasch,
in his book The Culture of Narcissism.   His concern is not violence
and sex, but it may be of more fundamental importance than either.
According to Lasch's analysis, one harmful effect of a mediated electronic medium is that it "undermines our sense of reality."[46] This
comes about because instead of real events we daily consume great
quantities of pseudo events, mediated events.   Eventually our capacity to separate image from reality is eroded.[47] A related result,
Lasch contends, is the creation of a "cynical awareness of illusion"
in children that may lead to an inability "to take any interest in anything outside the self."[48]   This awareness of illusion is fed by con-
tinual exposure to television "spectacles."   The child becomes im-
pervious to surprise, cool and detached, jaded.   It might be said the
child is robbed of its capacity for wonder and its capacity to empa-
thize imaginatively with others.   Lasch illustrates this with an account of a modern child's indifference to an event that formerly
elicited wonder in most children: "... at the circus ... she leaned
back on her padded seat, my four-year-old ... anticipating pratfalls,
toughly, smartly, sadly, wisely, agedly, unenthralled, more wrapped
up in the cotton candy than in the Greatest Show on Earth."[49]
Children's librarians apparently have had similar experiences with
children, as can be seen in a chilling little poem titled "Children
in the Library":[50]

> Children in the library
> stand no longer by your knee.
> Children turning page on page
> are not children, have no age.
> Have no heed, no hand to take;
> go at will, with whom they like.
> ....
> ....
> ....
> Children, children, gone for good
> into the world, into wood.
> ....

What are we to make of this apparent change in children?
What do we understand childhood to be today?   What do we want
it to be?   These are questions of importance for children's librarians, and to answer them will require knowledge.   Childhood, as

we have known it in the twentieth century, did not mature as a concept until the nineteenth century.[51] Childhood thus is a relatively modern concept and that concept is changing. Consider the change in child care. Today the care of children is being franchised in the same manner as McDonald's hamburgers. Child care is now referred to as a "growth industry." Kinder-Care Learning Centers is the largest of the chains in the United States, with 500 branches in 300 cities, and Kinder-Care has just acquired Mini-Skools, a Canadian chain of 88 centers. Gerber Products, manufacturers of baby food, has entered the business also with 30 centers.[52] What will be the effect of this change on children? What will be the effect on mothers? Will the role of mother become that of mere incubator? In a world already dangerously overpopulated, the need for more incubators can be questioned. Children's librarians need to understand why this type of change occurs, understand how social conditions alter the very concept of what a child is. They need that knowledge not only to evaluate more carefully the possibly differing effects of the media but also to evaluate prescriptions for the improvement of childhood that are periodically put forth by one or another well-meaning group.

Every prescription of what childhood ought to be rests on an assumption of what human society ought to be--socially, politically, and economically. These assumptions need to be examined. This can be illustrated with a study done at Simon Fraser University, Burnaby, British Columbia.[53] The Study is a content analysis of two series of readers used in the primary grades in British Columbia.

The overall conclusion of the study was that the world depicted in the stories contained in these readers was to be deplored and should be replaced. It was a world made up of dominance. People dominated animals, parents dominated children, males dominated females. In short, as interpreted by the researchers, it was a world of hierarchy and ranking, a world of inferiors and superiors, of subordination and superordination.[54] The prescription to cure this alleged malady of differentiation and hierarchy was to make everyone equal--banish all hierarchy. That seems fine at first glance. But we must ask, What is the price and do we want to pay it? A possible high price not addressed in the study is the fundamental question of how the human being, the child in our context, achieves personal identity. The differing roles and hierarchies deplored in the study may serve an important purpose. Without such differentiation it may be impossible for the human being to achieve a sense of self-identity.

In Canada and the United States, we have always had private identities, we have always been individual persons. We have never been simply undifferentiated members of groups. Are we in the process of changing that? Marshall McLuhan thought so. In his predictions for the 1980s he predicted that private identity will be replaced with group identity.[55] And he noted that "when people feel a threat to their identity ... they become very anxious and

even violent."[56] Perhaps we will want to replace private identity
with group identity, perhaps not. But either way, we need to know
what we are doing when we prescribe for the child. We need to
have at least some notion of what the consequences of our prescription might be, its social, political, and economic consequences; we
need to know what kind of world we may be helping to bring into
being.

We have a common saying that we take entirely for granted
and from which we take comfort. We say blandly, confidently,
"Children are our hope for the future." Are they? Are we making
that possible? Perhaps children's librarians can help make it possible through deeper understanding and revitalization of their historic
mission and through deeper understanding of the consequences of
social change and its meaning for childhood. With many aspects of
our society showing strain and instability, there is no service in the
public library more important than children's service. It is the
base upon which future library usage depends. If it is to contribute
to solving our common problems, resources will be needed to
strengthen it. One resource is knowledge. If well-equipped with
knowledge, children's service can help shape the future--the jewel
can help remove tarnish from its setting.

References

1. John Berry and others, "Cadres for the Library Future," Li-
    brary Journal 15:156 (15 Jan. 1980).
2. Neil Sutherland, Children in English-Canadian Society: Fram-
    ing the Twentieth Century Consensus (Toronto: Univ. of
    Toronto Pr., 1976), p. 19.
3. Peter C. Newman, "The Man of History," Macleans 93, no. 1:18
    (7 Jan. 1980).
4. Christopher Lasch, The Culture of Narcissism: American Life
    in an Age of Diminishing Expectations (New York: Warner
    Books, 1979), p. 128-29.
5. Mae Benne, The Central Children's Library in Metropolitan
    Public Libraries (Seattle, Wash.: School of Librarianship,
    Univ. of Washington, 1977), p. 15, 33, 45: Michael Wessells
    and others, A Survey of Children's Services in Ohio Public
    Libraries. 1979 (Columbus, Ohio: Ohio Library Association,
    1979), p. 30-31; Barbara Rollock, "Services of Large Public
    Libraries," in Selma K. Richardson, ed., Children's Services
    of Public Libraries (Champaign-Urbana, Ill.: Graduate
    School of Library Science, Univ. of Illinois, 1978), p. 92,
    95; Judith A. Drescher, "What's the Picture? The Library
    Administrator and Children's Services," Illinois Libraries
    58:784 (Dec. 1976).
6. Benne, Central Children's Library, p. 34; Wessells, A Survey
    of Children's Services, p. 13.
7. Wessells, A Survey of Children's Services, p. 8.
8. Herbert Goldhor, "Summary," in Selma K. Richardson, ed.,

Children's Services of Public Libraries, (Champaign-Urbana, Ill.: Graduate School of Library Science, Univ. of Illinois, 1978), p. 168.

9. Crystal M. Bailey, "Response," in George S. Bonn and Sylvia Fabisoff, eds., Changing Times; Changing Libraries (Champaign-Urbana, Ill.: Graduate School of Library Science, Univ. of Illinois, 1978), p. 127.
10. Cornelia Ives, "One County's View of Library Service without Age-Level Specialists," American Libraries 11:205-6 (April 1980).
11. Benne, Central Children's Library, p. 17-24. See also "Report of the Co-Ordinators of Children's Services of the Large Public Libraries in Canada," mimeographed (n. d.): Rollock, "Services of Large Public Libraries," p. 92.
12. Margo Sassé, "The Children's Librarian in America," Library Journal 98:213-17 (15 Jan. 1973).
13. So common is this perception that the three following examples appeared in one issue, Illinois Libraries 58 (Dec. 1976): Jane A. McGregor, "Leadership in the Library Profession," p. 815; Tamiye Trejo, "Planning in Concert," p. 820; Leslie Edmonds, "Babes in Library Land: Where We Are and What to Do about It," p. 826.
14. F. William Summers, "What You Want the Future to Be ... Children's Services and Library Administrators," School Library Journal 24:80 (Oct. 1977).
15. Philip Elliott, The Sociology of the Professions (New York: Herder & Herder, 1972), p. 144.
16. U. S. Department of State, Background Notes--Canada (Pubn. 7769, Oct. 1979), p. 5-6.
17. Daniel Bell, The Coming of Post-Industrial Society (New York: Basic Books, 1973), p. 14-15, 20-21, 26. The concept of postindustrial society has been challenged recently by sociologist Amitai Etzioni. He believes it will not last because we will be unable to afford the many service enterprises characteristic of such a society. We will return to being industrial. See Amitai Etzioni, "In Future: Who Killed Postindustrial Society?" Next 1:20 (March-April 1980).
18. Timothy Ferris, "Hopeful Prophet Who Speaks for Human Aspiration," Smithsonian 11:136 (April 1980).
19. Jim Foulds, "You Can't Go Home Again," Interchange 7, no. 4:11 (1976-77).
20. Adele M. Fasick and Claire England, Children Using Media (Regina, Saskatchewan: Regina Public Library, 1977), p. 1.
21. Ibid., p. 19.
22. Ibid., p. 21.
23. Ibid., p. 8.
24. Ibid., p. 26.
25. Northrop Frye, p. 35.
26. Fasick and England, Children Using Media, p. 1.
27. N. V. Scarfe, "Can You Teach Hostile Students?" Education Canada 14, no. 2:22-23 (June 1974).
28. Brian Burnham, "Human Values Education," Education Canada

15, no. 1:4-10 (Spring 1975); Tom R. Williams, "Our Value
Dilemma, " Education Canada 14, no. 3:10-15 (Sept. 1974).
29. W. Gordon West, "Adolescent Deviance and the School, " Interchange 6, no. 2:54 (1975).
30. Spencer G. Shaw, "The Children's Librarian as Viewed by Library School Educators, " in Selma K. Richardson, ed. , Children's Services of Public Libraries (Champaign-Urbana, Ill. :
Graduate School of Library Science, Univ. of Illinois, 1978),
p. 38.
31. Gerald J. Kleisinger, "Alcohol and Drug Education: Improvement Needed?" Education Canada 18, no. 4:54-58 (Winter
1978).
32. C. Michael Bryan, "Cannabis in Canada--A Decade of Indeci-
sion, " Contemporary Drug Problems 8, no. 2:169, 188 (Summer 1979).
33. John G. Corbett, "Canadian Cities: How 'American' Are They?"
Urban Affairs Quarterly 13:384 (March 1978).
34. K. M. Chrysler, "Canada Has Second Thoughts about Its Open
Door to Immigrants, " U.S. News & World Report, 3 Oct.
1977, p. 60.
35. Peter Carlyle-Gordge, "Wasteland ... Canada: Our Own Urban
Ghetto, " Macleans 27:54 (Nov. 1978).
36. Mary Ashworth, "The Education of Immigrant Children in Canada, " English Language Teaching Journal 31, no. 4:266 (July
1977).
37. That our national life resembles a war of all against all has
been noted by more than one commentator. See Lasch,
Culture of Narcissism, p. 102, 122, 127, 132. Lasch does
not liken the Hobbesian state to pluralism as I have done.
For a discussion of the future of pluralism see E. J. Mi-
shan, The Economic Growth Debate (London: Allen & Unwin,
1977), p. 62. For a popular cogent comment see A. J. Vogl,
"Conversations: Bill Moyers, " Next 1:22-24 (March-April
1980).
38. Education USA 19, no. 52:377 (29 Aug. 1977). The scores fell
again in 1978-79.
39. Carl Bognar and others, "Back to the Basics--An Introductory
Survey, " Interchange 7, no. 4:1-17 (1976-77).
40. Education USA 22, no. 27:202 (3 March 1980).
41. Gwen Liu, "Literacy News, " Ontario Library Review, Sept.
1979, p. 214; Ann Makletzoff, "Literacy in Ontario, " Ontario
Library Review, June 1978, p. 119-23.
42. See Lasch, Culture of Narcissism, p. 74, for a summary of
the major reasons. The entire book is an analysis of the
reasons Lasch thinks most important.
43. Howard Gardner, "Programming the Media Researchers, "
Psychology Today 13, no. 8:12 (Jan. 1980). Other important
research on the effect of television on children is being done
at Yale University: Jerome L. Singer and Dorothy G. Singer,
"Come Back, Mister Rogers, Come Back, " Psychology Today
12, no. 10:56, 59-60 (March 1979).
44. Gardner, "Programming the Media Researchers, " p. 12-13.
45. Ibid.

46. Lasch, Culture of Narcissism, p. 97.
47. Ibid., p. 96-98 and throughout.
48. Ibid., p. 159-60.
49. Ibid., p. 159.
50. Norma Farber, "Children in the Library," Horn Book, June 1976, p. 269.
51. Philippe Ariès, Centuries of Childhood (New York: Vintage Books, 1962), p. 10 and throughout.
52. "Growth Industry," Parade 13:6 (April 1980).
53. Rowland Lorimer and others, "Consider Content: An Analysis of Two 'Canadian' Primary Language Arts Reading Series," Interchange 8, no. 4:64-75 (1977-78).
54. Ibid.
55. Marshall McLuhan, "Living at the Speed of Light," Macleans 93, no. 1:32-33 (7 Jan. 1980).
56. Ibid., p. 32.

THE WILL TO SURVIVE*

Marilyn L. Miller

American librarianship is at a turning point. Libraries face the
pressures of changing clientele, accountability, budgetary restraints,
inflation, expensive technology, and censorship. Children's librarianship has been neither better nor worse than the rest of the profession in coping with these matters. Unlike its counterparts, however, it faces an additional challenge: assuring children access to
the resources, staff, and facilities they need. Failure to meet this
challenge will lead children's librarianship into a crisis state.

        Problems of access for children loom large because young-
sters depend on adult advocates and lack mobility and voting power.
In the January 1981 issue of Library Quarterly, Lillian Gerhardt
provides a timely case study of the Prince George's County (Md.)
Memorial Public Library's efforts to assure total access to children.
[1] Such reports raise questions that the entire library profession
should consider: Where will children get resources? What kinds
will be available and accessible? What resources do children want
and need? Who will assist youngsters in locating, retrieving, and
using them?

Just when we felt it was safe ...

Such questions began arising just when many children's librarians
thought they had reached the base level of providing the necessities
in public and school libraries and could devote their attention to improved service. The direction public library service to children
has taken has resulted from changes in the school library system
nationwide. The mid-1970s saw the burgeoning of thousands of elementary school libraries that were well designed, attractive, amply
equipped, stocked with a variety of resources, and administered by
certified school library media specialists. Complementing the developing national school library system were public library children's
departments that were visually pleasing, well stocked, staffed, and
free from decades of being the community's only source of organized

*Reprinted by permission of the American Library Association and
the author from American Libraries, 12:6 (June 1981) 369-72.
Copyright © 1981 by Marilyn L. Miller.

library service and programs for children.   However, instead of
being able to move ahead in the '80s, librarians began facing retrenchment in school libraries and developing new patterns for serving children in public ones.   Furthermore, the new patterns began
evolving on the erroneous assumption that school libraries with adequate personnel and quality programs guaranteeing access existed
nationwide.

Today, retrenchment is either stopping school library development in many areas, particularly at the elementary level, or producing ravaging cuts in adequately staffed programs with ample materials budgets and good facilities.   It is causing cuts in positions held
by young, recently educated school librarians who have been trained
to act simultaneously as media specialists, instructional designers,
and team teachers.   Retrenchment also is resulting in the critical
loss of district-level school library coordinators and state-level
school library and instructional media personnel.   These professionals were largely responsible for the success of school library programs of the '70s.   They developed state standards for school libraries, upgraded certification and accreditation standards, and created inservice education programs for media staffs, classroom teachers, and administrators.   Their work in interpreting the role of the
school library media program to boards of education, community
leaders, and colleagues has yet to be adequately credited.   Many
district and state school library coordinators are now losing their
jobs simply because they have the least seniority in their departments.   Children's librarians will miss them as the movement toward increased use of communications technology in instructional
programs continues.

Two examples illustrate the seriousness of these developments.
An $800,000 budget cut recently devastated the Michigan State Library,
which had to pare staff using the "last hired, first fired" principle.
As a result, Michigan, long a pioneer in school library media and
instructional technology, will have no state leadership in these areas
without help from institutions of higher education and the state school
library media association.   In Connecticut, 275 of the state's 715
elementary schools now have no professional library services, and
220 have only a half-time or less certified staffer.   Many of these
schools are located in rural areas with little or no access to public
libraries.

Fast-food for young minds

Turning points in public library service to children seem to revolve
around three factors: use of the generalist approach in providing
library service; the changing status of the central children's library;
and developing school/public library cooperative relationships.

In the Spring 1981 Top of the News, Margaret Kimmel discusses the generalist approach of one urban library.[2] She describes
implications of the philosophy that regardless of differing creative

abilities, interests, attitudes, and special knowledge, public librarians can serve all clients equally well.   This attitude can be discon-
certing to children's librarians, who always have seen themselves
at the heart of youngsters' education within the library.   Kimmel
says the generalist approach confuses providing information with education.   It thus muddles the traditional view of children's librarianship as an opportunity to assist youngsters in using, interpreting,
and restructuring learning with new information and creative literature.

Kimmel also questions the benefit of acquisitions policies in
which demand vies with quality: the purchasing, for example, of
more than 300 copies of a popular book but only six copies of a
special, high-quality work.   Such policies contradict what children's
librarians believe about youngsters and what they have learned through
experience about library materials, services, and programming.
For this author, they raise the question, "Do we really want our
public libraries to become the fast-food chains of the mind?"

Branches in sharper focus?

Historically, children's rooms and staffs of large-city public libraries have been the national trend setters for collection development,
programming, and services for children.   Changes in the status and
influence of these libraries are documented in a fine study by Mae
Benne.[3]   The changing perception of the role of the central children's library is evident in Lowell Martin's recent recommendations
for the Philadelphia Free Library (AL, March 1981, pp.118-19).
Martin suggests branch libraries serve as youth agencies employing
children's and young adult librarians.   He recommends that each
branch enlarge its collection to serve youngsters up to age 15, increasing the traditional service age to children by one year.   In
Martin's plan, the branches would maintain their heavy emphasis on
preschool programs.   The central children's room would feature
reference and research collections and would no longer circulate materials.   Martin suggests continued cooperation with schools, but he
believes the public library should no longer purchase materials for
school assignments.   Recommendations such as these will have a
definite effect upon the future of children's librarianship and youngsters' ability to access materials.

Other turning points in children's librarianship are the trends
toward networking, multitype library cooperation, resource sharing,
and in some areas, school-based public library service.   Such movements may help eradicate barriers children now face in accessing
library materials, such as discrimination by those who believe service to adults is more important than service to youth.

In the past five years, public library administrators, educators, and children's librarians have attempted to define the competencies needed for serving children in public libraries.   The librarians have been criticized thoroughly for concentrating too much on

children's literature, for lacking knowledge of evaluation and research techniques, for not possessing management skills, and for not knowing enough about child development.

Defining children's librarian

A study underway by Julie Todaro of the University of Michigan library school will be helpful in deciding what the field expects of the children's librarian. It will poll children's librarians and their coordinators, public library directors and personnel officers, and library educators on the desirability of various competencies for librarians working with young people. The results should be especially helpful to library schools.

How can children's librarians help guide children's services in this era of change? One way to begin is through self-education --including study of the professional literature for current developments and trends. Children's librarians must extend their knowledge of many aspects of management, automation, and information science. They must broaden their expertise on the role books play in the development of children's cognitive and affective abilities. Children's librarians also must learn to plan more effective programs, such as those that help preschoolers develop their psychomotor skills.

Self-educators might benefit from reading Dorothy Butler's Cushla and Her Books [4] or the December 1980 Illinois Libraries. The former describes the work of parents who used books to implement developmental theories of Piaget, Bruner, Gesell, and others, thereby motivating their mentally retarded baby. The latter, devoted to learning about children, features excellent articles by a variety of specialists in child growth and development, education, and librarianship. The proliferating books on developing materials and techniques for the gifted child also can be useful. Many of their suggestions can be adapted to materials and programming for all youngsters.

With the current emphasis on continuing education in librarianship, children's librarians have ample opportunity to extend their knowledge in management or information science each year. Courses in child psychology, child growth and development, and learning theory also are available at most colleges and universities. The Association for Library Service to Children offers educational programs, such as an all-day workshop on management at ALA's 1981 San Francisco conference.

As individuals, children's librarians must become more involved in local and state library developments, for there is strength in sharing. As travel expenses increase and fewer can make ALA conferences an annual affair, state conference programming will become increasingly important.

The library school dilemma

Within their state and national associations, children's librarians
must exert pressure for examination of library school curricula
and recommended programs that prepare children's library specialists. An analysis of current library school catalogs shows that all
ALA accredited schools in the United States offer classes in the selection of children's and young adult materials. Many also have
courses covering storytelling, the history of children's literature,
and programming. But 72 percent do not have specialized courses
for youth-services librarians in subjects such as public relations,
grantseeking, staff development, networking, and interlibrary cooperation. These same schools have required or strongly recommended specialized courses beyond the core and introductory levels
in other areas of library service. Why not for children's services?

Management courses miss

Library school curriculum committees should take a close look at
the content of introductory-level management and public library administration courses for generalists and future administrators who
will eventually develop, support, and evaluate children's services.
Who teaches these courses? What are the sources of the readings
and examples they use? Who are the visiting lecturers? What are
the sites for field trips? A good theoretical approach to management is available in most library schools, but the opportunities for
application are missing, along with the chance to develop the subtle-
ties and intricacies of designing, developing, implementing, and
evaluating programs for public library children's specialists. Children's librarians should be lobbying ALA's Committee on Accreditation and library schools to remedy this situation.

The public children's library field also needs to continue
developing a research base. Although children's librarians can use
research findings from a variety of fields, the volume of specialized
research in their field by library school faculty members and doc-
toral students is slim and focused on children's literature. Practitioners can take up the slack by becoming skilled in research and
evaluation and applying the results to library problems.

As children's librarians participate in their state library associations and ALA, they should encourage and support cooperative
efforts among the Association for Library Service to Children, the
Young Adult Services Division, and the American Association of
School Librarians. These divisions must have committees gathering
data, developing case studies, proposing experiments, supporting
research, and exerting political pressure. Together, ALSC, YASD,
and AASL represent a sizable proportion of ALA.

Divisional councilors will further gains for youth services
within the association. Those representing young people's divisions

already have demonstrated their persuasive abilities. At the 1981 Midwinter Meeting, they actively explained their positions to council members. To maximize their influence, perhaps the three youth divisions should begin taking a stand on ALA presidential candidates.

Children's librarianship is historically and currently a vital part of our profession. Patterns of service must and will change as society changes. To lead the way, children's specialists should be articulate, knowledgeable, and caring individuals who know their field. They must be able to enter the political arena of professional associations and work for change both there and in their own communities.

References

1. Lillian N. Gerhardt, "Children's Access to Public Library Services: Prince George's County Memorial Public Library, Maryland, 1980," The Library Quarterly, 51, Jan. 1981, 20-37.
2. Margaret Kimmel, "Baltimore County Public Library: A Generalist Approach," Top of the News, 37, Spring 1981.
3. Mae Benne, The Central Children's Library in Metropolitan Public Libraries, School of Librarianship, University of Washington, Seattle, 1977.
4. Dorothy Butler, Cushla and Her Books, Boston, The Horn Book, Inc., 1980.

PARENTS AND STUDENTS COMMUNICATE THROUGH LITERATURE*

Pat Scales

Too many parents express interest only when they disapprove of
books their children read. Few of them ever communicate a genuine excitement for the reading experience. This fact is evidenced
by the increasing number of censorship cases and declining reading
scores among the students in this nation.

Educators are certainly alert to these existing problems, but
the numerous strategies for solving them can be questioned. Public
demand has forced a greater emphasis on the teaching of reading
skills; therefore, books are used primarily in the instructional process. Yet, opportunities to stress recreational reading are often
neglected because of individual and societal biases, teacher accountability, and a limited knowledge of the literature.

Because today's parents have less time to spend with their
children, reading is not a top priority in many homes. Even parents who have enjoyed books with their preschoolers tend to lose
interest once their children begin to read independently.

Adult Fears

When children reach their "middle years" and individual interests
emerge and reading choices change, parents who appear uninterested
in their children's reading habits may only be frightened because of
their restricted knowledge of the literature. They remember from
their own childhood ardently collecting the Hardy Boys, Nancy Drew,
and the Bobbsey Twins, and though such series have survived the
years, children today are more interested in reading the humor of
Beverly Cleary, the mysteries of John Bellairs, and the fantasies
of Lloyd Alexander.

Adults confront an even greater misunderstanding concerning
the reading needs of young people in contemporary adolescent literature. Don't Slam the Door When You Go, Early Disorder, Killing

*Reprinted by permission of the author and publisher from Voice
of Youth Advocates, 4:2 (June 1981) 9-11. P.O. Box 6569, University, AL 35486.

Mr. Griffin, Are You in the House Alone?, About David, and Love Is a Missing Person are titles which evoke attention from both adults and young adults. Unfortunately, while the young are reading and discussing the books, adults are only reading the blurbs. They read words such as rape, pregnancy, abortion, drugs, suicide, and divorce, and they rush to schools, libraries, and book stores to complain about the literature their children are reading.

They want to protect their children from the mores of a changing society and teach them that all of their hopes and dreams will be fulfilled. Mothers have fond memories of Betty Cavanna's Going on Sixteen and Maureen Daly's Seventeenth Summer, and they expect their daughters to flock to these titles with the same enthusiasm. Dads are anxious to share The Deerslayer, Huckleberry Finn, and Robinson Crusoe, while grandparents proudly present leather-bound editions of Alcott, Brontë, and Dickens.

Attempts to share such reading experiences are certainly based on good intentions, but today's youth are more concerned with the pressures of their own world. They are willing to discuss the books they are reading, but they want to talk with open-minded adults who share their concerns.

The Issues

The issues are crucial. Are current reading programs in public schools effective for developing positive attitudes toward reading? Are educators concerned enough for the reading direction of the young to initiate programs that will stress the values of adolescent literature to parents?

Such issues have been carefully evaluated by the faculty and staff at Greenville Middle School (Greenville, SC), and the results have produced new designs in the reading curriculum. The reading program at this middle school is centered upon one premise--that the more students read, the better they read. Germane to this philosophy is the belief that faculty, students and parents must share reading experiences in order to achieve the ultimate goal of developing good, life-long reading habits.

The Program

Once a month parents are invited to the school's library for a special program planned by the librarian. Entitled "Communicate Through Literature," the four-year-old program has three primary objectives: (1) to develop positive communication between parents and their children through the use of literature; (2) to encourage a better relationship between the school and community by involving the parents in the school program, and (3) to create a supportive atmosphere for intellectual freedom by providing parents with the opportunity to study and analyze young adult literature.

Discussions concerning reading interest of young adults, special needs of the reluctant reader, and the importance of reading
together as a family challenge parents to make reading a major part
of their home environment. Efforts are made to identify and analyze
the unique personal needs of the adolescent, and parents are encouraged to relate these needs to their children's reading choices.

The meetings are held at 10:00 a. m. while students and
teachers proceed with their library activities. Parents see the library at maximum use, and students are fascinated by their parents'
discussions. Library cards are issued to parents, and they are
urged to use the library collection at any time. Immediately following the monthly meeting, they browse among the shelves and seek
reading suggestions from observing students. Between meetings,
many parents send messages requesting certain titles, and students
provide the necessary courier service.

Parent Response

Various feelings for the literature have surfaced. Parents who were
once troubled by their children's request for "a sad book" now realize that such emotions and moods are common and necessary to
the maturing process. They are beginning to relate a child's need
for escapist literature to an adult's desire to view soap operas.
Parents who initially viewed with guarded interest books dealing with
such social issues as drug abuse, child abuse, alcoholism, divorce,
and teenage pregnancies now realize that a desire to read about such
subjects is not necessarily an indication that the reader is unhappy
with his or her own life or engaged in wrong-doings. It is, however,
an indication of natural curiosity to know and understand the conflicts
which surround and threaten his/her world.

Several parental perceptions of the literature have evoked
concern. One mother who noted the negative portrayal of parents
in many of the young adult novels commented, "I certainly hope
that my son doesn't view me this way. He probably does. Maybe
I should think about this." Another mother expressed an extreme
dislike for the "open endings" so common to contemporary literature.
Upon discussing the issue with an eighth grader, she was surprised
when the girl responded, "I like to supply my own endings. That
way I can make it as happy or sad as I want." Though this mother
accepts the idea that such endings provide the reader with an opportunity to think creatively and critically, she still prefers the comfort of the definite ending of the "happily ever after" novel.

Most of the adults do not share their children's interest in
science fiction, but will readily read and discuss realistic fiction.
They are not especially fond of the "thriller" or the didactic novel,
but find a refreshing enjoyment in humor. They like historical fiction and short stories, but are bored with the superficial "series"
novel.

Controversy Minimal

Books which have been banned or questioned in many public and
school libraries are openly discussed in these parent meetings.
Each person's views are valued and a mutual respect for individual
opinions has developed among the group. The school has experienced
no problems with censorship, and the majority of the parents have
accepted "such books" with overt enthusiasm. As one mother stated,
"I would rather my daughter read Forever at home and discuss it
with me than snicker over isolated passages with her friends at a
slumber party."

One usually conservative parent became so thrilled with Judy
Blume's Deenie that she chose to express her approval to the librarian in writing. "Thanks for asking me to read Deenie; otherwise I
might not have taken the time ... I find it honest and true to the
world of the adolescent ... I prefer its answers to mine! I hope
my daughter will read it soon. She is very interested now that she
knows I've had the privilege."

A father has expressed disbelief that anyone could question
The Cay. "It's such an important book. I'm happy that my son
wants to read it a third time."

A consistent number of parents have become actively involved
and have alternately been willing to share the program with others.
Parents from other middle schools have asked if they could join the
group, and local community clubs have requested that the program
be shared with them. Public librarians have willingly participated
in the monthly meetings, and the P. T. A. has endorsed the school's
entire reader guidance program by occasionally providing financial
support.

Future plans include inviting participation from parents of
children who attend the five "feeder" elementary schools. This invitation will amplify the current program by providing parents the
opportunity to identify with the school's reading program before their
children face the difficult transition to middle school.

Improvements Needed

The faculty of Greenville Middle School is aware of several problems
with the existing program. Because of the meeting time, participation is now limited to non-working parents. There are plans, however, to expand the program to include night meetings. These meetings should solicit more involvement and open lines of communication
to a larger percentage of the school community.

Informing parents of meeting dates is perhaps the major
problem. Because there is no budget for postage, students are asked
to deliver announcements of meetings. Unfortunately, many of the
notices are found on school buses or tucked away in lockers.

This problem is currently being evaluated by the parents and improvements are being planned for next year.

Rewards

The rewards of the program are numerous. Adults and students are reading together, parents have grown sensitive to the reading needs and interests of middle schoolers, and faculty members feel encouraged by the students' excitement for books. The school administration enjoys the positive reactions expressed by the parents, and local book stores and public library branches indicate that the entire school community has acquired a zealous taste for young adult literature.

Reading can become a fad, or it can be as dreaded as a mathematics exam. Libraries can become as popular as the local teen hang-out, or they can be as quiet as the football stadium on a Monday morning. Parents and teachers can become involved in the reading experience of young adults, or they can take a passive attitude and risk a unique opportunity to communicate with one another.

Reading is a fad at Greenville Middle School, and the library is the most popular place in the building. But, most importantly, parents are involved in the reading experiences of their young adults. The enthusiasm for this involvement is best expressed in the following comment by seventh grader Kim Headley: "If I read a good book, I'll ask my Mom to read it. The books may help her see how I feel." Feelings are the basis for communication. Through literature parents and students ARE communicating!

IN DEFENSE OF FORMULA FICTION;

OR, THEY DON'T WRITE SCHLOCK THE WAY THEY USED TO*

Marilyn Kaye

One day not too long ago I visited a friend of mine in the children's room of a public library. It was early, the library had not yet opened, and I found her sitting at her desk, completely engrossed in a rather battered-looking book. When she saw me, she looked a little abashed and held up the book so that I could see the title: Betsy and Joe, by Maud Hart Lovelace. I felt a warm sense of recognition; it had been one of my favorite books during my pre-adolescent years. My friend sighed, laid the book down, and remarked--a little sadly--"You know, they just don't write schlock like this anymore."

She's right. They don't, at least not for adolescents. Gone are the days of Betty Cavanna, Rosamond Du Jardin, Anne Emery, Lenore Mattingly Weber, Maud Hart Lovelace, ad infinitum. Ad nauseam, some might say, but not me. I can conjure up a clear picture of myself, fifteen to twenty years ago, poring over those books, devouring them, and drifting away into a fanciful world of proms and class rings and love at first sight. The plots and the characters certainly bore no relation to my own dateless, promless world, and even at the age of twelve I had a sinking suspicion that they never would. They were pure escape. It was with pleasant anticipation that I could open each one, secure in the knowledge that everything would work out neatly and to my satisfaction: the girl and the boy would get together, the boy would make captain of the football team, the girl would get the lead in the class play, whatever. There would be small problems and minor disappointments along the way, but in the end they would all be resolved, and everyone would live happily ever after.

This is what escapist, formula literature is all about. It provides us with an experience we can anticipate. We know what's going to happen, but that in no way diminishes our enjoyment. As John Cawelti wrote in his study of popular formulas, Adventure, Mystery and Romance (University of Chicago Press, 1976): "Since

*Reprinted by permission of the author and publisher from Top of the News, 37:1 (Fall 1980) 87-90.

the pleasure and effectiveness of an individual formulaic work depends on its intensi-fiction of a familiar experience, the formula creates its own world with which we become familiar by repetition." The experience he refers to is not a "life" experience; it's a literary one. These are imaginary worlds he's talking about; not imaginary in the sense of high fantasy, but worlds of reordered and reworked reality. These are the worlds of Harold Robbins, Jacqueline Susann, and countless others--worlds that, for the most part, simply are not currently available in adolescent literature.

Today we have realism and relevance. Adolescent novels speak to real life, to the actual problems and crises, fears and anxieties of contemporary youth. They probe the mind of the adolescent, they give him or her characters to relate to, situations they can recognize in their own day-to-day, real-life experience. Plots are often original and inventive, with twists and surprises and a satiric humor that suits the bizarre reality of today's world. Some of these works may be ponderous and self-consciously grim, but many others are fine, high-quality works of literature. This is wonderful, and I only wish there had been authors like M. E. Kerr and Robert Cormier during my adolescence.

But at the same time I ask: is this all we can offer them? Is there no room in the adolescent literary world for a little light escapism, some formula fiction to take them away from the realities of their confused, crisis-prone lives? As adult readers, we have plenty of opportunities for escape; we have our gothic and contemporary romances, our westerns, our spy stories, our murder mysteries. Adolescents certainly have access to these, too, but would it not provide them with additional pleasure if they had a formula fiction of their own, which dealt with characters their own age, with settings with which they can identify, with their own "standard conventions?"

The standard convention is a primary aspect of formula fiction. Cawelti writes that standard conventions have a "primary relation to the needs of escape and relaxation" and that "well-established conventional structures are particularly essential to the creation of formula literature and reflect the interests of audiences, creators, and distributors."

We are all familiar with conventional plots; those are the ones we dismiss as "trite" and "predictable" in our YA book reviews. And they are trite and predictable, but why must we perceive these qualities as having completely negative connotations? True, these characteristics may negate the potential value of the work as "high" literature, but how successful are these works when examined within the scope of their own genre? Do they provide a pleasant, satisfying means of relaxation? If the answer is yes, then why not simply accept them for what they are and judge them only in terms of how well they meet the criteria for good escapist reading?

Plot conventions, even if unappealing to the elitist in all of us who wants to provide adolescents only with "good" literature, can be grudgingly accepted; but what do we do with character conventions? Because when we talk about character conventions, we are ultimately talking about--shudder--stereotypes. And suddenly we're confronted with visions of those wretched personifications that we have, for the most part, successfully eliminated from literature, many of which have been based on erroneous and harmful perceptions of alleged ethnic and racial characteristics. But there are other kinds of stereotypes, or stock characters, that dwell within the realm of standard convention: the romantic heroine, the mysterious, handsome stranger with a secret past, the macho private eye. We know them, and we recognize them each time we read our own favorite type of formula fiction.

Some of them used to exist in adolescent fiction: the shy teenager who prayed for a date, the poor rich kid who longed for real affection, the kindly, upright parent, à la "Father Knows Best," who doled out words of comfort and wisdom. Are these harmful stereotypes? I think not. One could argue that both plot and character conventions will give our readers false expectations, poor values, fraudulent role models, and an implausible vision of life. Yet again, as adults we allow ourselves the privileges of unrealistic literature. Ah yes, one might argue, but we know the truth. We may thoroughly enjoy a gothic romance, but at the same time we know that a knight in shining armor will never sweep us off the ground and carry us away to his castle on the hill. We know that we're not going to carouse with the jet set in Monte Carlo or find ourselves seduced by a handsome baronet in an English manor. We can indulge ourselves in these vicarious reading experiences because they will not affect our expectations of what life has to offer. Children and adolescents, on the other hand, are impressionable; if we give them pulp about senior proms, lighthearted and carefree high school stories, they will believe them, and we will be deceiving them. We're afraid that due to their lack of experience, they won't recognize these works as escapism. We allow them their pure fantasy and science fiction because they're so obviously unrealistic, but we won't let them have the personal fantasies that exist in escapist literature. We have declared that since real life rarely offers neat resolutions, we won't mislead our readers by giving them happy endings in their literature. But whom are we kidding? They know what real life is like; they're living it. Would it be so terrible, so earth-shattering, to let them escape it once in a while? If formula fiction were the only type of literature available to young adults, we would all be justified in demanding more realism; but we have many gifted authors writing realistic fiction. We can afford to let our young adult readers have a little fluff.

Take the romantic "junior novel," for example. It doesn't really exist anymore, at least not in the Du Jardin tradition. There's very little romance in the contemporary adolescent "love story"; we give them sex, we even give them clinical, step-by-step descriptions of sex--but there's no passion, no heart-fluttering, dreamy, head-

in-the-clouds, sentimental love.   There are no Heathcliffs, no Mr.
Rochesters, no tall, dark, handsome strangers; instead young adults
get penises named Ralph and relationships that are often more neu-
rotic than romantic.   At the end of Norma Klein's It's OK If You
Don't Love Me, the heroine visualizes a heaven where "all the women
in the world who thought of themselves as feminists will have to line
up and take their turn justifying all the times they were crazily,
dopily in love."   We won't even let our protagonists fall in love
without feeling guilty about it!

    Adolescents have a right to the same sort of light, formula
fiction available to adults.   Mysteries with plenty of suspense and
adolescent protagonists.   Dreamy, idealistic romances.   Glamorous
career stories where the emphasis is on succeeding, rather than on
coping.   Pure frothy entertainment: no messages, no insights, no
role models.   We have our Barbara Cartlands, Victoria Holts, Har-
lequin Romances, Agatha Christies, Mickey Spillanes: why shouldn't
adolescents have their own pleasant means of escaping reality?   With
all the solid, honest, realistic literature available to young adults
today, there's no reason why we can't accommodate a little schlock.

EXCERPTS FROM MY BOUBOULINA FILE

E. L. Konigsburg

Last November when I was a delegate to the White House Conference on Library and Information Services, I went to Washington armed with a large manila file full of materials on censorship. I have labeled this file BOUBOULINA. Bouboulina was the name Zorba gave to Dame Hortense, the painted old courtesan in Kazantzakis's novel. I figure that censorship has been around about as long as prostitution. Did not ancient kings cut off the heads of bearers of bad news? Besides, whores and censors have several things in common: No one ever admits to being one, both can look alluring, and both like to think of themselves as serving a public good. There is one more thing they have in common, but I'll get to that later.

I shlepped my Bouboulina File around the Washington Hilton for the entire length of the conference and did not once get an opportunity to open it. Like Gracie Fields, I felt that I had "brought my harp to the party, and nobody asked me to play." But now this conference has.

And so I have delved into my Bouboulina File and plucked some notes from it. All of them involve an author's--often my own --dealings with censors from the left and from the right.

A recent addition to my file is an article from my hometown newspaper, the Florida Times-Union, on a new school textbook.[1] On December 18, 1979, the paper carried an article that reads as follows: "The Duval County School Board Monday voted to allow stickers to be placed over objectionable parts of its new human growth and development textbook. The board's vote on the merits of altering the textbooks came without discussion. The action will allow the school system's curriculum division to pay employees to apply stickers over sections of the book which deal with abortion, masturbation, and homosexuality. The course, which will be taught with parental permission, is scheduled to begin next fall."[2]

A follow-up article on January 28, 1980, showed pictures of

*Reprinted by permission of the author and publisher from Library Quarterly, 51:1 (1981) 68-79. The University of Chicago Press; © 1981 by The University of Chicago.

the taped-over pages. Goodheart-Willcox, the publishers, had provided the adhesive stickers. John Flanagan, vice-president of
Goodheart-Willcox, said that if the board reorders about 3,000 books
this spring, his company will make a special revised book available.
Ah! Bouboulina, Bouboulina.

     In the follow-up article there appeared a statement about the
book's author, Verdene Ryder: "Mrs. Ryder did not offer any objections to the Duval board's action because she feels the book is
valuable because of the variety of other topics it includes, such as
family economic planning, child development, birth control methods
and death. Along with the book, there are suggested class activities,
including a mock wedding, a trip to a funeral home and child care"
[3, p. B3]. (An altogether reasonable trade-off. In this school system where in the 1978-79 school year there were 4,468 teenage
pregnancies out of a total teenage schoolgirl population of 28,000
[that is, more than one in seven Duval County schoolgirls between
the ages of 13 and 19 got pregnant], I think that a mock wedding is
a suitable class activity, for weddings are, indeed, a mockery.)
Ryder is quoted as saying, "The students need that information. We
cannot protect them from what they will find in the real world when
they go to college or to work."[3]

     Allow me to read another statement by a different author.
This statement appears in an introduction to a paperback edition of
his work:

          The natural desire of an author is to be read by as
     wide a circle of readers as possible, and when I was given
     to understand that only by cutting it could my novel be pub-
     lished in this series, I consented without a minute's hesi-
     tation. A novel is not like a fugue, for instance, which
     if you cut, say twenty bars from it, would be rendered
     meaningless.... A novel is a very loose form of art....
     It is also a very imperfect form of art.
          The novelist, a working man who wants to earn his
     living, is obliged to conform to the methods of publication
     common to the time at which he writes. Balzac ... always
     short of money, was paid so much a line, and he ...
     though the greatest novelist of them all, was capable of
     writing pages which had nothing to do with the story he
     had to tell.
          The author of a piece of fiction is ... influenced by
     fashion. At the time [of this book] many novelists, pos-
     sibly incited by the deep impression made on them by
     Samuel Butler's The Way of All Flesh, were impelled to
     write semi-autobiographical novels. Such a book was
     [this].... The author writes to disembarrass himself of
     painful memories; he is not concerned with the reader but
     only with his own liberation.... A writer is a fool if he
     thinks that every word he wrote is sacrosanct and that his
     work will be ruined if a comma is omitted.... A novel
     is not a scientific work nor a work of edification. So far

as the reader is concerned it is a work which purports to offer him intelligent entertainment. If this book, in this shortened version, finds new readers who get just that from it I shall be well satisfied. [4, pp. v, vii]

That was W. Somerset Maugham writing about Of Human Bondage.

It appears that both of these authors' consenting to expurgation have the same motive: to sell books. We can stop here and say that in the end Mammon rules us all. But I don't think we should stop here. I think there are important differences between Ryder's consent and Maugham's, and I think we ought to explore those differences. One way to start is to examine the books from the reader's point of view.

What does a reader get from picking up an expurgated copy of Of Human Bondage? If it is a first reading, he may never know --for without that introduction, who would?--that the book is a shortened version. In this way Maugham's form of censorship is more insidious than the very obvious, pasted-over version of Ryder's. But suppose the reader does find out? Suppose he learns that his copy of Of Human Bondage has been cut, and he wants to read the uncut story? Chances are excellent that he will be able to get the full-length novel from a library or a bookstore without much trouble. In any case, he does get intelligent entertainment. Maugham himself says, "A novel is not a scientific work nor a work of edification."

Contrast this with what a reader using Ryder's book learns. First of all, Contemporary Living [1] is not a work of fiction. It is a textbook, and the reader will be a student. The book will be presented to him in school, not as optional, and if it is entertainment, Ryder has lost control of her material. The student immediately sees that certain facts--not personal, semiautobiographical, authorial facts but impersonal, authoritative information that is supposed to be truthful and helpful--are being kept from him. The sticker procedure has the virtue of obviousness. But the covered-up version of this text, given to him in school, tells him something else too. It tells him that this censorship is sanctioned. With only a little thought he can trace those sanctions from the writer to the editor, the publisher, the teacher, the school administration, and, ultimately, the board of education, a duly elected body of government. It takes no leap of faith for him to realize that censorship by government is sticker approved.

He learns something else. He learns what this chain of command thinks about him, the student, the reader. There is a word for what it is. About that later.

What, then, are some of the distinctions between what Maugham has done to Of Human Bondage and what has been done to Ryder's Contemporary Living? One important difference is implicit in the question I just asked, and that is the difference between active

and passive: Maugham did; Ryder was done to. What Maugham did
to his own work was personal and eccentric. What was done to
Ryder's was impersonal and bureaucratic. And, finally, what Maugham did was done by the artist himself in the name of simplifying
and refining. What was done to Ryder was done by a whole chain
of command in the name of morality, the fancy feathers hiding the
real Bouboulina.

The censors call it "guidelines." The censors call it "applying local standards." Those words, "guidelines" and "local standards," would make one think that the word for what the censors feel
toward the students is "protective." But that is not the word.

To help find the word that best suits what the censor feels
toward the reader, let us examine that chain of command: the editors, publishers, teachers, and school administrators. I believe
that the fate of Ryder's Contemporary Living embodies all of these,
and I would like to show how it is done, one at a time, with examples from my Bouboulina File.

Let us first examine censorship of an author's work by an
editor. I would like to read to you a three-way correspondence
concerning me, my editor at Atheneum, Jean Karl, and some editors of a New York textbook publishing house. The correspondence
all took place late in 1977, except for the last letter which was dated
January 6, 1978.

It begins with this letter to me from my editor at Atheneum:

Dear Elaine:
    We have had a request to adapt material from From the
Mixed-up Files of Mrs. Basil E. Frankweiler [5] for a textbook. I am enclosing the material that came from the publisher. Do look it over and see what you think. If you
don't like it at all and don't approve of what they are doing,
just say so, and I will tell them.
    Best wishes, Jean Karl.

The letter she enclosed was as follows:

Dear Mrs. Konigsburg:
    I am writing in the hope that you will allow us to use an
excerpt from From the Mixed-up Files of Mrs. Basil E.
Frankweiler in the revision of our sixth grade reader. There
are two reasons why I am very anxious to use this particular
piece. First, it is a representative selection of a delightful
book that I want to share with our readers. Secondly, I am
planning to follow your story with a photo essay/article on a
very exciting Children's Museum in Connecticut. It is my
hope that the two pieces taught together will give children a
new, more positive approach to museums, both traditional
and experimental. I hope they will be inspired to explore
museums and your other works with equal fervor.

Due to space considerations, I have been forced to cut several passages from Chapter Three. Your suggestions and criticisms on the editing would be greatly appreciated.
Very sincerely,
Editor, Reading Basics.

Chapter 3 of From the Mixed-up Files of Mrs. Basil E. Frankweiler deals with Claudia Kincaid and her brother Jamie who, in running away from home, end up in New York City. They arrive at the Metropolitan Museum of Art where they intend to live in comfort and a bit of luxury. They take a map from the information stand, and Claudia selects where they will hide during that dangerous time immediately after the museum is closed to the public and before all the guards leave. She decides that she will go to the ladies' room and Jamie will go to the men's room. She instructs Jamie to go to the one near the restaurant on the main floor. The following conversation ensues:

"I'm not spending a night in a men's room [Jamie said]. All that tile. It's cold." ...
Claudia explained to Jamie that he was to enter a booth in the men's room. "And then stand on it." ...
"Stand on it? Stand on what?" Jamie demanded.
"You know," Claudia insisted. "Stand on it!"
"You mean stand on the toilet?" ...
"Well, what else would I mean? What else is there in a booth in the men's room? And keep your head down. And keep the door to the booth very slightly open," Claudia finished.
"Feet up. Head down. Door open. Why?"
"Because I'm certain that when they check the ladies' room and the men's room, they peek under the door and check only to see if there are feet. We must stay there until we're sure all the people and guards have gone home."
[5, pp. 35-36]

That passage is part of chapter 3, and chapter 3 is what the publisher wanted to use for its new sixth-grade reader. I looked over the materials they had sent via my editor and sent the following letter:

Dear Jean:
Enclosed are the materials from the publisher. I think it will be fine for them to use part of my book From the Mixed-up Files of Mrs. Basil E. Frankweiler if they use the material as I have edited it per the suggestion in their letter. I have cut out as much as they have in the interest of saving space without destroying the characterizations of the two children and without leaving information dangling in the manner they did on pages 3 and 6 of their copy. If they should decide that the material needs further editing, I would like to see it before it goes to print.
Sincerely. ...

Next in this little saga comes a letter from my editor at Atheneum:

> Dear Elaine:
>   I am enclosing material in this letter that came from the
> textbook publisher today. I think this is ridiculous. I would
> say to them "Go fly a kite." Do let me know what you think.
>   Sincerely, Jean Karl.

The letter that she wanted to tell them to go fly a kite about is as
follows:

> Dear Miss Karl:
>   I'm so sorry to trouble you again--I'd hoped we were
> through with From the Mixed-up Files of Mrs. Basil E.
> Frankweiler. But alas, standing on toilets just didn't make
> it through editorial conference last week.
>   Would Elaine Konigsburg be kind enough to take a look at
> our deletion?
>   Manuscript page attached.
>   With thanks, Rights and Permissions, School Department.

I reread the standing-on-toilets section, and I didn't think it
was so very bad. And so I wrote the following letter directly to
the Rights and Permissions Editor of the Department of Reading
Basics:

> Dear [Mrs. Editor]:
>   During the past year I have appeared on several different
> talk shows, some TV, some radio--local productions in var-
> ious parts of the country: The South, The Midwest, The
> West. Last spring I was interviewed on one of New York
> City's public radio stations. Something happened at that ses-
> sion that I would like to share with you.
>   My editor and I arrived early, even before the interviewer
> got there. The lady who produces the show met us in the
> studio where the interview was to take place. She was a
> native New Yorker; she knew that I had arrived from Jackson-
> ville, Florida. She explained to me that the interviewer would
> concentrate on questions about my newest book and would in
> no way embarrass me by asking personal questions such as
> how many times I was married and/or divorced. I realized
> that she was trying to put me at ease; she couldn't know that
> it has been a decade since I have experienced any nervous-
> ness about public appearances. Being a good daughter--this
> was an older woman--I listened to her politely and smiled
> a great deal. I have very large front teeth, and sometimes
> my smile appears overabundant and anxious. The producer
> then attempted to reassure me further by telling me that the
> interview would be on cassette and, thus anything embarrass-
> ing that I might accidentally say could be edited out. I
> smiled my long-tooth smile again.
>   The producer fixed her eyes hard on me and repeated,
> "Cassette."

Being patient, I repeated my nod and my smile.
"You know cassettes?" she asked.
I couldn't believe that she would think that I didn't, so I
returned a puzzled look.
Then she repeated, upped volume, lowered speed. "Cas-
settes. You have cassettes?"
Finally, I realized what she was asking. She wanted to
know if I, having arrived from Jacksonville, Florida, had
ever heard of cassettes.
I politely reassured her that I had cassettes.
Elsewhere, everywhere I have gone throughout the country,
everyone has always assumed that I know cassettes.
I fear, [Mrs. Editor], that you are worried about receiving
irate letters from people in The South, The Midwest and The
West concerning your excerpt from From the Mixed-up Files
of Mrs. Basil E. Frankweiler. I can only ask you to trust
us out here. Everyone out here assumes that everyone knows
about cassettes, Sara Lee pound cake and flush toilets, and
we all assume about each other that we use each of them as
the occasion and/or need arises.
Something in me does not want to believe that an editorial
board at your company is as provincial as a provincial New
Yorker.
I stand with Claudia and Jamie Kincaid firmly on the toilets in the booths of the ladies' and men's rooms at the Metropolitan Museum of Art. Won't you please join us?
Sincerely, Elaine Konigsburg.

There followed two phone calls.

The first was from the woman to whom I had addressed the
letter. She told me that they had had several conferences on the
toilets--I guess I should say about the toilets--but they were afraid
that they would get irate letters from people Out There. "Out
There" is anywhere not in New York. It was such a short passage,
wouldn't I consider letting them take it out?

I said no.

That very morning there followed a second phone call from
the editor of the editor. She said that there was a question of
safety involved, that some child might read about standing on the
toilets and try it and fall in.

I told her that I didn't believe that.

I also mentioned that the book had been read by hundreds and
hundreds of children for over a decade, and I had never heard of
anyone falling into a toilet as a result of reading my book. I also
told her that I had been to places in Kenya and Greece where the
only way you could use it was to stand on it.

She said that she would confer again about the toilets and
call me back.

Well, she didn't.

Instead I got a final letter from Jean Karl:

Dear Elaine:
    You will be interested to know that since you will not allow
the children not to stand on the toilets, the publisher has decided not to use the selection. I think they are being absurd
and hope it doesn't bother you too much that they won't be
using it.
    Sincerely, Jean Karl.

Now, what has kept this particular publishing house from allowing mention of toilets in a textbook? I touched on an answer in
my reply to them; I said that they didn't trust us. That was a
gentle word. There is a more accurate one. We'll get to it a little
later. For the moment let this exchange stand as an example of
how censorship of an author is applied by an editor.

Next in the chain of censorship command is the publisher.
Clyde Robert Bulla once reported that a textbook publisher asked
him to achieve "sexual balance" in one of his stories that included
a girl, a boy, an old woman, and a pony by changing the sex of the
pony. What do you think prompts a textbook publisher to make such
a request of an author? To whom is he paying respect by making
such a request? The word we are looking for is not "respect."

The book passes from the editor through the publisher and
inevitably falls into the hands of the teacher. Teachers, too, don't
call it by name, but they do it. Take this letter from my Bouboulina File. It was addressed to my publisher and forwarded to me.
It is from Camden, New Jersey.

Dear Sir:
    Last month I ordered four books from your company from
the catalog which you had sent. One of the books which I
ordered was Altogether, One at a Time, [6] invoice #14635
by Konigsburg. I am writing now to tell you that the women
who are in charge of our school library felt that they could
not use this book on our library shelves, because there were
two places where it is inappropriate for children's reading,
namely pages 7 and 15. Unfortunately, I am not able to return the book because it has already been stamped.
    However, I wanted to let you know that it is the opinion
of many people that these pages are entirely unsuitable for
children, and should be advertized [sic] as such.

Page 7 of Altogether, One at a Time is within the story "Inviting
Jason," an account of a ten-year-old's first sleep-over birthday
party. It contains the following passage: "Our first game was a
drawing contest to see who could draw the best. We drew girls.
With their clothes off. Grown-up girls" [6, p. 7]. The other unacceptable passage is part of the story, "The Night of the Leonids."

In it our hero, Lewis, is describing the relationship that he has
with his Park Avenue grandmother. He says, "Grandmother doesn't
take me everywhere she goes, and I don't take her everywhere I go;
but we get along pretty well, Grandmother and I" [6, p. 15]. Then
there is a drawing of one of the places that Lewis doesn't take his
grandmother. It shows a door with a sign MEN on the outside.

      I hope you don't think that I write only about public toilets.
I don't. But I do seem to have this little problem: I use them a
lot.

      I did not deign to answer the teacher from Camden, New
Jersey, and I want to tell you why. That letter was written on
March 31, 1971; I received it on April 8, 1971, the very day I read
in the New York Times that a federal grand jury indicted May De-
Rose and nine other Gloucester Township and Camden City officials
for bribery and extortion. I decided that in a town where the politics were filthy, children deserved to have library shelves free of
the likes of "Inviting Jason" or "The Night of the Leonids."

      To track Bouboulina's shamelessness from editor, through pub-
lisher, through teacher, and on to its inevitable government connection, I must share with you the most disturbing set of correspondence
that I have in my file. Disturbing because it came from a school
administrator. And disturbing because it came dressed with cheeks
painted rosy like virtue. I shall not spare names. The letter came
with a cover note from my editor at Atheneum:

> Dear Elaine:
>   There is a new system for book selection in Maryland
> where everything is subjected to all kinds of minority scru-
> tiny, and I think the enclosed letter comes as a result of
> this. I have not answered the letter except to acknowledge
> its receipt. If you want to answer it, fine. If you want me
> to answer, I will. Or if you prefer that we say nothing at
> all, we can do that, too. I think it is interesting that it has
> taken this long for us to get as strong a letter as this.
>   Best wishes, Jean Karl.

The letter was from Montgomery County Public Schools and was
dated June 17, 1976, our bicentennial year. It is addressed to the
Children's Book Editor at Atheneum.

> Re: Altogether, One at a Time by E. L. Konigsburg
> To Whom It May Concern:
>   Some of our librarians have questioned the language in
> "Momma at the Pearly Gates." Specifically, the objection is
> to "I bet there's no niggers in Heaven" and "Haven't you ever
> heard of Nigger Heaven" on page 72. We believe the story
> has many positive elements, and we would appreciate your
> asking the author to consider the use of the word Black in-
> stead of nigger. We also believe that the description of
> "Nigger Heaven" would be offensive to all Black Americans.

In September we will be alerting our librarians to what
we consider an inappropriate short story in this collection
and we would hope that a new revision of this particular
short story will be forthcoming.
Sincerely yours,
Frances C. Dean, Coordinator
Division of Evaluation and Selection
Department of Educational Media and Technology.

I chose to answer Ms. Dean.   I sent her the following letter and
sent carbons to Mrs. Nancy C. Walker, head, Department of Educational Media and Technology, Montgomery County Schools; to Dr.
Charles M. Bernardo, superintendent of Montgomery County Schools;
as well as to my own editor, Jean Karl.   Here's what I wrote:

Dear Ms. Dean:
"Momma at the Pearly Gates" takes place in the 1940's,
a time when the term black was unknown to the blacks as
well as to the whites of eastern Ohio.   As a writer, I cannot do as you ask me to; to change my story would be dis-
honest.
I have read "Momma at the Pearly Gates" to audiences of
children of mixed races, and they have never had any doubt
about how cleverly Momma picks up Roseann's weapon, the
word nigger, and cudgels her with it.   In the year of its publication I chose to read that story to an assembly of children
in one of our local all-white, church-affiliated schools that
was founded to avoid court-ordered integration.   The entire
audience broke out in loud, spontaneous applause where on
page 73 Momma says, "You can go down farther than that
for all I care."
I predict that black Americans will feel patronized at your
alert that there is "an inappropriate short story" in ALTO-
GETHER, ONE AT A TIME.   Patronized and cheated.   Cheated
of a black heroine who triumphs over being called nigger to
become the heroine of her own short story as well as the
heroine of the collected elementary grades of a segregated
white school in Jacksonville, Florida in 1971.
Sincerely, E. L. Konigsburg.

I called it "patronizing" here, and that word is close to what
the censors feel toward their readers.   Close, but not exact enough.

I have never received a reply, and I don't know if Altogether,
One at a Time remains on the shelves of the schools of Montgomery
County.

On January 28, 1979, I picked up our morning paper, that
same Florida Times-Union that I mentioned earlier, and found a two-
column headline that read, "Avoid All Censorship, Says School Librarian."   Imagine my surprise when I read, "Mrs. Francis [sic]
Dean, immediate past president of the American Association of
School Librarians, ... questioned if a parent has the right to keep

'your child or my child from reading a book we might find worthwhile? A censor, then, in my opinion, is one who inflicts his or her beliefs on me by denying me free access to any medium of communication reflecting the past or present.'" The article has a final paragraph in which Mrs. Dean is quoted further: "'We, as individual citizens, may not like a particular work and may find some books particularly offensive,' she said. 'But as a school person it is not our responsibility to quarrel about how an author has exercised his rights under the First Amendment.'"[7]

Can you believe that from a woman who would ask an author to change a story? That from a woman who would write a veiled threat that unless the book is changed, it would be removed from the shelves of Montgomery County, Maryland?

What is Mrs. Dean saying? What were the editors who didn't want Claudia and Jamie on the toilet seats saying? What are the teachers and the publishers and the school boards saying? I know. I know the word, but I can't say it yet.

Let me be gentle. Let me transfer this treatment of an author's work to another medium, one that has less history as an art form. Let me say that instead of making a textbook, we are going to make a movie out of a book. We recognize that some of the material has to be shortened, just as Maugham had to shorten Of Human Bondage. There are often changes that must be made so that the work can be translated into an audio-visual medium. But let us suppose that the book is a noncontroversial one--or about as noncontroversial as any book can be. Let us suppose that it is not only nonsexist, but that it is also nonsexy. Let it be an adventure story. Let it be Charles Portis's True Grit. Suppose you loved the book, and you went to the movie, and you found that you loved it, too. But as you leave the theater, you ask yourself, why did the heroine in the movie not lose her arm the way the heroine in the book did?

You answer, the Movie People.

You answer, the Movie People didn't want her to.

You answer, the Movie People thought that I couldn't take it or wouldn't take it or would be offended. The Movie People thought that I wouldn't pay admission to see True Grit if the heroine lost her arm. The producer and the director (read: publisher and editor) got together and decided that I, the audience (read: reader) would not understand.

And the word for what the Movie People have shown me is "contempt." And that's an ugly word. And I don't deserve it.

What the textbook publishers and editors are showing their readers is contempt. What the teacher in Camden and Mrs. Dean's evaluation committee in Montgomery County are showing their readers is contempt. I say that anyone who looks at the word "nigger" in "Momma at the Pearly Gates," like anyone who looks at the word "nigger" in Huckleberry Finn and who does not see beyond the word, who refuses to see where the author's sentiments lie, is showing contempt for that author. And anyone who properly sees where that author's sentiments lie and does not trust others to do so is showing contempt for them. And, as an author or as a reader, I take that personally; I don't know any other way to take it.

And that word "contempt," the proper word for the feeling that censors have for the users of their services, shows a fourth trait that whores and censors have in common.

And I say to the textbook companies, with their worried minds about offending someone, anyone, with their ready stickers to paste over more objectionable parts, I say that there are some people who deserve to be offended. And no one deserves it more than those Bouboulinas who show contempt for the reader.

And that is what I have to say about the basic difference between what Maugham did to shorten Of Human Bondage and what the Duval County Board of Education did to Ryder's Contemporary Living. The difference was a difference in attitude toward the reader. One did not show contempt; one did.

My basic motive for writing as I do, for changing, revising, and honing as I do, is to communicate with as many children as want to meet me in my books. I may offend some; some readers are prickly. Sometimes I am. But I respect all of my readers. Where in the world of literature for children is there a place for someone who does not respect its audience? What children who read my work deserve contempt? They deserve intelligent entertainment, and I don't know any way to give that, just as I don't know any way to take it, except personally.

References

1. Ryder, Verdene. Contemporary Living. South Holland, Ill.: Goodheart-Willcox Co., 1979.
2. Pope, Margo C., and Anderson, Mike. "Board Okays Stickers for Sex Education Text Books." Florida Times-Union (December 18, 1979), p. B1.
3. Pope, Margo C. "Reviewers' Reactions on Book Vary." Florida Times-Union (January 28, 1980), pp. B1, B3.
4. Maugham, W. Somerset. "Introduction." Of Human Bondage. New York: Pocket Books, 1950.
5. Konigsburg, E. L. From the Mixed-up Files of Mrs. Basil E. Frankweiler. New York: Atheneum Publishers, 1967.
6. Konigsburg, E. L. Altogether, One at a Time. New York: Atheneum Publishers, 1971.
7. Callahan, John. "Avoid All Censorship, Says School Librarian." Florida Times-Union (January 28, 1979), p. B2.

BOOK SELECTION PRESSURE

ON SCHOOL LIBRARY MEDIA SPECIALISTS AND TEACHERS*

Jerry J. Watson and Bill C. Snider

School media specialists and teachers read and rely upon critical book reviews as an influential factor in selecting books for children. Book reviews appearing in professional journals allow one to read of a book's content, plot summary, important characters, and theme or concept based upon literary and graphic standards of excellence. Reviews of children's books are rather terse and concisely written depending upon the journal's audience and purpose, space allotment, and the critical analysis skills of the reviewer.[1] Some journals have an additional policy of actually coding or rating particular book titles that are reviewed. Ruth Stein's book reviews in Language Arts, for example, contain the symbol (+) indicating a high judgment of literary and graphic elements, or the review might be signaled by the symbol (-) indicating substandard components. The Bulletin for the Center of Children's Books provides an even more elaborate rating system for recommending or not recommending a book, e.g., *, R, ad, M. One journal, The Horn Book, and a review organ, Booklist, review only books that are recommended reading fare for children, and no coding system is employed. Thus there exists a multitude of coded rating systems for recommending or not recommending books for children's reading fare from which teachers and librarians must make their selection decisions.

Once the decision has been made to purchase a book, the services of a book jobber may be utilized rather than ordering a book directly from a publisher. Until recently book jobbers functioned solely to conveniently provide books placed on order. As of 1978, Follett Library Book Company, a national book jobber located in Crystal Lake, Illinois, has implemented a practice of enclosing a warning pink bookmark in certain books that contained what some media specialists had identified and complained of as objectionable content that might arouse censorship problems or that some librarians or teachers might find not appropriate for children. The bookmarks read, in part,

*Reprinted by permission of the American Library Association and the author from School Media Quarterly, 9:2 (Winter 1981) 95-101.

> Attention librarians and teachers. Some of our customers
> have informed us of their opinion that the content or vo-
> cabulary of this book is inappropriate for young readers.
> Before distributing this book, you may wish to examine it
> to assure yourself that the subject matter and vocabulary
> meets your standards. [2]

The warning makes no references to literary or artistic merits of
the book.

A great deal of controversy concerning this warning bookmark
practice surfaced among circles within the American Library Association (ALA), notably the Intellectual Freedom Committee. Judith
F. Krug, director of the ALA Office of Intellectual Freedom, stated
that such a practice "would result in arbitrary or unjustified rejection of titles by librarians selecting materials for their collections."
[3]

In an attempt to gather information from the Follett Library
Book Company, Krug wrote a letter requesting specific facts regarding the purpose and habit of the book company's policy of inserting
the pink bookmark. In reply, Charles R. Follett assured Krug that

> the bookmark is in no manner intended to influence the requi-
> sition of any one title prior to purchase. The librarian be-
> comes aware of the book after receiving her (his) order.
> The decision to keep or return any title on the basis of con-
> tent is entirely up to that librarian's professional judgement.
> [4]

In addition, Follett enclosed seventy-eight letters from customers which the Office of Intellectual Freedom used to compose
the following statistics:

● There were seventy-eight letters, six of which were against
  the bookmarks (these six letters were from two public li-
  braries, three schools, and one university, mostly from the
  Northeast or Midwest).
● The pro-bookmark letters were from twenty-nine different
  states, predominantly from public schools and from the
  Midwest.
● Area of the country:

West	16
South	12
Northeast	13
Midwest	29
undetermined	2

● Type of library:

elementary school	35
junior high school	9
high school	2
public school (no breakdown)	9
parochial school	11
public library	1
undetermined	5

● Reasons for objections:

offensive language	25
inappropriate	22
immoral	1
offensive illustrations	6
violence	3

● Thirteen letters specifically mentioned being in favor of the bookmarks.

The strong support of the warning pink bookmark system practiced by the Follett Library Book Company is evident by the number of favorable letters. The majority of pro-bookmark customers were from elementary public schools located in the midwestern region of the nation. The influence of such a warning system upon book selection processes undertaken by teachers and school librarians prompted this study.

Design of the Study

This exploratory study was designed to measure the resistance of teachers and media specialists to a warning symbol found in book reviews when making book selections for a children's collection. There is little empirical evidence regarding the extent of such influence upon book selectors who read children's book reviews that warn about offensive language, inappropriate content, immoral themes and actions, offensive illustrations, or violence. One such manner in which a book review may be notated is by a warning symbol (*) accompanied by a footnote that explains the symbol identifying objectionable content.

Two questions were asked: (1) When making selections for a children's book collection, are book selectors influenced by a warning symbol attached to a book review to such an extent that they will avoid ordering the book? (2) Is there a difference when selecting warning symbol books for different age groups of children, e. g. , picture books (N-grade-2d grade), average readers (3d grade-5th grade), advanced readers (6th grade-8th grade)?

To answer the questions, forty-five children's book reviews written by Ruth Stein and published in the journal Language Arts (NCTE, October 1978-June 1979) were selected to test the influence of a warning symbol upon book selectors when selecting books for a children's collection. All reviews chosen for the study had been written favorably and assigned a recommended (+) symbol by Stein. The recommended symbol for all reviews was deleted during the test and a substitute warning symbol (*) was randomly placed beside nine of the forty-five book reviews. The substitute warning symbol was explained in a footnote, which stated that the book had received at least five complaints because of "offensive language, inappropriate content, immoral theme or concept; offensive illustrations; or violence. " No wording of the reviews was altered, except in the case of characters' names and book titles. Reviews were altered to eliminate easy recognition of known books, and no other bibliographic information was provided in an attempt to control personal bias regarding names of authors, illustrators, or publishers.

To ensure that each book review would receive a warning symbol for the administration within each population sample, five different forms of the same book reviews were tested. The population sampled in the study consisted of 197 undergraduate and graduate students enrolled in children's literature classes at two major midwestern universities: the University of Iowa and Michigan State University. The sample consisted primarily of white, middle-class female students enrolled as education and library science majors.

All subjects were provided an instrument of forty-five book reviews and asked to imagine themselves in a situation where budgetary funds would allow for the purchase of thirty titles for a children's book collection. Each title chosen was to be circled on the book review instrument. Of the thirty total titles chosen, ten would be picture books intended for primary- and primary-age children; ten titles would be for average readers (middle grades); and ten titles would be chosen for advanced readers (upper grades).

Fifteen book reviews for three age levels were provided for possible selection. Three book reviews were randomly assigned a warning symbol (*) in each of the three age categories for a total of nine warning symbols appearing among the book reviews. As only ten book titles could be chosen and five rejected in each age category, it was hypothesized that if book selectors had a low resistance to a warning symbol to avoid, then no (*) book title or only one (*) book title would be selected. If resistance to a warning symbol was high, then book selections would include an average of two warning symbol titles. It was also assumed that book selectors may reject books rated with a warning symbol as frequently for older children in the upper grades as for children in preprimary and primary grades.

Results

Book selectors were asked to select ten books for three different age groups from a book selection tool containing forty-five reviews of books written for children. For each age category fifteen book reviews were provided and three books were marked by a warning symbol beside three randomly selected titles. As only ten book titles could be chosen for each age group, five titles had to be rejected. It was allowed that if a book selector included one (*) book among the ten selected books, there was no avoidance effect acting upon the selector. If the book selector included two (*) books among the five rejected books for each age group, it was assumed that the warning symbol exerted the avoidance effect upon the book selector's decision when choosing books for a children's book collection in that particular age group.

A z statistic for each of three different age groups was computed to test the null hypothesis: there is no difference in the X number of warning symbol books selected than the population X of two warning symbol books selected for each of three age groups of children. The data reported in Table 1 show that when asked to select ten books for each of three age groups, the book selectors did avoid selecting two warning symbol books for each age group (<.05 level). The X number of (*) picture books selected for the preprimary and primary age group was less than two (*) books (X = 1.45 (*) books). The X number of (*) books selected for the middle-grade group was less than two (*) books (X = 1.44 (*) books). The X number of (*) books selected for the upper-grade group was less than two (*) books (X = 1.57 (*) books).

The null hypothesis was rejected and the alternate hypothesis was rejected and the alternate hypothesis was accepted: the X number of warning symbol books selected is different than the population X of two warning symbol books selected for each of three different age groups of children. Book selectors do not have a high resistance to book reviews marked by a warning symbol (*) and an avoidance effect acts upon the decision to reject books marked by a warning symbol.

Analysis of variance using a treatment by subject design was employed to test the second null hypothesis: there is no difference in the X number of warning symbol (*) books selected from a book selection tool for three different age treatment groups of children when randomly selected book reviews have a warning symbol attached to them.

It was assumed that the warning symbol books would be rejected equally across all three age groups. In Table 2, the findings indicate that no statistical difference exists between three different age groups when book selectors reject book reviews containing a warning symbol (F=2.07). The null hypothesis is accepted.

Discussion

This investigation was prompted by recent concern among teachers and media specialists who rely heavily upon written children's book reviews as a selection aid when choosing books for children's reading, and for those same professionals who utilize the services of a book jobber when ordering books for children's reading. Children's book review services are provided by various professional journals and review organs that may incorporate a symbolic coding system to aid the book selector in determining purchase or rejection of the reviewed book. Until recently, the sole function of the book jobber was to provide a convenient and efficient ordering service for teachers and media specialists who had already decided upon the books needed to fill in missing gaps and to bring balance to a collection of children's reading fare.

Table 1

Warning Symbol (*) Books Selected

Age Group	N	X	SD	Variance	z statistic
Preprimary and Primary Picture Books (N-2d grade)	197	1. 45	0. 98	0. 96	7. 524*
Middle Grades (3d-5th grade)	197	1. 43	0. 87	0. 76	8. 974*
Upper Grades (6th-8th grade)	197	1. 57	0. 90	0. 82	6. 636*

*< 0. 05

Table 2

Variance Between Age Groups

Picture Book, Middle- and Upper-Grade Groups	DF	Sum of Squares	Mean Squares	F-Ratio
Subjects	197	288. 33	1. 46	
Treatment A	2	2. 31	1. 15	2. 07
Interaction	394	219. 68	0. 55	
Total	593	510. 33		

There are two important findings as a result of this exploratory investigation. One finding indicates that a book review warning symbol system exerts a negative choice-avoidance influence upon adult book selectors when choosing books for children. Book selectors view the warning symbol as a stigma to a book's value. The second finding indicates that regardless of the intended reading age, adult book selectors reject to a great extent children's books based on reviews identified by a warning symbol. In spite of the favorably written text, children's book reviews marked by a warning symbol alleging objectionable content, e. g. , "offensive language," "offensive illustrations," "violence," "inappropriate," or "immoral," are strongly rejected by adult book selectors for children across all age groups from preprimary through upper grades.

Providing a balanced children's book collection rests upon several factors. Book selectors base decisions upon the reading needs and interests of children, budget and curriculum needs, space, and community standards as well as how highly recommended the book is by reviewers.[5] Most book reviews are rated according to high standards of literary merit and graphic achievement as perceived by the reviewer who has proven abilities in discerning such artistic and subjective qualities. Obviously, not all books reviewed receive the same evaluation from different critics regarding excellence in literary elements and illustrations as found in books written for children. The results of this study reinforce the need of book selectors to read more than one selection aid when choosing books. Several book reviews should be read and compared to help determine the final decision: to order or to reject.

There is possibly one area of book analysis in which there could be closer agreement among reviewers. Unfortunately, this is in the area of determining objectionable content and subject matter that may be deemed unsuitable for children's reading. To label a children's book as "inappropriate" or "immoral" because it contains "offensive language," "offensive illustrations," or "violence" would not be a difficult task. Such "offensive" elements are often easily spotted and do not even require full reading of the context. Book censors have readily engaged in such practice for years. Professional children's book reviewers, trusted for their assumed objective and critical analysis skills, might identify and denounce objectionable content only when such objectionable elements are judged to be blatantly, excessively, and exploitively used in a shocking and startlingly distasteful style.

There are presently no known professional staff book reviewers writing for Booklist, The Horn Book, or Language Arts who openly and singularly condemn a book because objectionable content has been identified. Warnings about such possibly hazardous content is provided by lay practitioners reviewing children's books in School Library Journal (SLJ), which provides in its annual policy statement the following item:

> Reviews are expected by many to be an early warning system, a bulwark against taxpayer protest and the censor. Reviewers need to identify controversial subjects and illuminate how they are handled, without stumping for any side. This leaves the final judgment to the person with the final responsibility--the librarian-selectors who alone can determine the appropriateness of a given book to their children. [6]

Book selectors may appreciate book reviews containing fore-warnings of objectionable content that may provoke censorship problems when the book is placed into circulation. Possibly, a more negative effect may result in encouraging acts of self-imposed censorship to be committed by the book selector. Such a deleterious reaction, long considered the most insidious form of censorship, could possibly promote an attitude among the insecure, uneducated, or novice book selectors that children's books to be chosen are only those considered safe and which reflect only the moral standards of the adults of a community. Obviously the values, temperament, and expectations of a community must be considered when selecting books for children. But as Ken Donelson has argued, children's maturity, intelligence, and sensitivity are the prime qualities to be considered first when selecting books for children, not the adult standards of a community. [7]

Implications from this study clearly show that book selectors avoid selecting children's books containing objectionable content as identified by someone else. Although all the adults tested in this study were university students enrolled in children's literature classes with many practicing teachers and librarians participating, none had received an explicit instructional unit on book selection policy and ways to defend against censorship. Further research studies should be designed to measure the effect of an instructional unit on changes in attitudes, skills, and concepts when books for children are selected and to what effect undue fears and concerns of censorship problems are eradicated. Axiomatic theories have long been held that education and development of personal attitudes, concepts, and skills are viable and worthwhile components of a professional's training to adequately defend against outside influence and interference.

Another strong implication resulting from this study indicates the force and influence of a warning symbol made upon book selectors. Symbols accompanying a book review are indeed noticed by book selectors and such symbols exert a tremendous and powerful effect upon final book choices. As Belland found, a favorable book review is the most important factor considered by media specialists when selecting books. [8] Some professional review journals include symbols to rate a variety of qualifying evaluations made by reviewers about books. Some reviews are not accompanied by an evaluation symbol, and some selection tools, as in this study, use only one symbol. SLJ incorporates only one symbol, a star (★) denoting "excellent in relation to others of its kind."[9] One might wonder if a star (★) rating would be withheld because of objectionable content identified in the book. To read and carefully weigh the analysis and evaluation offered by book reviewers in various selection aids should be obvious from the results of this study. Further studies should attempt to ascertain the influence upon book selectors who read and respond to a variety of symbolic rating codes employed in review journals. Such information may be helpful to editors of selection tools as well as teachers and media specialists.

In no case is this investigator advocating the use of a book review warning symbol to be attached to book reviews. Media personnel and teachers who rely on book reviews found in contemporary selection tools should realize the basic importance, with limitations, such reviews provide. Some book reviews may not be extensive enough, or provide adequate critical analysis; however, book selectors should judge the suitability of a book after the book has been thoroughly read and evaluated according to their own professional criteria and not those of an outside source.

Book vendors may rationalize their position as an outside source providing book warnings. A member of the Follett Library Book Company has explained,

the practice began as an economic measure because of an
enormous amount of returns of certain titles; however, nine
out of ten librarians still keep the book after it arrives with
such a warning. [10]

This information encouragingly reflects the selector's independence;
yet implications from this study advise that if such a warning system were used in the company's order catalog, then very few of
those books might originally be ordered. However severe economic
pressures have become, this investigator trusts that such book jobbers do not justify the inclusion of a warning symbol in book order
catalogs. Media personnel recently identified seven items of information found in catalogs considered important: "applicability to curriculum, reading level, grade level, review source, copyright date,
price, and learner verification. "[11] None specified the need to fore-
warn of objectionable content. Nat Hentoff, critic and children's
book author, has labeled the Follett Company's pink slip policy "appalling" and "disgraceful"--"an invitation to censorship. "[12] Perhaps
a study should be designed to determine whether or not 90 percent
of book selectors would indeed retain and recommend for children's
reading such books that did contain a warning pink bookmark.

To avoid any undue pressure from book jobbers and perhaps
to save budgetary funds for acquisition, book selectors may heed the
suggestion of Robert Leider to order directly from the publisher. [13]
Apparently, little else can be done to persuade book jobbers to avoid
influencing the appropriateness of children's books. Waiting for improved economic conditions and writing letters of protest may bring
some degree of satisfaction to discontented members of the profession. However, for those members in higher education and others
planning in-service and conference meetings, the best long-range
policy would be to take up a charge of renewed interest and energy
in providing sound educational advice to persons responsible for selecting books for children. Concentration in the areas of book selection, book evaluation, and book protection in censorship cases
needs immediate practical and thorough attention. Teachers and
media specialists as book selectors for children, either currently in
practice or in preparation for their profession, should be provided
with opportunities to develop well-rounded perspectives and strong
convictions regarding book selection policies. Professional members
need the confidence- and armor-building defenses that such workshops
and units of study may provide when voices of complaint are raised
in defiance against literary selections chosen for children's reading.
The pressures of outside warning devices need not perform a crip-
pling effect upon teachers and librarians.

References

1. Virginia Witucke, "A Comparative Analysis of Juvenile Book
     Review Media," School Media Quarterly 8:153-59 (Spring
     1980).

2. "Midwinter Notebook," American Libraries 10:132 (March 1979).
3. Ibid.
4. Statistics on Follett letters. Memorandum from Office of Intellectual Freedom, American Library Association, Nov. 13, 1978.
5. Kay Vandergrift, "Selection: Reexamination and Reassessment," School Media Quarterly 6:103-11 (Winter 1978).
6. Pamela D. Pollack, School Library Journal 27:53 (Sept. 1980).
7. Kenneth L. Donelson, "Obscenity and the Chill Factor: Court Decisions about Obscenity and Their Relationships to School Censorship," in James E. Davis, ed., Dealing with Censorship (Urbana, Ill.: National Council of Teachers of English, 1979), p. 72.
8. John Belland, "Factors Influencing Selection of Materials," School Media Quarterly 6:113 (Winter 1979).
9. Pollack, SLJ, p. 53.
10. "News," School Library Journal 27:16 (Sept. 1980).
11. Phyllis Van Orden, "Promotion, Review, and Examination of Materials," School Media Quarterly 6:122 (Winter 1978).
12. "News," SLJ, p. 16.
13. Robert Leider, "How Librarians Help Inflate the Price of Books and What to Do about It," American Libraries 11:559-60 (Oct. 1980).

RELATIVE IMPACT OF PRINT AND DATABASE PRODUCTS

ON DATABASE PRODUCER EXPENSES AND INCOME--

TRENDS FOR DATABASE PRODUCER ORGANIZATIONS

BASED ON A THIRTEEN YEAR FINANCIAL ANALYSIS*

Martha E. Williams

Introduction

Since the advent of online database services there has been considerable discussion regarding the negative impact that the online use
of databases may have on the subscriptions to the hard copy counterpart products (the so-called migration phenomenon). [1, 2] This question
has been raised primarily with respect to the secondary bibliographic
services where print products existed and were marketed prior to the
existence of the computer-readable database and its subsequent implementation online. Some A&I publishers maintain that because an alternate form of the same file is available, new sales of print products are
not made, existing subscriptions are cancelled, or both. Some vendors
of online search services maintain that the use of databases online introduces the file to new users and generates new sales of hardcopy
(print) products. † Some users of online services maintain that database producers are "ripping them off" by charging "high prices" for
the online file when (they think) it exists as a "by-product" of the computer composition of the print product.

Most discussions of migration have been made in the absence
of hard data to substantiate allegations. This paper provides 13
years' worth of hard data on the income, expenses and prices of
one organization which produces both databases and printed abstract-

*Reprinted by permission of the author and publisher from Informa-
tion Processing and Management, 17:5 (1981) 263-76. Copyright ©
1981 by Pergamon Press, Ltd.
†Throughout this paper the term "database products" is used to refer to those products that are marketed in the form of a database.
In fact all products are generated from a master database and in
that sense are products of a database--print products (sometimes
referred to as paper or hard copy products) and database products
(sometimes referred to as tape products or C-R products) are both
products of a master database.

ing and indexing (A&I) services. Although the date relate to one
organization, private discussion with other database producers indicates that the trends shown by the data are not atypical. The purpose of this paper is to confirm some allegations and dispel others
by displaying the facts and pointing out trends with respect to one
major database producing organization.

Although I have alluded to the so-called "migration phenomenon," I maintain that the existence or non-existence of migration
is immaterial. The very term "migration" seeks to lay blame, and
the blame is laid on a technology and a service whose time has come.
Online use of databases is an important technology that is here to
stay until another technology proves more efficient, effective or in-
expensive and thereby is able to displace it. The fact that printed
products compete with computer readable products in the information industry is not unusual. In many industries, or companies
within an industry, competing products are marketed. In the database field, one segment of the information industry, producers are
selling multiple forms of the same information and it is very likely
that one form may outstrip the others. This is not necessarily bad;
it is an intended good, but there can be difficulties with respect to
timing and pricing.

In this paper I have analyzed 13 years' worth of data relevant
to the finances of an A&I publisher that is also a producer of machine-readable databases. Data are presented in terms of both real
dollars and constant dollars adjusted in accordance with the Consumer
Price Index (CPI). The CPI base year is 1967† and the restated
(constant dollar) value equals original dollar cost x (CPI(x)/CPI(y))
(where x refers to period x and y refers to period y)[3]. Data are
presented in the form of graphs, and a discussion of the trends indicated
and interpretation of each graph or set of related graphs precedes their
presentation. In order to maintain confidentiality with respect to actual
dollar revenue and expenses, the ranges are not given on the figures.
Orders of magnitude are indicated, but specific dollars are not. The
database producing organization is not identified, though many will be
able to guess its identity. The database organization is simply referred
to as the organization or the producer.

There are some general trends that can be observed regarding this database producer's financial picture, relating to the online
use of the database, batch use of the database, and print products.
The cost for production of all products has increased. As a result
of online use of the file, database revenue (in the form of royalty
income), connect hours, and number of online users have increased;
but, at the same time, there has been a decrease in the number of
(and income from) database leases and licenses and a slight decrease
in the number of (and income from) print product subscriptions. The

---

†The CPI base changes every 13 years. The 13 years of this study
coincide with the 13 years of the CPI with a 1967 base. A new
base will be established in 1980.

general problem facing the organization is that of assessing the trade-offs between increased income from one class of product vs decreased income from another class of product while cost of operation continues to go up.

Major sections of this paper include discussions of income, expenses, excess of income over expenses, prices, the products a user gets for his money, and possible approaches the organization might take in the future to ensure a proper ratio of income to expenses.

Income

Figure 1 shows the income for the organization in real dollars (R$) for all products combined, for paper products, for the database, and for miscellaneous products. The same graph also provides the same data in constant dollars (C$). Income associated with print products includes subscriptions to current publications and sales of back issues, and it includes both domestic and foreign sales. Income associated with the database includes: income from leasing and licensing the database, fees, tape duplication charges, usage royalties, print charges, etc., associated with the acquisition of the database by foreign and domestic clients for batch and online use of the file. Income associated with miscellaneous products includes a potpourri of microform products, vocabulary tools and user aids, some of which were dropped when they did not prove to be profitable; the volume of income from miscellaneous sources is so small that it does not show up on Fig. 1 after 1976. In no case is income from contracts or interest from investments shown, as those types of income are incidental to the requirements of a self-supporting A&I print and database service.

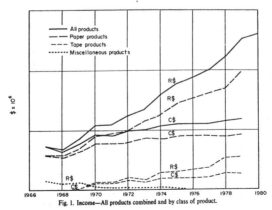

Fig. 1. Income—All products combined and by class of product.

The "All Products" curve shows that total income in real dollars, between 1967 and 1979, has more than tripled, i. e. has increased 246%. By itself that kind of increase is impressive, but

one must also consider the nature of the products that are responsible for the income, their respective contributions to it, the cost
of producing the products, and the relationship of expense to income.
Figure 1 also shows total income, for the same time period, in constant dollars. In constant dollars, income increased only 63% (with
a slight decrease in 1968) as opposed to the impressive 246% increase
reported in real dollars.

Income from miscellaneous products dropped 84% in real dollars and 87% in constant dollars between 1967 and 1975 when several
products were dropped. Miscellaneous income is too small to merit
further discussion.

Overall, the constant dollar revenue picture is positive, but
it is obvious that growth is tapering off. One should also bear in
mind that while the dollar revenue for the organization is up 63%,
the size of both the database and print products is nearly 50% larger
in terms of the number of abstracts produced per year, and the
product is greatly improved with more quality control.

Paper products income

The increase in annual revenue for paper products was 247% in real
dollars over the 13 years; in constant dollars the increase was 59%
or slightly less than the increase for all products combined. The
increase in real dollars from 1970 to 1979 was 120%; from 1974 to
1979 it was 59%; and from 1978 to 1979 it was 17%.

The income associated with printed products has increased
very little between 1974 and 1979, and the increase is due to the
increase in prices rather than to an increase in number of subscriptions sold. In fact, the total number of subscriptions decreased 7%
as did the number of subscriptions for each of the three print products individually. There was a slight increase in subscriptions from
1973 to 1974, but since 1974, the year the file went online, the number has decreased slightly each year. This does not necessarily
imply a cause:effect relationship--that may or not be the case and
we simply do not know--it is simply a fact to be reckoned with.
The two phenomena coexist and cannot be ignored.

Database income

The database income increased 2192% in real dollars over the eleven
years from its initiation. The percentage increase sounds more
impressive than the actual dollar figures would indicate. The database was started in 1969 and the first year brought in less than
$ 50,000. Thus, the percent increase is high because the base from
which it is calculated is so low in comparison. The database income
in 1979 was twenty times what it was in 1969, but this represents
only one-fifth of the revenue for the organization. If one were to
omit the first year of the database and calculate percentage increase

Communication and Education   221

from 1970 to 1979, the increase is 320% rather than 2192%. The
increase from 1974 to 1979 is 92% and from 1978 to 1979 it is neg-
ligible. In constant dollars the database income increased 1064% in
eleven years, 32% from 1974 to 1979, and decreased 6% from 1978
to 1979.

Although database income represents only one-fifth of the
product revenue, it provided the largest percentage increase and
merits further investigation. The major elements of database income are lease/license income and online royalty income. The
database was first leased in 1969 for in-house use in batch systems;
it was first licensed for batch use in 1971; and the first online licenses were let in 1974. The database was first costed as a separate line item in 1974.

Lease/license income and online royalty income in real and
constant dollars are shown in Fig. 2. Lease/license income increased 1367% from 1969 to 1978 (highest year) but only 1063% from
1969 to 1979 because there was a decrease of 37% from 1978 to 1979.
The decrease occurred because some database leases and licenses
were dropped. Fewer organizations are spinning tapes in-house now
that they can access the same information online and formulate their
search strategies themselves (thereby maintaining a reasonable amount
of confidentiality), and fewer batch search services are operating
than in earlier years. It is interesting to note that the lease/li-
cense income in 1974 and 1979 are almost identical. The peak in
1978 was due to an increase in the number of tape licenses to foreign countries. In constant dollars, lease/license income rose
491% from 1969 to 1979, was about identical in 1974 and 1978 and
declined 28% from that point to 1979.

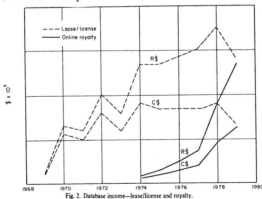
Fig. 2. Database income—lease/license and royalty.

The royalty income from online searching is the most promising element of database income. It rose 1400% from the start
year in 1974 to 1979 (950% in constant dollars). Royalty income
has risen steadily with no peaks and valleys, and between 1978 and
1979 when lease/license declined, royalties increased 49% (37% in
constant dollars).

Connect hours: an indicator of growth

Since royalty income is a function of price, a better indicator of
the growth of online use of the database is connect hours.   The
database was put up by four online services in 1974 and use has
more than quadrupled in the five years (see Fig. 3).   The number
of connect hours increased 376% overall and the percent increases
for each year relative to the prior year are 50, 47, 38, 25 and 26%.
Recognizing that in each subsequent year the base is larger than before, the outlook is positive.   In fact, in real numbers the growth
from 1978 to 1979 is just double what it was from 1974 to 1975.
With one exception, 1977-78, the size of the increase in real numbers (Fig. 3, dashed line) has increased steadily.

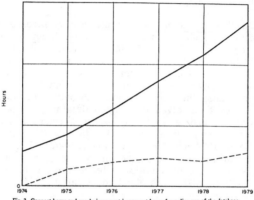

Fig. 3. Connect hours and yearly increment in connect hours for online use of the database.

Percent revenue by product

Any analysis of an organization's revenue should include a look at
the contribution each product makes toward the total product revenue.   Total production revenue can be broken down into specific
products or classes of products.   In this analysis (Fig. 4) I have
separated out print revenue, database revenue and isolated one subset of database revenue--online (royalty) revenue.   In 1968 the organization produced printed A&I tools only.   Thus, 100% of revenue
was related to print products.   In 1969 their first database leases
were instituted and accounted for 3% of income, and in 1979, print
products accounted for 78% of product revenue, while the database
accounted for 22% of revenue.   Royalties are the hope of most producers of online databases and although they reflect the use of the
file, it is necessary to recognize that they do not yet constitute a
large fraction of total income for A&I publishers who produce competing print and tape products.   For this database in 1979 they make
up 11% of the total of all product revenues.   As one can see in Fig.
4, the print products are declining in terms of percent revenues
while the database is increasing.   Although there is a slight increase
for print products from 1978 to 1979, the reason is that the non-U.S.
market, (specifically, developing countries) has purchased subscriptions and back issues of the A&I publications.   The U.S. market is

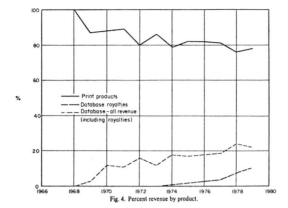

Fig. 4. Percent revenue by product.

considered to have reached saturation. Further sales to developing countries are anticipated and for a while they will ofset the drop in sales of print products to the U. S. market.

Expense

We have looked at the revenue situation for one database producer-- A&I publisher organization. It is now necessary to look at the other side of the coin to assess the health of the organization. First of all one must recognize the fact that, in this case, all products of the organization are either abstracts or references for serial or monograph publications, or indexes that point one to the abstracts or references. Thus, all the intellectual, management and production-processing efforts that go into creating the basic records, whether they are eventually published in hard copy print form or in computer-readable database form, should be associated with the master database. Neither print nor tape products could be provided without it. Production of the same print products today without use of computers and associated technologies would be prohibitively expensive and would undoubtedly price the A&I products out of the market, so let's face the situation squarely. The master database is a sine qua non for all the products. The distribution tape is not just a by-product of a printed publication. Both tape and print are direct and intended products of the master database and costs should be associated accordingly. Costs that are related to print products alone, such as paper, printing and binding should be costed to print products, and costs that are associated with tape products only, such as reformatting to various standards, tape duplication and distribution, etc. should be costed to the tape products.

Total expense

We have seen the increase in revenue over the past 13 years and will now look at the increase in expenses. Both income and expenses

have nearly tripled in the same time period. Product revenue more
than tripled and expenses did not quite triple. This might sound as
if revenue would exceed expenses, but expenses started from a larger
base and in fact, in 1979 expenses exceeded product revenue by several hundred thousand dollars. [Since the organization has some
contract, dividend and interest income, the total income vs expense
difference is only a few thousand dollars in the red.] This is the
first time since 1972 that the balance sheet has been in the red. A
discussion of the excess of income over the expenses or "profit" is
given in a later section.

Salaries and benefits vs materials and services

The information has been called into play to decrease manual efforts.
The cost of labor is high and automation is often considered a good
way to control expenses. This organization has increased automation and is continuing to do so. It has increased efficiency considerably and continues to do so. Total expenses can be broken into
two major categories, (1) salaries and benefits and (2) materials
and services. From Fig. 5 we can see that the largest increases
have been in materials and services rather than in salaries and benefits. From this we can conclude either that the automation efforts
have paid off or that materials and services have increased rapidly.
In fact, both are true.

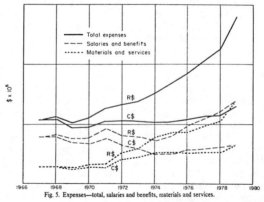

Fig. 5. Expenses—total, salaries and benefits, materials and services.

Total expenses increased 165% in real dollars but in constant
dollars they increased only 23% in 13 years while the basic product
increased in size by 96% (nearly twice as many abstracts). Thus,
productivity increased significantly more than expenses, the quality
of the products improved, and more output products were produced
from the basic production processing effort. It is obvious that the
efforts to increase automation and efficiency have paid off. Salaries
and benefits increased 81% in real dollars and they decreased 16%
in constant dollars. Materials and services increased 400% in real
dollars and they increased 132% in constant dollars. Materials and
services quintupled and a large cost element within this category is

paper, printing and binding. From 1978 to 1979, expenses increased 14% in constant dollars (25% in real dollars), salaries and benefits increased 6% in constant dollars (16. 5% in real dollars), while materials and services increased 23% (35% in real dollars).

Cost per abstract

Another way of looking at expenses is to look at the average cost of producing a surrogate or abstract. Since, within this organization, all products in all forms are related to abstracts, I have taken the total expenses of the organization and divided by the number of abstracts produced and reported that as the cost per abstract. I realize that one could report a significantly lower cost by removing the costs associated with future planning, research and development, marketing and anything else that is not directly related to production of abstracts, but in fact, when an organization produces nothing other than abstracts in multiple forms and combinations, the simple and straightforward approach of calculating cost per abstract in terms of total expenses is appropriate.

While the increase in expenses over the 13 year period was 165%, the increase in cost per abstract was only 37%. As shown in Fig. 6, the cost per abstract in 1967 was $20. 59 and in 1979 it was $28. 16. There was a decrease in cost per abstract between 1968 and 1971. In 1968 automation of the production of abstracts began and the database was released in 1969. Unfortunately, the early automation efforts were not entirely satisfactory and serious quality control problems became evident (the inconsistencies may have existed prior to automation; automation does point out inconsistencies that might not otherwise be seen). There were management problems at the same time, and in 1972, a new executive director was appointed. The new director added a bibliographic control staff to improve the quality of the products, but this naturally increased expenses and consequently, the real dollar cost per abstract went up.

Although the real dollar cost per abstract has increased 37% in 13 years, the constant dollar cost per abstract has decreased 36%. It has decreased from $20. 59 to $13. 15 while the quality of the abstract has improved (consistent bibliographic format). The lower cost reflects good management and improvements through automation. Although a bibliographic control department was added in 1972 and the start-up costs are seen in a higher cost per abstract in 1973, the constant dollar cost per abstract has decreased 7% from $14. 16 in 1973 to $13. 15 in 1979.

One more way of looking at the cost per abstract is to remove the costs that are directly related to print products and tape products. If one removes the cost of paper, printing and binding, the real dollar cost per abstract for 1979 becomes $21. 88 or $10. 22 in constant dollars. If one removes the tape preparation cost, the real dollars cost becomes $27. 88 or $13. 02 in constant dollars. If

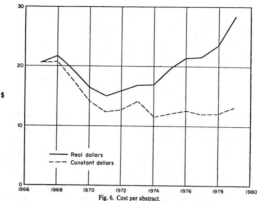

Fig. 6. Cost per abstract.

one removes both direct print and tape expenses, the cost per abstract, which is the cost to create the basic file from which all
products are generated, then becomes $21.59 in real dollars or
$10.08 in constant dollars. This is the cost per abstract for the
master database from which both print and tape products can be
generated. This cost must be allocated fairly to both types of products. At present, the lion's share is allocated to print products.

Excess of income over expenses

One measure of the success of a corporation is the excess of income
over expenses. In for-profit corporations this is called profit and
may be distributed to stockholders. In the case of not-for-profit
corporations the term profit is not used. The excess of income over
expenses is limited by IRS regulation and the funds must be used to
further the ends of the corporation. There are no stockholders and
no funds are distributed for anyone's personal benefit. The organization being analyzed is a not-for-profit corporation.

Figure 7 shows that at the close of 1968 the organization faced
serious problems as it was operating several hundred thousand dollars in the red; it nearly broke even in 1970 and by the end of 1972
it was in the black. By 1975 it was operating several hundred thousand dollars in the black or 1883% up from the low of 1968. Although it remained in the black until the year ending in 1979, the
trend from 1975 has been downward. The shape of the constant dollar curve is the same but the range is smaller. The downward trend
has been a definite worry since it began in 1976. However, to some
extent, the concern was offset by the knowledge that a portion of the
expense was due to capital expenditures for a new computer and software. The negative position that appeared in 1979 cannot be allowed
to continue, as no non-subsidized organization can be viable if it remains in the red for more than a short time.

Prices

Print product prices

The cost to the organization for generating its products was treated
in the section on expenses. I will now look at the cost to a user
or client of using or acquiring the various products. The organization produces three major print products. In Fig. 8 these are la-
belled A, B and C. For the 11 years from 1969-1979 the real dollar price of each of the print products increased by more than 100%.
A increased 137%, B 131% and C 121%. The constant dollar picture
is quite different; all remained almost static (product A increased
2.2%, B 18% and C 14%), despite the fact that the number of surrogates published in them nearly doubled. Thus, it is obvious that
productivity and efficiency nearly doubled.

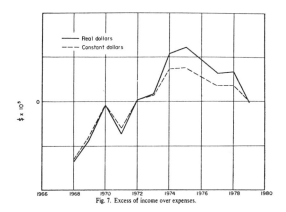

Fig. 7. Excess of income over expenses.

Database (tape) product prices

Tape products (Fig. 9) were made available in 1969 for lease (for
in-house use) and in 1971 for license (for resale to others). From
1969 to 1979 the lease fee increased only 23% and from 1971 to 1979
the license fee increased only 32%. The 1980 fees in both cases
were increased 7%. In constant dollars, lease/license fees decreased
steadily from their initiation to 1979. The lease fee declined 42%
and the license fee 29%. The constant dollar lease fee increased
8% in 1980 and the constant dollar license fee increased 4%. Because online use of databases was new, the producer was afraid that
higher fees might cause a decline in use or lower the rate of growth.
It is only in retrospect that one can say that the decision may have
been erroneous. Unfortunately, one seldom has an opportunity to
measure such events against a control.

Online royalty charges

The license fee is the base cost an online vendor must pay to use

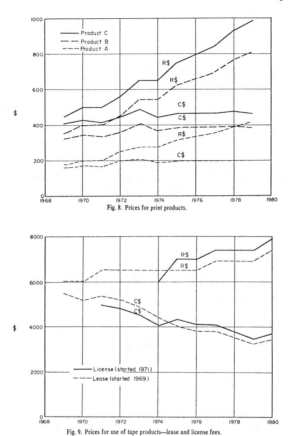

Fig. 8. Prices for print products.

Fig. 9. Prices for use of tape products—lease and license fees.

a database and offer services from it to his clients. In addition to
this basic charge, he must also return to the database producer a
royalty, which in this case is based on connect hours. The database producer established a royalty rate in the first year of online
availability, 1974, in the absence of knowledge about the likely success of the product online. In fact, an outside study had been conducted in 1968 to project the income picture for leasing and licensing
the database and for use charges. The consultant erroneously predicted heavy income from leases/licenses and very little income
from use royalties. Because he did not anticipate high use of the
database online, the royalty fee was set low and established a poor
precedent. The rate of 10% of the connect time charge was established and continued for three years. Although quoted in terms of
a percentage, I have provided it in terms of a rate per hour. As
shown in Fig. 10, the rate more than doubled (up 188%) from 1974
to 1979 but in constant dollars has increased only 50%.

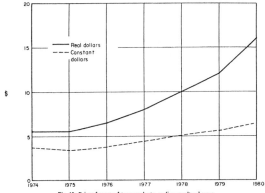

Fig. 10. Prices for use of tape products—online royalty charges.

The initial rates were 10% of connect time; thus, in those years the online vendors took in nine times as much money for the use of the file as the producer. Even as late as 1979, when online use of the file was hardly experimental (although many aspects of pricing are still unknown), the vendors received approximately five times as much money for the use of the file as the producer. One cannot help but wonder if it really costs five times as much to put up and maintain a database online (including the cost of training, advertising and marketing) as it does to produce it in the first place. Certainly the cost of developing and maintaining an online system is high, and when only a few databases are mounted, the cost per database must be high if the system costs are distributed over the total number of databases and their usage. When the number of databases available on a given system is large, and total use is high, however, then it would seem that the share of the fixed cost allocated to each database could be reduced.

Online connect fees

Royalty payments paid back to database producers are a fraction of the online connect fees charged by online vendors. I do not intend to present the pros and cons of connect time as a basis for charging. Most bibliographic systems use that basis for charging, and it is readily understood by users. In contrast, however, most numeric database systems do not charge on a connect hour basis.

The producer's database was put up on four online systems in 1974 (Fig. 11). Two charged $30/hr, one $95/hr and one $55/hr. By 1976 both the $95 and $55 services changed their fee to $65 where it has remained to date (System A decreased 32% and system D increased 18%). Both of the $30 services increased their fees-- one to $40 (system B increased 33%) and the other to $45 (system C increased 50%). In constant dollars all but the $95 fee have remained fairly steady.

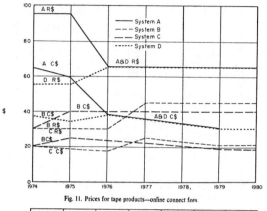

Fig. 11. Prices for tape products—online connect fees.

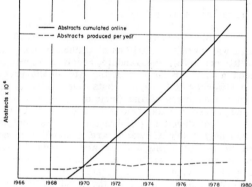

Fig. 12. Number of abstracts produced per year and abstracts cumulated online.

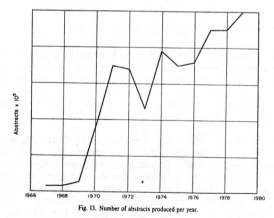

Fig. 13. Number of abstracts produced per year.

What Does the User Get for His Money

The online user pays a connect hour rate plus a fee for printing references. He may purchase various other services, but they do not bear on the discussion at hand. The royalties paid to the database producer from the connect hour fees are what the user pays (indirectly) to the producer for use of the file. The number of surrogates (in this case abstracts) in the file is what the user gains access to for the rate he pays. Figure 12 shows the number of cumulated records (abstracts) online and the number of abstracts produced per year for 1967 to 1979. The number of abstracts produced per year has doubled and the upper limit reached is a function of hardware/software limitations rather than a reflection of the applicable material in the field. The steep jump after 1969 (Fig. 13) is a function of automation which permitted more productivity with the same staffing. Expenses and income should be functions of the number of abstracts.

The number of abstracts produced each year is not the only consideration a user should keep in mind when using a database online (one generally searches more than one year at a time). He should also be aware of the number of abstracts that have been cumulated in the online file. In this case, (see Fig. 12) when the database was brought online, it was brought up in 1974 with records for the years from 1970 to 1973. The file has not been subdivided or broken into time segments, so the user accesses the entire file in each search. Even though the online connect charge was nearly the same in 1979 as in 1974, the amount of material searched was more than twice as large in 1979. And, because the online file is an inverted file, the connect time for searching the file would be very little more for the larger file. Thus, the user is getting more per dollar of connect time. Since the purchasing power of the dollar has been nearly halved between 1974 and 1979, the connect time has been constant and the online database has doubled, one can see that the user is getting four times as much for the dollar in 1979 as in 1974.

Possible Future Directions

The successful operation of an organization can be measured in terms of the relationship of income to expenses. If they are identical the organization breaks even but has no margin for difficult times and no margin to use for research or for the development of new products, etc. The excess of income over expenses is called "profit" in for-profit corporations and is simply referred to as "excess income over expenses" in not-for-profit corporations. I have used the term loosely here and employed the term "profit" even though we are dealing with a not-for-profit corporation. Regardless of what it is called, it is the chief indicator of the health of the organization. In the case of the A&I database organization studied, the profit picture has declined since 1975. Although it was in the black by a small margin as late as 1978, it went into the red a bit in 1979. Although the decline in "profits" started one year after

the database went online, this does not imply a cause:effect relationship, but there is a need to face the fact that expenses are increasing and profits decreasing.

    Overall there are several concurrent phenomena or trends.
Online use of the database is increasing as is income from online
use, but at the same time profit is decreasing and the number of
subscriptions to the print products is decreasing. The decrease in
subscriptions may be the result of any one or combination of the
following: price increases for print products, budget decreases in
the subscriber organizations, migration, or other reasons. However,
when facing the concurrent phenomena, the database producer should
not be concerned with assigning blame--particularly when the cause
is something that cannot be corrected by the database producer (as
is the case here). He should recognize the facts and act to increase
revenue and to offset the loss of profit. Actions the organization
might take to correct the situation are of several types and they relate to expenses, efficiency of operation, marketing, products and
services offered and pricing.

    Expenses. The organization might try to decrease expenses.
In fact, this has been done and they have reached the point where
further decreases would affect the quality of the products. In constant dollars, expenses have increased only 24% in three years; thus,
there is little additional that can be done in this area.

    Efficiency of operation. Efficiency has been increased. The
organization now produces twice as many abstracts per dollar as it
did in 1971, despite the devaluation of the dollar.

    Marketing. In the area of marketing one might suggest sell-
ing more print products, but every indicator shows that the domestic
market is saturated and that in a few years the foreign market will
also be saturated. The organization might attempt to increase online usage. This is being done via education/training/marketing
activities and by putting the file up on more online systems; two
more online search services are expected to mount the database in
1981. Lease/license revenue is anticipated to be up 10% in 1980,
correcting the beginning of a downward trend that occurred in 1979.
Online royalties are estimated to be up 110% in 1980 and the real
dollar increase is expected to be three times what it was the prior
year. A new marketing director has been hired, and he will monitor these efforts. Good marketing is essential but alone will not
solve all of the problems.

    Products. The organization might develop new products or
discontinue some of the existing ones. Since the end-of-year projections for 1980 are positive for the lease/license and royalties
for the database, these cannot be considered candidates for termination. The print products, however, are expected to produce only
66% of product revenues as opposed to 78% in 1979. Sixty-six percent is still the major portion of income even though it is declining
and will continue to decline. Print products cannot be considered

for termination at this time. However, if the trend continues, serious consideration might have to be given to this possibility in a decade or two. New products might be introduced; this is a tack which is being seriously investigated. Several possible products have been costed out and decisions will be made shortly.

Services. New services could be introduced. This has been seriously considered and the producer has introduced a brokerage-type search service using the major online vendor systems. Another possibility for a new service would be the initiation of an online search service operated on the producer's computer. This would not be cost effective if only one database were offered, but it might be feasible if the organization were to function as the heart of a distributed network, tying in to other related databases (offering numeric databases, bibliographic databases, modeling systems, and various packages for manipulating numeric data and producing reports). [4] Another possible configuration would be the development of a cooperative organization or consortium of database producers for offering online services. These latter possibilities are difficult and costly to implement, but they might offer a means of recovering more of the revenue from the use of a database for the producer. The present arrangement compensates the online vendor more than the database producers for the use of the producer's database. The possibility of offering online services through a distributed network or through a consortium is a consideration which should not be rejected out of hand.

Pricing. Pricing of products is another means of affecting revenue. Prices can be increased, decreased, or the pricing scheme can be changed. The increases, decreases and revised schemes can be associated with print products, lease/license fees, online use charges, print charges and display charges. Today, most A&I databases are dependent on print products to cover a major portion of the master database. If database prices were to be increased to the point where the database was paying its own way, then the prices of the print products could be decreased--perhaps enough to delay the day when a serious consideration of phase-out would need to be made. Increasing the price of the database necessitates someone's absorbing the increase. If the online vendors choose to absorb the price increase and hold to the price they charge the user, then the producer will increase revenue if the use remains static or increases, the user will not pay more, and the online vendor would decrease his profits if the volume of use is static and increase revenue if the use increases. If the online vendor passes on the increase to the users, then the users will pay more and the effect this might have on volume of use is unknown. Unfortunately, a database producer does not have the luxury of tracking price variations as a research investigation wherein controls are employed and one factor is varied at a time. The database producer is in a real life, real market situation. Faced with a negative balance for the year 1979, there is no way to stay in business without increasing revenues and this generally means increasing prices. Both the user and online vendors must recognize the fact that database production is expensive and that databases must bring in enough money to support their production. Without databases, the online vendors would have nothing to offer and the users would have nothing to search.

References

1. T. P. Barwise, Online Searching: The Impact on User Charges of the Extended Use of Online Information Services. 75pp. International Council of Scientific Unions Abstracting Board, Paris, France (1979).
2. Loene Trubkin, Migration from Print to Online, Online Reviews pp. 5-12 (March 1980).
3. Statistical Abstracts, 1978, p. 482, Table No. 781.
4. M. E. Williams and T. Brandhorst, Future trends in A&I database publication. Bull. Am. Soc. Information Sci. 5(3), 27-28 (1979).

Professor Williams has prepared a follow-up article to "Relative Impact of Print and Database Products on Database Producer Expenses" scheduled for publication during 1982 in Information Processing and Management. The follow-up article reports that all of the recommendations made were acted upon and the organizations' financial picture went from a loss to the second highest "profit" in its history.

CORPORATE GHOSTS IN THE PHOTOCOPYING MACHINE*

Irving Louis Horowitz

Since the Williams & Wilkins decision of 1972, it has been clear that the issue of copyright in the United States has essentially involved two relatively large-scale principles. The first is the right of the people to have, unimpeded, without artificial restraints, and with the exception of areas of national and military security, as much information as they want. Indeed, recent executive orders have extended the right to know into the area of private dossiers in an effort to combat the capacities of a society to gather and maintain privileged information. The second is the right to compensation or payment for work done. This right to compensation for copyrighted material is not some selfish effort to create payments for a priestly class, but quite the contrary: to establish the principle that intellectual or creative work deserves the same consideration as manual labour.

The antinomy between knowledge and property is at the source of present dilemmas which have plagued and beset librarians and information agencies, on the one hand, and publishers and authors, who are usually found on the other side of any argument, on the other. The present legislation fails, to put it bluntly, because it tries to adjudicate the claims of those who believe in the right to know against the claims of those who believe in the rights of compensation. The upshot has been that neither side has been made content. Librarians and publishers, two groups that desperately require each other's co-operation and assistance, have been placed extraordinarily at loggerheads.

In general, librarians have argued that the new copyright legislation has changed library procedures for the worse: that they must engage in police activities to determine what is and what is not proper use of copyright materials; that they have had to engage in bookkeeping and auditing to keep records of such use; and that they have had to go back in time to an older library concept, when the lion at the gate meant keeping people out rather than encouraging broader use of the facilities. Specific queries concerning revisions in the 1976 U.S. copyright legislation involve concepts no librarian

*Reprinted by permission of the author and publisher from Scholarly Publishing, 12:4 (July 1981) 299-304. Copyright © 1981 by The University of Toronto Press.

can accept with equanimity: How should librarians interpret fair use? How should periodicals more than five years old be treated? Such questions suggest procedures that require an unacceptable bureaucratic manipulation of people and massaging of events.

Publishers, from their point of view, are equally frustrated by what they feel, and with equal justification, are highly ambiguous aspects of current copyright legislation. They point out unmistakable evidence of the near total collapse in the sale of special issues or special articles for classroom and educational purposes; the purchase of one copy of a periodical or book for a master file which is then photocopied in multiples and dispersed to libraries in a wider system; the wholesale random extraction of data, tabular material, and technical information from copyright material and the use of this material in data banks without regard to the cost of composition, authorship, or any of the processes involved in creating the material. All this is done in the name of a doctrine of fair use which new copying technology has made obsolete. That this fact was not recognized in the 1976 legislation has opened up an area of intolerable ambiguity for publishers and librarians alike.

The law dislikes ambiguity--above all the kind of ambiguity which increases rather than decreases the abuse intended to be removed by legislation. Present copyright law must, at the level of cognition, be put into the category of metaphysics rather than pragmatics. Fair use mandates that do not permit the making of multiple copies of the same material go on to list a series of exceptions that can only be characterized as effective loopholes in the legislation. Current guidelines require a degree of record-keeping on the part of librarians--for instance, no more than five orders for copies from a given periodical can be filled during a calendar year for articles less than five years old--yet the legislation permits different responses for light and heavy use at the discretion of a library clerk. It establishes a Copyright Clearance Center which itself has no uniform rules for granting permission since each publisher sets his own fees for copying. Current legislation makes participation in such a centre entirely optional with no penalty for non-membership and no rewards for participation. The reasoning behind this is that copyright owners believe they have the right to assess the value of their materials, and should not be subject to mandatory licensing.

It is essential to alleviate the copyright muddle and restore norms of cooperation and confidence between the two great communities of librarians and publishers, who serve writers and readers alike. Any fundamental solution would have two elements: one technical, the other corporate. Let us address each in turn.

At the technical level, several copier controller systems are now in place and have the capacity to provide the name of the person using the copier, the name of the document being copied, the department using the particular document, and the number of copies being made. All this information can be recorded individually and summarized. Several such systems are programmed to record and print out data for billing clients such as lawyers, advertisers, public relations officers, management, and consulting and professional organizations of all kinds. Several models of copier controller even have the capacity to prepare summaries in computer printout for auditing purposes by project, department, division, and ultimately by periodical to the copier. The librarian need only insert his or her coded card and the ISBN or ISSN numbers borne by the book or periodical into a small terminal attached to the copier. If the card is valid, and the information accurate, a central recorder transmits this information to the photocopying machine, which is instantly activated, permitting the user to make copies. As those copies are being made, the equipment can record a fee to be transmitted to the Copyright Clearance Center or to the owners of these materials directly. Many copying machines have long had a special document button which charges the user for the reproduction of bulk matter such as books or journals at a different rate.

The technology now exists that would audit the use of copyright materials, encouraging maximum usage and satisfying the librarian's concern for the unimpeded flow of information, while permitting simple, accurate record-keeping and procedures for compensating copyright holders. ISBN and ISSN systems exist that provide exact identification of material in copyright, permitting compensation to publishers and authors. Let me emphasize that this technology is fully available and in place. I am not speculating about inventions that are yet to be.

This brings us to the most vexing and troubling issue: namely, the corporate ghosts in the photocopying machines. Librarians and publishers have confronted each other as adversaries, although in reality each needs the other, while manufacturers have stayed out of the conflict and walked away with enormous profits from reproducing copyright materials. Xerox, Minolta, IBM, and a handful of other manufacturers currently have the capacity to install controlling devices such as I have described, but choose not to do so in order to encourage wider numbers of people and agencies to install their equipment. The weakening of copyright that has resulted from uncontrolled copying occurs to the greater loss of the community of knowledge as a whole. It is an odd situation, in which the manufacturers of photocopiers can take relatively low risks and reap relatively high profits, while ignoring with impunity an industry called publishing which takes relatively high risks for relatively low profits. This dichotomy is untenable. It is ludicrous that these parties to the copying of copyright material have thus far successfully avoided taking any responsibility for the current confusion about copyright legislation.

There are serious legal problems involved in holding manufacturers accountable for unrestricted copying. Many of the photocopying manufacturers both sell and lease their equipment: what should be the relationship between proceeds generated as a result of leased versus sold equipment? Manufacturers have no direct control over licit or illicit use of their equipment: how then can

they be expected to be liable in situations of copyright abuse?
Further, how can one legislate that abuse should be corrected by
a manufacturer? Is this tantamount to charging a gun manufacturer
rather than the user with manslaughter? Perhaps a way out is to
draw a parallel with a defective product. Is the use of a malfunc-
tioning car the fault of GM or Ford, or of the user? In a period
when such relationships of manufacturer to consumer are being
widely debated in both law and custom, in one industry after another,
perhaps photocopier manufacturers have some culpability for illicit
copying.

These are serious questions. They remain questions to be
addressed, and not glossed over to avoid shared responsibility. To
further complicate issues, both IBM and Xerox are directly involved
in the world of publishing itself. They have subsidiary organizations
with vital concerns for the protection of copyright. If these interests
are to be served in a healthy way, without creating an unintended
monopoly of information, then the major photocopying agents must
become co-operative in the most intimate meaning of that word. They
should begin by modifying their hardware to permit users to compen-
sate copyright owners and to permit the widest dissemination of information while reimbursing authors and publishers for their materials.

At present, each copying machine is provided with a copyright notice based on the 1976 legislation which can be either ignored
or peeled off, and has absolutely no binding value. Photocopier manufacturers should be required under law to supply their machines
with copyright controllers to permit systematic recording of the
name of the user, client, ISBN or ISSN number, number of copies,
amount to be billed, where payments are to be automatically rendered, and any other requested information for later computer printout. Such equipment must also have automatic clearance, so that no
copies will be billed to the next user. The ISBN and ISSN system
is now nearly universally used and recognized. The Copyright Clearance Center, with all of its imperfections and crudities, is also in
place. Finally, the technology, copyright controlling devices, also
exists and is being marketed.[1]

The only weakness remaining is the sloth of tradition, the
reluctance of major copier manufacturers to provide at point of sale
or rental the controlling equipment which comes with the proper
copyright controller devices. I therefore urge those agencies considering copyright revision at this time to move the discussion at
once from a futile fratricidal struggle between professional publishers and professional librarians to a common concerted effort to
make photocopying manufacturers aware of the magnitude of the
problem, and to make them legally responsive to the needs of users
and owners of information alike. Only when responsibility for fair
compensation for use of copyright material is accepted by the manufacturers of copiers no less than by librarians and publishers will
the present inadequacies of most current copyright law be resolved
in a manner acceptable to all interested parties.

Commissioner James F. Davis, who found in favour of Williams and Wilkins and against the Department of Health, Education and Welfare, put the matter most succinctly in noting that "the issues raised by this case are but part of a larger problem which continues to plague our institutions with ever-increasing complexity --how best to reconcile, on the one hand, the rights of authors and publishers under the copyright laws with, on the other hand, the technological improvements in copying techniques and the legitimate public need for rapid dissemination of scientific and technical literature." We must keep in mind that the essential purpose of copyright is not to restrict use, but to benefit the arts and sciences by compensating people who create.

The rise of a new technology, the dawn of an era when information is electronically stored and transmitted rather than recorded solely on printed paper, requires that librarians and publishers, in their quest to serve users and creators alike, must confront the realities of this new technology. This further means dealing directly with the industries and manufacturers in this new world of copiers and computers. Ignoring these facts will ensure that, whatever solutions now are found, several years hence further revisions will have to be considered, perhaps at a period when the balance of forces will weigh yet more heavily against those who believe that copyright encourages creativity no less than it protects those who create.

Reference

This paper is adapted from a presentation to the public hearing of the Copyright Office, Library of Congress, held in New York City on 28 January 1981.
1.   One such device, manufactured by Manitou Systems in Chicago, is in use in Levi Strauss, duPont, Simon & Friedlander, the University of San Francisco, and scores of other industries, banks, law firms, and accounting firms. See New Product Marketing, May 1977, pp. 24-5.

Part IV

THE SOCIAL PREROGATIVE

SHIFTING BOUNDARIES IN INFORMATION*

Anita Schiller

Less than ten years ago, libraries began to contract for online
search services, and introduce them to library users. Since then,
the services have become well established. As this occurred, libraries became the initial linking agents between large electronic
stores of information and the American public. Access by the public-
at-large to major scientific, educational, and social science databases
began to become available, and libraries were the pivotal intermediaries.

    This was a spectacular development. A new technology opened
up the possibility for libraries to offer a level of service that just a
short time before would have seemed almost unimaginable. Developments have moved so rapidly, that though the terminals have barely
been plugged in, predictions of the library's ultimate demise are
now being widely circulated. Scenarios from outside librarianship
also depict transformational changes in nearly every aspect of our
lives--in the workplace and the family--in economic, educational,
cultural, and legal institutions and arrangements.

    These predictions come at a time when information as a re-
source has taken on a new economic value, and the information sector of the national economy is seen by some to be its driving force.
They are based not only on the present capabilities of the technology,
but also on expectations of growing mass consumer markets.

Library and public

Libraries constitute only a tiny portion of the computer/communica-
tions market. Even when we look at only that limited segment of it
with which libraries are most familiar--the online bibliographic utilities and search services--we see only a portion of those databases
which are publicly available. In addition, the converging of computer
/communications technologies, and efforts, both here and abroad, to

*Reprinted by permission of the author and publisher from Library
Journal, 106 (April 1, 1981) 705-09. Published by R.R. Bowker Co.
(a Xerox Company). Copyright © 1981 by Xerox Corporation.

develop systems for the consumer market, have resulted in several
varieties of information services with varying capabilities.   The
search systems now used by libraries represent only one of many
types to be directed ultimately toward individual consumers and end
users in homes and offices.

Despite these qualifications, libraries have a significant relationship to the developing consumer market for electronic information systems.   This is due both to the informational nature of the
library's role, and to its public character.   It is their public information function, in fact, that made libraries the sought-after intermediaries between the search services and the general public.   For
example, OCLC has turned to libraries as intermediaries in several
of its "home delivery of information services" projects.   The irony
here is that if electronic information services tend ultimately to displace libraries, this will have as much to do with the now shifting
public-private sector boundaries, and the erosion of the public character of the library's role, as with the shift from print to electronic
technology.

The shift to profit

In some ways, what is now taking place in libraries can be seen as
a microcosm of much broader changes which are taking place in society.   Traditional functions of libraries have included the collection,
storage, organization, and retrieval of information for use.   Today,
these functions, on a vastly expanded scale, are being performed
by information technology.   At the same time, the production and
processing of information, which were essentially peripheral, not-
for-profit activities, have become primary, for-profit activities.
This has brought library functions nearer to the mainstream of economic activity.   While traditionally, ownership of information has
not been particularly profitable, today information is increasingly
defined as a commodity to be bought and sold.   The public information function that libraries serve is seen to have a new-found value
in the private sphere.   Yet while we tend to perceive the capabilities of the technology independently from its institutional forms, and
quite separately and distinctly from the organizational arrangements
for the distribution of its products, the utilization of online search
services in academic and public libraries has been closely linked to
an expanding private sector role in information.

The primary goal of the Information Industry Association
(IIA) is "to promote the development of private enterprise in the field
of information and to gain recognition for information as a commercial product."[1]   The introduction of user fees for online search
services constitutes a major shift in this direction, and in the public-
private sector boundaries in the library information sphere.   Other
examples are less obtrusive.   One concerns the source of the service itself, which resides externally, outside the library, most typically in the private sector.   The increasing role of bibliographic
utilities and regional library networks also suggests an increasing

shift toward new financial arrangements, and away from traditional
tax support for public institutions. Possibly even more interesting
is the growing role of the private sector in decisions concerning the
national bibliographic record. Historically, the responsibility for
standards in this area has resided with the Library of Congress,
and the national and international library communities. More recently, however, private sector organizations have also begun to
be represented. [2] Other examples include the growing emphasis
on specialized, on-demand information products and services which
are marketed like traditional commodities; and on document delivery,
ordered and paid for on an individual basis.

As these changes occur the very definitions of the public and
private sectors begin to change, and the distinctions between them
become blurred. This point is noted in the Annual Review of Information Science and Technology for 1978, which was, incidentally,
the first volume in the series to include a chapter on public-private
sector interaction. [3] There the authors use the term "public sector" to designate governmental organizations, and "private sector" to
designate nongovernmental organizations. They also note the currently increasing discussion of private, for-profit organizations "in
marked contrast to the earlier literature emphasizing the private
sector information systems developed by scientific and technical societies."[4] It is interesting too, that in common usage, the terms
"publicly available" and "commercially available" appear to have become synonymous.

While definitions of "public" and "private" sector vary, and
while the distinctions between them have already become so blurred
that both terms convey very imprecise meanings, what seems most
important in attempting to understand current trends is recognition
of the increasing proprietary interest in information as a profitable
resource as opposed to the diminishing concern for the social interest in information as a shared resource.

Even the government increasingly relies on the market model
to define its own informational activities. For the National Technical Information Service (NTIS), for example, cost recovery has been
a major principle of operation, and this agency has been expanding
and extending its domain, absorbing, duplicating, or displacing publication and dissemination functions of the U.S. Government Printing
Office and its depository library system. At one point, NTIS even
sought to secure copyright for its publications. Ironically, this was
opposed, both by the IIA, and the American Library Association.
Current trends suggest, however, that portions of public information
may be shifted from the public to the private domain along with federal contracts that are awarded to outside information organizations.
A recent Supreme Court decision ruled, for example, that the Freedom of Information Act "does not apply to research prepared by a
private group, even when the research is financed by the U.S. Government and the research records are in the government's possession."[5] To cite another example, the Smithsonian Science Information Exchange (SSIE) has been supported for the most part by

public funds, but its database was initially offered exclusively by
one of the commercial search services, at an hourly fee which was
among the highest charged for any database to be offered by any
search services.[6]

   Considering that these two organizations, NTIS and SSIE, have
been most vigorous in promoting cost recovery, it should also be
noted that both organizations have mandates that cut across all mis-
sions and disciplines. They are the only centralized sources of scientific and technical information which deal with dissemination of the
results of all federally sponsored research and development.

Government marketing

There are many other examples of the vanishing borderline between
the federal government and the private sector. Beyond supplying
research and development support for the advancement of information
technology, the federal government has also financed market studies
for information services. Two pilot projects for introducing the
search services in libraries illustrate the point. Each of these projects, the first in academic libraries, and the second in public libraries, precede the wider implementation of search services in these
types of libraries.[7] Each was supported by the National Science
Foundation, and each was directed toward the following concerns:
Was there a clientele which would find searches of machine readable databases useful? Would users be willing to pay for searches?
How could fees for service be implemented? The results, in both
of the studies, were generally affirmative, and indicated as well,
some of the mechanics for providing the service. Despite variations in applications, and alternative arrangements for support which
were established in some libraries, these pilot projects essentially
became the models for implementing the new services, particularly
in academic libraries.

   It is not unusual for the federal government to sponsor studies which assist market development, not only for particular technologies, but for individual firms as well. One recent announce-
ment of a small grant to an individual researcher states that, "The
goal will be to develop the presentation to the point where the students will learn to perform searches of ... files using the computer
services of the ... [X] Company's online search system."[8]

   In 1972, a major report on the implications of information
technology for society was issued by the Conference Board. According to a key chapter in this report, "the blurring of the distinction
between public-private spheres may be the single most important
political development during the next generation."[9] Events during
the past decade seem to support this prediction.

   Librarians have been involved in the changing public-private
sector relationships relatively early. The increasing utilization of
libraries as intermediaries by the private sector, to supply public
information services has been a major source of this involvement.

Impact on access

Due to their own position in the information field, librarians have
become aware, ahead of the general public, of some significant issues surrounding access to information which relate both to the electronic technology and the growing role of the private sector. Both
the capabilities of the technology and private sector interest in its
application have developed new forms of information access. At the
same time, new restrictions on access have begun to develop. The
first of these concerns the "free or fee" issue.

Recently, however, the questions, "who 'owns' the bibliographic records?"; or "who 'owns' the data?"; or "who 'owns' the
information?" have begun to surface more often. These questions
have been raised frequently at conferences of librarians, information scientists, and the online services community. The ownership
questions have become a source of growing uncertainty for information users, as "stakeholders" in the information field assert what
they regard as their proprietary rights.

Interest in this issue increased dramatically when OCLC announced that third party use of bibliographic records in its database
would be prohibited in its new contractual arrangements. There was
considerable protest, and a set of OCLC hearings where testimony
from librarians and library network representatives strongly opposed
restrictions on a library's use of its own cataloging records. OCLC
decided to modify its position, and generally to allow third party
use.

The issue of property rights to information has not been resolved. The U.S. Constitution states that "The Congress shall have
power ... to promote the progress of science and the useful arts,
by securing for limited times to authors and inventors the exclusive
right to their respective writings and discoveries." Despite the en-
actment of the Copyright Law of 1976, and the issuance in July 1978
of the final report of the Commission on New Technological Uses of
Copyrighted Works (CONTU), the new rules of the game are seen by
some to be inadequate to apply to the changing technology and the
changing economic role of information in society. There is growing
uncertainty and doubt about the rights of information consumers, end
users, and intermediaries.

A hostile environment

As conflicting interests within the information sector itself emerge,
a major problem has become the right to use information once it
has been acquired. One database producer, for example, has stated
that use of information from its database is restricted to the geo-
graphical site where the printout is delivered by the search service.
It may be difficult to comprehend precisely what this means, or whether, in fact, this particular injunction would hold up in a court of
law. Yet the restriction exemplifies a growing set of restrictive

arrangements now being asserted as the legitimate rights of one or another stakeholder. These restrictions limit information use. In recent print publications stringent warnings have begun to appear. One newspaper, closely reflecting the views of the IIA, claims "All rights reserved. Reproduction of material appearing in Information World is forbidden without written permission."

At a national online meeting in 1980, after a panel discussion on copyright and related database royalty issues emphasized the legal rights of database producers, one member of the audience objected to the stress on user restrictions. He noted that it would certainly be reasonable for an end user to include citations from an online search in a paper for publication. While he was reassured that this was indeed a legitimate use, this interchange at a forum of experts suggests that an environment is being created which is hostile to the sharing of information. Current developments in the information field must not simply be hailed as extending information access, but examined as well, for the restrictive impact they may have on the intellectual process.

When information is organized, patterned, and distributed on the basis of proprietary interest, the dissemination process itself is being transformed. The costs involved in this transformation may serve to accelerate its impact. As Theodore Lowi pointed out, almost a decade ago, "... while the cost of information is going to drop precipitously, the cost of being informed will not."[10]

While it is possible that some progress will be made in defining some of the issues of ownership and access to bibliographic records and data as the Network Advisory Committee and other groups consider these issues, the rights of information users remain in doubt. In the present environment, the social imperatives of information access are beginning to take second place to proprietary interests.

User charges affect the ability to acquire information in the first place. Questions concerning data or information ownership add barriers to information use.

Information quality

Another issue concerns information quality, and user knowledge of what the databases include, or the sources from which the data derive. While there are several examples in existing online databases, the growth of mass market information systems suggests additional problems. The British Post Office's Prestel System, for example, does not require information providers to distinguish advertising from other information. A lack of such differentiation could make it more difficult for consumers to evaluate critically the information they receive.[11]

Another concern is monitoring--not only for individual sur-

veillance--but also for purposes which may lead to reducing the
range of information that is supplied. For example, one of the
new home information systems claims that its computer configuration "gives us the ability to monitor what people are looking at, for
how long, and in what sequence."[12] IBM's Chief Scientist Lewis
Branscomb recently touched on this development: "Yet somehow I
worry, " he stated, "that the electronic libraries of the future will
have in them only the information someone knows we want to know.
That's probably not the information we most need to know."[13]

Libraries and information issues

When libraries began to utilize the commercial online search services, they did so in order to offer enhanced service to library users.
The new services were regarded simply as supplements to existing
services. Similarly, the use of OCLC for library cataloging was
regarded as a more efficient way to perform that operation. Yet,
in contrast to traditional arrangements, when libraries began to contract with external suppliers for online information or online cataloging service, they thereby became intermediaries in a much larger,
and very different kind of informational system, with impacts on library services to users, collections, staff, organization, and support
that have only begun to be seen. These impacts affect the character,
form, and content of the information which library users and information consumers obtain, and the way in which information is used.

       Looking into the near future, Lancaster has stated that "li-
braries are becoming in a sense 'disembodied.' A research 'library'
of the future ... need not contain any printed materials at all. It
can be a room containing a terminal and nothing more."[14]

       Lancaster defines the present major professional tasks of a
librarian as threefold: first, the selection of materials; second,
their intellectual organization; and, third, providing various types
of question-answering and literature-searching services. In the
electronic world, however, "since any information source is accessible on demand, and items are not physically 'owned,' the only selection activity is the selection of which source to access for any
particular purpose." "Because the electronic sources are not owned, "
he continues, "they require no organization by the librarian."[15]

       Whatever the positive and negative impact of this forecast,
it is clear that a shift in public-private sector boundaries is involved in this technological transformation.

       It is also clear that its growing social impact needs to be
further explored, and that social criteria for information access
need to be asserted with as much vigor, imagination, and initiative
as has been applied to extending the new technology.

       As the new technology is applied, and as the long awaited
end user community begins to participate directly, new tensions in

the information economy may emerge, along with new efforts to rectify the growing imbalance between the public and private interests in the information society.

References

1. "The 1976 Information Year in Review, " Information Action, February 1977, p. 5.
2. See "Who Owns the MARC Format?, " Advanced Technology Libraries, July 1979, p. 5-6.
3. Berninger, Douglas E. & Burton W. Adkinson, "Interaction between the Public and Private Sectors in National Information Programs, " in Martha E. Williams, ed. , Annual Review of Information Science and Technology 13, Knowledge Industry Publications, 1978, p. 3-36.
4. Ibid, p. 13.
5. "Supreme Court Decisions on Freedom of Information Act, " Information Reports and Bibliographies 9, No. 4, 1980, p. 2.
6. For a description of the funding and organization of the SSIE, see Need To Strengthen Financial Accountability to the Congress, Washington, D. C. , U. S. General Accounting Office, 1977, p. 15-19.
7. See Alan R. Benenfeld, et al. , Nasic at MIT: Final Report, March 1974-28 February 1975, MIT Electronic Systems Laboratory Report (ESL-R-543), February 1975; and Roger F. Summit and Oscar Firschein, Investigation of the Public Library as a Linking Agent to Major Scientific, Education, Social and Environmental Data Bases. Final Report, Information Systems Programs, Lockheed Palo Alto Research Laboratory, October 1977.
8. "The Incorporation of Computer-based Literature Searching Methods into an Existing Programs [sic] of Independent Study in Chemistry, " Information Hotline, September 1980, p. 20.
9. Lowi, Theodore, "Government and Politics, " in Information Technology: Some Critical Implications for Decision Makers, N. Y. : The Conference Board, 1972, p. 147.
10. Ibid, p. 137.
11. For a recent report on this and other pertinent questions, see Federal Trade Commission, Media Policy Session: Technology and Legal Change, Washington, D. C. : USGPO, 1980.
12. "Merrill Lynch and CBS/Publishing Join Viewtron Test, " IDP Report, May 24, 1980, p. 3-4.
13. Branscomb, Lewis M. , "The Technology of Information, " a paper delivered at the Conference, "An Information Agenda for the 1980's, " sponsored by the American Library Association, June 27-28, 1980, New York University. (Processed, p. 140.)
14. Lancaster, F. Wilfred, "The Future of the Librarian Lies Outside the Library, " Catholic Library World, April 1980, p. 391.
15. Ibid.

BETWEEN GIN AND TWIN: MEETING THE

INFORMATION NEEDS OF THE THIRD WORLD*

Ziauddin Sardar

Introduction

Access to knowledge and information and to the channels through
which it is conveyed has now become important for both domestic
development and international trade and economic gains. The developing countries realize that information has now become the chief
raw material and the principal product of modern economy. They
have become acutely dependent on the industrialized countries for it
--a dependency which is producing all the adverse repercussions
which are normally associated with technological dependency.

The developing countries are thus forced to ask four basic
questions about the world's pool of scientific and technological information. Who shall have access? For what purpose? What will be
the procedure for granting or denying access? And what are the
costs involved and how are they to be allocated? The Third World's
concern with these questions has led to the demand for a New International Information Order; a demand that is parallel to the developing countries' struggle to establish a New International Economic
Order (NIEO). The first articulation of this demand was made at
the United Nations Conference on Science and Technology for Development (UNCSTD) held in Vienna in August 1979.

The proposal for GIN

UNCSTD was a continuation both of the series of UN conferences
held during the 1970's on specific development issues and is a part
of the North-South dialogue over the establishment of NIEO. The
developing countries, represented at UNCSTD by the Group of 77
(now more than 120 developing countries) believe that science and
technology play an important role in the establishment of NIEO. At
UNCSTD, the Group of 77 declared that "global and fundamental
structural changes are required in the existing distribution of scien-

*Reprinted by permission of the author and publisher from Aslib
Proceedings, 33:2 (February 1981) 53-61.

tific and technological capacities in the world. "[1] In the pursuance
of this goal, the developing countries made three specific demands.
Firstly, they called for the establishment of a funding mechanism
which would raise up to $2 billion by 1985, not just by voluntary
contributions but also through compulsory automatic contributions.
Secondly, they asked for a new inter-governmental committee to
govern the new financing system, oversee the UN science and technology activities, and report directly to the General Assembly.
Thirdly, the developing countries demanded a new Global Information
Network (GIN) that would facilitate the transfer of scientific and technological information to the Third World.

What happened to the first two demands of the developing
countries, both at UNCSTD and various UN Sessions on "The Vienna
Programme of Action on Science and Technology for Development"
(UNCSTD's recommendations), has been widely reported and analyzed.
[2] This paper concentrates on the third demand of the developing
countries: the establishment of GIN.

The Third World's demand for GIN is based on the belief that
a global network would reduce their information dependency and provide them with a certain amount of access to world's scientific and
technological information.   The developing countries argued for a
global network that gives open access to developing countries to scientific and technological information from the industrialized nations
as well as information-on-information.   UNCSTD's Draft Programme
of Action stated the position of the developing countries in these
words:

> International organizations should act as a tool for syste-
> matic exchange of information on experience on different
> countries in all fields pertaining to the application of sci-
> ence and technology for development.   In this connexion,
> continuing consideration should be given to the establish-
> ment of a global and international information network,
> within the United Nations system, where emphasis will be
> placed on priority needs of the developing countries.[3]
> The developing countries also argued that as the developed
> countries have a monopoly of scientific and technological
> information they should "make their information resources
> readily accessible to users from developing countries" and
> allow access to "their specialized information systems."
> [4] GIN, the developing countries demanded, should in-
> clude the following features:
>
> (a) the network should be designed to meet particularly
> the needs of the developing countries and to provide access
> to information for users who contribute to problem-solving
> activities and decisions relating to development;
> (b) the network should operate inter alia as a channelling
> mechanism facilitating contact between users and suppliers
> of information;
> (c) in each country there should exist one national focal

point for its different subnetworks while at the same time
there should be, at the world level, under the auspices
of the United Nations, a global central focal point;
(d) each national focal point should have the information-
on-information for its country; the global focal point should
have the same for the world;
(e) users should be able to get the needed (information or)
information-on-information from the national or from the
global central focal point;
(f) the global central focal point should be able to collect
information (on information) from any focal point and send
it to users upon request;
(g) the global central focal point and individual country
focal points should be managed by qualified personnel who
are capable of easily, promptly and clearly understanding
the requests for information and of directing the requests
to the appropriate source;
(h) each focal point should have the appropriate communication facilities so as to be able to receive or supply information as fast as needed, either directly through the
individual national focal points or through the global one.
[5]

The industrialized countries considered the developing countries' demand for GIN, and particularly its design criteria, "too ambitious." They argued that the technical problems involved in setting up such a system were too complex. In particular, the developed countries argued that it is not technically possible to set up a
global information system that can perform both the retrieval and
referral functions. There were heated debates on the Third World's
demand that "the users should be able to get the needed (information
or) information-on-information from the national or from the global
central focal point." The industrialized countries objected strongly
to the words "information on."[6] The developed countries conceded
to the Third World's demands that GIN should have a world-wide
referral system on the understanding that the global central focal
point does not have to be in a single place. Different disciplines,
like fisheries and agriculture, could have focal points in different
places. However, the industrialized countries refused to negotiate
on the issue that individual users should have direct access to the
central focal point. They also argued that the problems of the users were being overlooked by the developing countries. On this
point, the developing countries had to give in and it was decided that
only national users will have access to the global central focal point.
[7]

The final accord on GIN was the only real victory of the
Third World at UNCSTD. The developed countries agreed to set
up GIN within the UN system largely as a referral system providing
information-on-information to all national focal points and to act as
"complaints bureau." In case of difficulty in getting a response
from a national point, the global focal point would take measures
to ensure the required information is provided. However, the global

focal point will not perform the function of information retrieval; this function will be performed largely by national focal points. The developed countries also agreed to "make those resources which are readily accessible to their own nationals also readily accessible to users from developing countries." They will also allow access to the results of their research and development "relevant to the social and economic development of developing countries." The two basic questions of who decides what is relevant, and what is the criteria of relevancy were not discussed at UNCSTD. Omitted too from the agreement is the question of confidentiality. While the developed countries showed considerable concern over access to confidential information, nothing was resolved at UNCSTD.[8]

Much of the onus of developing GIN has been placed on the Third World. Before the developed countries can meet their part of the agreement, developing countries must establish national scientific and technological information systems that could be linked to GIN. Moreover, for GIN to function properly, the national focal points must provide significant backup. The national information systems are required to have storage facilities on information concerning development of science and technology, national capacity in science and technology, information pertaining to foreign sources of technology and supply and sources of foreign capital and their conditions, and information pertaining to national users of science and technology.[9]

The final agreement to establish GIN sums up the characteristics of the network in the following words:

> Priority should be given to covering scientific, technical, socio-economic, legal and other aspects needed for decision-making in the selection and transfer of technology. The existing information systems within the United Nations and other international bodies set up for the exchange of scientific and technological information and which are also serving as industrial technology data banks should form an integral part of the proposed global network. Data from the developed and developing countries on available technologies, conditions of licensing, identification of suitable experts, engineering and consultancy services and the like should be widely available so as to promote their effective utilization, thereby strengthening the concept of the global information network.
> The developing and developed countries should participate in, and make better use of the existing scientific and technical information systems and take such steps as would enable their own information systems to be coupled to the global information network and ensure that all support is provided for the effective use of this global network.[10]

Post-UNCSTD developments

The UNCSTD accords were approved by the UN General Assembly

on 19 December 1979 without a formal vote. The UN also agreed to
set up a new policy unit to help implement the recommendations of
UNCSTD contained in "The Vienna Programme of Action on Science
and Technology for Development." Both the establishment of the new
unit, which is called the Centre for Science and Technology for Development (CSTD), and its staffing have been heated issues at the
UN. The main function of the Centre is to service the inter-governmental committee (IGC) established to oversee the UNCSTD Fund
that has been established, coordinate various programmes concerned
with the implementation of the Vienna accords and to further stimu-
late programmes to promote science development activities in the
Third World.[11]

What steps are taken to establish GIN depends both on the
facilities and authority of CSTD and the financial resources available
to implement the Vienna accords. As the developed countries have
not given much support to CSTD and as it is staffed by low-level
UN executives, it is doubtful whether agreements on GIN would actually be implemented. Moreover, the new fund has been pushed
to the wayside by the industrialized nations.

The developing countries came to UNCSTD with a demand for
a fund of $2 billion, to be raised over a five year period. At the
conclusion of UNCSTD, the original demand of the Third World was
cut to $250 million to be raised over two years. The developed
countries agreed to set up an initial fund of $250 million to imple-
ment the recommendations of UNCSTD over a two year period. The
principal contributors to the fund were to be the US and the Organization of the Petroleum Exporting Countries (OPEC). OPEC had
agreed to meet any figure that the US was willing to contribute.
However, the US contribution, put at $50 million over two years,
was reduced in January 1980 by President Carter to $15 million.
The OPEC countries were forced to reconsider their commitment
and now plan to set up their own special fund. A UN Pledging Conference held in March 1980, raised only $36 million. However,
even this figure would not be reached as the US House Appropriation
Committee has cut the US contribution to the UNCSTD Fund and has
completely refused to support the fund.[12] It is now obvious that
there will be no financial resources to implement the UNCSTD recommendation: GIN is, therefore, destined to be a paper proposal.

How good is GIN, anyway?

Even if financial support was forthcoming and GIN was to be established, what contribution would it make to science development in
the Third World? A global information system, on the pattern of
GIN, would hardly be a panacea for Third World information dependency. GIN would accomplish, in all probability, a unidirection flow
of information from the developed to the developing countries. There
are three information agencies, namely UNISIST, the Canadian International Development Centre and DEVSIS (Development Science Information System), that are already working on these lines. Thus it

would seem that GIN would be duplicating the efforts of existing
agencies.   The crucial requirement of promoting the transfer of
information within the Third World would be swamped by the flow of
information from the developed to the developing countries.   As 97%
of this information is not geared to the needs and requirements of
the developing countries, it will only force western patterns of development and dependency.[13]   What makes the Third World's demand for GIN really irrelevant is the fact that much of the information the developing countries seek can be retrieved in many countries
around the world simply by using a small portable computer terminal.

Much of the information on science and technology for development is available on vast numbers of commercial information systems.   It is not possible for any country to control or censor this
information because of the great volume and the widespread and uncontrolled nature of agencies providing it.   However, much of the
information that can be retrieved is by no means politically neutral.
The developing countries using them have to be sure of their needs
and use the available information with political understanding.   The
paradox is why the UN agencies have not as yet undertaken steps to
enable developing countries to use the vast array of available databases more fully.   Here, the cost is no problem as a developing
country can gain access to these databases at less cost than that
involved for one expert provided by the UN agency.[14]

However, even if we overlook the available databases and the
ease with which they can be tapped, there are a number of fundamental political and economic questions that must be answered before
GIN can be established (see Table 1).   The answers to many of these
questions will not come easily; and it seems reasonable that these
questions should be settled before financial support for GIN is sought.

In the final analysis, however, it seems more appropriate
for the Third World to develop an information network of its own
design, geared to meeting its own specific needs.   Let there be a
demand for TWIN--the Third World Information Network.

Table 1: Basic questions relating to the development of a Global
Information Network (GIN) as proposed by UNCSTD

POLITICAL
          Who has what share?
          Who pays?
          Where is the global focal point to be centred (in various
               fields)?
          Where will the national/regional focal points be?
          Whose data is chosen?
          Which order is the data to be taken?
          How many similar one/or combine?
          What will be the language of documentation (English, Russian,
               Arabic, Hindi)?

ECONOMIC
>How much will it cost a developing country to subscribe?
>Can it afford to subscribe?
>What will be the capital expense?
>Exchange rates?
>Will there be different rates for national and private users?
>Payment pro-rata to what: use, GNP, number of users, etc.?

RELEVANCE
>Do the developing countries really need it?
>Cui bono? Who benefits, ultimately?

TECHNICAL
>Can the Third World countries develop their information in-
>frastructure to the desired level?
>What/whose hardware? Software?
>Are transmission lines available for a developing country to
>use such a network?
>What will be the language of output?

TWIN--An alternative to GIN

What immediate benefits could be derived by developing countries
opting out of the global information race and cooperating amongst
themselves for information? The developing countries themselves
generate only about 3% of the world's total scientific and technological information. But this information is of great value to the Third
World itself: scientific, technological and economic information generated in one developing country is of vital importance to another
at the same level of development and with similar scientific, technological and economic problems. Moreover, much of this information is not under bibliographical control and is not readily accessible. More specifically, the developing countries will benefit from:

>(a) improvements in the coverage and timeliness of informa-
>tion transfer by assessing material at or near its source in
>the Third World;
>(b) avoidance of unnecessary duplication of material and wast-
>age of scarce resources;
>(c) advantages derived from the use of local linguistic skills
>for transforming document description into the language of the
>sharing system; and
>(d) generation of local resources and full use of the available
>technical manpower rather than reliance on imported consult-
>ants.

In addition, there are some outstanding information problems
in the Third World that can only be solved by developing countries
cooperating for information amongst themselves: the difficulties produced by the increasing volume of Third World technical and scientific literature that never sees the light of day in the Western com-

munication system, faulty distribution practices among the UN agencies, understocked and understaffed libraries in the developing countries, the lack of compatibility among the various existing information
systems and the lack of adequate information infrastructure in almost
all developing countries.

So what should be the objectives of TWIN?   What would be its
design criteria?

The objectives of TWIN should be to provide a network for
making cooperatively available existing and planned information
sources for the benefit of the users throughout the Third World.
This will involve: improvement, adaptation and further development
of existing systems in the Third World; the coordination of these
systems; the cooperative establishment of new small-scale information systems on specific needs of the Third World; the provision of
appropriate facilities throughout the Third World for communication
and reprocessing of information; and the cooperative utilization of
information resources of the industrialized nations by the Third World.

The essential function of TWIN would be to provide a medium
for access to the exchange of information relating to science and
technology--originating largely in the developing countries. As much
as three-quarters of this information exist in unpublished or semi-
published reports and documents in government ministries and institutions and national and international agencies.

Although TWIN would store information generated largely by
the developing countries, it would also provide a means of access
to relevant scientific and technical information generated in the industrialized nations and would be capable of connecting with other,
already existing networks. It should, thus, provide the following
functions:

(a) the network should be able to transmit data to any major
Third World city for current awareness and retrospective
searches; furthermore, it should be possible to send the results of searches to another location in the Third World;
(b) the network should be able to make selective dissemination of information (SDI) to Third World scientists and tech-
nologists with profiles stored in the system;
(c) the network should be able to take on the function of location and acquisition of documents and online cataloging;
(d) the network should be able to provide assistance in locating the database most appropriate for the needs of individual
users. In other words, it should be able to fulfil a referral
function in guiding enquirers to the most relevant database;
and finally,
(e) the network should be able to gather statistics on its own
usage and performance which will be needed for the identification of problem areas (for example, frequency of breakdown,
overload conditions, user behaviour and so on) and for the
purpose of network management and control.

Is TWIN taking shape in the Middle East?

In fact, a network of this nature is already evolving in the Middle East as a result of rapid technological, legal, economic and manpower developments. This is not a planned coordinated development, but unconnected incidental and haphazard happenings. However, some independent, incidental developments may converge to produce some type of network. The changes that are responsible for these developments are worth stating:

(a) satellite communication: most Arab countries have grand satellite stations in full operation and three Arab satellites (ARABSAT) to improve communications amongst the Arab countries are to be launched in the next few years. (Amongst the more likely services that ARABSAT will offer include a rural telecommunication service, a remote monitoring service, computer communications, land mobile services, teleconferencing and electronic mail);[15]
(b) microwave communication: most Arab countries are in the process of completing their individual microwave communication networks which are linked across their borders; in case of Tunisia, Algeria and Morocco, the linkage spans the Mediterranean to the European networks;
(c) computer installations: more and more government agencies, universities and business organizations are computerizing their operations and despite the acute shortage of manpower and countless problems there is a steady growth;
(d) Arab news agencies: Arab news agencies are developing rapidly, using networks of telephone-linked teleprinters and increasingly relying on computerized photocomposition.

These trends, together with the large geographic area of the Middle East, a substantial population base, and capital and manpower shortages in certain countries are all factors which indicate the emergence of a computerized system of collecting, processing, transmitting and consuming information. Obviously such a system would not perform the functions of TWIN but it could be used as a basis for the development of TWIN. The hardware is already there and will undoubtedly grow. The challenge before the information scientists in the Third World in general, and the Middle East in particular, is to turn this haphazard, random development into something positive and planned.

For the developing countries too, it is a better proposition to work with other developing countries to develop an information system that is designed to meet their specific needs and requirements than gamble with a global information network of the restricted nature of GIN. At least in this option they have an opportunity to solve their political and information problems together, rather than bargain with the uncompromising industrialized nations from a position of weakness.

ACKNOWLEDGEMENTS

I would like to thank Dr. Peter Norr of the British Library Bibliographic Division, for his valuable help and advice in writing this
paper.

References

1. Group of 77 get it all together, Retort Issue 1, p. 1. 20 August
   1979. See also note 2, below.
2. The complete report and detailed analysis of issues involved can
   be found in the UNCSTD newspaper, Retort, which was published daily during the conference. (Complete sets of Retort
   are available from the NGO Forum on Science and Technology
   for Development, 122 East 42nd Street, New York, NY 10017,
   USA.) See also various reports by David Dickson and Ziauddin Sardar in Nature 280 (23 August 1979) 620-622; 280 (30
   August 1979) 710-712; 281 (6 September 1979) 1-5. See also
   Ziauddin Sardar, A Retrospect on UNCSTD: Heads I win,
   tails you lose. Impact International 28 December -10 January
   1980, p. 12-25. For a complete listing of UNCSTD documents
   see Learning Resources in International Studies, Science and
   Technology for Development: International Conflict and Co-
   operation--A Bibliography of Studies and Documents Related
   to UNCSTD, New York, 1980 (six volumes).
3. UNCSTD Draft Plan for Action, A/CONF. 81/L. 1 19 July 1979
   p. 27.
4. Ibid., p. 34.
5. Ibid., p. 34-35.
6. Sardar, Z., Information--the haves give way. Retort Issue 7,
   p. 2, 28 August 1979.
7. Sardar, Z., Global network controversy. Retort Issue 8, p. 7,
   29 August 1979.
8. Sardar, Z., Accord on global information system. Retort Issue
   10, p. 2, 31 August 1979.
9. Sardar, Z., G77 wins on global information network. Nature
   281 (6 September 1979) p. 4.
10. United Nations. The Vienna Programme of Action on Science
    and Technology for Development. New York, 1979, p. 21.
11. Dickson, D. UN agrees on science and technology centre.
    Nature 282 (20-27 December 1979) p. 767. For a more de-
    tailed account of the controversy over the UNCSTD Fund and
    the CSTD, see Broad, W. J., UN at odds over science cen-
    tre. Science, 207 (25 January 1980) p. 387-391.
12. Dickson, D. Congress turns sour on technology fund. Nature
    286 (7 August 1980) p. 547.
13. Sardar, Z. The information game--can the Third World win?
    Retort Issue 5 p. 4-5, 24 August 1979.
14. See the report of the International Society for Community De-
    velopment, How to gain access to information on science and
    technology for development from databases through computer

telecommunication systems, submitted to UNCSTD, A/CONF 81/BP/NGO/* & A/CONF 81/BP/NGO/17/Add 1, 15 August 1979.
15. Al-Mashat, A.   The Arab view of satellite services.   Intermedia 8 (5) September 1980 p. 18-19.

INDIAN MANIKINS WITH FEW REFERENCES*

Gerald Vizenor

Encyclopaedia Britannica has sponsored the creation of a dozen tribal manikins, dressed (more or less) in traditional vestments, for promotional exhibition at various shopping centers.

The sculptured figures--named for Black Hawk, Pontiac, Cochise, Massasoit, and other tribal leaders from the footnotes of dominant cultural histories--will stand like specters from the tribal past at the Burnsville Center during the second week of September and, later, at the Maplewood Mall.

What is most unusual about this exhibition of anatomical artifacts is not that tribal leaders are invented for a place in a diorama to promote the sale of books, but that few of the tribal names celebrated in plastic casts are entered in the reference books published by the sponsor of the manikins.

"The Indian leaders whose likenesses appear in this exhibition represent every major region of the country and span more than four centuries of history," the editors write in the illustrated catalogue which is sold to promote their reference books. "Some were great military leaders who fought valiantly to defend their lands. Others were statesmen, diplomats, scholars and spiritual leaders."

Nine manikins are feathered and the same number are praised as warriors. Black Hawk, the catalogue reveals, "established his reputation as a warrior early in life. He wounded an enemy of his tribe at the age of 15 and took his first scalp the same year."

Three figures bear rifles; but only Massasoit, the manikin who associated with the colonists, is dressed in a breechcloth and holds a short bow. In addition to those mentioned, the other manikins are named Joseph, Cornplanter, Powhatan, Red Cloud, Sequoyah, Tecumseh, Wovoka and Sacagawea, the one female tribal figure in the collection.

The editors consulted with "scholars in the fields of Indian

---

*Reprinted by permission of the author and publisher from the Minneapolis Tribune, September 5, 1981, Editorial Page.

history, anthropology and ethnology, " and point out that the tribal biographies in the catalogue are the "product of hundreds of hours of research involving scores of sources of information." Such claims seem ironic, because the sponsors were not able to consult their own published references for all the tribal names used to promote their books.

Encyclopaedia Britannica is published in two parts: the Micropaedia, a 10-volume ready-reference and index; and the Macropaedia, 20 volumes of information in greater depth. Tecumseh is the only tribal name, of the dozen manikins in the exhibition, which appears as an entry in the Macropaedia.

The tribal names Black Hawk, Powhatan and Wovoka are not entered in the current edition of the Micropaedia, but their names and figures are promoted at shopping centers.

Cornplanter is given short notice in the Micropaedia, while in the ephemeral exhibition catalogue the famous Seneca chief is featured on five full pages. One page is a color photograph of a ridiculous manikin dressed in a red cape with four wide silver arm bands, an earring and nose ring, a green and white feathered headpiece and holding a peacepipe.

Joseph, the celebrated leader of the Nez Percé, is the only tribal figure whose photograph, from a portrait painting, appears in the reference books. Joseph the manikin is dressed in a capote made from a Hudson's Bay Company blanket.

Sequoyah and the Sequoia National Park receive about the same space in the Micropaedia, but it is the trees, not the person for whom the giant trees were named, that appear in the color photograph.

The manikin of Wovoka, spiritual founder of the Ghost Dance religion, was created from photographs, while the other manikins, for the most part, were imagined from historical descriptions. "It may seem odd, " the editors of the catalogue write, "that Wovoka is shown dressed in white man's clothes, but this is the costume he typically wore as did many other Indians." The other manikins, however, are dressed in what appear to be romantic variations of tribal vestments.

The manikins of Black Hawk and Sequoyah, for example, are based on the portraits painted by Charles Bird King, who is best known for his romantic embellishment of tribal figures. Sequoyah, the tribal scholar who developed a writing system for the Cherokee language, wears a cloth around his head like a turban, bears a peace medal around his neck and smokes a narrow pipe in the imaginative portrait by King. Sequoyah the promotional manikin has lost his peace medal and pipe, but the figure has been decorated with red and white feathers, like egret plumes, for the shopping-center tour.

Most of the sources of visual information, portraits and historical descriptions which the sculptors used to imagine the manikins
are not reliable.   Portrait painters, photographers, explorers, trad-
ers and politicians have, with few exceptions, created a romantic
savage in perfect opposition to the theologies of civilization.   "For
one person to have tried to separate fact from fiction in every instance would border on the impossible," explain the editors of the
catalogue.

To create manikins from the archives of racism and frontier
romances, even with the consent of anthropologists and ethnologists,
for the promotion of reference books which do not include most of
the names of the tribal leaders, is no less an invalidation of tribal
humanism in the present than the denial of tribal languages and re-
ligions was in the past.

LIBRARY CENSORSHIP AND THE LAW*

Clifton O. Lawhorne

> A library is a mighty resource in the free marketplace
> of ideas.... It is specially dedicated to broad dissem-
> ination of ideas. It is a forum of silent speech.

Such was the wording of the decision in Minarcini v. Strongsville
City School District, rendered by the United States Court of Appeals
for the Sixth Circuit.[1] In the 1976 precedent-setting decision, the
court ruled that the removal by the Strongsville School Board of
Joseph Heller's Catch 22 and Kurt Vonnegut's Cat's Cradle from the
high school library was unconstitutional. Specifically the court said
the action taken by this Ohio school board, because the content of
the books was considered distasteful and objectionable, violated the
student's First Amendment "right to know."[2]

The decision was grounded on the fact that a school board,
as is any public library board, is an agency of the state. And the
Fourteenth Amendment to the U.S. Constitution prevents a state from
depriving individuals of their liberty without due process of law.
Further among those liberties the state cannot deny is freedom of
speech and press and its First Amendment corollary, recognized
here, of a right to know. As the Court of Appeals in this case
stated:

> Neither the State of Ohio nor the Strongsville School Board
> was under any federal constitutional compulsion to provide
> a library for the Strongsville High School or to choose any
> particular books. Once having created such a privilege
> for the benefit of its students, however, neither body could
> place conditions on the use of the library which were re-
> lated solely to the social or political tastes of the school
> board members.[3]

Basically, then, the state--through its school board--had
created a "library forum" for a free flow of ideas. And once government creates a public forum for expression--like a public park,

*Reprinted by permission of the author and publisher from Arkansas
Libraries, 38:2 (June 1981) 8-13.

town hall, auditorium, or even a student newspaper--courts throughout the country have been consistent in saying that government cannot regulate what is expressed in that forum.[4]

    Nevertheless there has been a rash of attempts in recent
years to prevent various types of expression in library forums.
These censorship efforts, according to records at the American Library Association, have especially accelerated since the election of
President Ronald Reagan. In fact, these records show that complaints about specific library books have increased fivefold since
Reagan's election and the conservative tide that followed.[5] Judith
Krug, director of the library association's Office for Intellectual
Freedom, states that censorship efforts have been aimed at separate
books in thirty-three states in the first six months after the election.[6] And many of the efforts have been successful.

    Why these successes when the law appears clear? The answer
is that the law is not clearly enunciated. The United States Supreme
Court has not issued a specific library censorship opinion binding
on the entire nation, and decisions of lower federal courts--while
setting precedents--are not binding except in their districts. Also
while all lower federal courts in all jurisdictions have recently held
that books cannot be banned from libraries to discourage or suppress
particular social or political ideas, these courts are not uniform concerning the banning of books with "obscenities and explicit sexual
interludes, " particularly when those books are in school libraries.
[7] But what specifically have the courts held in library censorship
cases? What is this right to know? And what, if any, censorship
"exceptions" have been allowed by the courts when dealing with
school libraries? These questions will form the focus of this study,
which will attempt to shed some light on where, at this time, the
legal lines on library censorship have been drawn.

    In drawing these lines, the logical place to start is with
guiding pronouncements of the United States Supreme Court concerning censorship generally. These began fifty years ago, in 1931,
when the Court ruled in Near v. Minnesota that the First and Fourteenth Amendments prevent a state from suppressing publications
except on very narrow grounds.[8] Exceptions specifically listed in
that case were publications that interferred with war efforts, that
incited acts of violence, or that were obscene. The Court also held
in the 1938 case of Lovell v. Griffin that freedom to publish meant
little without freedom to circulate what was published. Here the
Court made clear that the press freedom clause of the Constitution
protected circulation of "every sort of publication which affords a
vehicle of information and opinion."[9] And finally, when the national
government tried to suppress publication of the Pentagon Papers, on
the grounds that publication interfered with the Vietnam War effort,
the Supreme Court would not allow the censorship, stating:

        Any system of prior restraints of expression comes to this
        Court bearing a heavy presumption against its constitutional
        validity.... The Government "thus carries a heavy burden

of showing justification for the imposition of such a restraint."[10]

The sum total of these Supreme Court decisions, binding on
the nation as a whole, is that any effort to censor publication or
circulation automatically carries a presumption of unconstitutionality
that is hard to overcome.

Yet censorship efforts abound.[11]   The thrust of these efforts, so far as libraries are concerned, is toward what complainants call "obscene materials." And obscenities, under law, can be
suppressed. Such suppression was listed as permissible in the
Near case, and the Supreme Court has consistently ruled that obscenities are not protected by the Constitution.[12]   Nevertheless,
the definition of obscenity has been so tightened in recent years that,
legally few works can actually be censored on this basis--either at
the publication or circulation stage.

So what is obscene? The Supreme Court has said that to be
obscene a work must be patently offensive by describing the ultimate
sex act or by lewdly exhibiting genitals and, when considered as a
whole in accordance with community standards, must appeal to the
prurient interest and must lack any serious literary, artistic, scientific or political value.[13]   This standard has been strictly enforced
when censorship cases have gone to the courts. For instance, the
Fifth United States Circuit Court of Appeals, which has jurisdiction
over most Southern states, in 1980 ruled that Penthouse and Play-
boy magazines, despite what some called patently offensive pictures,
were not obscene. The reason? The magazines, the court said,
could not be considered "piecemeal by individual articles."[14] They
had to be considered in entirety and they included significant literary
and political material. This is a typical decision.

Legally, then, librarians have little to fear from those wish-
ing to censor books on the basis of what they call obscene portions
or passages. They find this out when they stand their ground. Only
last year, a county librarian in North Carolina successfully "bucked"
county commissioners by refusing to bow to their demands to prevent
youngsters access (without parents' permission) to Judy Blume's
Wifey.[15]   And a Davis County, Utah, librarian was by a 1980 court
order reinstated to her job after being fired for refusing to remove
David DeLillo's Americana from library shelves.[16] Also a county
librarian in Virginia ignored threats of prosecution for refusing to
remove Sidney Sheldon's Bloodline, Harold Robbins's The Lonely Lady,
and Philip Roth's Goodbye, Columbus from library shelves. Virginia
law, similar to that of other states, prohibits prosecution of library
employees for disseminating materials claimed to be obscene.[17]

The problem, of course, is that legalities and practicalities
do not always mix. One reason is that librarians are caught in the
middle of often countervailing pressures. Also many librarians are
answerable to politically motivated board members who may have
different views on censorship. While the boards cannot legally fire

librarians on First Amendment issues, [18] reasons aside from these
issues can be generated to accomplish the same end. Because of
this and because some librarians desire to follow what is believed to
be "prevailing community standards," many have "caved in" to censorship pressures.[19] This is especially true of school librarians,
who are (1) dealing with a younger clientele and (2) are answerable
to boards that have extreme political motivation. Censorship pressures in schools are widespread, and it is in the school arena that
most of the recent court law has been made concerning the banning
of library books.

While this recent court-propounded law is not uniform, it
comes down stronger for wide-open circulation than many book ban-
ners would desire. Perhaps the primary reason for this is the fact
that schools are no longer seen as serving in loco parentis. The
death knell to this old concept came in the 1969 decision of the
United States Supreme Court in Tinker v. Des Moines Independent
School District, which stated public school officials have no absolute
authority over students--and that students as well as teachers keep
their First Amendment right of speech and expression within the
schools.[20]   Even more appropriate, though, was this statement
by the Court:

> In our system, students may not be regarded as closed-
> circuit recipients of only that which the State chooses to
> communicate. They may not be confined to the expres-
> sion of those sentiments that are officially approved.[21]

Freedom of speech could be limited in public schools only
when it would "substantially interfere" with discipline, the Court
said. This decision, which overturned censorship by school authorities of "silent" expression, the wearing of black armbands to protest the Vietnam War, has been the basis for overturning other censorship efforts in schools.

Perhaps this was nowhere more evident than in the United
States Supreme Court decision of 1973 in Papish v. University of
Missouri Curators.[22] Here the Court would not let the university
ban circulation of an underground newspaper with a political cartoon
of a policeman raping the Statue of Liberty and captioned with the
words "mother fucker acquitted." Neither, the Court said, could
the student editor be expelled. The Court said the "dissemination
of ideas--no matter how offensive to good taste--on a state university campus may not be shut off in the name alone of 'conventions
of decency.'" This and other court decisions make it clear that
the circulation of just about any type material on college campuses
--including college library forums--is beyond censorship.

However, court decisions concerning junior and senior high
school libraries leave questions concerning censorship. While generally protecting the dissemination of ideas in public school libraries, courts have not been so clear about protecting dissemination of
offensive language and explicit sexual materials. This is because of

the variable obscenity theory, sanctioned by the Supreme Court, which allows sexually explicit material not obscene in a constitutional sense for adults to be regulated when children are involved. [23]

Such regulation was involved in the first major school library case of the last decade--President's Council, District 25 v. Community School Board No. 25, decided by the United States Court of Appeals for the Second Circuit in 1972. Here a school board, after receiving complaints concerning Piri Thomas's Down These Mean Streets, ordered that the book be kept on the junior high school "reserved" shelves, available for check-outs to parents only. Several students and parents, joined by the junior high principal and librarian, brought suit. The court held that the action was taken because of "obscenities and explicit sexual interludes, " that there was no evidence that the board's action was political or that any particular ideas were suppressed. [24] Specifically, the court said the librarian was not penalized and teachers still were free to discuss the book with students; hence there was "no showing of a curtailment of freedom of speech and thought. "[25] The precedent set here, obviously, was that undefined "obscenities and explicit sexual interludes" could be banned in children's libraries.

It was after this decision, though, that the United States Supreme Court began to seriously acknowledge the right to "receive information and ideas. " In fact a series of cases was decided to the effect that freedom of speech "necessarily protects the right to receive. "[26] Finally in 1976, in Virginia State Board of Pharmacy v. Virginia Citizens Consumer Council, Inc., the Supreme Court stated that First Amendment protection extends "to the communication, to its source, and to its recipients both. "[27] It further held that people could bring action on a First Amendment right "to receive communications. "

The Virginia State Board case had just been decided when Minarcini v. Strongsville City School District, the case discussed at the beginning of this article, hit the United States Court of Appeals for the Sixth Circuit. And this court, which has jurisdiction over Michigan, Ohio, Kentucky, and Tennessee, said the Supreme Court decision had established "firmly both the First Amendment right to know ... and the standing of student plaintiffs to raise the issue. " [24] It was clear, then, that students had a First Amendment right to sue if books were removed from libraries, as court after court began to recognize.

One of these federal court cases, Right to Read Defense Committee v. Chelsea School Committee, resulted when a Massachusetts school board banned an anthology, Male and Female Under 18, from the high school library because of one poem, "The City To A Young Girl. " Threats of removing the librarian and English teachers also were made by board members, and an action was brought for the right to read by parents, teachers, and students. The court ruled in this 1978 case that the board's removal of the book from library shelves was an infringement of the First Amend-

ment rights of both students and faculty and ordered that no action
be taken against the librarian or teachers. [29] The court said:

> What is at stake here is the right to read and be exposed
> to controversial thoughts and language--a valuable right
> subject to First Amendment protection. [30]

The gutteral language in the poem, according to the decision,
was "vivid street language" and "tough" and "legitimately offensive
to some" but was not obscene. Then the court said:

> If this work may be removed by a committee hostile to
> its language and theme, then the precedent is set for
> removal of any other work. The prospect of successive
> school committees "sanitizing" the school library of views
> divergent from their own is alarming, whether they do it
> book by book or one page at a time. [31]

Here then, in a decision from still another judicial circuit,
the First, a court refused to allow a book to be banned from a high
school library because of vulgar language and theme.

Language, however, was not the issue in a 1979 New Hamp-
shire case. The issue was content, and a United States District
Court ruled in Salvail v. Nashua Board of Education that it was con-
stitutionally impermissible for a school board to remove Ms. magazine from library shelves because of objections concerning content
on lesbianism, gays, witchcraft, contraceptives, and communism.
The court said the First Amendment was violated because the "political content of Ms. magazine more than its sexual overtones" led
to the removal from the library forum. [32] The court said students
had a right to know about their material and that board members
could not remove it solely because of their political or social views.

To an extent--and only to an extent--this last phrase brought
disagreement from the United States Court of Appeals for the Seventh
Circuit in still another case. This court, which has jurisdiction over
Illinois, Indiana and Wisconsin, said in 1979 that it is permissible
for boards of education "to make educational decisions based upon
their personal social, political and moral views."[33] However, the
court also ruled in this Indiana case, Zykan v. Warsaw Community
School District, that academic freedom and "freedom to hear" at a
secondary school level prohibits boards from imposing "a pall of
orthodoxy" over offerings in the classroom or libraries. [34] While
this decision itself did not force the board to replace the book Go
Ask Alice, it did send the case back for retrial to give those bringing suit an opportunity to show that censorship was "taken in the
interest of imposing some religious or scientific orthodoxy or limit-
ing a particular kind of inquiry."[35] If this were shown, the court
said, the removal would be unconstitutional.

This reasoning was pretty well adopted by the United States
Court of Appeals for the Second Circuit in late 1980, in deciding

the two latest federal court library cases. In one of these cases, Pico v. Island Trees Union Free School District, a school board on Long Island had banned nine school library books, including Bernard Malamud's The Fixer, Kurt Vonnegut's Slaughterhouse Five, and Desmond Morris's The Naked Ape. They were banned because they contained "either vulgar and indecent language, profanities, explicit sex, sexual perversion, poor grammar, glorification of sex and drugs, or anti-Jewish, anti-Black, or anti-Christian remarks."[36] The court said this suggested the board in banning the books was offering views with regard to God and country "for the purpose of establishing those views as the correct and orthodox ones for all purposes in the particular community."[37] If so, the court said, this was unconstitutional. Hence the case was sent back to district court for retrial to see if the school board was unconstitutionally banning ideas from the school library. [38]

Interestingly enough, however, the same court on the same day ruled in another case, Bicknell v. Vergennes Union High School, that removal of books from school libraries because of vulgar and indecent language is not unconstitutional.[39] Here the school board had removed Richard Price's The Wanderers from the library and had placed Patrick Mann's Dog Day Afternoon on a restricted shelf. The court stressed there was no suggestion that the books were removed because of their ideas or because the board was politically motivated. Even those bringing suit said censorship was because of language alone.

The lesson from these two recent Second Circuit cases, perhaps, is that boards cannot ban books because of their ideas or themes or because of political views or to impose some orthodoxy concerning views but that they can censor because of vulgar and indecent language. However, this could be an erroneous lesson. This Second Circuit Court, the same one that allowed books to be banned in the 1972 President's Council case, is the only federal court in the last 10 years to specifically allow censorship of school library books to stand without challenge. And the court's jurisdiction is limited to New York, Vermont and Connecticut.

Further, not all federal courts agree that books in school libraries can be censored for vulgar and indecent language. One in Massachusetts, in the First Circuit, has ruled specifically that school library books cannot be removed because of vulgar, tough, offensive, or controversial language. The courts, then, have differences of opinion. This also is shown in rationale used to strike down book censorship. For instance some courts stated school libraries are public forums in which boards cannot regulate on the basis of political or social ideas. Others have stated that regulation on that basis is okay provided there is no "pall of orthodoxy" imposed by censorship actions. The lines, then, are not clearly drawn and likely will not be until some definitive ruling comes from the United States Supreme Court.

Nevertheless, there are points of agreement in decisions

already handed down. All federal courts taking up the issue have made it quite clear that librarians and teachers cannot be removed for disagreeing with boards ordering censorship. And all courts agree that students and teachers alike have First Amendment rights in the school setting. More importantly, however, the rulings have been consistent that library books in schools cannot be censored because of ideas.

But are school libraries different than other libraries? Yes and no. Yes because of variable obscenity standards which some courts interpret as allowing greater control over youth literature than over adult literature. No, in that city and county libraries-- like school libraries--are agents of the state, and the state is prohibited by the Fourteenth Amendment from depriving individuals of their First Amendment rights, including the "right to know." And this is so regardless of availability of the particular books in places outside the libraries. The significant thing in censorship is that a state library uses "its public power to perform an act clearly indicating that the views represented by the forbidden book are unacceptable."[40]

References

1. Minarcini v. Strongsville City School District, 541 F. 2d 577 at 583-3 (6th Cir. 1976).
2. Ibid. , p. 583.
3. Ibid. , p. 582.
4. See Vanessa Orlando, "Censorship Runs Rampant," Student Press Law Center Report (3:2, Spring 1980), p. 10.
5. "Calls For Banning of Library Books Rise Sharply Since Reagan Victory," New York Times, Dec. 11, 1980, 28:3.
6. "Censors and the Library," ABC telecast Nightline, April 22, 1981.
7. See President's Council, District 25 v. Community School Board No. 25, 457 F. 2d 289 at 291 (2nd Cir. , 1972) for example.
8. Near v. Minnesota, 283 U.S. 697 (1931).
9. Lovell v. Griffin, 303 U.S. 444 at 452 (1938).
10. New York Times v. United States, 403 U.S. 713 (1972).
11. See Snepp, v. U.S. , 5 Med. L. Rptr. 2409 (1980), Progressive v. U.S. ,(5 Med. L. Rptr. 2441 (1980) for censorship efforts by the U.S. government.
12. Roth v. U.S. 354 U.S. 476 at 484-5 (1957) was the first decision on this matter by the Supreme Court, and it still is the precedent.
13. Miller v. California, 413 U.S. 15 (1973).
14. Penthouse v. McCuliffe, 5 Med. L. Rptr. 2531 (5th Cir. 1980).
15. Library Journal, Jan. 15, 1981, p. 123.
16. Ibid.
17. "Virginia Library Fights For Books That Minister Labels Obscene," New York Times, Dec. 14, 1980, 95:3. Arkansas has, for instance, a similar law, Ark. Stat. Ann. 41-3508.
18. Bronti v. Finkley, 63 L. Ed. 2d 574 at 582, where the Supreme

Court says public employees cannot be fired for speech or beliefs. This has been the basis for many lower court decisions preventing punishment for First Amendment activities.

19. See "Book Burning" series in Arkansas Democrat, April 26, May 3, in which several school librarians are quoted as "holding" purchases to books that are in good taste.
20. Tinker v. Des Moines School District, 393 U.S. 503 (1969).
21. Ibid., p. 911.
22. Papish v. University of Missouri Curators, 410 U.S. 670 (1971).
23. Ginsberg v. New York, 390 U.S. 629 (1968); FCC v. Pacifica Foundation, 438 U.S. (1978). See Ark. Stat. Ann. 41-3582.
24. President's Council, District 25 v. Community School Board No. 25, 254 F.2d 289 at 292-93 (2nd Cir. 1972).
25. Ibid., p. 293.
26. See Kleindienst v. Mandel, 408 U.S. 753 at 762-3 (1972) and Procunier v. Martinez, 416 U.S. 396 at 408-09 (1974).
27. Virginia State Board v. Virginia Consumer Council, 425 U.S. 748 at 756 (1976).
28. Minarcini v. Strongsville City School District, 541 F.2d 477 at 583 (6th Cir. 1976).
29. Right To Read Defense Committee v. Chelsea School Committee, 5 Med. L. Rptr. 1113 at 1117, 454 F.Supp. 703 (D.Mass, 1978).
30. Ibid. 5 Med. L. Rptr. 113 at 1121.
31. Ibid., p. 1121.
32. Salvail v. Nashua Board of Education, 5 Med. L. Rptr. 1096 at 1110, 469 F.Supp. 1269 (D.N.H., 1979).
33. Zykan v. Warsaw Community School District, 631 F.2d 1300 at 1305 (7th Cir., 1980).
34. Ibid., p. 1306.
35. Ibid.
36. Pico v. Board of Education, Island Trees Union Free School District No. 26, 638 F.2d 404 at 416, 436 (2nd Cir., 1980).
37. Ibid., p. 417.
38. One of the three justices felt there was sufficient evidence already to show unconstitutionality; another felt the allegations had to be proved. See decision, p. 418.
39. Bicknell v. Vergennes Union High School Board of Directors, 638 F.2d 438 at 441 (2nd Cir., 1980).
40. Pico v. Board of Education, 638 F.2d 404 at 435.

"GOD FORBID THAT SODOMITES CONTROL THIS COUNTY"*

Nat Hentoff

Washington County in Southwest Virginia is a farming community of some 44,000 souls. Among last year's big stories were the all-time record set for burley tobacco prices and Abingdon High School's victory in the Southwest District football championship.

Something else happened, and is still going on, in the town of Abingdon that is of national import. A fundamentalist Baptist preacher, the Reverend Tom Williams, has declared war against 23-year-old Kathy Russell, director of the Washington County Public Library in Abingdon. The library, says Reverend Williams, buys, maintains, and issues hardcore pornography, which even children are allowed to check out. And as everyone knows, adds Williams, "The cumulative results of pornography on a young person are practically equivalent to the sad effects felt by the victim of a child seducer."

The books in question are: Sidney Sheldon's Bloodline, Harold Robbins's The Lonely Lady, Philip Roth's Goodbye, Columbus, Muriel Davidson's The Thursday Woman, and Jacqueline Susann's Once Is Not Enough.

There is much more of this "perverted filth" in Kathy Russell's library, the Reverend Williams keeps reporting, but there is a limit to how much of this one man of God can be expected to ingest. Christ, after all, was only crucified. He did not have to read Jacqueline Susann.

The odds in this war would appear to be heavily on the side of Tom Williams. Churches sternly abound in Washington County; and deposited in some of the public phone booths of Abingdon, you can find copies of such crucial religious pamphlets as "Your Last Warning." And on the bumper sticker of Reverend Williams's car is the proclamation: "God Is in Control." Many folks in the county agree, and see this battle over the public library as vital to God's continuing dominion.

*Reprinted by permission of the author and publisher from the Village Voice, February 11-17, 1981, p. 8.

One retired Baptist minister wrote to the <u>Bristol Herald</u> <u>Courier</u>: "I am proud of our county that bears the name of our first president. Let us keep its good name. I ask every concerned citizen who believes in a moral, clean society and a God-honoring Christian society to stand with us, and protest strongly against the use of our tax dollars to pay for these filthy books.... As a Christian gentleman, I think it is not right for our tax money to pay for something that has been wrong all down through the ages."

In a letter to the same newspaper, a woman gave this heartfelt cry: "God forbid that sodomites control Washington County."

Another woman, whose ancestors have been in southwest Virginia for centuries, fervently supports Reverend Williams: "I was 24 years old before I knew a homosexual existed. I was raised on a farm and none of the farm animals, not even dogs, acted in that manner. How low has society fallen? ... This type of trash [in the library] poisons the minds of our children. No wonder there is so much rape and murder."

On the other hand, there are those, like Lowry Bowman, editor and publisher of the <u>Washington County News</u>, who are embarrassed by the wolf packs of censorship. They are tarnishing the good name, as Bowman sees it, of a place where generations of governors, congressmen, generals, and judges were born. "We helped turn the tide of the American Revolution in 1780," Bowman writes, "and helped give the world the high ideas of the Bill of Rights," which begins with the First Amendment.

As for Kathy Russell--the slight, soft-spoken, quite shy center of this vortex of the word--she comes on clear and strong. She will not be a party to the bending of the First Amendment: "It is in everyone's interest for libraries to make available the widest diversity of views and expressions, including those which are extreme, distasteful, unorthodox or unpopular with the majority.... The library is not a repository of ultimate truth or a storehouse of only that which most people see as good, honest, moral or worthy."

Before chronicling the testing of Kathy Russell and the rather surprising outcome of her ordeal (at least as of now), it's useful to explain why the events in Abingdon have significance far beyond Washington County.

Ronald Reagan would appear to be neither passionately for nor against the Bill of Rights. In this respect, he is indeed the moyen American. In California, he did oppose Proposition 6, a referendum that would have prohibited homosexuals from teaching in the public schools. ("What if an overwrought youngster," Reagan said, "disappointed by bad grades, imagined it was the teacher's fault and struck out by accusing the teacher of advocating homosexuality? Innocent lives could be ruined.") But, while Governor of California, Reagan, both through his appointments to the Board of

Regents and in his own pronouncements, revealed a decidedly dis-
torted view of academic freedom.

Yet, Reagan is not (I knock on wood) Nixon. In this Administration, attempts to regulate speech and to control thought are less
likely to come directly from Reagan than to be made in his name.
(The resurrection, for instance, of Congressional committees charged
with sniffing out "subversives.") And, on the state and local levels,
there will be hordes of amateur, as well as legislative, thought police who have taken Reagan's election as the good people's mandate
to clean up libraries, schools, and other places where dangerous
ideas and filthy language are being nurtured so that they may further
infect the Republic.

This has already begun. The Reverend Jerry Falwell of Virginia notes with satisfaction that his Moral Majority has experienced
its most rapid period of growth since the November elections as
more Christian Americans feel compelled to join the war on "secular
humanism, the established religion of America." (It was Falwell,
Alan Crawford reminds us in Thunder on the Right, who, in 1977,
called for a return to the McCarthy era, and urged that all Com-
munists be registered. "We should stamp it on their foreheads and
send them back to Russia." Where else does secular humanism
lead but straight to Communism?)

In Illinois, North Carolina, Utah, Texas, and many other
states, the legions of the Moral Majority and like-minded purgers
have, since November, descended, in increasing numbers, on school
and public libraries, while also scrutinizing school textbooks. In
Texas, for example, a book used in an advanced math course is
highly suspect because it contains no absolutes. Children need absolute values, in math as in everything else.

Or, as the Reverend Tom Williams of Abingdon explains,
"The majority of society is now turning away from permissiveness.
We need some absolutes. That's one of the cries of the people who
elected Reagan."

God is an absolute. Or rather, the God of the Christians.
All them other gods are worth about as much as the prizes in Crack-
erjack boxes. Not that our new political clerics are, for instance,
anti-Semitic. "There is not one anti-Semite in a Bible-believing
church in America," Jerry Falwell told a Washington session of the
National Religious Broadcasters on January 27.

But Falwell, of course, is smoothing out his act now that
he is a nation-wide spiritual leader. In September 1979, in recommending to his followers that they abjure anti-Semitism, the then-
regional Falwell said that the only reason some of them didn't like
Jews was that Jews "can make more money accidentally than you
can on purpose." He later explained that that was a joke, son.

The hunt, in any case, is for books that do not belong in a

Christian society. And that most certainly includes the kinds of books designated as pornographic by the folks who feel, as they put it, "validated" by the election of Ronald Reagan. Pornography is antithetical to Christian family life. Those under its influence, the Reverend Tom Williams warns, "destroy not only themselves but the society of which they are a part.... Uncontrolled aggressive and sexual feelings (such as murder and indiscriminate sex) which served our caveman ancestors long ago cannot be tolerated in civilized nations."

Not only pornography, however, must be uprooted from our libraries. There are pestilential ideas that cannot be allowed to circulate in a Christian country without fatally weakening it. The fiery Christians going after these ideas have, until now, been mainly operating in the schools. "Textbooks," proclaims Jerry Falwell, "are Soviet propaganda. Textbooks are destroying our children. [We must] rise up in arms to throw out every textbook not reflecting [our] values." But soon public libraries, too, will be scoured of unChristian ideas. This at least is the fierce prayer of many in Ronald Reagan's time of deliverance.

An index of these inquisitors' diligence comes from Judith Krug, director of the American Library Association's Office for Intellectual Freedom. I have known Judy, and marveled at her skills, for a long time; and one of the many reasons for her effectiveness is that she shuns hyperbole. So that when she told me last November that reports of library censorship around the country had increased fivefold that month, I had a clear sense of the embattled years ahead.

There was a slight decline in December, due, I suppose, to the attention that must be paid to the birth of some folks' Savior, but the mistral of censorship is blowing strong again. The importance of the war in Abingdon has to do with the fact that it is the first full-scale, prolonged clash between the forces of light and darkness (depending on your angle of vision) in the Reagan years. Also, it has turned out to be a classic primer for other beleaguered librarians on how to deal with this kind of bruising campaign. More of that next week.

Even if you don't believe in censorship, however, there are corollary questions in the Abingdon conflict (and all others of this sort) that raise intriguing questions. For instance, one antagonist of librarian Kathy Russell wrote to the <u>Bristol Herald Courier</u>:

"I believe a person has the right to collect, keep and house any type of reading material and other literature. However, it is his private right and, therefore, we should not be expected as taxpayers to collect, keep and house any material which is morally degrading, offensive to society or pornographic in its content or nature."

Suppose a public library has a section of anti-Semitic and

racist books. The real thing, not books about anti-Semitism and racism. Should infuriated Jews and blacks have no recourse when part of their tax money goes to pay for the purchase of such books? Think about it, and write in what you think.

And what about children? Should kids be allowed to check out anything they find in the library? Or should parents have a right to restrict what their children read? Or, wouldn't it be easier and socially beneficial--since not all parents pay that much attention to what their children do, in or out of a library--to prevent certain books and magazines in a library from being read by any children, up to a certain age?

Meanwhile, as the Reagan months go on, I shall be reporting from time to time on the forays of the Moral Majority and others of the thought police. It should be kept in mind that they are true believers, every bit as zealous in their conviction that they are saving the nation as are their natural antagonists, the much smaller band of civil libertarians (perforce including librarians).

Nothing you say will make these censors-touched-with-grace quail. Not even the specter of book-burning. Says the Reverend George Zarris, chairman of the Moral Majority of Illinois: "I would think moral-minded people might object to books that are philosophically alien to what they believe. If [their libraries] have the books, and they feel like burning them, fine."

There has been no bonfire yet in Abingdon. That's because of Kathy Russell. I last saw her a few weeks ago in Charlottesville and asked her how rough the war has been. "It's been difficult at times," she said in the softly falling speech of her native Virginia. "You know, those times when you're by yourself, and you really do wonder what's going to happen. But I did what I had to do. As a librarian, I had no choice."

THE NEW BOOK BURNERS*

William F. Ryan

When I spoke to Kathy Russell, director of the Washington County Public Library in Abingdon, Virginia, she told me that her nemesis, the Reverend Tom Williams, had expanded his list of allegedly dirty books to some two hundred titles. That very night--February 23, 1981--he held a meeting at his Emmanuel Baptist Church to muster the local vigilantes of decency. In attendance were his right-hand man, Bobby Sproles, chairman of the County Board of Supervisors, and the Reverend Donnie Cantwell, chairman of the Virginia chapter of the Moral Majority.

"The meeting last night was packed out," Sproles said to me the next morning. "Three hundred people, probably more. A very fine meeting. We don't have any plans to take the library to court. Our position is simply that we object to the issuance of pornography with tax dollars. We'd like to put it to a referendum locally. We're only interested in Washington County, where we pay taxes."

And the Reverend Williams was right on track. "We're just simply formulating plans to use the political process to correct our problem," he commented to me. "People should register to vote for county supervisors who identify themselves with this moral issue. I'm sure that those familiar with authors could determine what books in the library are obscene. In my experience, authors who write pornography write nothing else. It should be handled by the library board, eight people appointed by the Board of Supervisors. I'm sure the library board must change. But that will happen when we elect people to the Board of Supervisors with a sense of decency and moral standards. It could be solved simply if the present Board of Supervisors would act responsibly."

For the Reverend Tom Williams, the responsible acts would be the appointment of a new library board to systematically remove books written by Harold Robbins, Sidney Sheldon, Jacqueline Susann, and a gallery of others.

Harry Dean, executive director of the Virginia Moral Majority, has offered Williams assistance to organize--on a local basis.

*Reprinted by permission of the author and publisher from Free Inquiry, 1:3 (Summer 1981) 14-18.

A slim paperback from Avon Books could well be the most
hated--and the most vulnerable--of the modern day "youth runs wild"
novels on the New Right's hit-list. First published in 1971 by Pren-
tice-Hall and adapted for television as one of ABC's "Wednesday
Movie of the Week" attractions, Go Ask Alice is enjoying a record
of praise and persecution far beyond the understanding of any rational
and unbiased critic of either literature or social trends.

The book is based, its editors claim, on the actual diary of
a fifteen-year-old drug-user. Its authorship is anonymous. Its contents are the almost-daily ups and downs of a bright and terribly disturbed teen-age girl over the course of a single year. In her search
for acceptance and friendship, she is Mickey-Finned twice with drugs
--the illegal and frequently lethal variety still called "psychedelic"
in 1971. She slides into severe drug dependency, runs away from
home twice, is committed to a mental hospital for most of a summer, and fears for herself and her family when she tries to stay
drug-free and yet remain in the same high school in the same town,
surrounded by the same dopers and juvenile psychopaths who had
ruined her life. Her family is affluent, and the account of her
homelife reveals no basis for maladjustment, mistreatment, or lack
of love. Her sexual encounters seem always the side-effects of losing control with marijuana or heavier opiates. She seems never to
seek out sexual abandon, and her "diary"--whether it is the truth
or, as I suspect, a fiction--contains no erotic detail or titillation
of any sort. The sad account abruptly and quite chillingly ends with
an editor's note to the effect that the diarist was found dead in her
home just days after the last entry was written. She died of an
overdose, presumably of tranquilizers. A suicide? An accident?
A murder by former comrades in the teen-age underground who feared
exposure at her hands? At the close of the book, the terrible questions remains. The title, incidentally, is taken from Grace Slick's
forgettable lyrics to "White Rabbit," a big-selling record in the late
1960s. At the time of the record's unfortunate popularity, the life-
style portrayed in Go Ask Alice had great appeal for those American
teenagers who longed for a bizarre existence within a subculture, all
but gone as the 1970s waned and thoroughly debunked by such bohe-
mian elders as Gershon Legman as early as 1967.

The point: so-called "flower power" and "peace-and-love hip-
piedom" have been hosed off contemporary American life, across
class lines and across the map. But the drugs remain. We know
more about them, and we have no good excuse to use them or act
messianic about them. Still they proliferate. Kids in grade school
can score on pot and reds and KW more easily then they can swipe
booze from the household liquor cabinet. So the book Go Ask Alice
remains, and for good reason. As a literary scholar, I found it no
treasure. But I read it and gulped. When I closed the book at the
last page I knew that probably few teen-agers who read it cover-to-
cover would ever be tempted to take drugs again. Its redeeming
social value, therefore, is beyond dispute. Moreover, any truly
responsible parent would recognize that the rationale for publishing
Go Ask Alice and offering it to young people in classrooms, libraries,

or in stores, is absolutely in keeping with what the U. S. Supreme Court would call contemporary community standards.

In view of the foregoing argument, the sinister purpose is not in Go Ask Alice--a truly ironic title!--but in the book's attackers, and in full measure in its loudest attackers on the fundamentalist Right.

Edward B. Jenkinson, in Censors in the Classroom, has cited the banning of Go Ask Alice in public schools and libraries in the east and midwest since 1976. Of particular alarm is the case in Warsaw, Indiana, where eleven high-school English teachers were fired in 1978 for refusing to stop the use of Go Ask Alice and such other worthwhile novels as Sylvia Plath's The Bell Jar in their curricula. High-school students in Warsaw have sued the school board, with the help of an attorney, to reinstate Go Ask Alice and several suspended courses, claiming a violation of their First Amendment rights. But that suit has been repeatedly dismissed in U. S. District Court.

When Ron Marr, Canadian fundamentalist and editor of The Christian Inquirer, was still calling his organization the Council for National Righteousness, he wrote a pamphlet entitled The Unbelievable Truth About Your Public Schools. On the first page he scourged Go Ask Alice under a section headed "Dirt, Sex, Drugs in School Books." Then, "with sincere apologies to every clean mind," he reprinted a passage from the book, but deleted two sentences from the original. Those two sentences might have made the context somewhat clearer. The sampling from Go Ask Alice tells of when the diarist and her runaway friend, Chris, are lured to a party at the home of their wealthy employers in San Francisco. The two teen-age girls are drugged into a stupor against their will and raped by rich deviants who are flying on "speed." The Reverend Marr doesn't bother to explain any of the context, or the naivete of the runaways, or the motivation for the diarist's setting down what took place. He leaves out what would be obvious to anyone who read the actual book--that the fifteen-year-old girl uses such words and phrases as shitty, rotten, stinky, dreary, fucked-up life and cocksucker and sonsof-bitches and low-class shit eaters because she is feverish, angry, and fearfully on the edge of total nervous collapse.

The Reverend Marr's scare tactics--using vulgar words to upset those who are so neurotically righteous that such words alone keep them from reading books--are cosmetic to any clear thinker. Moreover, his motives are clearly printed on the same pages as his ravings about "secular humanism" and "atheism" and the rest. He doesn't want tax dollars to buy students' copies of Go Ask Alice.

Gordon Parks, at age sixty-eight, is one of the most widely acclaimed artists in the United States. A full list of his awards for photography, motion-picture direction, and musical composition would stagger the compilers of Who's Who volumes and celebrity registers. In 1963, Harper and Row published Gordon Parks's autobiographical

novel, The Learning Tree, a moving account of a black youth's
growing up in the rural eastern Kansas of the 1920s. In 1968,
Parks wrote the script and produced and directed the film rendition
of The Learning Tree for Warner Brothers.

The movie's appearance was the occasion for the release of
the Fawcett Crest paperback edition of The Learning Tree, which
made this fine book accessible to teen-agers in public high-schools
and in multiple copies in the young-adult sections of public libraries.
This novel has an appeal broad enough to span generations, regions,
and social classes. Moreover, The Learning Tree need not rely on
any tradition of black novels and novelists in the United States. It
can stand on its merits alongside almost anything by Philip Roth or
Joyce Carol Oates, as much as it can be compared to renderings
of black experience by Richard Wright or Jean Toomer.

The Gordon Parks novel could nonetheless be forgotten--lost
in the high-velocity shuffle of American letters and publishing, as is
the fate of most contemporary fiction. If The Learning Tree has a
lasting reputation, its distinction could well rely on the fierce and
unwarranted ill will fueled by misguided vigilantes of decency and
the moral life.

In his work on classroom censorship, Dr. Jenkinson traces
the suppression of The Learning Tree as far back as May 1973, when
a fault-finding school-board member in Asheville, North Carolina,
took it upon herself to remove four books from a high-school library
and to then dispatch a check to the principal to cover the cost of the
volumes. One of the four was The Learning Tree. Jenkinson also
cites a case in early 1978, when a group calling itself Citizens
United for Responsible Education (CURE) was unsuccessful in its
campaign to have The Learning Tree removed from high-school libraries in Rockville, Maryland. The right-wing cotillion had charged
that the novel contained "denigrating racial epithets toward both blacks
and whites" and "cheap, explicit passages on sex."

Only adults who can't or won't read contemporary fiction in
any genre would sincerely accuse The Learning Tree of explicit passages on sex. The erotic experiences of the boy Newt are subtly
and poetically told. Gordon Parks obviously found lurid detail unnecessary for his account of a male youth's self-discovery and loss of
innocence. As for the complaints of vulgar language, racial epithets,
and the like--again, they are examples of a collective herd-neurosis
unable to cope with words, words within a fictional context. And,
again, it is the motives of the censors that are suspect, rather than
those of author or publisher. The sinister purpose comes into
sharper focus with the current fracas over the Parks novel.

In April 1980, two parents in Spokane County, Washington
complained about the use of The Learning Tree in a sophomore
English reading program at Mead High School. A public hearing
was called and two hundred people crowded in. An ad hoc committee of five was selected to review the facts and submit a recommendation to Mead School Superintendent Eugene Regan.

"I selected the committee," Regan told me recently. "Three
board members, three staff. They evaluated the book and designed
an alternative plan. The Learning Tree is supplemental reading for
sophomore English classes. The teacher can make the selections.
If the youngster elects not to read it, we now furnish an alternative
program. The Moral Majority found this unacceptable as a plan and
took us to court in August 1980. Michael Farris was their private
attorney. Since then he has ascended to executive director of Moral
Majority of Washington."

Subsequently, Michael Farris made headlines for the state
chapter of the Moral Majority by demanding that public libraries in
Washington open their records. The Moral Majority wanted to know
who was checking out a sex-education film entitled Achieving Sexual
Maturity. The state librarian refused Farris's request, and the
Moral Majority suit was dismissed on February 23. When approached
by reporters after the hearing, Farris said that he had won, even
though the suit will not be reactivated. The publicity he had generated was victory in itself. Farris told the press that he would
see that indecent literature was removed from the schools.

The Learning Tree, at this writing, is still in court. On
December 31, 1980, Farris filed a formal complaint against the
book in U.S. District Court for Washington's Eastern District in
behalf of three plaintiffs designated as "taxpayers." Only one of the
three, Carolyn Grove, is named as a parent as well. The five persons named as defendants are members of the Mead School Board.
The complaint alleges that The Learning Tree contains:

    a. swearing
    b. profanity
    c. obscene language
    d. explicit description of premarital sexual intercourse
    e. explicit description of other lewd behavior
    f. specific blasphemies against Jesus Christ
    g. excessive violence and murder

Among the bill of particulars--and I quote: "Plaintiffs have strong,
religiously based convictions against using their tax dollars to promote or glorify swearing, profanity, obscene language, explicit
descriptions of pre-marital sexual intercourse, explicit descriptions
of other lewd behavior, blasphemies against Jesus Christ, and excessive violence and murder [italics added].... Plaintiffs believe
the teaching of this book tends to inculcate the anti-God religion of
humanism which is antithetical to Plaintiffs' beliefs and which vio-
lates the free exercise and no establishment of religion clauses of
the First Amendment."

The Farris complaint further states that his Moral Majority
clients are entitled to damages to be proved by trial, to attorneys'
fees, to court costs, and to a permanent injunction against further
use of The Learning Tree in the Mead school district.

Counsel for the school board defendants is Gerald Gesinger, deputy prosecuting attorney for Spokane County and an elected official. I spoke to Gesinger on March 10. "We will prepare a pretrial motion to dismiss the complaint," he told me. "The Washington Education Association is affiliated with the National Education Association, and they have indicated that they are going to intervene. The American Civil Liberties Union will enter as amicus curiae. No brief has been filed so far and no trial date set. We will hopefully try for hearing on a motion to dismiss in the next four to six weeks."

Responding to a query from me, Michael Farris enclosed photocopied pages from the paperback edition of The Learning Tree. He marked off a section of dialogue, early in the book, when twelve-year-old Newt is being prodded by his chum Beansy to describe his first sexual experience (which Newt doesn't describe very well at all!). A few pages later, Farris underlined a paragraph in which Newt's older brother, Clint, is drunk beyond control and yelling that Jesus Christ is "the long-legged white son-of-a-bitch!" This paragraph, Farris labeled as "blasphemy." The third sample is an admittedly bawdy chapter opening in which young boys are peeping at young girls' exposed flesh from under the bleacher seats in a ballpark. Humorous, but harmless I think. Farris labeled the section "Vulgar Scene." The pages immediately following he labels profusely as "vulgar language and description of vulgar acts," a drunken car theft as a "steeling [sic] scene" and a circled "Goddam" on the printed page as "profane word." Farris's letter to me, dated March 3, 1981, is far more interesting.

"My observation is that the public schools censor objectionable material from the curriculum," he wrote. "The standards employed by the public schools are far more restrictive than the First Amendment would permit as pertains to society in general.

"For examples, books portraying all men as doctors and all women teachers are censored for being sexist. The Little Black Sambo series has been censored for being racist. Certainly these types of materials are protected by the First Amendment, yet the ACLU and the press has [sic] raised no hue and cry over the removal of these kinds of texts from the public schools.

"Apparently, to them, it depends on whose values you trample on. Books that trample on liberal values can be censored, those that trample on Christian values are protected by the First Amendment.

"In other words, the First Amendment allows more in society than is allowed, or should be allowed, in our public schools.

"Given that premise, the question is how do we decide what is appropriate to use as required reading material in the public schools.

"... The Learning Tree ... has no place in our public
schools as required reading material. Remember this is not a
question of what is permitted but what is required.

"The First Amendment also requires neutrality to religion and
religious people in the public school. This book is not neutral. Just
as Madalyn Murray O'Hair was able to remove required Bible reading, so too this book offensively coerces the conscience of Christians
required to read it."

The Farris argument isn't entirely without merit. But, as
Superintendent Regan specified to me, the Parks novel was supplemental reading and an alternative plan was devised for students to
substitute other literary works for The Learning Tree, within the
same sophomore English reading curriculum. Given that Mr. Regan
wan't making up this solution for my benefit, and wasn't lying when
he told me that the alternative plan was unacceptable to the Moral
Majority, the "what is permitted" and "what is required" distinctions
of Mr. Farris could be quite afield of the actual circumstances in
his case.

I continue to be curious about how serious a thrust toward
censorship is resulting from the muscular Christianity of the Moral
Majority. Judith F. Krug, director of the American Library Association's Intellectual Freedom Committee, has said that censorship
cases have increased alarmingly in number since last spring. "The
North Carolina Moral Majority is active in censorship, more so
than other state chapters," she told me. "But the adversary is not
the Moral Majority per se--it's the anti-intellectualism per se.
People who are afraid to think or will not think. I find it rather
amusing that self-styled conservatives have decided that, in the name
of God, they can dictate how a person makes choices about what to
read. It amounts to fascism."

Dorothy Massie is a Human Relations Specialist with NEA's
Teacher Rights division. "I would agree with Judy Krug," she said
to me, "except I know that the censorship activity from the Right
has spanned all of last year. The North Carolina affiliate of Moral
Majority has launched a project on a statewide basis in schools and
libraries. On the surface it's dirty words, explicit sex, depressing
material, women's history, or minorities. I suspect a façade with
all this. I am beginning to think that in the ultimate, it will be a
church-state conflict. I get the impression that the pro-family people who criticize secular humanism really want tuition tax credit for
Christian schools. The attack is on public school education. And I
believe racism underlies it. And I see a continuing spread of at-
tacks on sex education everywhere."

So does Dr. Sol Gordon, America's most visible sex educator.

Early this year, the fate of a National Public Radio station,
sorely in need of public funds to survive, may have been sealed--
in a sarcophagus. On the afternoon of January 17, WVWR-FM, the

NPR affiliate at Roanoke's Virginia Western Community College,
aired a tape of "Myths of Human Sexuality," a lecture first presented to the students at the University of Texas and taped by NPR
Station KUT there.   The author and speaker is Dr. Sol Gordon, professor of psychology at Syracuse University and director of the Institute for Family Research and Education.

Sol Gordon is an entertaining speaker and an idealist for sex
education--good sex education.   He personally feels that much of
what passes for sex education in schools--where it truly exists at
all--is worse than inadequate.   Gordon's irreverence is toward the
taboos and ugly shibboleths that have haunted the knowledge of sexuality since the subject was first whispered aloud.   He does not
stand for promiscuity or even premarital sex, as his Bible-hoisting
detractors have claimed for a dozen years.   He merely stands for
frank, open, courageous discussion, the banishment of mirages and
phantoms disguised as true erotic experience.   He has never endorsed abortion out of hand--contrary to much exurban and backwoods
opinion--because he has never been philosophically sure that it should
be applied on the scale that some of its champions would like to
guarantee.   His most salient message is a talisman for anyone who
claims to be fighting in Heine's "liberation war of humanity"--that
human love relies on a multitude of human possibilities and that human sexuality doesn't top the list.

The God-fearin' folks in the Roanoke listening area didn't
hear the message as well as Dr. Gordon and others would have
hoped.   Worse, the Saturday broadcast--the fact of it--was used
as a cudgel over the heads of station personnel when WVWR came
to the Virginia General Assembly on Monday, February 2--at funding
time.

What transpired in Richmond during those budget discussions
involving WVWR and its future was reported in different ways on
different wire services and in different newspapers.   On February
23, when most of the smoke was drifting away from the controversy,
I spoke to Steve Mills, the station manager.

"The controversy stemmed from our airing the program at
the time that we did--when we needed funding," Mills told me.
"We are in a difficult position because of the licensing of the station.   Before we went to the Virginia General Assembly, we sent
out letters to our contributors, asking them to write to elected officials.   One of the people who received our letter was upset about
the Sol Gordon broadcast.   This is the Bible Belt.   He wrote to
NPR, got a transcript of the tape, and sent it on to Lacey Putney,
an Independent delegate from a county near Lynchburg.   I appeared
before the House Appropriations Committee.   I was questioned by
Delegate Putney, who said he had received a number of complaints
from constituents who didn't want the station to be funded with their
tax money--because of the broadcast.   I said we had a commitment
to provide programs that are topical in nature.   We don't want to
offend anyone--however, we do provide controversial material.   Putney admitted that he had never listened to the station before.

"The Roanoke Times carried a front-page story written out of the Richmond bureau. They missed a few things. They reported that I said we would never air such things like that again. I did say we would use more discretion. The problem was that we aired it around 1:00 P.M. A local TV critic defended us but claimed that Putney was just doing his job. Five letters to the editor came in support of us. The radio-TV editor later wrote a follow-up on the mail he received about it. One letter came from a woman from CAUSE--Citizens Against Unacceptable Sex Education. She claimed that Sol Gordon had called himself 'polymorphous perverse' and she had interpreted that description as 'child molester.'

"We had requested $179,000 to run the station for another year. We received $60,000 and were told to sell the station by December 31. We must identify new owners, and we haven't done that yet. It's been a problem whether we should be run by a community college system at all."

Steve Mills only regrets that Delegate Putney didn't hear the Sol Gordon talk. "After the broadcast," Mills said, "we had requests for transcripts from the City of Lynchburg Health Department and from Randolph Macon College. We've gotten a number of letters in support of Dr. Gordon--and us. Dr. Gordon appeared at the Roanoke Hotel at the Invitation of the Junior League. Some people wanted to ban the Junior League after that."

Ironically, the WVWR affair transpired almost in the back-yard of Jerry Falwell's Lynchburg bastion of the Moral Majority. The feelings harbored by them good clean folks about sex education are no secret.

"We are coercing the conscience of boys and girls and usurping the right of parents when we require them to watch men having erections, women displaying their genitals and both sexes masturbating as does the film 'Achieving Sexual Maturity,'" reads Michael Farris's letter to me.

"Sex education does not work for the purposes of preventing venerial [sic] disease or pregnancies," he goes on. "Teenage abortion and pregnancy rates have doubled in Washington State in the last six years despite declining population of school age children and despite increased sex education.

"The Michigan Department of Public Education has recently concluded that sex education can only be honestly justified on the basis of teaching teens how to have a happy sex life. They have concluded that sex education does nothing to relieve the problems of teen-age pregnancy and venerial [sic] disease.

"I would submit that sex education, as it is being taught today, is a contributing factor in the rise of these problems.

"I believe in the Constitution and the Bill of Rights. But I also believe in responsibility. Kids coming out of the public schools today know how to use condones [sic], smoke dope, and have intercourse, but they can't read. To me the inability of a child to read and especially the inability to write articulately, poses a far greater threat to our society than any imagined threat of censorship. "

Somewhere embedded in that deathless prose could well be a statement about why the Moral Majority dislikes the process of self-discovery and would prefer that public officials ban any guidance for students toward that discovery--specifically, the guidance to be found in The Learning Tree and in the texts and talks of Sol Gordon. The answer to that one: the Moral Majority and their ilk are very bothered by what they understand as values clarification. They should be, considering the problems they have clarifying their own.

So if you have any further questions, class ... better go ask Alice.

DISMISSAL WITH PREJUDICE*

Sue Fontaine

One veteran reporter called it an anti-climax. In one sense, it was. The Washington State Library (WSL) was prepared to argue its position in court. However, Michael P. Farris, the state head of the Moral Majority, which had filed suit against WSL for its refusal to release the names of persons borrowing a sex education film, asked for dismissal just before the case was to be heard.

Members of the library community had expressed hope that a court hearing would result in a ruling supporting the library's stand--a ruling which would set a precedent in the courts for protection of patron privacy. Farris's request for "dismissal with prejudice" erased that hope. (Dismissal with prejudice means that the library cannot be taken to court again on the identical case.) Still, much was gained from the experience, and sharing it may prove helpful to other libraries. There is increasing pressure, nationwide, from those who would seek to control what others read, view, or hear. While the issue at stake in Washington was that of "unreasonable invasion of privacy," it is clearly correlated to intellectual freedom.

The Moral Majority's ultimate goal was to learn which schools in Washington State had shown the film, so that the information could be used to bolster its proposed legislation calling for closer parental/community control of sex education in the public schools.

The State Library's immediate goal was to protect the identity of those who had borrowed the film and to do so within the confines of the Public Disclosure Law of Washington State, which calls for open public records related to state business.

To provide both facts and perspective, a diary of events which led to the courtroom is presented here with full background information and comments:

JANUARY 29: Michael Farris, head of the Washington

---

*Reprinted by permission of the author and publisher from Library Journal, 106 (June 15, 1981) 1273-77. Published by R. R. Bowker Co. (a Xerox Company). Copyright © 1981 by Xerox Corporation.

State Moral Majority, telephoned WSL's film department on
the Evergreen State College campus and asked for a list of
borrowers of a film titled "Achieving Sexual Maturity." The
individual who handles WSL's film bookings informed Farris
that WSL's policy is to hold circulation records confidential.
The name of the Assistant Attorney General who is assigned
to the State Library was supplied. Farris promptly contacted
him, announcing that he would bring action against the library
to obtain the records. Meantime, WSL's policy was forwarded
to the attorney , who began to review the policy in the context of the Public Disclosure Act and other documents to see
if the library was exempt from provisions. Farris was asked
to put his request in writing; until this formal request was
received, the library planned no action and gave no statements to the press.

It is important to note from the onset that WSL had a policy
firmly in place and that it had been well communicated to staff members. The policy is in the staff manual and is reinforced in orien-
tation/training sessions.

The Privacy of Circulation Records policy (see box) was
adopted by the appointed State Library Commission in 1972. It is
based on that adopted by the American Library Association in 1971.

This policy gave WSL's administration something tangible to
turn to as it took an official stand, and was later a key in bolster-
ing the defense prepared by WSL's attorney. The Washington State
Library Commission, as well as the Washington Library Association,
had also adopted the Intellectual Freedom policy recommended by
ALA in 1971.

FEBRUARY 5: WSL received "a formal demand under the
Washington Public Disclosure Act" for a list of "all public
school districts and their employees who have received from
your library the film 'Achieving Sexual Maturity.'" The letter advised that appropriate legal action would be taken with
"no future notice to you if you fail to recognize your obliga-
tion...." The letter was dated February 3.

Both the State Librarian, Roderick G. Swartz, and the Deputy
State Librarian, Nancy Zussy, had experienced previous demands for
circulation records. In both instances the complainants were directed
to the proper authorities to obtain the necessary subpoenas, but failed
to return. In some instances libraries have been able to deter legal
action by demonstrating that a search for patron identity would be
an involved, laborious process which would put undue strain on the
library's conduct of daily business.

In this case, however, the records were readily accessible.
WSL's general intent is to eliminate circulation records as soon as
materials are returned since they are unnecessary after that time.
Film circulation records, however, require a longer retention period

> ## Privacy of Library Circulation Records Policy
>
> 1. The circulation records of the Washington State Library are confidential regardless of source of inquiry.
> 2. Circulation records shall not be made available to anyone except pursuant to such process, order, or subpoena as may be authorized by law.
> 3. Upon receipt of such process, order or subpoena, consultation shall be made with the legal officer assigned to the library to determine if such process, order, or subpoena is in good form and if there is a showing of good cause for its issuance.
> 4. If the process, order, or subpoena is not in proper form or if good cause has not been shown, insistence shall be made that such defects be cured before any records are released. (The legal process requiring the production of circulation records shall ordinarily be in the form of subpoena duces tecum (bring your records), requiring the librarian to attend court or the taking of his or her deposition and may require him to bring along certain designated circulation records.)
> 5. Any threats or unauthorized demands, (i. e., those not supported by a process, order or subpoena) concerning circulation records shall be reported to the State Library Commission and Attorney General.
> 6. Any problems relating to the privacy of circulation records which are not provided for in the above five paragraphs are to be referred to the Chief of Reader (Information) Services or to the State Librarian.
>
> Washington State Library
> Commission
> Adopted 5/23/72

than those of books because the films must be checked for damage, cleaned, rewound, and repackaged for the next client. Unreliability of mail deliveries, the unpredictability of some patrons in returning films on the due date, and limited staff support led to our decision to retain the film circulation records up to six months. The current list of persons borrowing Achieving Sexual Maturity contained some 25 names. Because the film was heavily used, the library had three copies--one purchased soon after the film was produced (1973) and two gift copies. The library was immediately able to determine a part of the Farris request to supply the names of school districts or schools which had borrowed the film. A detailed check revealed that only the names of individuals appear on the records. The attorney advised that under present disclosure laws the library would be in a stronger position to protect individuals than agencies. Whether these persons are, or are not, school employees remains uncertain.

FEBRUARY 6: The Associated Press broke the story in

the Seattle "Post-Intelligencer." To the administration's
knowledge, the information was not provided by WSL staff.
News media from Washington State, from Oregon, from NBC
in Los Angeles, and elsewhere pursued WSL staff by telephone over the weekend of February 7 and 8. Staff was informed that all calls from the media should be referred to
the State Librarian's office or to the Public Information Officer (PIO). In the absence of the State Librarian, the Deputy State Librarian and the PIO handled the calls. The State
Librarian and the PIO took calls at home over the weekend.
The message stated that WSL's attorney was exploring the library's position with regard to the Public Disclosure Act and
that it would be inappropriate to share any information until
a formal reply had been given to Farris. The library's policy on privacy was confirmed, with stress put on the fact
that it was in line with the national policy and the ethical position of the library profession. Reporters were told that
WSL hoped to have its response to Farris after 3 p.m. Monday afternoon (February 9) and would make it public as soon
as it was delivered to him.

Central to WSL's response to the media at this point--and
throughout the next three weeks--was its policy of open communication between the administration and the Public Information Office as
well as a pattern of open communication with the media. WSL's
PIO reports directly to the State Librarian. The State Librarian
and Tom Bjorgen, Assistant Attorney General, met with the PIO
shortly after Farris's visit to the film library. They discussed
the facts of the case and the potential responses to both Farris
and to the media.

FEBRUARY 9: WSL's attorney advised that the library
could stand firm in its denial, based on its policy and on the
Washington Administrative Code (WAC 304-20-060(4). He advised the library that the policy and regulation do not conflict
with the Public Disclosure Act (42.17 RCW), since "library
circulation records of the type we are here declining to disclose come under certain exceptions to the disclosure requirement of the Act." Calls were then made to each of WSL's
five Library Commissioners, who had been kept informed of
the dispute as it developed. Each reaffirmed support for the
existing policy and the library's stance. The State Librarian
prepared a letter to Farris, which read in part:

In answer to the first part of your demand, the records
of the Washington State Library do not indicate that any
public school districts have checked out or received the
film "Achieving Sexual Maturity...." In answer to the
second part of your demand, the Washington State Library
declines to disclose the names of public school district
employees who may have checked out or received this film.

The letter cited the administrative and statutory codes above,

and stated WSL's belief that the records were exempt "in
that disclosure would constitute an unreasonable invasion of
privacy" and that disclosure "would impair a vital governmental interest of the State Library, ... would violate the
guarantee of freedom of speech contained in the First Amendment to the United States Constitution, ... and ... may well
tend to inhibit persons in checking out material of unconven-
tional political, social, or other persuasions."

The PIO was well-informed and anticipating the activity, so
it was a fairly easy matter to prepare an official press release
within the hour after the decision. The release cited the Assistant
Attorney General's opinion and contained the following statement by
the State Librarian, portions of which were subsequently quoted
widely in the press:

> State libraries, along with other tax-supported libraries,
> are citadels of education and information. Their purpose
> is to provide access to information and ideas from all
> points of view. The release of records would have a
> chilling effect on the use of libraries for the purposes
> for which they are intended. Fear of public disclosure,
> particularly among those who read or view controversial
> or unorthodox materials, would result in deterring citizens
> from seeking information through their libraries.

The rejection letter was delivered to Michael Farris. The
State Librarian personally took the release to the AP reporter who
had broken the story and had persistently pursued it. The PIO
simultaneously delivered the release to the United Press. Had it
not been late afternoon, WSL might have also photocopied the release
for some 30 other members of the Capitol Press Corps. However,
at this time of day, they are generally absent from their offices.
In addition, it was certain that the news could be shared because
the wire service and representatives of individual media occupy the
same office space. Under other circumstances, a news release of
this importance might also be mailed to media statewide, but it was
obvious that this news, sent via the mails, would have been "old
hat" when it arrived. Every newspaper, broadcast station, and news
service that had telephoned for information was telephoned again, and
new calls were answered. To give libraries that find themselves in
the national news an idea of what to anticipate, the PIO returned--
or accepted--more than 30 telephone calls between 5 and 8:30 p.m.
Each inquirer was given the State Librarian's "chilling effect" comment and the attorney's opinion. The PIO attempted to answer both
simple and detailed questions, such as: "How many names are on
the list?" "How long have you had the film?" "How many copies
do you have?" "Supposing there were school names on the records,
what would you have done?" "Could anyone steal into the State Library Film Department at night and pull a 'filmgate?'" "Exactly
what are your circulation procedures, and why?" It was here that
the open and continuous communication paid off. The PIO had been
able to anticipate many of the questions, and those which were posed

unexpectedly or could be handled by the State Librarian or the Attorney General were listed with the promise of obtaining a direct response in the morning. Many of the reporters, including network TV newspersons, and reporters from Sixty Minutes, asked to talk directly to either the State Librarian and/or the attorney, and interview times were scheduled.

Later, addressing the Washington State Information Council, the PIO stated:

> Since our case was coming before the courts, we had to be judicious, but at the same time, we wanted our point of view to be heard. Having an administrator who was accessible to the press, at ease and articulate with regard to the professional ethics involved, and firm in his convictions, was a plus that cannot be underestimated. In addition, having a willing, articulate, and dedicated Assistant Attorney General who made himself available almost on an hourly basis to handle "sticky" questions was a key factor in being able to respond to media promptly and accurately.

FEBRUARY 10: The attorney continued a search for citations on similar cases. A Whatcom County Librarian who moved to Washington after experiencing a similar problem in Nevada called to supply several citations and the opinion of the Nevada Attorney General. ALA's Intellectual Freedom Office responded promptly with a packet of papers which included the opinion of the Attorney General of Texas, who supported protection of library circulation records. However, WSL's attorney could locate no record of a similar case being brought to trial.

FEBRUARY 11: The Moral Majority filed its petition for disclosure in the Superior Court of Washington State, Thurston County. Although this was clearly an "invasion of privacy" dispute, the issue of censorship began to take shape. The media, the ministry, the educators, and the curious were demanding to see the film. The film was soon fully booked until August 1981. On February 10, however, one copy had been returned. Since returned films remain in the film library for approximately a week so that they can be checked, cleaned, and packaged for the next borrower, it was possible to temporarily respond to requests for viewing of the film on site. An appointment was made to show it to the reporters at 1 p.m.

Here another sort of pressure occurred. Many arrived with cameras, which they wished to bring into the screening room. The film library head explained that the film was protected by copyright and that she could not grant permission for pictures to be taken of even one frame. One of the press people telephoned his attorney while the film librarian, in turn, called WSL administration. She was advised to maintain her stand on the copyright, and WSL's attorney was then contacted.

Meanwhile, the PIO talked to Preston Holdner of the Media Guild, which distributes the film. Holdner had been previously cooperative in helping the media round up copies of the film when none were available at the State Library. He now offered to negotiate individually with the media to release certain portions of the film under certain conditions. He stated that he welcomed the showing of the film in its entirety if the media thought it was appropriate for airing, but that he did not wish scenes or audio to be used out of context. Later, one TV station did air portions of the film, apparently with Holdner's permission. The film received various "ratings" from the press who viewed it, but none of the stories reported it as "pornographic" or "erotic."

The delivery of the petition to the courts was accompanied by a 10 a.m. press conference which was held by the Moral Majority's Farris and well attended. In the petition Farris asked for: 1) names of school districts borrowing the film, 2) the dates of the showing of the film, 3) the number of persons viewing the film, 4) the grade level of the students seeing the films, 5) whether the classes are coeducational and whether they are compulsory or voluntary. It stated that WSL had attempted to "stonewall" the Moral Majority's request for information rather than simply eliminating identifying details regarding school employees. Accompanying the petition, however, was a document which WSL's attorney referred to as "an offer of settlement." The compromise offered by Farris was the following: The library would provide a list of cities to which the film has been sent. The Moral Majority would then supply a list of public schools, with their addresses, which were located in each of these cities, which WSL would review and match.

In response to the petition and the Farris press conference, a new group came forward to voice an alternative to the Moral Majority. It was the "Immoral Minority," which had been formed in November to protect free speech and to prevent encroachments on privacy by "small religious sects" and "zealots." It now had a focus for its cause, and its members arrived on the scene with T-shirts, bumper stickers, buttons, and an articulate spokesman, Bob Shirley.

WSL's approach, meantime, continued to be "low key" as it responded to all inquiries. In the interim between the delivery of the first demand and the scheduling of the court hearing for February 23, the library had communications challenges to consider beyond those with Farris and the media. The PIO drew up the following "crisis communications" list:

1. Be sure staff is continually informed. (The news release was immediately posted, and staff was kept up to date in the weekly staff newsletter as well as verbally.)
2. Organize communications with Library Commissioners.
3. Consider relationships with the Governor/Legislature.
4. Keep the Governor informed. (A personal letter from the State Librarian went to him with a packet of information.)

5. Keep the library community informed. (Progress
    reported in WSL's bi-weekly newsletter to public and
    academic library directors and in Password, the news-
    letter sponsored by state associations and WSL.)
6. Inform the national library press. (The news release
    was mailed and phone calls were returned.)
7. Respond to all press inquiries.
8. Keep management/PIO/attorney communications open and
    organized.
9. Let each key person involved know when unusual questions
    or activities occur with media and inform all involved as
    to how we responded.
10. Prepare positions or statements in anticipation of major
    turns in events and inform all involved.
11. Remind staff through the newsletter that all media inquir-
    ies are to be directed to the State Librarian's office or
    the PIO.
12. Consider possible need for "Letters to the Editor."
    (These poured in without any encouragement.)
13. Consider a method of alerting Friends and other support
    groups should the need arise. (Many volunteered.)
14. Get advice/material from ALA's Intellectual Freedom Of-
    fice and the Civil Liberties Union.
15. Consider the need to prepare news releases, hold press
    conferences, etc. in the light of day-to-day events.
16. Keep files of all contacts, background materials (includ-
    ing the reviews of the film, which was a CINE Golden
    Eagle award-winner), news clippings, etc.
17. Thank those who offered support. (Letters were sent to
    citizens, the library community, and editorial writers
    who had expressed support.)

Tending to the above tasks, along with "business as usual,"
kept the State Library staff busy until February 23, the day scheduled for the hearing.

FEBRUARY 17: WSL delivered its official reply to the
"offer of compromise" by Farris. Before so doing, a careful check was made of the addresses in the records. The
response said in part:

The Washington State Library appreciates your offer of
compromise ... in furtherance of the same purpose, the
library has checked the addresses to which our records
indicate the film has been sent and has ascertained that
none of these addresses is that of a public school district,
public school district office, public school, or public school
office. We would be happy to supply you with an affidavit
confirming these results.... The upshot of this situation
is that the compromise you proposed would be futile....
We cannot in good conscience attempt to bind you to a
settlement which we know will result in no benefit to you
or your client.

More press inquiries, more speculation, and numerous media
interviews with Farris followed. Over the three-week period our
general assessment was that the press was fair to the library, pro-
fessionally objective, but personally sympathetic. Farris was by
far the most flamboyant figure for media focus. In early interviews
he stated that the Moral Majority was $9000 in debt and that he had
not been paid a salary since November. A month later he reported
that the group had raised some $14,000. The Immoral Minority also
received media attention and also stated that support funds were coming in from all over the country. WSL received several dozen letters from librarians, friends, and just plain citizens encouraging its
stand, and only one negative letter. At the legislature, verbal encouragement was given, some of it from people from the conservative
camp. Legislators and legislative staff asked for "Love Your Library" buttons, sold earlier as a part of the project by the Washington Library Trustees Association.

The upshot of the legislative interest was the spontaneous
introduction of not just one, but three, bills aimed at specifically
exempting library circulation and other identifiable records from the
Public Disclosure Act. The Washington Library Association worked
with the State Library in developing the language of SB4194 and
HB476, which appeared to be the most comprehensive of the bills
introduced. Also introduced was the Moral Majority's bill on sex
education in the public schools, which requires, among other stipu-
lations, that parents approve all material to be presented to students
in any sex education effort.

FEBRUARY 23: Although the Assistant Attorney General
for WSL had received an indication from Farris that he might
drop the suit, he had prepared an excellent 16-page brief,
based on the State Library's policy position and on two primary points of law: 1) that disclosure would be an unconstitutional invasion of privacy under a long line of cases cited
in the brief, and 2) that disclosure would violate the Freedom
of Speech clause in the First Amendment.
A few minutes before the scheduled hearing, Farris informed
WSL's attorney and Judge Gerry Alexander that he was dropping the suit. Judge Alexander, however, asked both the
plaintiff and the defendant to make statements in the courtroom, which was packed with onlookers, media personnel,
and TV crews. Washington is one of the few states which
allows cameras in the courtroom.
Farris stated that he had dropped the suit because he "got
what he wanted" and would pursue his quest for information
on sex education materials directly with the public schools.
WSL's attorney stated that "the library did not compromise
its position in any way. We refused from the outset to di-
vulge the names of any individuals, and have not retreated
one iota. We are prepared to argue our case on its merits."

The media then conducted extensive interviews with the attorney, the State Librarian, Farris, and Bob Shirley of the Immoral

Minority, in the halls outside the courtroom. WSL subsequently issued its second news release, which contained the attorney's statement.

    Because the issue (invasion of privacy) is likely to occur in
other libraries, both the attorney and the State Librarian expressed
regret at the lost opportunity to get a court decision. With every
reason to believe that the State Library's position was a strong one,
a hearing might have proved valuable to the profession as well as to
WSL. The dismissal of the case, however, did relieve WSL of a potential financial risk. Had the State Library lost the case, it would
have been liable for all court costs. Since state agencies are
charged for Attorney General services, it even now faces an unan-
ticipated expense in that regard.

    If HB476 is passed in the current legislative session, it will
protect the State Library from further encroachments. At least five
states are known to have library records specifically exempted;
among them, Florida, Iowa, and Minnesota.

    In converting "negatives" into "positives," the issue of the
circulation records has caused greater interest in funding the automated circulation system proposed by WSL, The Evergreen State College, and the Timberland Regional Library. WSL and Evergreen are
seeking their share of the funding for this online, turn-key system
from the legislature. The dispute also made the State Library highly
visible at a time when the legislature is drastically cutting state
agency budgets, a visibility which could possibly help. The Library
Commission has now adopted a "Freedom to View" policy and is
working on a "Freedom to Hear" policy.

    To summarize, these are factors which helped the State Li-
brary: 1) an adequate policy firmly in place; 2) a firm governing
commission; 3) a good file of intellectual freedom materials, policies
and other background materials, such as the reviews of the film;
4) a fully informed knowledgeable staff; 5) daily communications patterns; 6) a dedicated attorney; 7) fair news coverage, plus supportive
editorials; 8) a fully supportive library community locally, statewide,
and nationally; and 9) citizens who came forth with vocal and visible
support for the library's stand.

LIBRARIANS AS POLITICAL ACTIVISTS*

Ethel Manheimer

> The librarian should be a careful student of his own
> town. He should know its history and topography, its
> life. To this end he should have a personal acquaint-
> ance with the city officers, the party bosses, the labor
> leaders, members of the board of trade, manufacturers,
> leading women in society, with the clergy, with the
> school superintendent and the teachers, with those who
> shape the charitable organizations, with reporters, po-
> licemen and reformers. To what end? Broadly that he
> may catch the spirit of the civic life and relate the li-
> brary to the whole as the organs to the body. Mary
> Salome Cutler, Library Journal, October 1896

In post-Proposition 13 California, many librarians were jolted into
action when they realized that their libraries and jobs could be dec-
imated through other people's actions. When Californians voted themselves a substantial property-tax reduction in June 1978, sharply curtailed budgets were to affect libraries, both school and public, in
most cities, towns, and counties. Schools faced the additional financial constraints that resulted from declining enrollment. Library
closings--as well as reductions in service, staff, hours, and book
budgets--have been described and well documented in the library
press.

Less well known are some California success stories--situa-
tions in which action by librarians and the community at the local
level enabled libraries to maintain their positions or even grow, in
spite of the general shrinkage of local budgets in the state.

Most recently, the city of Berkeley voted for a new tax that
will totally fund the operation of the Berkeley Public Library at pre-
Proposition 13 levels, with a small inflation factor added. The library's budget is now independent of the city's general fund and the
library is no longer in competition with other city services (such as
police, fire, health, recreation) for dwindling revenue.

*Reprinted by permission of the author and publisher from School Li-
brary Journal, 27:5 (January 1981) 29-31. Published by R. R. Bowker
Co. (a Xerox Company). Copyright © 1981 by Xerox Corporation.

How did Berkeley become the first and only community in California to levy a new tax on itself in order to rebuild and maintain a quality library program? Part of the answer lies in the nature of the community, its dependence on the library, and the library's success in meeting the community's needs. A city of 110,000 in which 45 percent of the population have active library cards, Berkeley's per capita circulation is triple the average for the state.

But this relationship between the community and the library is not enough to explain the passage of Measure E (the local tax bill) in these times of voter antipathy to government and taxation. This came about in a city where a sharp political split resulted in public opposition to the measure, where the city's major newspaper editorialized against the measure, where the Chamber of Commerce opposed it, and where the approval of two-thirds of the electorate was needed to pass the bill. The support given by the sponsoring political party--Berkeley Citizens Action--was vital, but victory at the polls can be attributed to a campaign characterized by the close cooperation of three distinct groups: the Friends of the Berkeley Public Library, the library's Board of Trustees, and the library staff. The board unanimously supported the measure, and individual members participated effectively in public debates. The Friends kicked off the campaign with a $5000 contribution; the unpaid campaign manager and other Friends worked vigorously and untiringly through the eight weeks of election activities. The significant and unstinting work of the librarians and other staff members gave the campaign much of its energy and effectiveness.

Motivated, inspired, and led by library director, Regina U. Minudri, the staff of the Berkeley Public Library gave up many hours of their own time (no electioneering on the job) to plan events and strategy, to raise money, to do the nitty-gritty work of campaigning (and to enjoy a victory celebration). Though most of us were politically inexperienced and naive, we learned quickly, and we discovered that our skills and competencies as librarians were transferable to the political arena and stood us in good stead as campaigners. What did we actually do in the campaign? We researched library history; we wrote letters to the editor; we helped compose campaign literature; we scanned voter lists to find names of library patrons, supporters, and friends; we folded, stuffed, addressed envelopes; we walked precincts dropping literature (i.e., went door-to-door through preselected neighborhoods leaving our campaign literature and urging anyone who'd talk with us to vote for the measure); we distributed our literature at supermarkets, at churches, at concerts, meetings and fairs, we "sniped" signs; we telephoned friends and strangers asking for their endorsement of the measure and for contributions to finance our campaign; we walked to work wearing signboards, taking different, heavily trafficked routes each day; we stood at tables outside the libraries giving information and soliciting funds; we spoke at meetings of senior citizen groups, of parents' organizations, of church and civic groups, of any group that would let us in.

On election day, we got up at 4:00 a.m. to walk precincts again. This time, we went in cooperation with the political party that put Measure E on the ballot, hanging voter cards on every door-knob in town so every Berkeleyan left home election morning with a reminder to vote "Yes on E" and with the address of her/his polling place. When the polls opened and again after work, we went and stood the legal 100 feet from polling places, greeted voters, and reminded them to vote for the libraries.

Why did the librarians and other library staff get so involved, give as much time, energy, and money to this campaign? Particularly, we wondered, why did the staff working with young people (traditionally or stereotypically the most reticent, politically) become activists? How was their activism affecting their lives, both personally and at work? What benefits accrued to Linda Perkins, supervising program librarian for Young People's Services, and to staff members, Joan Akawie, Jean Leiby, Carol Naito, Heo Park, Martha Shogren, as they gave up much of their leisure time for two months?

Commitment to the library and its mission, to their coworkers and to the community as well as a desire to "fight back" against the effects of Proposition 13 stimulated these young people's librarians' participation. For the most part, they were glad they got involved. They felt that their effort, as part of a committed working group, was important to the campaign and could make a difference in the election's outcome. They expressed satisfaction with the large number of their colleagues who were working (but felt disappointment and some tension at work with those who were doing nothing for the campaign or grumbling); they were gratified by the number of friends and library supporters who joined in at work meetings and other campaign efforts.

Working with other people at concrete tasks was energizing; "joining in the fight makes you feel good" even though there was also anxiety and sleeplessness. All the librarians we talked to felt the hardest and most unpleasant task they performed in the campaign was asking for money. Several expressed disappointment that so few librarians from schools and from other library systems joined in. Said one Berkeley librarian, "We're all part of the library movement: I hope I'll respond when other libraries need help." These young people's librarians enjoyed working with and getting to know community people and colleagues from all the departments and branches of the library. All were leery of involvement with the city's political parties and the partisan issues on the ballot. Without exception, before knowing if Measure E would win or lose, these young people's librarians knew that if another campaign for library funding became necessary they'd be active campaigners again. Jean Leiby summed it up, "It's the only way you can make your voice heard."

Mount Diablo USD Librarians Organize

For the past two years, librarians in the Mount Diablo Unified

School District (Contra Costa County) have been making their voices
heard. Drastic personnel cuts were announced by their board in
July 1978; newly instituted collective bargaining required their sympathetic supervisor to hew to the management position; the librarians
knew their own immediate action was necessary to save the library
program. The librarians organized themselves into Library Staff
United (LSU), an ad hoc group separate from their grade level staff
organization. They became their own advocates, delivering their
message to teachers and administrators, to their teachers' association officers, to parents and to the board. LSU asked the California
Media and Library Educators Association (CMLEA) and the American
Association of School Librarians (AASL) for advice and action; both
groups came through with information, letters and telegrams of support to the administrators and board members, and Alice Fite, executive secretary of AASL, visited the district to help. LSU, at its
own expense, retained an attorney knowledgeable in the laws pertaining to education and school libraries. But it has been the constant
activity of LSU and the individual librarians in it that made the difference.

Under the leadership of LSU's first two presidents, Lynn
Pryer and Laurene Martin, the group has used a variety of strategies including the assignment of a number of librarians to be at
each school board meeting, so that their specialty is always represented. They've asked parents and teachers who are supportive of
library service to write letters to newspapers and to call board members. Out of this appeal, a parent, Jan Fezatte, organized a parents advocates group to support better library services in the district.
The librarians met with administrators to tell them what librarians
do in the schools and how the libraries fit into and serve the total
curriculum. For one of many library presentations to the board,
LSU organized an authors' night with the cooperation of local writers.
On the evening of a school board meeting, a dinner for the writers
and the board members was followed by an autographing session for
students. A huge turnout of students and their parents graphically
displayed to the board the vitality and significance of the librarians'
literature programs.

Through LSU, the librarians have mutual support and problem
solving assistance, strengthening their own skills and the program.
They prepared and publicized a library curriculum continuum, which
though never adopted by the board, informed the entire district of
their plan of instruction. LSU worked even more closely with the
teachers' association than they had before--some became building
representatives--resulting in greater recognition of the librarians
as teachers.

What does LSU have to show for its herculean efforts? During the first year, the board retained three-and-one-half elementary
library positions they'd planned to eliminate through attrition. In
the secondary schools, the librarians were involved in planning the
realignment of a reduced clerical staff. Since then, a new board
attempted to eliminate elementary librarians, but LSU and its now

numerous library supporters were ready for the threat; the board was convinced and the program was saved. When eight schools were closed recently, the parents of many transferring students exerted pressure on the district to provide better library facilities or services in the new schools their children would attend.

Clearly the Mount Diablo Unified School District librarians are devoting many after-school hours to LSU's planning activities. They've gone out to the community, provided information about their program, and found the support they needed to keep their programs alive and save their jobs.

A Matter of Survival

How many librarians have remained aloof from all political involvement, feeling the issues were too remote or that they should not take an active role? How many believe that "my involvement won't make any difference," or "what will be, will be," or that politics is a dirty business? How many other reasons have we given ourselves to justify doing nothing in the political arena? If we think libraries are worth fighting for, then we librarians must lead the fight. Insofar as libraries are funded by citizens to serve the citizens and must compete with other public services for revenue, it is clear that we must generate our support from the citizenry in the political arena. And, as Betty McDavid, past president of CMLEA, Northern Section, said, "It's a never-ending job. There are always new people, new groups to whom we must communicate our message."

It has been said that libraries have no natural enemies, but neither do they have natural political allies. It is up to us librarians to recruit our allies. Alice B. Ihrig once pointed out that "the political process turns the good will enjoyed by librarians into the ultimate support dollars."[*] The day of the low profile is over. Librarians must be politically aware and politically adept in order to survive in the decade of the '80s and beyond.

---

*Ihrig, Alice B. "Librarians and the Political Process," in As Much to Learn as to Teach (Shoe String, 1979), (p. 83-93)

NOTES ON CONTRIBUTORS

DANA L. ALESSI, Regional Sales Manager for Blackwell North American and D. H. Blackwell Ltd., is based in Houston Texas.

RUSSELL BAKER, newspaperman, writes the "Observer" column which appears regularly opposite the editorial page of The New York Times and in the New York Times Magazine.

JOHN CALVIN COLSON has taught in six library education programs in the United States and Great Britain. He currently resides in Sycamore, Illinois.

PENELOPE COWELL, a graduate of the College of Librarianship, Wales, holds the post of librarian at Gawthorpe Hall in Lancashire, a house owned by the National Trust.

LEIGH ESTABROOK, librarian and sociologist, is an Associate Professor at the Syracuse University School of Information Studies.

SUE FONTAINE, Washington State Library Public Information Officer at the time she wrote her article on the Moral Majority, is now Associate Chief of Public Relations at The New York Public Library.

MICHAEL HALPERIN heads the Reference Department at Drexel University's library, Philadelphia, Pennsylvania.

KATHLEEN HEIM, Assistant Professor, University of Illinois Graduate School of Library and Information Science, chairs the American Library Association Committee on the Status of Women in Librarianship.

NAT HENTOFF, well known for his championship of first ammendment freedoms, is a columnist for the Village Voice, staff writer for the New Yorker, teacher, and author of numerous books on music, education, and politics.

IRVING LOUIS HOROWITZ, Distinguished Professor of Sociology and Political Science, holds the Hannah Arendt Chair at Rutgers University, Livingston College.

MARILYN KAYE is an Assistant Professor at the College of Librarianship, University of South Carolina.

ELAINE L. KONIGSBURG, winner of the 1968 Newbery Award for

From the Mixed-up Files of Mrs. Basil E. Frankweiler, lives in Jacksonville, Florida.

TIM LA BORIE is librarian at the School of Library and Information Science library, Drexel University, Philadelphia.

CLIFTON O. LAWHORNE is Professor of Journalism, University of Arkansas at Little Rock.

PHILIP LENTZ, a reporter for the Philadelphia Bulletin, is also a freelance writer.

MAURICE B. LINE, Director General, British Lending Library Division, also holds the title Professor Associate, University of Sheffield, Postgraduate School of Librarianship and Information Science.

GERTRUDE LONDON is Emerita Associate Professor, School of Library Science, University of North Carolina, Chapel Hill.

ETHEL MANHEIMER, formerly librarian at Alto-Edna Maguire Elementary School, Mill Valley, California lives in Berkeley where she was treasurer of the successful campaign to fund the Berkeley Public Library at pre-Proposition 13 levels.

MARILYN L. MILLER is Associate Professor at the University of North Carolina, Chapel Hill, School of Library Science.

BRIAN NIELSON is Head of the Reference Department at Northwestern University in Evanston, Illinois.

NEIL A. RADFORD serves as Librarian, University of Sydney, Sydney, Australia.

WILLIAM F. RYAN, a freelance reporter and novelist, resides in Arlington, Virginia.

ZIAUDDIN SARDAR is Middle East Science Consultant of the British journal New Scientist.

PATRICIA SCALES is Media Specialist at the Greenville (South Carolina) Middle School.

ANITA SCHILLER, frequent contributor to library literature, is Data Services Librarian at the University of California, San Diego.

BILL SNIDER teaches in the areas of educational psychology, measurement and statistics at the University of Iowa College of Education.

GERALD VIZENOR, writer and teacher, holds appointments at the University of Minnesota and the University of California at Berkeley.

LUCY WARNER, a former Assistant Editor of School Library Journal, is a freelance writer and editor working out of Boulder, Colorado.

JERRY J. WATSON is Assistant Professor, Children's Literature, at the University of Iowa College of Education.

MARTHA E. WILLIAMS, editor of the Annual Review of Information Science and Technology and On-line Review, directs the Information Retrieval Research Laboratory at the University of Illinois at Urbana-Champaign.

PAULINE WILSON is Associate Professor at the Graduate School of Library and Information Science, University of Tennessee, Knoxville.